Cultural Differences and Economic Globalization

Economic globalization is the process of increased integration among nations, characterized and fostered by the three elements of international trade in goods and services, international capital flows, and international migration. In recent decades, international economic integration has increased both in depth (more pronounced bilateral connections) and in breadth (connections have become more commonplace). Thus, the global economy has become increasingly integrated. Societies receive tremendous net benefits from economic globalization. However, accessing these benefits may be limited by cross-societal cultural differences.

This book examines cultural differences as a potential impediment to economic integration. Relying on rigorous statistical and econometric techniques, the analyses indicate that higher transaction costs, due to greater cultural distance, inhibit both the volume of trade flows and the successful completion of trade deals. Cultural distance appears to also reduce foreign direct investment, as well as diverting investment to less culturally-distant destinations. Likewise, this book finds a negative relationship between migration flows and cultural distance. Additionally, it considers the common criticism that repeated and intensified integration diminishes cultural differences, resulting in cultural homogeneity.

This book offers the first comprehensive examination of the relationships between cross-societal cultural differences and economic globalization. It will be of great interest to scholars and students who study globalization, international economics, and cultural studies.

Roger White is Associate Professor of Economics and Douglas W. Ferguson Chair in International Economics at Whittier College, California, USA.

Routledge Studies in the Modern World Economy

For a complete list of titles in this series, please visit www.routledge.com.

124 Financial Globalization and Regionalism in East Asia
Edited by Takuji Kinkyo, Yoichi Matsubayashi and Shigeyuki Hamori

125 Successful Business Dealings and Management with China Oil, Gas and Chemical Giants
EurIng. Henry K. H. Wang

126 State Building and Development
Edited by Keijiro Otsuka and Takashi Shiraishi

127 International Economic Development
Leading issues and challenges
Edited by Fu Lai Tony Yu, Wai Kee Yuen and Diana S. Kwan

128 Innovation, Globalization and Firm Dynamics
Lessons for enterprise policy
Edited by Anna Ferragina, Erol Taymoz and Kamil Yilmaz

129 International Remittance Payments and the Global Economy
Bharati Basu with James T. Bang

130 The Open Society and its Enemies in East Asia
The relevance of the Popperian framework
Edited by Gregory C. G. Moore

131 The Economics of Knowledge Generation and Distribution
The role of interactions in the system dynamics of innovation and growth
Edited by Pier Paolo Patrucco

132 Japan's Aid
Lessons for economic growth, development and political economy
Edward M. Feasel

133 The Geographical Transformation of China
Edited by Michael Dunford and Weidong Lui

134 The Economics of Cooperative Education
A practitioners' guide to the theoretical framework and empirical assessment of cooperative education
Yasushi Tanaka

135 Comparing Post War Japanese and Finnish Economies and Societies
Edited by Yasushi Tanaka, Toshiaki Tamaki, Jari Ojala and Jari Eloranta

136 Measuring National Income in the Centrally Planned Economies
Why the west underestimated the transition to capitalism
William Jefferies

137 Crises in Europe in the Transatlantic Context
Economic and political appraisals
Edited by Bruno Dallago and John McGowan

138 The International Monetary System, Energy and Sustainable Development
Edited by Sung Jin Kang and Yung Chul Park

139 Capitalism and the World Economy
The light and shadow of globalization
Edited by Toshiaki Hirai

140 Irish Economic Development
High-performing EU state or serial under-achiever?
Eoin O'Leary

141 Banking on Equality
Women, work and employment in the banking sector in India
Supriti Bezbaruah

142 Poverty, Inequality and Growth in Developing Countries
Theoretical and empirical approaches
Edited by Atsushi Maki

143 Decentralization and Infrastructure in the Global Economy: From Gaps to Solutions
Edited by Jonas Frank and Jorge Martínez-Vázquez

144 The Global Commercial Aviation Industry
Edited by Sören Eriksson and Harm-jan Steenhuis

145 International Trade, Competitive Advantage and Developing Economies
How less developed countries are capturing global markets
Caf Dowlah

146 Chinese Entrepreneurship
An Austrian economics perspective
Fu-Lai Tony Yu and Diana S. Kwan

147 Corruption, Economic Growth and Globalization
Edited by Aurora Teixeira, Carlos Pimenta, António Maia and José António Moreira

148 Low-carbon, Sustainable Future in East Asia
Improving energy systems, taxation and policy cooperation
Edited by Soocheol Lee, Hector Pollitt and Park Seung-Joon

149 The Local Impact of Globalization in South and Southeast Asia
Offshore business processes in services industries
Edited by Bart Lambregts, Niels Beerepoot and Robert Kloosterman

150 Moving Out of Poverty
An inquiry into the inclusive growth in Asia
Jonna P. Estudillo and Keijiro Otsuka

151 Cultural Differences and Economic Globalization
Effects on trade, foreign direct investment, and migration
Roger White

Cultural Differences and Economic Globalization

Effects on trade, foreign direct investment, and migration

Roger White

Routledge
Taylor & Francis Group
LONDON AND NEW YORK

First published 2016 by Routledge

2 Park Square, Milton Park, Abingdon, Oxfordshire OX14 4RN
52 Vanderbilt Avenue, New York, NY 10017

Routledge is an imprint of the Taylor & Francis Group, an informa business

First issued in paperback 2020

British Library Cataloguing in Publication Data
A catalogue record for this book is available from the British Library

Library of Congress Cataloging in Publication Data
White, Roger, 1967-
Cultural difference and economic globalization : effects on trade, foreign direct investment and migration / Roger White.
pages cm
1. International economic integration. 2. International trade. 3. International finance. 4. Emigration and immigration. I. Title.
HF1418.5.W485 2015
337–dc23
2015020555

ISBN: 978-1-138-89180-7 (hbk)
ISBN: 978-0-367-66862-4 (pbk)

Typeset in Times New Roman
by Swales & Willis Ltd, Exeter, Devon, UK

Contents

Figures

Tables

Preface

> "Culture is a matrix of infinite possibilities and choices. From within the same culture matrix we can extract arguments and strategies for the degradation and ennoblement of our species, for its enslavement or liberation, for the suppression of its productive potential or its enhancement."
>
> Wole Soyinka, Nigerian Nobel Laureate

> "Globalization is not something we can hold off or turn off . . . it is the economic equivalent of a force of nature – like wind or water."
>
> Bill Clinton, Former President of the United States of America

In the above quote, Bill Clinton describes globalization as a force. While there may be a tinge of hyperbole in the former President's words, the sentiment rings true. Globalization is a powerful process that confers tremendous benefits. The garnering of these benefits, however, may result in the imposition of costs. Accordingly, the overall merits of globalization are often heartily debated. One aspect of globalization that seems to receive a great deal of attention is the corresponding interaction among people from quite dissimilar cultures. It is often claimed that globalization weakens or homogenizes cultures. This may be true; however, might cultural differences hinder or limit the process of economic globalization by adding to related transaction costs? Before focusing too intently on the relationship between cultural differences and economic globalization, we should first gain a better understanding of what culture is or represents, and what the process of globalization, particularly economic globalization, entails.

The opening quote from Wole Soyinka speaks to the nature of culture. The quote also simultaneously offers a succinct definition and an explanation of culture. The words are direct and the meaning is clear, but the words also convey that culture is not easily defined. Culture is a vague term. Perhaps we can say that culture is an embodiment, but what it is, in any specific sense, is very much context-specific. In fact, culture may be so context-specific that differences across cultures are more easily identified and defined than are the respective cultures.

We can say that our differences, in terms of beliefs, attitudes, norms, values, social mores etc., make us unique. Further, our differences as individuals and our collective differences as societies, to the extent that they are meaningful when we engage in economic activities, likely result in higher associated transaction costs. These higher costs, in turn, are expected to translate to a reduced level of economic interaction with those who are dissimilar from us as individuals, or who differ from the societies in which we live. In a few words, the effect that our differences have on economic interactions is what this book, more or less, is about.

We seek to understand the relationship between cross-societal cultural differences and three specific facets of economic globalization: international trade, foreign direct investment, and international migration. We posit, from the outset, that cultural differences correlate with higher related transaction costs and that these costs manifest to hinder economic globalization. Given the importance of culture and the potential for tremendous gains to be received from international economic integration (i.e., economic globalization), a more complete understanding of the influences of cultural differences on trade, foreign direct investment and migration is valuable. Similarly, gaining an understanding of how economic globalization may affect cultural heterogeneity is also of considerable importance.

In this work, we extend the related academic literature by seeking a more detailed understanding of the relationships between cultural differences and economic globalization. We hope that the information provided here is useful for policymakers and of interest to students, researchers, academicians, and members of the general public.

Acknowledgments

I wish to convey my gratitude to the administration of Whittier College for their continued funding and overall support of my research efforts. Specifically, I wish to thank Charlotte Borst, Dean of the faculty, for bringing me to Whittier College, and our College President, Sharon Herzberger, for appointing me as the Douglas W. Ferguson Chair in International Economics. Accordingly, I wish to acknowledge the generous research support provided by the Ferguson Chair. Ashling Massoumi and Patrick Rubalcava provided outstanding research support. Funding support for student research assistants, provided by the John Murdy Chair in Business and Economics, is gratefully acknowledged. Lastly, very special thanks are in order to Michelle Espaldon for her friendship, patience, and loving support, and to Scout for just being her usual, wonderful self.

Part I

Globalization, economic integration, and cultural differences

This book addresses an important topic in international economics that, thus far, has received only scant attention. Our goal is to provide information that contributes to a better understanding of the potential influences of cultural differences on international economic interactions. More specifically, we seek to provide new information, garnered largely from econometric analyses, on the relationships between cross-societal cultural differences (i.e., the "cultural distance" between countries) and three distinct facets of economic globalization: international trade, foreign direct investment (FDI), and international migration.

The importance of our topic is underscored by the fact that we live in a world that has become increasingly interconnected while also being populated by individuals and societies that are incredibly diverse in their attitudes, beliefs, traditions, values etc. In short, economic activities are among the most common means by which international interactions occur, and these activities often involve quite dissimilar peoples and cultures. We have, however, a very limited understanding of the extent to which bilateral trade flows, FDI, and international migration are influenced by cultural differences. The work presented here seeks to improve our understanding of these relationships. Further, the results and conclusions provided in this work are beneficial, in a more general sense, as they afford a more complete understanding of the world in which we live.

We begin with some basic questions. What does the word "culture" represent? What are we referring to when we use the word? What is meant when we use the term "globalization" or the phrase "economic integration"? Defining these words and concepts, which are quite vague, even in a general sense, is necessary, as doing so provides the context for the analyses that follow in later chapters. Once our working definitions are in place, we provide an overview of the three most recent waves of globalization, while placing our emphasis on aspects of economic integration. This allows us to provide details of the degree to which economies have (or have not) integrated into the global economy, and to discuss related changes that have occurred over time.

In this initial portion of the book, we present several globalization indexes and discuss their construction. We also provide information about the component dimensions on which each of the indexes is based, placing a particular focus on the dimensions that are most related to international economic interactions.

Complementing our discussion of the three most recent periods of globalization, we introduce four composite measures of the cultural distances between countries. We make connections between cultural differences and the three waves of globalization where appropriate. Finally, we introduce and discuss a number of other variables that are used in later chapters as proxy variables for cultural differences.

By introducing the concepts of cultural distance and economic globalization, providing descriptive overviews of both concepts, and presenting the research questions that we address, this initial portion of the book sets the stage for the analyses that follow in Chapters 5 through 8. Moreover, these first four chapters provide the foundational material on which the contents of later chapters build.

1 Introducing culture and globalization

We live in a world that is characterized by extraordinary differences. In a sense, it is our differences that define us as individuals. That is, they permit us to identify as unique members of our communities and societies. Collectively, at a societal level, our cultural identities are informed by our individual and group differences. These differences represent who we are, in a collective sense, and they sometimes result in frictions that color the nature of the interactions we undertake. At a societal (or economy-wide) level, we see key differences among economic systems that have evolved over lengthy periods of time – decades, generations, and centuries. From what may be described as traditionally market-centric, capitalist economies, to the former members of the Soviet Union that continue their transitions, at varying paces, toward greater market-orientations, to the new traditional economies that feature religiously-influenced economic doctrines, the differences that exist between societies often manifest in the form of increased transaction costs. Even among groups of countries that share similar economic structures, we often see considerable and pronounced cultural differences that may result in diminished economic interaction.

The increased transaction costs that correspond with cultural differences may limit, or hinder, international trade flows. They may also make foreign direct investment (FDI) less likely to occur, and they may make international migration more costly and, therefore, a less common occurrence. In short, our cultural attributes make ourselves and our societies unique, but our differences may also impact our ability to benefit from economic interaction by raising the related transaction costs. In this book, we explore this possibility, examining the relationships between higher transaction costs, which may hinder economic globalization, and the greater cross-societal differences to which they may be attributable. Specifically, we employ a series of variables that represent cultural differences to consider whether cultural distance is a determinant of international trade flows. We also consider whether cross-societal cultural differences reduce FDI flows, and we examine a possible influence of cultural differences on international migration.

During the past 150 years or so, the world has witnessed three distinct periods of globalization. In a sense, these three periods, or "waves", of globalization can be thought of as eras within a more prolonged, almost continuous period of globalization that was interrupted by the start of the First World War and largely not restarted until after the close of the Second World War. The first two waves of globalization spanned the years, roughly, from 1870 through 1913 and from 1946 through about 1980. The disruption of international economic integration that is bookended by the two World Wars, along with the continued retreat toward isolationism during the interwar period, clearly delineates the first two waves of globalization.

The current and most recent wave of globalization differs from the previous two in that there was no interruption *per se* in the globalization process to separate the second wave from the third wave. It is true that, during each of the three waves, there has been a clearly observed increase in the intensity (or scale) of economic globalization; however, the end of the second wave of globalization and the start of the third was not marked by an interruption of the process. Beginning in the late 1970s and early 1980s, a larger number of developing countries became increasingly active in world markets. Further, following the collapse of the Soviet Union in 1991, the past two-plus decades have witnessed the increased integration of Russia and the former Soviet Republics, to varying degrees, into the global economy. Thus, even though a clear demarcation is lacking, marked changes can be found in terms of the scope of international economic integration as we move from the second wave to the current, third wave. In effect, one principal difference between the current wave of globalization and the prior waves is that today there is a broader cross-section of countries engaged in the global economy. In this sense, the globalization process is now more global.

Although we live in a world that can legitimately be described as more integrated, or connected than at any point in human history, economic interactions – such as international trade in goods and services and international factor movements (FDI flows and migration) – occur in a space that is characterized, in part, by great differences between countries. As these differences may correlate with greater frictions and, hence, higher transaction costs, it seems reasonable to examine the relationship between cultural differences and economic globalization. To that end, in this book, we examine the influence of cross-societal cultural differences as a potential impediment to international economic integration.

The analysis that follows is considerably data-focused. This means that rigorous statistical and econometric techniques are employed as we consider whether higher transaction costs, potentially attributable to greater cross-societal cultural differences (i.e., "cultural distance"), inhibit the volume of trade flows and/or the successful completion of new trade deals. Likewise, we consider whether cultural distance reduces foreign direct investment and, as noted, we explore a potential relationship between cultural distance and international migration. Our econometric analysis begins with an examination of the general relationships between cultural distance and these three facets of economic globalization. We then turn to examine, as far as possible, the common criticism that repeated economic interaction and intensified economic integration diminish cultural differences and result in a loss of cultural diversity (i.e., that economic globalization leads to greater cultural homogeneity).

Defining culture and globalization

It is necessary to establish, at the outset, working definitions of the terms "culture" and "globalization". Admittedly, as has been noted, these are rather amorphous terms. Perhaps this might explain why such a great number of possible definitions exist. Even so, it is beneficial to consider a sampling of definitions from the variety that has been offered, as doing so allows us to identify commonalities across definitions and, from these commonalities, to construct working definitions to guide the efforts that are presented here.

A handful of definitions for the term "culture" from the more distant past include: "those historically created designs for living, explicit and implicit, rational, irrational, and non-rational, which exist at any given time as potential guides for the behavior of men" (Kluckhohn and Kelly, 1945, p. 45). Echoing this definition while also focusing largely on behavior, Linton (1945, p. 32) defines culture as "a configuration of learned behaviors and results of behavior whose component elements are shared and transmitted by the members of a particular society." Similarly, Parson (1949, p. 8) emphasizes behavior, but also mentions the transmission of culture across time by stating that culture is "those patterns relative to behavior and the products of human action which may be inherited, that is, passed on from generation to generation independently of the biological genes." Reflecting what appears to have been a commonly-held view that culture is narrowly related to behavior, Useem and Useem (1963, p. 169) state that "[c]ulture has been defined in a number of ways, but most simply, as the learned and shared behavior of a community of interacting human beings." Here, the transmission of culture may be implied by the mention of interactions. Even so, the emphasis in these early definitions of culture is clearly on the topic of behavior.

More recent attempts to define culture indicate that the narrow, behavior-focused definition persists. One example is Damen (1987, p. 367), who describes culture as the "learned and shared human patterns or models for living." Damen further asserts that these "patterns and models pervade all aspects of human social interaction. Culture is mankind's primary adaptive mechanism." A second, more succinct, example is provided by Hofstede (2012, p. 51) who defines culture as simply "the collective programming of the mind which distinguishes the members of one category of people from another."

Following the social sciences' cognitive revolution of the 1950s and 1960s, many anthropologists have incorporated artifacts, mentifacts, and sociofacts when crafting definitions of culture. Huxley (1955), for example, posited that cultural traits effectively take on lives of their own and move from one generation to the next. One example comes from a very generic, yet contemporary, definition of culture. The Merriam-Webster Dictionary (2015a) defines culture as "[t]he beliefs, customs, arts, etc., of a particular society, group, place, or time." In this dictionary definition of culture, which may appear simplistic and/or vague, we see the mention of i) artifacts (i.e., arts), ii) mentifacts (i.e., beliefs) and iii) sociofacts (i.e., customs). Although this definition may appear to be plain, and lacking in detail, we do see the three components of the definition appear in other, more complete/complex definitions.

Lederach (1995, p. 9) extends beyond behavior as the primary component of culture, defining it as "the shared knowledge and schemes created by a set of people for perceiving, interpreting, expressing, and responding to the social realities around them." Somewhat similarly, Kroeber and Kluckhohn (1952, p. 181) contend that culture is the "patterns, explicit and implicit, of and for behavior acquired and transmitted by symbols, constituting the distinctive achievements of human groups, including their embodiments in artifacts." Other succinct definitions have been offered. For example, Banks and Banks (1989, p. 367) define culture as "the values, symbols, interpretations, and perspectives that distinguish one people from another in modernized societies." A much more expansive definition is provided by Choudary (2015), who defines culture as the systems of knowledge shared by a relatively large group of people; a cultivated behavior that represents the entirety of past experience, values, and attitudes, which is represented by symbols, and artifacts and which is deliberately disseminated throughout a society and passed from generation to generation through social mores, traditions, and institutions. Here, it is knowledge, behavior, experiences, values, attitudes, symbols and artifacts that embody culture. Social mores, traditions, and institutions are the mediums by which culture is conveyed across time and, within time, among individuals and subgroups of society.

The broader definitions offered in the above paragraph move us from the narrow, behavior-based definitions and closer to the Merriam-Webster definition offered at the outset of this section. Other dictionary definitions are similarly expansive. For example, the Cambridge American English Dictionary (2015) defines culture as "the way of life of a particular people, especially as shown in their ordinary behavior and habits, their attitudes toward each other, and their moral and religious beliefs." Finally, a wonderfully phrased early definition of culture, offered by Sir Edward Burnett Tylor in 1871, is included in Murphy (1986, p. 14). According to Tylor, culture is:

> that complex whole which includes knowledge, belief, art, morals, law, customs, and many other capabilities and habits acquired by . . . [members] of society . . . Culture means the total body of tradition borne by a society and transmitted from generation to generation. It thus refers to the norms, values, standards by which people act, and it includes the ways distinctive in each society of ordering the world and rendering it intelligible. Culture is . . . a set of mechanisms for survival, but it provides us also with a definition of reality. It is the matrix into which we are born, it is the anvil upon which our persons and destinies are forged.

Regardless of the specific definition of culture one considers, it appears that more recent attempts to define culture (and even some early offerings) have included the three common attributes of i) artifacts, ii) mentifacts, and iii) sociofacts. The work presented in this book does not truly require a specific definition of culture. In fact, a set of definitions that, collectively, provide a broad yet meaningful description of what we are referring to when we use the term would seem sufficient. With this in mind, an acceptable working definition of culture that we will employ here is "the totality of behavior, beliefs, arts, institutions, and all other avenues by which a population, community, or a class collectively expresses its values and attitudes" (White, 2010).

Defining globalization may be more straightforward than arriving at an ideal definition for culture. The word 'globalization' is, in fact, a fairly recent addition to the English language. Boyd and Mackenzie (1930) are credited by the Oxford English Dictionary (2015) with the first written reference to the term 'globalization'. Even so, the term remained largely unused for decades. Illustrating the newness of globalization as a term, whether used to describe international economic integration or otherwise, a search of articles in *The New York Times* reveals that 'globalization' was not used in *The Times* until December 31, 1974, when the term was included in an article titled "Grappling with Multinational Corporations". (The article's focus is that year's annual meetings of the Allied Social Science Association.)

A decade-by-decade search of *The Times* during the period from 1851 through 2010 reveals an increase in the use of 'globalization' during recent decades. Corresponding with the increased usage has been a decrease in the use of the term "economic integration". Table 1.1 reports the number of articles, by decade, in which the corresponding words and terms are found.

The frequency of use of other key terms that are similar in meaning to "economic globalization", and the related processes that we examine in this work (i.e., trade, foreign direct investment, and migration), are noted in Table 1.1. Figure 1.1 illustrates the time paths of values presented in Table 1.1, while grouping terms to represent descriptors of i) globalization, ii) international trade, iii) foreign direct investment, and iv) international migration. Generally speaking, across the four groupings, we observe increased usage over time. Within each grouping, we also see some decline in the frequency of use for particular words or terms. Even so, while variation is found in the terminology used to describe the interactions that constitute what we may broadly label as economic globalization, the use of terms within the four groupings may reflect an increased prevalence of economic globalization in the day-to-day lives of many.

Although the word 'globalization' is a somewhat new addition to the English language, the activities associated with what we consider to be "globalization" have been ongoing, with ebbs, flows and periodic interruptions, since at least the latter half of the 19th century. Thus, globalization is certainly not a new phenomenon. Even so, the depth, breadth, and inclusiveness of prior waves of globalization pale in comparison to that which is observed today. Since about 1980, the extent and pace of global economic integration has been nothing short of astounding when considered in relation to earlier periods. Perhaps unsurprisingly, an increase in the number of definitions offered to describe globalization has coincided with this greater economic integration.

Table 1.1 Counts of *The New York Times* articles featuring certain words/terms, by decade

Words/Terms	*1851–60*	*1861–70*	*1871–80*	*1881–90*	*1891–1900*	*1901–10*	*1911–20*	*1921–30*
(1) globalization	0	0	0	0	0	0	0	0
(2) economic integration	0	0	0	0	0	0	0	7
(3) international trade	3	7	8	21	116	111	362	844
(4) exports	1,549	1,763	2,748	2,582	7,503	6,993	14,097	28,183
(5) imports	2,042	1,837	2,355	2,303	5,273	5,562	9,955	18,486
(6) foreign direct investment, direct foreign investment	0	0	0	0	0	0	0	0
(7) capital flows	0	0	0	0	0	1	0	7
(8) international migration	0	0	0	0	5	0	0	23
(9) immigration, emigration	2,261	1,863	2,130	2,591	3,018	3,808	4,283	9,090
(10) immigrant, emigrant	3,636	2,250	2,479	3,865	3,193	3,029	3,231	5,072

Words/Terms	*1931–40*	*1941–50*	*1951–60*	*1961–70*	*1971–80*	*1981–90*	*1991–2000*	*2001–10*
(1) globalization	0	0	0	0	1	160	681	1,792
(2) economic integration	8	182	370	595	472	194	159	94
(3) international trade	2,118	2,813	2,207	1,797	9,199	7,366	2,391	827
(4) exports	37,033	26,556	27,293	21,432	17,735	15,802	9,467	8,377
(5) imports	25,795	17,648	20,496	16,660	18,954	15,140	8,152	7,389
(6) foreign direct investment, direct foreign investment	1	3	5	67	97	79	114	168
(7) capital flows	12	1	11	70	163	165	127	113
(8) international migration	18	8	34	3	8	8	7	11
(9) immigration, emigration	7,294	8,676	8,176	4,075	7,209	7,012	5,540	7,192
(10) immigrant, emigrant	6,367	4,173	3,712	3,511	6,034	7,610	12,862	14,172

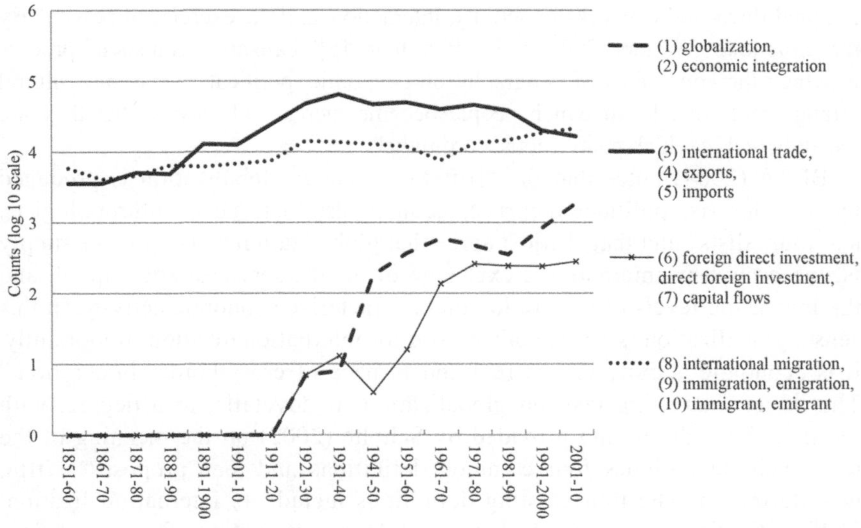

Figure 1.1 Counts of *The New York Times* articles featuring certain words/terms, by decade

Returning to the dictionary as a starting point for creating a working definition, we find globalization defined as "the development of an increasingly integrated global economy marked especially by free trade, free flow of capital, and the tapping of cheaper foreign labor markets" (Merriam-Webster, 2015b) and as "the process by which businesses or other organizations develop international influence or start operating on an international scale" (Oxford, 2015). Similarly, Shangquan (2000, p. 1) defines economic globalization as "the increasing interdependence of world economies as a result of the growing scale of cross-border trade of commodities and services, flow of international capital and wide and rapid spread of technologies." In each of these definitions, there is a strong emphasis on economic interactions.

More expansive definitions go beyond international economic interactions. Albrow and King (1990, p. 9) defines globalization as "all those processes by which the peoples of the world are incorporated into a single world society, global society." Similarly, Robertson (1992, p. 8) references the world when offering that globalization "refers both to the compression of the world and the intensification of consciousness of the world as a whole . . . both concrete global interdependence and consciousness of the global whole." Giddens (1990, p. 64) also passes on international economic interactions, focusing instead on the broad, inclusive, "global" aspect of the term. Specifically, globalization is said to be "the intensification of worldwide social relations which link distant localities in such a way that local happenings are shaped by events occurring many miles away and vice versa." A broader definition is provided by Held et al. (1999, p. 16) who assert that "[g]lobalization can be thought of as a process (or set of processes) which embodies a transformation in the spatial organization of social relations and transactions – assessed in terms of their extensity, intensity, velocity and impact – generating transcontinental or interregional flows and networks of activity, interaction, and the exercise of power." By the same token, Waters (2001, p. 3) offers that "[g]lobalization is a social process in which the constraints of geography on economic, political, social and cultural arrangements recede, in which people become increasingly aware that they are receding and in which people act accordingly."

BERA (2004) notes that the "[l]iterature about globalization is produced by sociologists, political theorists, economists, historians, anthropologists, and journalists" and that "[m]ost agree that globalization rests upon, or simply is, the growth in international exchange of goods, services, and capital, and the increasing levels of integration that characterize economic activity. In this sense, globalization is only another word for internationalization. Importantly, it is economic activity that is fuel and furnace of cross-border integration." This is an interesting take on globalization. It dovetails, to a degree, with the thoughtful discussion provided by Scholte (2002) on the meaning of the term. Scholte critiques four common definitions and then proposes a fifth, new definition. The four existing definitions include 1) internationalization, 2) liberalization, 3) universalization, and 4) westernization. The new definition offered by Scholte is 5) spatiality. The form of globalization that this book focuses on is most closely associated with what Scholte describes as internationalization and, indirectly and to a lesser extent, to what is labelled as liberalization. Before discussing the details of internationalization and of liberalization, it is useful to briefly discuss the three other definitions.

Universalization is described by Scholte (2002, p. 57) as "a process of dispersing various objects and experiences to people at all inhabited parts of the earth. On these lines, 'global' means 'worldwide' and 'everywhere'." A separate, yet related, definition is offered by Scholte (2002, p. 58) for westernization: "a particular type of universalization, one in which the social structures of modernity (capitalism, industrialism, rationalism, urbanism, etc.) are spread the world over, destroying pre-existent cultures and local self-determination in the process." Finally, Scholte (2002, p. 49) offers a new definition, spatiality, that "identifies globalization as the spread of transplanetary – and in recent times more particularly supraterritorial – connections between people. From this perspective, globalization involves reductions in barriers to transworld contacts. People become more able – physically, legally, culturally, and psychologically – to engage with each other in 'one world'." While these three definitions may be appropriate in certain settings, when discussing particular facets of globalization, or when considering globalization within particular contexts, it is the definition that Scholte labels as internationalization that is most fitting for the purposes of this book.

Internationalization is defined by Scholte (2002, p. 54) as "a growth of transactions and interdependence between countries. From this perspective, a more global world is one where more messages, ideas, merchandise, money, investments and people cross borders between national-state-territorial units." Additionally, there are elements of the 'liberalization' definition of globalization that are quite relevant for our purposes. Scholte (2002, p. 56) defines liberalization as "a process

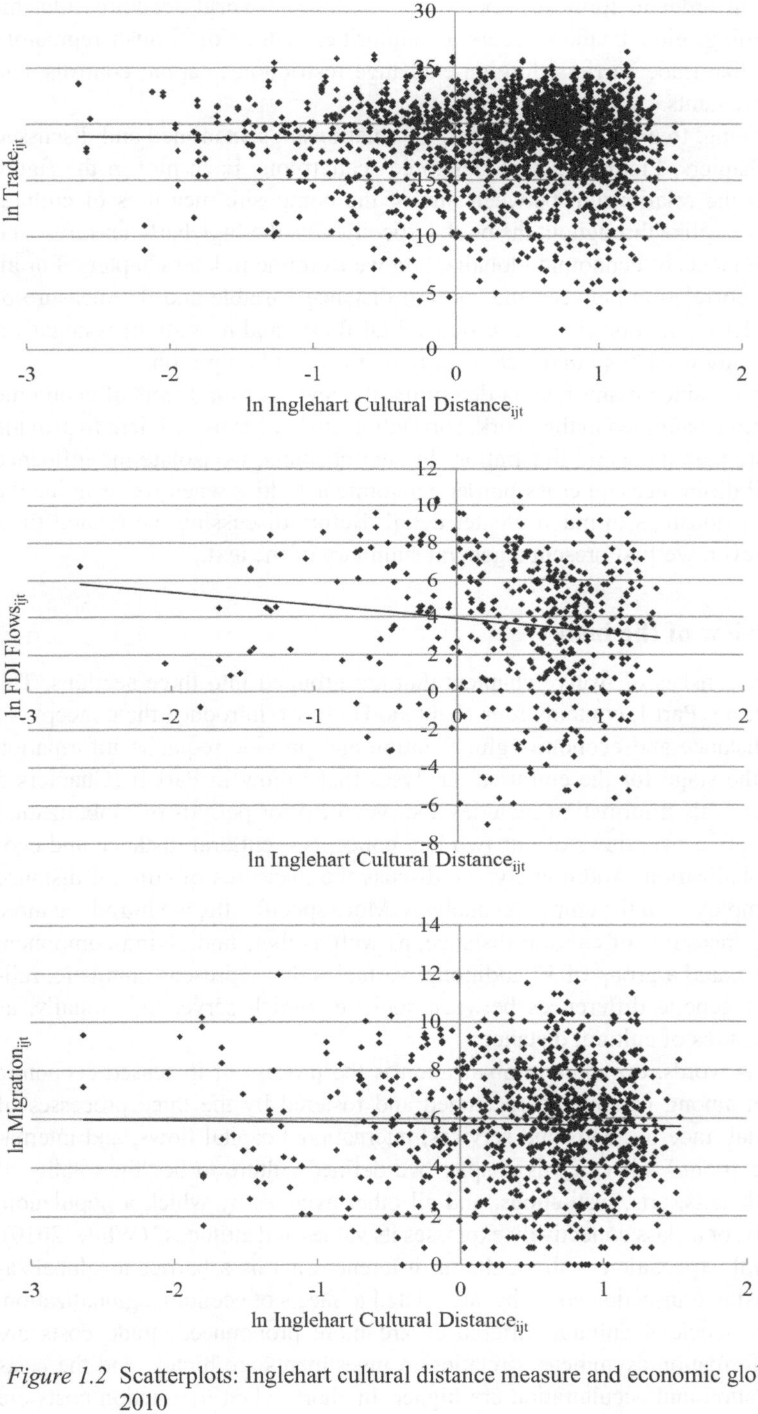

Figure 1.2 Scatterplots: Inglehart cultural distance measure and economic globalization, 2010

of removing officially imposed restrictions on movements of resources between countries in order to form an 'open' and 'borderless' world economy. On this understanding, globalization occurs as authorities reduce or abolish regulatory measures like trade barriers, foreign-exchange restrictions, capital controls, and visa requirements."

Previewing, to a very minor extent, the relationships examined and discussed in later chapters, Figure 1.2 includes three scatterplots. Each plot in the figure represents the relationship between one of the composite measures of cultural distance we utilize throughout the book – specifically, the Inglehart measure – and one of the facets of economic globalization we examine in later chapters. For all plots, the correlation between the cultural distance variable and the measure of cross-border interaction (i.e., trade flows, FDI flows, and migration) is negative; however, only weakly so in the cases of trade flows and migration.

Of course, since many factors determine the levels of the facets of economic globalization examined in this work, correlation analysis is insufficient to provide much more than a general illustration. In later chapters, we isolate the influence of cultural differences on cross-border economic activities when we examine the posited relationships in much greater detail. Before discussing the related findings, however, we first present a general summary of the text.

An overview of the book

This book consists of twelve chapters that are grouped into three sections. The initial section, Part I, contains four chapters. Here, we introduce the concepts of cultural distance and economic globalization and provide requisite information that sets the stage for the empirical analyses that follow in Part II (Chapters 5 through 8). This information includes a survey of prior periods of globalization and descriptive overviews of our two key concepts – cultural distance and economic globalization. Additionally, we discuss the measures of cultural distance that are employed in the empirical analysis. More specifically, we introduce three composite measures of cultural distance, as well as their underlying component dimensions, and a group of 17 additional variables that represent linguistic, religious, and genetic differences between societies which serve, individually, as proxy measures of cultural distance.

In a few words, economic globalization is the process of increased economic integration among nations, characterized and fostered by the three processes of international trade in goods and services, international capital flows, and international migration. Earlier in this chapter, we defined culture to be "the totality of behavior, beliefs, arts, institutions, and all other avenues by which a population, community, or a class collectively expresses its values and attitudes" (White, 2010). Our general expectation is that cultural differences act as a barrier to globalization by raising transaction costs that are related to facets of economic globalization. When cross-societal cultural differences are more pronounced, trade costs are higher, information asymmetries relating to investments are higher, and the costs of assimilation and acculturation are higher. In short, when transaction costs are higher, we anticipate reduced activity. Accordingly, we examine cross-societal cultural differences as a potential impediment to the three processes that, collectively, comprise the overarching phenomenon of economic globalization.

Thus far, we have introduced our topic in broad, general terms. We have explored what is meant when we use the terms 'culture' and 'globalization' and we have sought to provide working definitions of these concepts. Producing definitions for these terms is essential given our primary research topic/questions: to what extent, if any, do cross-societal cultural differences affect international trade flows, foreign direct investment flows and stocks, and international migration flows? We now offer greater detail regarding the structure of the book. Accordingly, the remainder of this chapter offers a general discussion of the book's focus, and detailed synopses of the current and remaining chapters.

In Chapter 2, we survey the three most recent waves of globalization while emphasizing economic integration as a facet of a more broadly-defined "globalization" process. Focusing primarily on the periods from 1870–1914 (i.e., a period of industrial and technological revolution in a large portion of the Western world) and 1945–1980 (i.e., a period marked by greater global cooperation, particularly among Western, developed economies), the degree to which economies have been integrated into the international economy is discussed using the results of prior research and data on trade flows, foreign direct investment flows and stocks, and international migration flows. Although we touch briefly on the present wave of globalization (1980–present), the emphasis of this chapter is largely confined to the two prior waves.

We introduce several measures of economic globalization in Chapter 3, and explore variations in the measures across time, countries, and country groups. From 1980 to the present, the KOF Economic Globalization Index scores have increased for 127 of the 131 countries for which complete data are available (Dreher, 2006 and Dreher et al., 2008). Further, the variance in index scores across these countries also decreased during the period. Since economic integration has increased both in depth (i.e., more pronounced bilateral connections) and in breadth (i.e., connections have become more commonplace), it is reasonable to say that the global economy has become increasingly integrated. The chapter includes a descriptive overview of the six globalization indexes we utilize in this work, along with discussions of their component dimensions and the associated country rankings.

To complement the discussion of economic integration presented in Chapter 3, we introduce four broad, composite measures of cultural differences in Chapter 4. The first measure is based on results from the first five waves (conducted from 1981 through 2009) of the World Values Survey and, where applicable, the European Values Survey. The second and third measures, based primarily on data collected during the late 1960s and early 1970s, are based on Hofstede's cultural dimensions. We employ a four-factor measure that permits more countries to be represented by the data, as well as a broader, six-factor measure of cultural distance. The fourth measure is based on data collected in the early-to-mid-1990s by the GLOBE Project. We also introduce 17 variables that collectively reflect linguistic differences/similarities, religious dissimilarity, and genetic distance. These variables are employed to represent cultural differences. We conclude this chapter by examining changes in the measures of cultural distance during recent decades as a means by which the evolution of cultural distances may be considered.

Having established what we can consider to be operational definitions of culture and globalization, we follow by examining the potential relationship between cultural differences and economic globalization and, conversely, how economic globalization may affect cultural differences. The second portion of the book consists of four chapters that introduce the general analytic framework used to conduct our analysis, and provide detailed analysis of the relationships between cultural distance and international trade flows, foreign direct investment, and international migration.

In Chapter 5, we present the theoretical bases and empirical frameworks that are employed, in turn, during our examination of the influence of cultural distance on international trade flows, foreign direct investment, and international migration. We also detail the specific research questions that will be addressed in subsequent chapters. The gravity model, initially developed by Tinbergen (1962), is commonly known as the workhorse for empirical studies of international trade. It has also been used frequently in the analysis of international migration (e.g., Lewer and van den Berg, 2008; White and Yamasaki, 2014). To examine foreign direct investment flows, we build upon the work of Blonigen and Piger (2011) who employ Bayesian statistical techniques to identify the most likely determinants of foreign direct investment flows. Coupled with the theoretical intuition that underlies this model's use, we discuss the choice of explanatory variables. Chapter 5 serves as a bridge from Part I to the analyses presented in Chapters 6 through 8. Throughout the analysis, we employ a variety of econometric techniques (i.e., ordinary least squares, feasible generalized least squares, the Tobit technique, and the zero-inflated negative binomial technique) as appropriate, given the data and the research question(s) addressed in the analysis.

We begin our presentation of the results obtained from our empirical analysis in Chapter 6, where the relationship between cultural distance and international trade is examined. We document that cultural distance inhibits both the volume of trade flows (an intensive margin, or trade-intensification, effect) and the successful completion of trade deals (an extensive margin, or trade-initiation, effect). The econometric specifications/methodologies employed largely follow the theoretical foundations of Anderson and van Wincoop (2003); however, augmented gravity specifications are also employed.

In Chapter 7, we examine the predicted determinants of international investment flows and stocks. Just as cultural differences are found to hinder international trade flows, we report a negative relationship between cultural distance and both FDI flows and FDI stocks. This finding is consistent across sample sizes, dependent variable series, and, perhaps most importantly, across the composite measures of cultural distance, the corresponding component dimensions, and the set of variables that are employed as proxy variables for the composite measures of cultural distance.

In Chapter 8 we again report a negative relationship between cultural distance and an aspect of economic globalization. In this instance, we find that international migration flows are diminished due to cultural differences between the source and destination countries. Again, the finding is consistent across measures of cultural distance.

Having explored, in Chapters 5 through 8, a general relationship between cross-societal cultural differences and international trade, foreign direct investment, and international migration flows, we close the book with a final section that consists of two chapters. In Chapter 9, we consider the potential influence of economic integration on cultural distance by examining the oft-mentioned criticism that economic globalization leads to cultural homogeneity. Thus, we turn our attention to our secondary research question that seeks to determine whether greater economic globalization results in a loss of cultural uniqueness.

Repeated interaction and intensified integration may result in a decrease in cultural differences and, if so, local mores may be replaced by global norms and ideas. It is also possible that greater interaction produces new mixtures of cultures and increased heterogeneity. Accordingly, we examine the hypothesis that increased interaction in the form of international trade, foreign direct investment and internal migration decreases bilateral cultural distance – an indication of cultural homogeneity – over a period from the early 1980s through the first decade of the current century.

In Chapter 10, we note that economic globalization confers tremendous net benefits to the involved societies; however, the ability to garner these benefits is limited, to varying degrees, by the influences of cross-societal cultural differences. With this in mind, we summarize the preceding chapters and close by briefly restating our most prominent findings, summarizing our work and offering broad, general thoughts on the topic.

2 Waves of globalization

Past and present

In this chapter, while emphasizing economic integration as a component of a more broadly-defined process labelled "globalization", we present an overview of the three most recent waves. While our primary focus is on the periods from 1870–1914 and 1945–1980, the degree to which economies have been integrated into the international economy during all three waves is detailed using the results of prior research and data on trade flows, foreign direct investment, and international migration. Given that we introduce a number of globalization measures in Chapter 3, and that the data necessary to produce these measures are typically not available for the years prior to the current wave of globalization, we wait until Chapter 3 to provide a detailed discussion of the current wave.

The first wave, 1870–1914

1870 marked the beginning of a significant period in the history of the global economy. This period ended with the outbreak of the First World War, which largely curtailed international trade, foreign investment flows, and international migration. Between 1820 and 1870, world trade as a share of Gross Global Product (GGP) increased from 2 percent to 10 percent (Maddison, 1995). Foreign direct investment had also increased significantly during this period, as had international migration. For example, between 1800 and the mid-1850s, the equivalent of about $2.1 billion was invested abroad (Graff et al., 2014). Even so, this total paled in comparison to the FDI outflows of $43 billion that occurred between 1870 and 1914 (Graff et al., 2014). While Great Britain and France accounted for the majority of pre-1870 FDI outflows, the United States and Germany joined Britain and France as major sources of foreign direct investment during the years from 1870 to 1914. In fact, these four nations accounted for 83 percent of 1914 global investment outflows and, when the FDI outflows from Belgium, the Netherlands, and Switzerland are also accounted for, these seven countries accounted for 95 percent of 1914 global FDI outflows (Graff et al., 2014). It is worth mentioning that the primary sources for foreign investment during this period were the United States and, effectively, a handful of European nations.

The recipients of foreign investment were more diverse. It is true that countries in Europe and North America received 51 percent of global FDI during the 1870–1914 period, with the remaining portion received by countries in Latin America (19 percent), Asia (16 percent), Africa (9 percent), and Oceania (5 percent) (Graff et al., 2014). As Table 2.1 indicates, during the four-decade-plus period from 1870 through 1914, world trade as a share of GGP continued to increase – from 10 percent to 18 percent: an impressive feat. As a share of GGP, however, the world stock of foreign investment increased to an even greater extent, more than doubling from 6.9 percent in 1870 to 17.5 percent in 1914 (Taylor, 2006 and Crafts, 2000).

Corresponding with the growth in trade and international investment, there was a marked increase in international migration, from 14.9 million international migrants worldwide during the 60-year period from 1821 through 1880 to 36.6 million migrants during the 35-year period from 1881 through 1915 (Ferenczi and Wilcox, 1929; Roberts and Byrne, 1966; and U.S. Census, 1960). Table 2.1 illustrates the substantial level of international migration during the 1870–1914 period. Roughly 10 percent of the total world population moved internationally – primarily from Europe to the Americas and from China and India to smaller nearby countries (World Bank, 2000). By contrast, in 2013, only about 3.2 percent of the world's population resided in a country different from that of their birth (UN, 2013).

Table 2.1 Measures of global integration, select years

Year	*Foreign Assets*	*Trade*	*Transport and Communications Costs (constant US$)*			
	(Percent of GGP)	*(Percent of GGP)*	*Sea Freight*[c]	*Air Transport*[d]	*Phone Call*[e]	*Computer*[f]
1820	.	2[a]	.	.	.	.
1870	6.9	10[a]	.	.	.	.
1890	.	12[a]	.	.	.	.
1900	18.6	.	.	.	.	.
1914	17.5	18[a,b]	.	.	.	.
1920	.	.	95	.	.	.
1930	8.4	18[a]	60	0.68	245	.
1940	.	.	63	0.46	189	.
1945	4.9	.	.	.	.	.
1950	.	14[a]	34	0.30	53	.
1960	6.4	16[b]	27	0.24	46	12,500
1970	.	22.4[a]–20[b]	27	0.16	32	1,947
1980	17.7	.	24	0.10	5	362
1990	.	26[a,b]	29	0.11	3	100
1995	56.8	.	.	.	.	.

Source(s): Crafts (2000)
a Maddison (1995)UNDP (1999)
b Crafts (2000)
c Average Ocean Freight and Port Charges per Ton.
d Average Revenue per Passenger Mile.
e Three minute telephone call from New York City to London.
f Index: 1990 = 100

Source: Dollar (2001).

The global reallocation of labor and capital, and the ensuing increases in production and trade in accordance with comparative advantage, resulted in an acceleration of economic growth. In the half century prior to 1870, worldwide, per capita incomes had increased annually, on average, by about 0.5 percent. During the first wave of globalization, the annual average increase in per capita income was approximately 1.3 percent (World Bank, 2002). Through the effective importation of capital and labor and the corresponding exports of primary goods, the economies that were most actively engaged in increasing economic integration (e.g., Argentina, Australia, New Zealand, and the United States), gained the most. In short, these countries largely left the rest of the world behind, especially those countries not engaged in globalization. It is noteworthy that, during this first wave of globalization, the primary trading powers, the source economies and recipients of a large share of global foreign investment, and the home and host countries for a high percentage of international migrants, were most often either European countries or countries that, historically, had strong ties to Europe. The vast majority of countries around the globe were essentially non-participants in international economic integration during this period.

The First World War, isolationism and the second wave, 1914–1980

The outbreak of the First World War in 1914 largely resulted in a cessation of global economic integration. This was neither surprising nor unprecedented. As noted in Taylor (2006), 90 percent or more of international trade disappears during wartime, and typically a decade is needed following a war's end for trade volumes to recover to their pre-war levels. Unfortunately, rather than seeking to restore global trade, investment, and migration flows to pre-war levels, a large number of countries chose to pursue nationalist agendas and, thus, retreated into isolation. Therefore, the countries that had been active globalizers during the first wave pulled back and the opportunities for countries that were not engaged in the international economy prior to the First World War dissipated. Between 1920 and 1950, there was a continued decline in transportation costs. Table 2.1 indicates that both sea freight costs and air transport costs were more than halved, while communications costs fell by an even greater margin. Even so, due to other barriers to cross-border economic activities, the observed levels of trade (as a share of GGP), foreign direct investment (also as a share of GGP), and the international migrant stock (as a share of world population) all declined from the beginning of the First World War through to the end of the Second World War.

An illustrative example of the retreat from the global economy is the post-First World War reversal of trade policies in many countries – moving from continued reductions in trade barriers or, at least, barriers held more or less constant, to the pursuit of "beggar-thy-neighbor" policies that sought to divert domestic demand for imports to domestically-produced goods. The result was a sharp decline in international trade flows. As is shown in Table 2.1, as a share of GGP, world trade declined from 18 percent in 1914 to 14 percent in 1950. Likewise, foreign assets as a share of GGP decreased from 17.5 percent in 1914 to 4.9 percent in 1945 before increasing, although only modestly and still far below pre-Second World War levels, to 6.4 percent in 1960.

A specific instance of a "beggar-thy-neighbor" policy was the Smoot-Hawley Tariff Act, which was passed in 1930 by the United States Congress. The act resulted in the imposition of import tariffs on over 20,000 imported goods. Further, the average tariff on dutiable goods imports increased from 40.1 percent in 1929 to 59.06 percent in 1932, and the average overall tariff rate for the United States, for both dutiable and non-dutiable imports, increased from 13.48 percent to 19.8 percent during the same period (US Census, 1975). Figure 2.1 illustrates, for the United States, the average tariff rates (on dutiable goods imports and on all imports), the share of total imports that were dutiable, and the levels of total imports during the period from 1870 through 1945.

The first wave of globalization (1870–1914) and the inter-war period (1914–1945) are identified in the figure. Passage of the Smoot-Hawley Act in 1930 is also marked. We see a near-continual decline in average import tariff rates during the first wave of globalization and through to the end of the First World War. The average tariff rate on dutiable imports remained relatively constant; however, for both tariff measures we see sharp declines beginning around 1900 and continuing through to the end of the First World War. Accordingly, during the period from 1900 through 1917, the United States' total imports increased at an average annual rate of 4.95 percent. This annual growth in imports was significantly higher than the corresponding 3.6 percent average annual growth rate observed between 1870 and 1899.

From 1914 to 1929, tariff rates largely remained level, with some increases being realized during the 1920s. Even so, the general increase in total imports

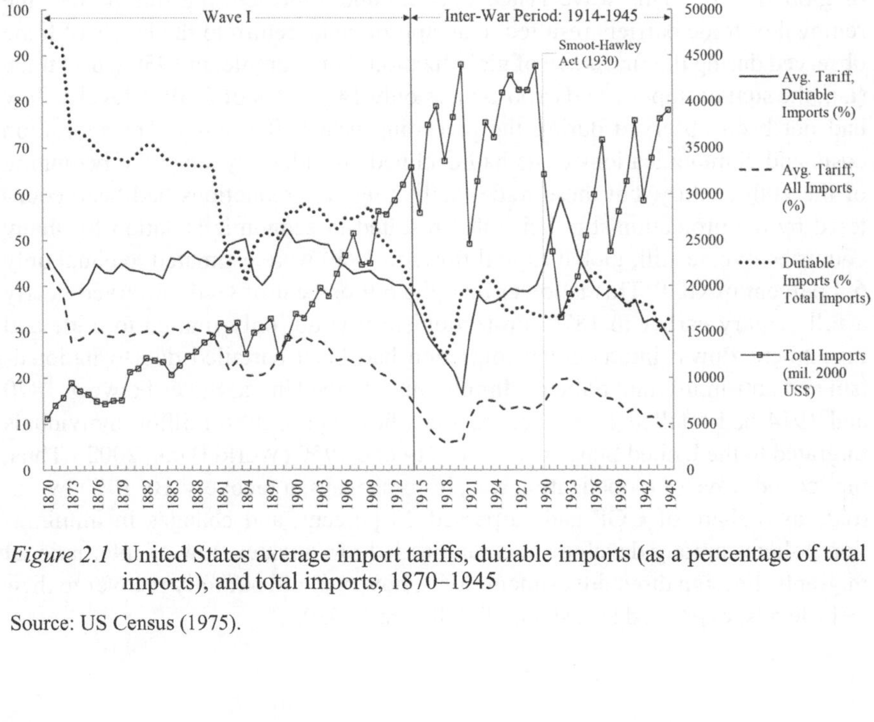

Figure 2.1 United States average import tariffs, dutiable imports (as a percentage of total imports), and total imports, 1870–1945

Source: US Census (1975).

continued until 1930. Between 1929 (the year prior to the passage and implementation of the Smoot-Hawley Tariff Act) and 1933, the total imports of the United States fell by a remarkable 55.3 percent. To illustrate how large a drop in trade this represents, the level of United States imports in 1933 was lower, in real terms, than it had been more than three decades earlier at the turn of the twentieth century. During the period from 1929 through 1933, the average overall import tariff of the United States and the average tariff imposed by the US on dutiable imports increased by nearly one half (46.9 percent) from 13.5 percent to 19.8 percent, and by more than one third (33.6 percent) from 40.1 percent to 53.8 percent, respectively. Even as import tariff rates started to decline, beginning in 1933 for dutiable imports and in 1934 for imports generally, total United States imports in 1945 remained below the level that had been achieved in 1920.

In response to the failed "beggar-thy-neighbor" policy of the Smoot-Hawley Tariff Act, the United States Congress passed the Reciprocal Tariff Act in 1934. The Reciprocal Tariff Act was an attempt to move to a more liberal trade policy. The act gave authority to the President of the United States to negotiate tariff reductions with trading partners, and served as a basis for subsequent bilateral trade agreements. Even with the act in place, the remnants of the Great Depression and the outbreak of the Second World War limited the dismantling of trade barriers prior to 1945. After 1945, governments moved to rein in protectionist policies. The corresponding reductions in trade barriers, along with further decreases in transportation costs and the establishment of the Bretton Woods system of quasi-fixed exchange rates, all contributed to increases in global trade flows.

The end of the Second World War marks the beginning of our second wave of globalization. This wave lasted until around 1980. During this period, the removal of trade barriers resulted in an approximate return to the levels of trade observed during the first wave of globalization. For example, in 1950 world trade (i.e., the sum of imports and exports) was only 14 percent of GGP. A level so low had not been observed during the preceding near-half century. Transportation costs and communications costs had declined considerably since the beginning of the 20th century, but these trade-facilitating cost reductions had been countered by the protectionist policies that resulted in economic isolation for many countries. Worse still, global capital flows in 1960 were estimated to equal only 6.4 percent of GGP. This is lower than the 6.9 percent of GGP observed nearly a full century earlier in 1870. Protectionism was not only limited to trade and investment flows; international migration had been curtailed due to nationalism and anti-immigrant policies. Immigration to the United States between 1870 and 1914 had totalled 15 million persons; however, only 6 million individuals migrated to the United States between 1914 and 1950 (World Bank, 2002). Thus, the second wave of globalization was, in some ways, a recovery. By 1970, world trade as a share of GGP had surpassed 20 percent, and changes in immigration policies among developed economies led to a greater flow of international migrants. Foreign direct investment flows, however, did not fully recover to their 1914 levels, expressed as a share of GGP, until 1980.

A brief introduction to the current wave of globalization

Figure 2.2 illustrates the time paths of world imports (both in real dollars and as a share of GGP), net FDI inflows (again, in real terms and as a percentage of GGP), and international migration (by number of migrants and as a share of world population) over the period from 1960 through 2013. Since 1980, there has been growth in both trade and foreign direct investment. Moreover, each has increased in absolute terms and as a share of GGP to previously unobserved levels. Similarly, there are more international migrants than at any prior point in our history; however, there has been a slight decline in the world stock of immigrants as a share of the global population. Many of the increases in these values can be attributed to the entry of developing economies and countries that had been members of the Soviet Union into the international economy. However, a portion of the increase, of course, is the result of greater intensity of interaction among the countries that had engaged internationally in the earlier waves.

Evidence of a shift in the international economic activity of developing countries is found in their general openness to international trade, in their successes in attracting foreign investment, and in the extent to which they contribute to the international migrant stock. In 1983, for example, developing countries (i.e., low- and middle-income countries that were not part of the USSR) maintained an average applied import tariff rate equal to 37.8 percent (World Bank, 2015a and 2015b). This rate decreased slightly to 27.7 percent in 1990, was nearly halved over the next decade to 14.4 percent by 2000, and declined further to 9.8 percent in 2007 (World Bank, 2015a and 2015b). In total, over just a quarter century, more or less the span of a single generation, the average applied import tariff rate of developing countries declined by nearly three-quarters (74.1 percent). Similarly, between 1980 and 2000, a period of only 21 years, the stock of inward

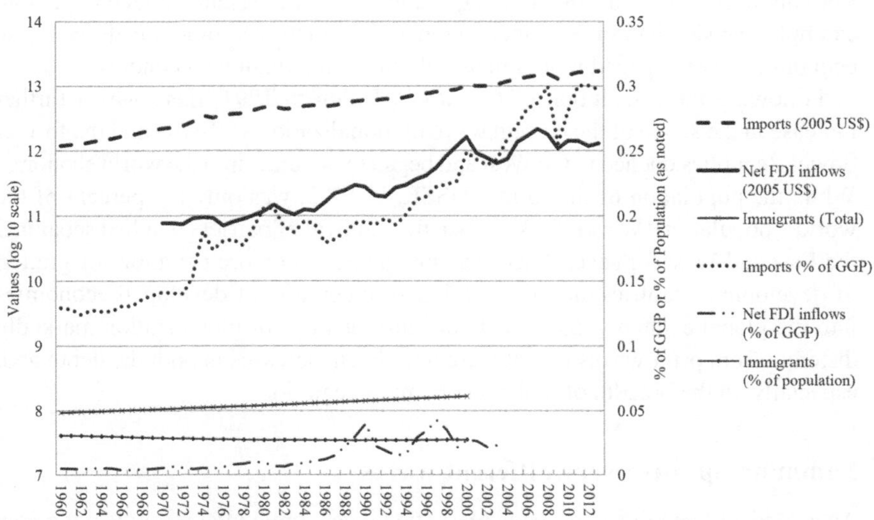

Figure 2.2 World trade, FDI flows, and immigrant stocks – counts and shares, 1960–2013

FDI in developing countries increased by a factor of more than seven from $241 billion to $1.98 trillion (Balasubramanyam, 2001). Additionally, over the same period, the number of international migrants who resided in developing countries increased from 52.1 million to 64.6 million (Zlotnik, 2005).

What is particularly striking is that, in 1982, a handful of developing countries (i.e., Bangladesh, China, India, Indonesia, and Pakistan) accounted for nearly one half (45.2 percent) of the world's population (World Bank, 2014). In that same year, the average annual incomes in these economies (measured in constant 2005 US dollars) ranged from as low as $245 (in Bangladesh) to $581 (in Indonesia), with the group average equal to only $299 (World Bank, 2014). An indicator of the relative lack of global economic engagement by these economies, at the time, is that their collective trade (i.e., the sum of their exports and imports) was equal to only 20.8 percent of their combined output (with imports equal to 10.9 percent of Gross Domestic Product – GDP – and exports equal to 9.9 percent of GDP) (World Bank, 2014). By 2012, these five economies still constituted a very large share (45.1 percent) of the world's population; however, their collective average annual income had increased to $2,072, and their trade intensity had risen to 51.9 percent of their combined output (with imports increasing as a share of GDP to 25.9 percent and exports, again as a share of GDP, increasing to 26 percent) (World Bank, 2014).

Corresponding with the increased trade volumes, there also has been an increase in FDI flows to developing economies. Likewise, the number of international migrants who reside in the global South (i.e., Africa, Central and Latin America, developing Asia, and the Middle East) increased from 51 million in 1985 to 78 million in 2005 (Ratha and Shaw, 2007). In fact, the absence of Bangladesh, China, India, Indonesia, Pakistan, and other similar developing economies from the global economic system prior to the 1980s left a large portion of the world's population unable to share in the potential benefits of economic globalization. Looking to Bangladesh, China, India, Indonesia, and Pakistan, collectively, as an example, we see that, on average, incomes have increased dramatically as these economies have engaged more intensively in the international economy.

Following the dissolution of the Soviet Union in 1991, there was a further increase in the scope of the current wave of globalization as Russia and the former Soviet Republics opened to the West and began to integrate into the world economy. While the population of the former USSR, in 1992, was only 5.4 percent of the world's population (World Bank, 2014), the removal of barriers that had separated the East and West for several decades, the greater and more common integration of developing countries, and the continued integration of developed economies into the global economy, have made the current wave of globalization markedly different from prior waves in that there have been increases in both the depth and, especially, in the breadth of global economic integration.

Summing up three very different waves

As is evident from this overview, international economic integration is not a new phenomenon. The first wave of globalization (1870–1914) was characterized by general decreases in the barriers to trade, by the development and diffusion of new technologies, and by declining transportation costs. The primary participants in the first globalization wave were European nations and countries that had been settled by European powers. For example, Jacks et al. (2006) estimate that total trade costs between the United States, the United Kingdom and France and their trading partners decreased by 10 to 15 percent from 1870 to 1913 and that these decreases accounted for 44 percent of the expansion in world trade observed during the period. The decline in trade costs is attributed to a number of factors, including reduced transportation costs stemming from technological advances (e.g., the use of steam-powered ships as opposed to sailing ships, an increased prevalence of railway use, and advances in communications), economic growth, productivity advances, and reduced tariff and non-tariff barriers to trade. While the United States was modestly active in terms of reducing tariff barriers during this period, its tariffs on imported goods were among the highest in the world at the outset of the First World War (Faubert, 2011).

The second wave of globalization (1945–1979) and the current wave (1980–present) have also been marked, generally, by reductions in tariffs and non-tariff barriers to trade. During these more recent waves, the United States has been among the leading proponents for reductions of such barriers. Additionally, since the end of the Second World War, we have witnessed greater technological transfers and the continuation of pronounced reductions in transportation costs. Further, the international financial system is more integrated now than ever before and, accordingly, international capital now flows more freely than it has during earlier periods. The second wave of globalization included more countries; however, the participants remained, generally, developed and market-oriented economies. It should be noted that there were exceptions and it was not solely developed economies that participated in this second wave of globalization. For example, the opening of Taiwan and South Korea to trade and international investment flows, and the subsequent economic success, was a powerful encouragement for other developing countries to follow suit (Dollar, 2001).

During the third wave (i.e., the current wave), we see the entrance of the majority of developing countries and of former members of the Soviet Union. Thus, the current wave of globalization is the first truly global wave. In conjunction with the timing of the end of the second wave and the current wave, and potentially resulting from the increased cross-border economic activity, the global economy has grown at an average annual rate of 3.5 percent (Dollar, 2001). This is a considerable improvement on the typical 0.5 percent annual growth in the world economy that was observed during the years from about 1820 through 1870 and the 1.3 percent average annual growth realized during the 1870 to 1914 period.

Effectively, although culture may appear to be in the background, perhaps, unrelated to the pattern and pace of economic globalization, it is linked (even if indirectly) to these three waves of economic integration. In the first wave, participants were largely limited to Europe, the United States, and a few other countries, often among those settled or colonized by major European powers. The second wave involved these industrialized, western, "first world" nations and a few developing countries, The wave did not involve the nations that comprised the Soviet Union (i.e., second world) or the majority of lesser-developed economies (i.e., third world). As noted, the most recent wave is largely global, with participation and increased integration being the norm and isolationism very much an exception. Thus, given the varied starting times and intensities of engagement in the global economy, it is not at all surprising to find countries currently at differing stages of globalization.

Nor is it surprising, again, given the different starting points/times and exclusions based on political considerations, colonial relationships, and relative stages of development, that there are stark cultural differences that correspond with the extent to which economies are currently globally integrated.

A result of some countries having been more engaged in the global economy and others less engaged or, in practical terms, not engaged at all, is that a clear unevenness in the extent to which national economies are globalized has emerged/evolved over time. Generally speaking, Western, industrialized, and post-industrial economies, having been more active in all three waves of globalization, are commonly among the most active in terms of international trade, foreign direct investment, and migration. Much of the developing world has, to varying degrees, embraced international economic integration since the 1970s, with a few of the countries in this cohort having been active in the global economy during the second wave of globalization. The former members of the Soviet Union, being among the more recent additions to the globalization process, face the hurdle of being late arrivals to engagement in the global economy and, thus, having to catch up with those countries that began the globalization process earlier, and of adapting to market-based economics after three quarters of a century (i.e., multiple generations), having generally been closed off from such institutions. As there are clear differences in the extents to which countries have been and are currently active in the global economy, and because these differences are such that they correspond with cultural differences, we discuss the current unevenness of economic globalization in much greater detail in Chapter 3.

3 The unevenness of economic globalization

Our introductory chapter provides a very brief overview of the three most recent waves of globalization. This overview is followed, in Chapter 2, by a more complete discussion of the first and second waves, dated from 1870 to 1914 and from 1945 to 1979, respectively. In this chapter, we extend the earlier, initial discussions by introducing a number of indexes to detail the most recent wave of globalization (i.e., the wave that began around 1980). In doing so, we show the extent to which countries are globalized, both generally and in terms of their economic interactions at various points in time. Accordingly, our focus is on several aggregate/overall measures of globalization (i.e., our four composite measures) and on the related dimensions that reflect the extent to which national economies are integrated with the global economy. Through the presentation and discussion of these indexes, we begin a broader discussion of globalization. Doing so serves to inform and frame the material that we present in later chapters, where we present the findings from our empirical examinations of the relationships between cross-societal cultural differences and different facets of economic globalization.

Components of globalization indexes and of economic globalization dimensions

The KOF Globalization Index

The globalization indexes presented in this chapter represent varying numbers of countries and span different time periods. Additionally, each measure is distinct in its construction. There are times, however, when we see considerable overlap in the composition of the underlying components that are used to construct the indexes. While we discuss several measures of globalization, the KOF Globalization Index provides coverage for the lengthiest time period – in this instance, annually from 1970 through 2011 – and includes the largest number of countries, ranging from 137 to as many as 191 countries depending on the year considered (Dreher, 2006 and Dreher et al., 2008). Thus, owing to its expansive coverage, in a sense, we rely on the KOF Index as our *de facto* measure of globalization.

The KOF Index is constructed based on information that represents three separate dimensions of globalization: 1) economic, 2) social, and 3) political. The overall index is a weighted composite of these three dimensions, ranging in value from 0 to 100, with higher values indicating greater degrees of globalization. The economic, social, and political dimensions carry weights of 36 percent, 38 percent and 26 percent respectively. Our primary interest lies in the examination of the relationships between various forms of international economic integration and cross-societal cultural differences. Although the economic dimension of the KOF Index is of considerable importance, we first look to the construction of the social and political dimensions, since doing so may allow for a better understanding of the overall KOF Globalization Index.

The social globalization dimension is constructed based on data that are categorized according to three sub-dimensions: 1) personal contact, 2) information flows, and 3) cultural proximity. The personal contact sub-dimension comprises one third of the social globalization value, data on information flows accounts for 35 percent, and cultural proximity represents the remaining 32 percent. The data used to calculate the personal contact sub-dimension includes telephone traffic (which carries a weight of 25 percent in the construction of the sub-dimension), transfers as a share of GDP (a 3 percent weight), international tourism (26 percent), the immigrant stock as a share of the total population (21 percent), and international letters per capita (25 percent). The information flows' contribution to the social dimension is based on the number of Internet users per 1,000 people (a 36 percent sub-dimension weight), televisions per 1,000 people (38 percent), and trade in newspapers as a share of the country's GDP (26 percent). Finally, the cultural proximity value is determined based on the number of McDonald's restaurants per capita (44 percent), the number of IKEA stores per capita (44 percent), and trade in books as a share of GDP (12 percent). By contrast, the political dimension is constructed using data that represent the number of embassies in the country (25 percent), the country's memberships in international organizations (27 percent), the country's participation in United Nations Security Council missions (22 percent), and the number of international treaties to which the country is a signatory (26 percent).

As noted, the economic globalization dimension of the KOF Index is of primary interest for the work presented here. It is based on 1) actual economic flows between each country and the remainder of the world and 2) the presence and extent of restrictions that impede international economic interactions. These two sub-dimensions are weighted equally to produce the economic globalization dimension. The economic flows that comprise the "actual flows" sub-dimension are the sum of the country's external trade as a share of its GDP (a weight of 22 percent), its FDI stocks as a share of its GDP (27 percent), total portfolio investment as a share of GDP (24 percent), and the amount of income payments made to foreign nationals, also as a share of GDP (27 percent). The components of the "restrictions" sub-dimension are hidden import barriers (a 24 percent weight in the sub-dimension), the average external tariff rate (28 percent), taxes on international trade as a share of current revenue (26 percent), and capital account restrictions (23 percent). Thus, the KOF economic globalization dimension is a composite that captures both observed international economic interactions and barriers that hinder such interaction.

The Centre for the Study of Globalisation and Regionalisation Index and the Foreign Policy/A.T. Kearney Globalization Index

Similar to the KOF Globalization Index, the Centre for the Study of Globalisation and Regionalisation (CSGR) Globalization Index includes a large number of countries and has a lengthy reference period. Specifically, the CSGR Index spans the period from 1982 through 2004 and includes values from as few as 27 countries in 1982 to as many as 103 countries in 2004. Moreover, the construction of the CSGR Index is considerably similar to that of the KOF Index. The CSGR Index and the KOF Index comprise the same three dimensions of globalization: economic, social, and political. The CSGR economic globalization dimension is constructed using data for four factors that include 1) the sum of the country's exports and imports (41.8 percent), 2) the sum of FDI inflows and outflows (9.2 percent), 3) the sum of portfolio investment inflows and outflows (22 percent), and 4) the sum of income payments made to foreign nationals and income payments from abroad that are received by domestic residents (27 percent). All four components are considered relative to the size of the nation's GDP. As before, the values in parentheses are the weights used to construct the dimension. While these four factors are nearly identical to those that comprise the actual flows sub-dimension of the KOF economic globalization dimension, there are minor dissimilarities and the weights vary across the two indexes. Additionally, while the actual flows sub-dimension of the KOF economic globalization dimension is similar to the CSGR economic globalization dimension, the KOF dimension includes factors that constitute the restrictions sub-dimension, while the CSGR dimension does not.

The CSGR Globalization Index was constructed with the notion of creating a complement to the Foreign Policy/A.T. Kearney (FP/ATK) Globalization Index. In fact, the CSGR Index uses many of the same variables in constructing its social dimension that are used as part of the personal contact and technological connectivity dimensions of the FP/ATK Index. Illustrating the similarities between the CSGR Index and the FP/ATK Index in terms of the construction of these dimensions, we see that the CSGR social dimension is constructed using data for immigrant stocks and inflows as shares of the population, worker remittances as a percentage of the country's GDP, tourist arrivals and departures relative to the population size, minutes of international telephone traffic, Internet users as a share of the country's population, the number of foreign films imported and domestic films exported, the value of per capita trade in books and newspapers, and the amount of international mail delivered and sent per capita. By comparison, the personal contact dimension of the FP/ATK Index is constructed using data on international travel and tourism, international telephone calls, remittances and transfers (i.e., worker remittances, compensation to employees, and other private transfers). The technological connectivity dimension of the FP/ATK Index is constructed using data on the number of Internet users and Internet hosts and the number of secure servers through which encrypted transactions are processed.

The political dimension of the CSGR Index is constructed based on data for the number of foreign embassies in the country, the number of United Nations peacekeeping operations in which the country participates, and the number of international organizations of which the country is a member. Similarly, the political engagement dimension of the FP/ATK Index is created using data that represent the country's international transfer payments made and its receipts, their personnel contributions and financial contributions to United Nations peacekeeping missions, the number of international treaties to which the country is a party, and the country's involvement in international organizations.

The economic dimension of the overall CSGR Index, as noted above, is created using data that represent the country's trade volume (i.e., the sum of its exports and imports relative to GDP), its FDI inflows and outflows, portfolio investment inflows and outflows, and international income payments made or received. Unsurprisingly, given that the overall CSGR Index was produced with the intention of being a complementary measure to the FP/ATK Globalization Index, the economic integration dimension of the FP/ATK Index is constructed using data on trade flows, FDI, portfolio capital flows, and international income payments and receipts. That is, the FP/ATK economic dimension is quite similar to the CSGR economic dimension, which itself is very similar to the actual flows sub-dimension of the KOF economic dimension.

The Ernst & Young Globalization Index

The Ernst & Young (E&Y) Globalization Index was developed by the Economist Intelligence Unit (EIU) in 2009 and provides annual coverage for a 20-year-plus time period (1995–2016) for the world's 60 largest countries, as determined by their GDP values. The E&Y Index is based on five "pillars" of globalization: 1) trade openness (which has a weight of 22 percent in the index), 2) capital flows (21 percent), 3) international exchange of technology and ideas (21 percent), 4) international labor movements (19 percent), and 5) cultural integration (17 percent).[1] Thus, as it lacks any explicit political dimension, the E&Y Index is most similar to the economic and social globalization dimensions of the KOF and CSGR Indexes.

The trade openness pillar of the E&Y Index is based on six factors related to international trade in goods and services. Specifically, the pillar is constructed using data for 1) total trade (i.e., the sum of imports and exports), 2) trade openness, 3) tariffs and non-tariff barriers, 4) ease of cross-border trading, 5) current account restrictions, and 6) the share of the country's trade that is with its main trading partners. Total trade data is from national accounts and has a 40 percent weight in the pillar's construction. Likewise, data for the share of the country's trade that is with its main trading partners is from national accounts and the factor has a weight of 20 percent. All other factors have weights equal to 10 percent and are constructed by the EIU using scales that range from 1 to 5.

The capital flows pillar of the E&Y Index is based on seven factors that are related to the international movement of capital and, more generally, to international finance. These factors are FDI stocks (in and out, as a share of GDP), portfolio capital flows (inward and outward, as a share of GDP), government policy towards foreign investment, expropriation risk, investment protection schemes, domestic favoritism by the government, and state control/ownership. The measures for FDI stocks and portfolio capital flows are based on data from the IMF International Financial Statistics, while the remaining factors are determined by the EIU using their 1-to-5 scale. The FDI stock measure has a weight of 50 percent in the pillar's construction. All other factors have equal weights of 8.3 percent.

The third pillar of the E&Y Index is the exchange of technology and ideas. The first of these three pillars is constructed using data on trade in information and communications technology goods, trade in creative goods and services, the number of broadband subscriptions per 100 people in the country's population, and the number of Internet users per 100 people. The trade measures are based on UNCTAD data and are constructed as the sum of relevant exports and imports as a share of GDP. Each trade measure has a weight of 30 percent in the pillar's construction. Data on the number of broadband subscriptions and on the number of Internet users are from the International Telecommunications Union. Each measure carries a weight of 20 percent in the pillar's construction.

The pillar that represents the international movement of labor is a composite measure based on three underlying facets: the net migration rate (per 1,000 members of the population), current transfers (inward and outward, as a share of GDP), and the ease of hiring foreign nationals. The data sources are the United Nations, the IMF International Financial Statistics, and the EIU's 1-to-5 ratings, respectively. The last facet, ease of hiring foreign nationals, has a weight of 20 percent and the other two facets carry weights of 40 percent. The final pillar, cultural integration, is also based on three underlying facets: tourism (in and out, per 1,000 members of the population), minutes of international telephone traffic per capita, and the openness of the national culture to foreign influences. All three facets carry the same weight of one third in the pillar's construction. The tourism data are from the World Tourism Organization, those for telephone traffic are from the International Telecommunications Union, and the measure of openness to foreign influences is determined by the EIU using the now familiar 1-to-5 scale.

The Maastricht Globalization Index

Echoing the construction of the E&Y Index, the structure of the Maastricht Globalization Index (MGI) reflects several facets of the FP/ATK Index. Currently available only for the years 2000, 2008, and 2012, the MGI is generated using data for seven dimensions. The global politics dimension is based on the number of foreign embassies and high commissions a country hosts and the number of international organizations to which the country is a member. A separate dimension that is not explicitly included in any of the other indexes is organized violence.

This dimension is generated using data on the country's trade in arms relative to total military spending. A third dimension, global trade, is based on the country's trade intensity (i.e., the sum of imports and exports as a share of GDP), while a fourth, global finance, is constructed from data on gross FDI stocks as a share of the country's GDP and from data on gross private capital flows, again as a proportion of GDP. The social and cultural dimension of the MGI is comprised of data on migrants per 1,000 members of the country's population and international tourism arrivals and departures per 100 members. The technology dimension is based on the number of Internet users as a share of the country's population, and on total (incoming and outgoing) international telephone traffic (measured in minutes) per capita.

Finally, unlike any of the other indexes, the MGI includes the country's ecological footprint as an environmental dimension. The logic underlying this dimension is that a country for which the footprint is greater than their biocapacity carries an ecological deficit. Likewise, a country can carry an ecological surplus. In these instances, there is a need to "export" or "import" space from the rest of the world in order to avoid rapid environmental degradation. This form of "trade" is not necessarily reflected in data on trade of goods and services, but would still imply greater involvement with the rest of the world. Another unique characteristic of the MGI is that it includes adjustments for countries' geographic attributes.

The DHL Global Connectedness Index

Similar to the E&Y Globalization Index, the DHL Global Connectedness Index is constructed using data on "pillars" of globalization. In this case, there are four pillars: 1) gross exports as a share of GDP, 2) FDI flows as a share of gross capital formation and portfolio equity stocks as a share of market capitalization, 3) international Internet traffic as a share of total Internet traffic and international telephone calls as a share of total calls, and 4) migrants as a share of the population, international students as a share of all students, and international tourists as a share of all arrivals. Thus, the DHL Index can be described as consisting of four broadly-defined facets: 1) trade, 2) capital movements and investment, 3) information flows, and 4) people (Ghemawat and Altman, 2014).

In addition to the four pillars of activity described above, the DHL Index takes into account the depth and the breadth of each country's international activity, as well as the directionality of their international interactions. The "depth" ratio reflects the extent of a country's international interaction (i.e., activities and flows) relative to its domestic activities. For example, in terms of international engagement, in absolute terms, the United States is among the most internationally-engaged economies in the world. However, given the size of the US economy, US international engagement is somewhat low relative to domestic activities and when considered in relation to that of other, smaller economies. The "breadth" facet complements the depth ratio. However, rather than measuring the degree of international engagement relative to domestic activity, the depth ratio represents the dispersion of a country's international activity (i.e., interaction) across other countries. Ghemawat and Altman (2014) offer inbound tourism in the Bahamas as an example of both depth and breadth. The Bahamas is ranked second in the world in terms of inbound tourists per capita. Thus, they have a high depth score for this facet. The vast majority (more than 80 percent) of tourist arrivals in the Bahamas are, however, from the United States. Accordingly, their breadth score is low for this facet. This example highlights the policy relevance of international flows (e.g., tourists, trade, capital, etc.) and the importance of including the directionality of international flows as part of the DHL Index.

Increases in the depth and breadth of globalization

Figure 3.1 illustrates the extent of globalization at three points in time. Panel A depicts globalization in 1970, a point near to the middle of the second wave of globalization (which began in 1945 and continued until about 1979). Panel B shows how globalized countries were in 1990, about one decade following the start of the current wave of globalization, and Panel C shows the extent of globalization in 2010 – 30 years since the start of the current period of globalization, and, of course, 40 years since the point depicted in Panel A.

Beginning with 1970 (Panel A) and looking first to the legend, we see that darker shading indicates higher index values (i.e., more globalization). As noted above, the KOF Globalization Index ranges from 0 to 100, and the shading for the Index is split into quintiles. Those countries that are not shaded are those for which data are not available. In the panel, we see that data are not available for Russia, other members of the USSR, a portion of southern Africa, and part of the Middle East. Even so, in 1970, the KOF Globalization Index is available for 137 countries. Among these countries, none are ranked at the highest level of globalization – that is, a score of 80–100. The country ranked as most globalized in 1970 is Belgium, which has an index value of 72.42. In fact, representative of the relative lack of globalization in 1970, there are only 12 countries that fall within the second highest quintile (i.e., the range of index scores from 60 to 80). Looking at the map we can see that this cohort includes Canada, a portion of Western Europe (e.g., Denmark, Ireland, and the Netherlands), Sweden, Norway, Singapore, and a few other countries. In fact, looking at Panel A, we see a number of countries (e.g., China and a number of countries in southeast Asia, Afghanistan, Somalia, Madagascar, Chad, Niger, and Benin) that are in the lowest quintile (i.e., index scores that range from 0 to 20). An even greater number have index scores that place them in the second lowest quintile (scores ranging from 20 to 40). This includes much of Central and South America, a large number of African countries, India, Pakistan, and several countries in Southeast Asia.

Turning our attention to Panel B, and comparing it to the situation depicted in Panel A, we first see that there are more countries for which data are available (fewer countries with no shading). Additionally, it is noticeable that the map, in general, has darkened. This illustrates the general movement of countries, during the 1970–1990 period, towards greater globalization. More specifically, slightly more than two thirds (67.1 percent) of the countries for which the 1970 KOF

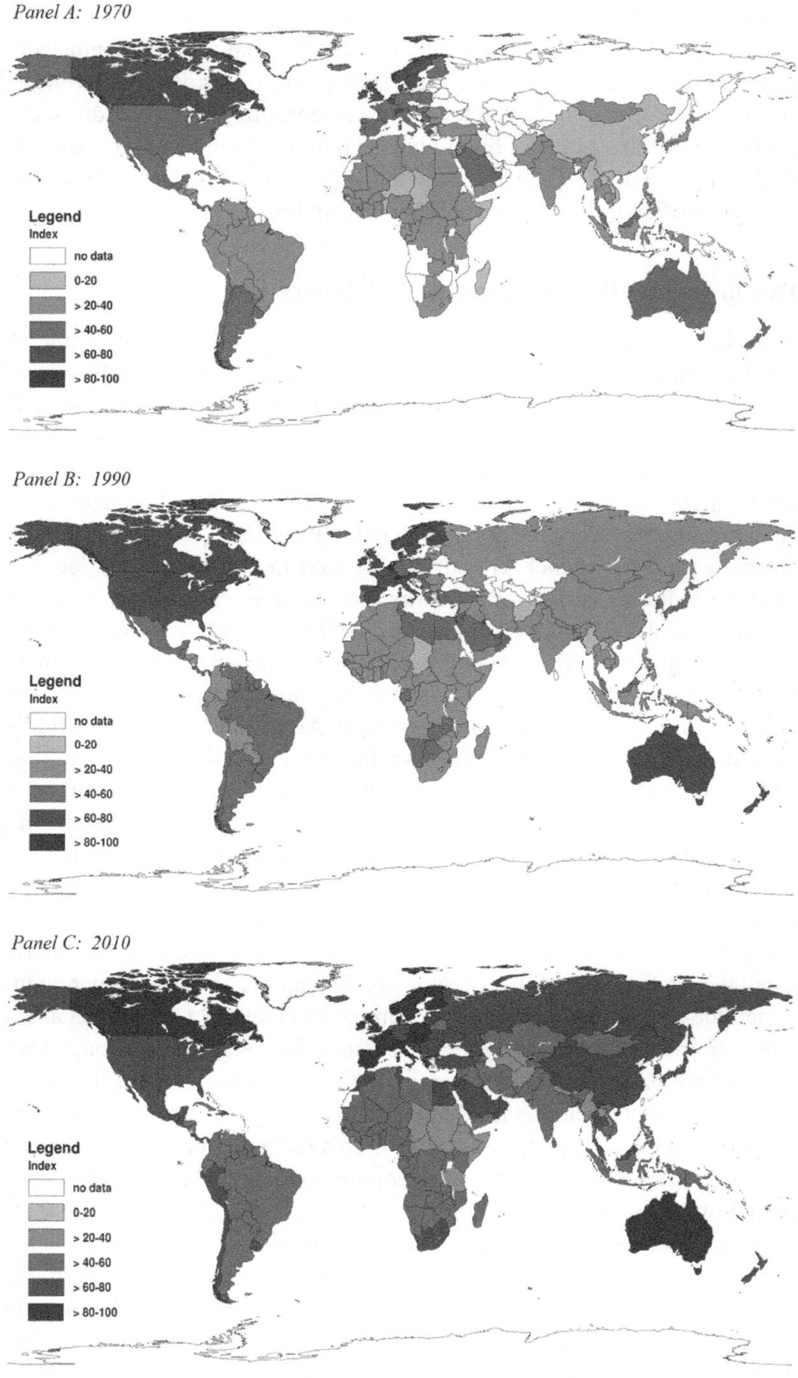

Figure 3.1 KOF Index of Globalization, 1970, 1990, and 2010

Index values are available (i.e., 92 of 137 countries) had scores between 0 and 40. By 1990, this share had decreased to 57.7 percent of the countries for which data are available (97 of 168 countries). By 2010, this figure had declined to only 14.4 percent (27 of the 187 countries for which data are available).

Corresponding with the absolute and proportional decreases in countries located in the bottom two quintiles, there has been an increase in the frequency with which countries appear in the middle and top two quintiles. Specifically, the shares (and numbers) of countries in the middle quintile (index values ranging from 40 to 60) increased from 24.1 percent (33 countries) in 1970 to nearly 29 percent (48 countries) in 1990, to almost half (48.1 percent or 90 countries) in 2010. Likewise, the shares (and, again, numbers) of countries in the top two quintiles (index values ranging from 60 to 100) increased from less than 9 percent (12 countries, all within the second quintile) in 1970 to almost 14 percent

Table 3.1 KOF Globalization Index, quintile distributions and inter-quintile movements

Panel A: Quintile Distributions

	1970	*1990*	*2010*
0–20	15 (10.9%)	7 (4.2%)	0
>20–40	77 (56.2%)	90 (53.6%)	27 (14.4%)
>40–60	33 (24.1%)	48 (28.6%)	90 (48.1%)
>60–80	12 (8.8%)	18 (10.7%)	46 (24.6%)
>80–100	0	5 (3.0%)	24 (12.8%)
No data	70	39	20

Panel B: Quintile Changes

	1970–1990	*1990–2010*	*1970–2010*
Moved up	42 (30.7%)	114 (67.9%)	120 (87.6%)
Moved up 1 quintile	42 (30.7%)	99 (58.9%)	88 (64.2%)
0–20 to >20–40	8 (5.8%)	2 (1.2%)	10 (7.3%)
20–40 to >40–60	18 (13.1%)	60 (35.7%)	52 (38.0%)
40–60 to >60–80	11 (8.1%)	23 (13.7%)	15 (10.9%)
60–80 to >80–100	5 (3.6%)	14 (8.3%)	11 (8.0%)
Moved up 2 quintiles	0	15 (8.9%)	32 (23.4%)
0–20 to >40–60	0	0	5 (3.6%)
20–40 to >60–80	0	12 (7.1%)	16 (11.7%)
40–60 to >80–100	0	3 (1.8%)	11 (8.0%)
Moved up 3 quintiles	0	0	0
0–20 to >60–80	0	0	0
20–40 to >80–100	0	0	0
Moved up 4 quintiles	0	0	0
0–20 to >80–100	0	0	0
No change	95 (69.3%)	54 (32.1%)	17 (12.4%)
Moved down	0	0	0

(23 countries) in 1990, to more than one third (37.4 percent or 70 countries) in 2010. The quintile distribution of countries, over the KOF Index, during the years 1970, 1990, and 2010 is presented in Table 3.1.

Returning our attention to Figure 3.1, Panel C illustrates the KOF Globalization Index values for the year 2010. Corresponding with the values presented in Panel A of Table 3.1, the further darkening of the map represents both the further globalization and an increase in the number of countries for which data are available. In 2010, 187 countries were represented by the index. While it is evident from the general darkening of the map that countries are becoming more globalized, it is perhaps equally, if not more, noteworthy that we are not seeing a retreat. That is, we do not see decreases in the extent to which countries are globalized. In fact, as we compare countries' 1970 KOF Index values to their 2010 values, we see 10 countries moving from the lowest quintile (index values ranging from 0 to 20) to the second quintile (values ranging from 20 to 40), 52 countries moving from the second quintile to the middle (i.e., third) quintile (values ranging from 40 to 60), 15 countries moving from the middle to fourth quintile (values ranging from 60 to 80) and 11 countries moving from the fourth quintile to the top quintile (values equal to or greater than 80). In fact, 120 countries moved from a lower quintile to a higher quintile over the 40-year period, with 88 moving to the next highest quintile and 32 moving up two quintiles. Another 17 countries did not change from their initial quintile during the 1970–2010 period. However, all 17 countries experienced increases in their index values (ranging from 0.61 to 19.07) during the period, with the mean increase equal to 12.34. Most striking is that not a single country moved to a lower quintile. A summary of the movements between quintiles is presented in Panel B of Table 3.1.

Comparing globalization indexes

Table 3.1 and Figure 3.1 combine to detail the KOF Globalization Index, in levels and changes in levels, at three points in time. While the KOF Index provides coverage for more countries and a longer period than other indexes, it is worthwhile to compare the KOF Index with other globalization indexes.

Table 3.2 lists the 10 most globalized countries, as identified by six different globalization indexes, using the most recent years for which data are available. Beginning with the KOF Globalization Index, we see that Ireland is ranked as the most globalized country in 2011, followed by Belgium, the Netherlands, Austria, Singapore, and so on. Looking across the remaining indexes, we see that five of the 10 countries identified by the KOF Index as being the most globalized – specifically, Singapore, Austria, Sweden, Belgium, and Denmark – are listed among the most globalized countries as determined by the 2004 Centre for the Study of Globalisation and Regionalisation (CSGR) Index. Similarly, Belgium, the Netherlands, Austria, Ireland, and Sweden are identified by both the 2011 KOF Index and the 2012 Maastricht Globalization Index (MGI) as being among the most globalized. Likewise, four of the top six countries listed in the 2007 Foreign Policy/AT Kearney (FP/ATK) ranking appear in the top 10 list of the KOF Index. Both the 2011 Ernst & Young (E&Y) Globalization Index and the 2011 DHL Global Connectedness Score include six countries that are listed among those included in the top 10 of the KOF ranking. In fact, the top seven most globalized countries, as identified by the KOF Index, appear on at least one of the other indexes presented in the table. More specifically, Ireland is found on all five of the other indexes. Belgium, the Netherlands, Singapore, and Sweden are found on four of the five non-KOF Indexes. Denmark shows up on three of the five indexes and Austria appears on two of the five. Portugal, Hungary, and Finland, which are ranked eighth through tenth on the KOF Index respectively, do not appear in the top 10 rankings of any of the other five indexes. However, Portugal is ranked as high as 18th (MGI), Hungary as high as 11th (E&Y), and Finland as high as 12th (E&Y).

The general consistency in rankings illustrates that, while the indexes are constructed in different ways (representing different facets or aspects of globalization),

Table 3.2 Top 10 most "globalized" countries, select years

Rank	*KOF (2011)*	*CSGR (2004)*	*E&Y (2011)*
1	Ireland	Singapore	Hong Kong
2	Belgium	Belgium	Singapore
3	Netherlands	Canada	Ireland
4	Austria	United Kingdom	Belgium
5	Singapore	United States	Switzerland
6	Denmark	Austria	Netherlands
7	Sweden	Sweden	Sweden
8	Portugal	Switzerland	Denmark
9	Hungary	France	United Kingdom
10	Finland	Denmark	Germany
Rank	*DHL (2011)*	*MGI (2012)*	*FP/ATK (2007)*
1	Netherlands	Belgium	Singapore
2	Ireland	Netherlands	Hong Kong
3	Singapore	Switzerland	Netherlands
4	Luxembourg	United Kingdom	Switzerland
5	United Kingdom	Austria	Ireland
6	Belgium	Germany	Denmark
7	Switzerland	Ireland	United States
8	Denmark	Sweden	Canada
9	Germany	Malaysia	Jordan
10	Sweden	France	Estonia

KOF: KOF Globalization Index
CSGR: Centre for the Study of Globalisation and Regionalisation Globalisation Index
E&Y: Ernst & Young Globalization Index
DHL: DHL Global Connectedness Score
MGI: Maastricht Globalization Index
FP/ATK: Foreign Policy-AT Kearney Globalization Index

include somewhat different cohorts of countries, and in some instances represent globalization at different points in time, they are somewhat alike in terms of how globalization is defined, and with respect to the rankings of countries as most (and least) globalized. However, while a set of top ten rankings is illustrative, it is worthwhile to compare all KOF Globalization Index values to the values of other indexes (or, where values are not available, to compare KOF Index values to index rankings) to determine how representative the KOF Globalization Index may be.

Considering the changes in CSGR Economic Globalization Index, we see that between 1982 and 2004 the value of the index for the world increased by 26 percent (from 0.111 to 0.14). Further, all geographic regions experienced increases in their corresponding index values over this period. Looking at individual countries, of the 70 countries for which values are available in both 1982 and 2004, 54 countries realized increases in their index values (77.1 percent) while 16 realized decreases. Owing to the similarities in the components and construction of the CSGR and KOF Indexes, it is not surprising to find that both indexes depict an increase in globalization during recent decades. Moreover, the similarities are reflected in the correlation coefficient between the two indexes that is equal to 0.8016.

	CSGR[a]	E&Y[b]	DHL[c]	MGI[d]	FP-ATK[e]
KOF	0.8016	0.8456	0.8581	0.8963	-0.8115

[a] Centre for the Study of Globalisation and Regionalisation Globalization Index

[b] Ernst & Young Globalization Index

[c] DHL Global Connectedness Score

[d] Maastricht Globalization Index

[e] Foreign Policy-AT Kearney Globalization Index Ranking

Note: For indexes except FP-ATK Index, higher scores imply "more globalized". For FP-ATK Index, higher rank (i.e., lower score) implies "more globalized".

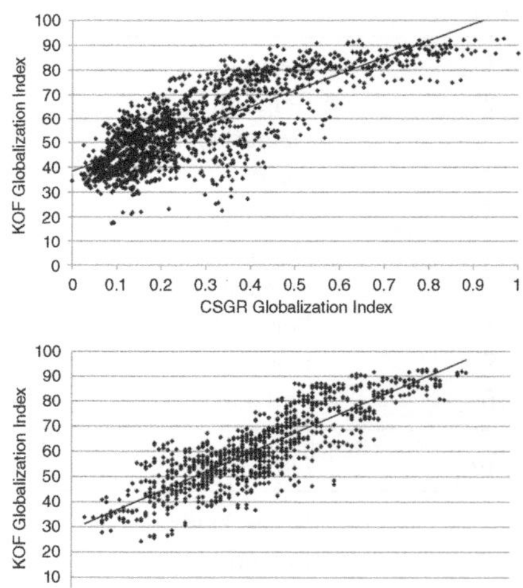

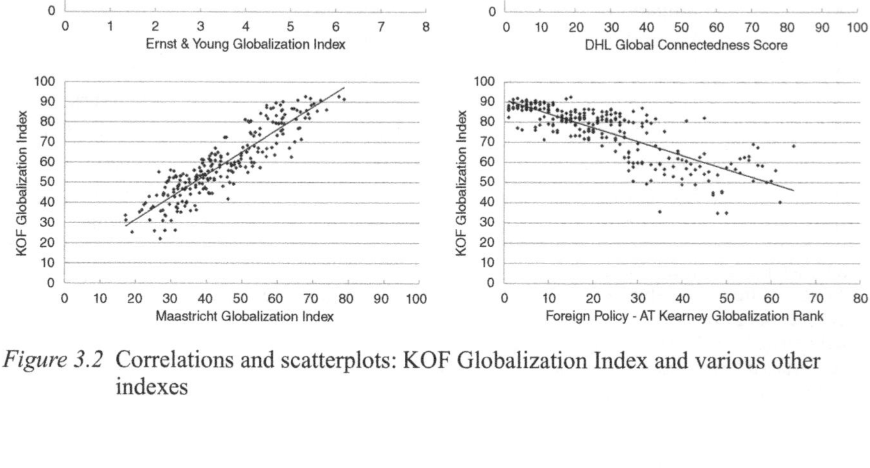

Figure 3.2 Correlations and scatterplots: KOF Globalization Index and various other indexes

We largely focus on the KOF Index values because they are available on a yearly basis for as many as 191 countries over the period from 1970 through 2011 and, thus, the KOF Index provides more expansive coverage than the other indexes. This does not, however, shape our depiction of the globalization process during recent decades. While each index is unique, that they seek to represent the same (or a similar) process leads to the unsurprising result that they are highly correlated.

Extending more generally from Table 3.2, in Figure 3.2 there is a correlation matrix that lists the pairwise correlation coefficients between the KOF Globalization Index and each of the remaining globalization indexes. There are also corresponding scatterplots that depict the relationship between the KOF Index (presented on the y axis) and each remaining index (located on the x axis). In all cases, there is a very strong correlation. For example, as noted, the correlation coefficient between the KOF Index and the CSGR Index is equal to 0.80. The Ernst & Young Globalization Index and the KOF Index have a correlation coefficient equal to 0.85. Similarly, the DHL Global Connectedness Score and the KOF Index have a pairwise correlation coefficient equal to 0.86, and the correlation between the Maastricht Globalization Index and the KOF Index is 0.90. This is the strongest correlation among the group; however, even the weakest correlation (0.8016 for the CSGR Index) is of considerable magnitude.

The scatterplot located in the bottom right corner of Figure 3.2 depicts a negative relationship between the KOF Index and the Foreign Policy/AT Kearney Globalization rank. The correlation between rank scores and index scores is -0.81. As the globalization rank is such that lower values correspond with greater globalization, higher values identify less-globalized countries. Thus, the negative correlation coefficient makes perfect sense. As noted, the pairwise correlation coefficients (in absolute value) presented in Figure 3.2 range from a low value of 0.80 to a high value of 0.90. Thus, it seems reasonable to assert that the KOF Globalization Index, given that it represents a larger number of countries and a longer time period than any of the other indexes, and correlates greatly with them, is a strong proxy measure for globalization, broadly defined.

We now turn our attention to the economic globalization component of the KOF Globalization Index and, specifically, to how the KOF economic globalization dimension compares to related component dimensions from the other five indexes. Figure 3.3 presents the correlation coefficients and scatterplots for the KOF economic globalization dimension (presented on the y axis) and the remaining globalization indexes (located on the x axis). Beginning with the CSGR Index, we see a correlation coefficient of only 0.48. While this is the weakest correlation found in either Figure 3.2 or Figure 3.3, it is a relatively strong one nevertheless. The Ernst & Young Globalization Index is based, in part, on dimensions that represent aspects of international finance and trade. The correlation coefficient between the Ernst & Young Finance dimension and the KOF economic globalization dimension is equal to 0.82. This is similar to the value present in Figure 3.2 of a correlation of 0.85 between the composite Ernst & Young Index and the KOF

	n pairs	Correlation with KOF
CSGR	2,049	0.4785
E&Y, Finance	983	0.8243
E&Y, Trade	983	0.7493
FP-ATK. . .		
Economic dimension rank	156	−0.688
Economic integration, Trade rank	156	−0.5928
Economic integration, FDI rank	156	−0.5569
Economic integration, Portfolio flows rank	61	−0.5411
Economic integration, Income payments rank	31	−0.7746
Economic integration, Investment income rank	30	−0.6584

See Table 3.1 notes.

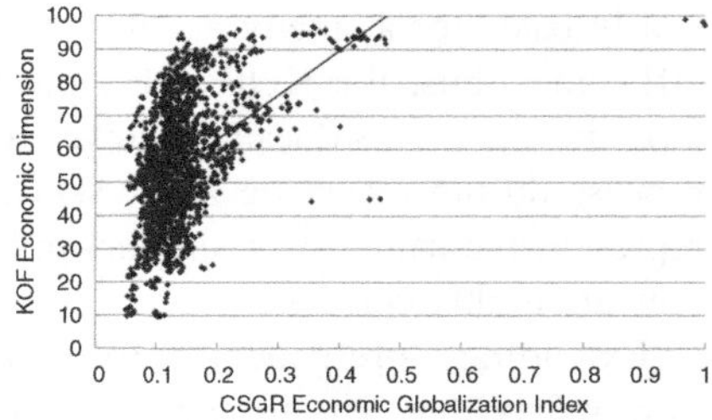

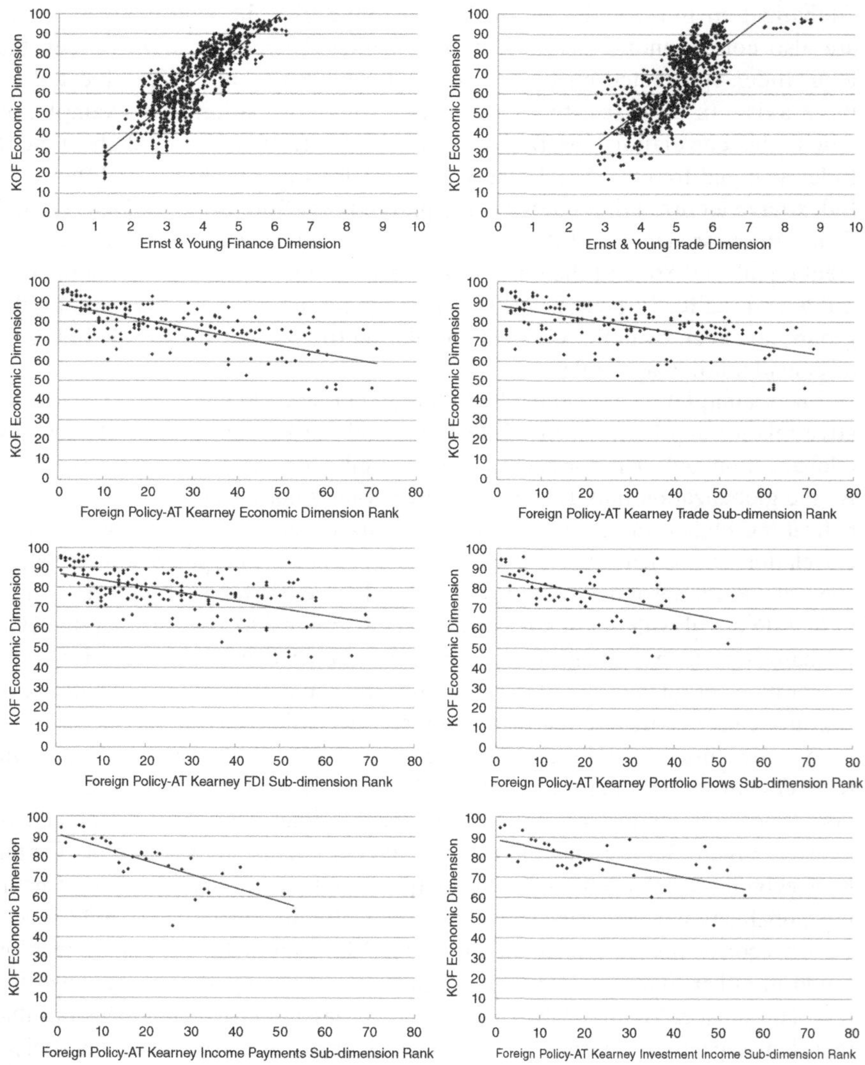

Figure 3.3 Correlations and scatterplots: KOF economic globalization and various other indexes

Index. Looking at the trade dimension of the Ernst & Young Index, we see a slightly weaker yet still strong correlation of 0.75.

The remainder of Figure 3.3 illustrates the correlation coefficients for the economic dimension ranks of the Foreign Policy/AT Kearney index and its sub-dimensions (trade, FDI, portfolio flows, income payments, and investment income) and the KOF economic globalization dimension. Both overall, for the KOF economic globalization dimension and the Foreign Policy/AT Kearney economic dimension rank, and for each of the sub-dimension ranks, we see correlation coefficients that range from -0.54 to -0.77. Again, because higher rank scores indicate lower levels of globalization, the negative correlations are expected.

In Table 3.3, we present the levels and ranks of the KOF economic globalization dimension and the overall KOF Globalization Index values for the years 1970 and 2011. We also include the level and proportional changes in values and ranks over the period from 1970 through 2011. The countries listed in the table are sorted by the proportional increase in the overall KOF Globalization Index. For example, China is listed first in the table. The 1970 and 2011 KOF Globalization Index values for China are 16.8 and 60.5, respectively. This represents a proportional increase of nearly 260 percent. That the next highest proportional increase in the overall index was 170.7 percent, for Rwanda, and that another 21 countries experienced proportional increases ranging from 100 percent to 166.3 percent, illustrates that China is a considerable outlier in the extent to which it has become integrated in the global economy since embarking upon its "Open Door" policy in 1978.

Even a cursory review of the rightmost column in Table 3.3 indicates that not a single country listed in the table experienced a decrease in its KOF Globalization Index between 1970 and 2011. The lowest proportional increase, 6.1 percent, is for Montenegro. The average increase in index value, across the cohort of countries, is 73.9 percent. This represents an increase in the average index value from 37.26 in 1970 to 60.96 in 2011. In terms of the average economic globalization dimension, the observed value increased from 72.05 to 93.98 during the period. The average proportional increase in the economic globalization dimension, again across the cohort of countries, is 70.7 percent. Unlike the overall KOF Globalization Index, for which not one country among the 116 presented experienced decreases over the time period, seven countries experienced declines in their economic globalization index values. These countries are Algeria (which experienced a 3.2 percent decline), Botswana (–4.4 percent), Burkina Faso (–7.3 percent), Ethiopia (–7.6 percent), Fiji (–1.4 percent), Luxembourg (–0.5 percent), and Malawi (–11.9 percent).

Figure 3.4 depicts the time path of the overall economic globalization index by continent during the period from 1970 through 2012. It is easily seen that the general trend, regardless of the geographic area depicted, is an increase in economic globalization. Throughout the period, the European nations are seen to be, collectively, the most globalized. Australia and New Zealand, forming Oceania, are consistently the least globalized, and the other regions are closely clustered

Table 3.3 Levels and changes in KOF economic globalization dimension and Globalization Index, 1970–2011

	1970			*2011*			*1970–2011*			*1970–2011*	
	Rank (Econ. Dimension)	*Econ. Dimension*	*Globaliz. Index*	*Rank*	*Econ. Dimension*	*Globaliz. Index*	*Δ Rank*	*Δ Econ. Dimension*	*Δ Globaliz. Index*	*%Δ Econ. Dimension*	*%Δ Globaliz. Index*
China	106	19.5	16.8	84	50.7	60.5	22	31.2	43.7	159.6%	259.9%
Rwanda	116	9.5	15.4	107	38.5	41.6	9	28.9	26.3	303.5%	170.7%
Nepal	114	13.0	14.5	114	27.6	38.7	0	14.6	24.2	112.7%	166.3%
Benin	105	19.8	16.8	110	35.5	41.8	−5	15.7	25.0	79.4%	148.8%
Korea, Rep.	71	32.9	26.8	62	59.9	64.8	9	27.0	38.0	81.9%	141.8%
Chad	104	20.0	15.9	106	38.9	38.0	−2	19.0	22.1	95.2%	138.6%
Albania	92	24.2	24.7	55	61.9	56.8	37	37.7	32.1	155.6%	129.9%
Thailand	80	28.3	28.6	36	68.8	65.3	44	40.5	36.8	143.1%	128.6%
Indonesia	76	30.6	25.0	69	58.0	56.4	7	27.4	31.4	89.5%	125.4%
Niger	102	20.4	18.2	109	35.9	40.8	−7	15.5	22.6	75.9%	123.9%
Madagascar	115	13.0	17.7	103	39.7	39.6	12	26.8	21.9	206.8%	123.8%
Peru	96	22.9	29.5	25	76.0	65.7	71	53.1	36.3	231.5%	123.2%
Uganda	109	17.3	20.5	88	49.5	45.4	21	32.1	24.8	185.7%	120.9%
Romania	75	31.2	32.8	51	64.1	72.2	24	32.9	39.5	105.5%	120.3%
Paraguay	90	25.8	27.3	77	53.5	57.5	13	27.7	30.3	107.5%	111.0%
Ghana	103	20.1	25.4	78	53.2	53.4	25	33.1	28.0	164.7%	110.4%
Mali	88	26.5	22.4	86	50.4	46.7	2	24.0	24.3	90.5%	108.4%
Azerbaijan	69	33.1	27.6	61	60.5	56.6	8	27.4	29.0	82.6%	104.9%
Sierra Leone	91	25.3	21.6	80	53.1	44.2	11	27.8	22.6	109.8%	104.5%
Moldova	42	44.1	31.4	47	64.8	64.1	−5	20.7	32.7	46.8%	104.3%
Haiti	112	14.7	19.6	90	47.2	40.1	22	32.5	20.5	220.8%	104.3%
Philippines	77	29.8	28.4	74	54.4	57.4	3	24.5	29.0	82.2%	102.0%
Burundi	113	14.0	16.0	116	23.1	32.1	−3	9.1	16.1	65.0%	100.4%

Honduras	87	26.6	29.6	49	64.7	59.0	38	38.1	29.4	143.0%	99.4%
Morocco	89	26.3	32.9	72	54.8	64.6	17	28.5	31.7	108.3%	96.4%
Dominican Rep.	93	23.8	31.3	68	58.3	61.2	25	34.5	29.9	145.2%	95.5%
Senegal	107	18.9	26.2	96	42.9	51.0	11	24.0	24.8	127.3%	94.7%
Congo, Dem. Rep.	97	22.6	21.6	73	54.6	42.1	24	31.9	20.4	141.2%	94.6%
Mongolia	48	42.6	28.7	30	73.3	55.7	18	30.7	27.1	72.1%	94.3%
Guatemala	78	28.7	31.3	66	58.9	60.7	12	30.2	29.4	105.3%	93.8%
Syrian Arab Rep.	110	16.9	23.2	93	43.4	44.7	17	26.5	21.5	156.8%	93.0%
Vietnam	65	37.3	25.2	65	59.2	48.6	0	21.8	23.4	58.4%	92.9%
India	108	18.5	26.2	99	41.7	50.4	9	23.2	24.2	125.7%	92.3%
Japan	100	21.2	34.0	92	45.4	65.0	8	24.3	31.1	114.4%	91.5%
Nigeria	72	31.7	29.5	52	63.8	56.5	20	32.1	27.0	101.3%	91.3%
Cyprus	28	49.7	44.6	11	84.5	85.3	17	34.8	40.7	70.0%	91.2%
Yemen, Rep.	55	40.6	25.5	63	59.8	48.6	–8	19.2	23.2	47.3%	90.9%
El Salvador	74	31.7	32.2	58	61.5	61.4	16	29.8	29.2	93.9%	90.6%
Hungary	40	45.4	45.3	7	86.8	85.9	33	41.5	40.6	91.4%	89.7%
Bulgaria	53	40.8	38.3	26	75.5	71.4	27	34.8	33.1	85.3%	86.5%
Turkey	73	31.7	36.6	79	53.2	68.2	–6	21.5	31.6	67.8%	86.3%
Egypt, Arab Rep.	85	26.8	31.0	91	46.0	57.2	–6	19.2	26.2	71.4%	84.8%
Cambodia	64	37.4	26.8	53	63.1	49.0	11	25.7	22.3	68.9%	83.3%
Tanzania	99	21.4	21.1	97	42.0	38.4	2	20.6	17.3	96.0%	82.3%
Colombia	86	26.7	32.8	70	57.2	59.3	16	30.6	26.5	114.7%	80.8%
Pakistan	95	23.0	27.9	108	36.1	50.3	–13	13.1	22.4	56.9%	80.5%
Malaysia	12	59.4	44.3	17	80.8	79.6	–5	21.4	35.3	36.0%	79.7%
Central African Rep.	98	21.5	19.9	112	34.7	35.6	–14	13.2	15.8	61.1%	79.4%
Mauritius	57	40.3	36.7	13	83.9	65.7	44	43.6	29.0	108.1%	79.1%
Jordan	44	43.1	39.0	39	67.8	69.5	5	24.7	30.5	57.2%	78.1%

(continued)

Table 3.3 (continued)

		1970			*2011*			*1970–2011*		*1970–2011*	
	Rank (Econ. Dimension)	*Econ. Dimension*	*Globaliz. Index*	*Rank*	*Econ. Dimension*	*Globaliz. Index*	*Δ Rank*	*Δ Econ. Dimension*	*Δ Globaliz. Index*	*%Δ Econ. Dimension*	*%Δ Globaliz. Index*
Poland	61	38.9	44.8	31	72.9	79.5	30	34.1	34.7	87.6%	77.6%
Kenya	83	27.3	26.6	102	41.0	46.7	–19	13.7	20.1	50.3%	75.6%
Ecuador	94	23.4	31.1	95	43.1	54.5	–1	19.7	23.4	84.4%	75.3%
Cameroon	101	21.0	24.9	101	41.2	43.6	0	20.1	18.7	95.9%	74.8%
Nicaragua	81	28.0	32.0	50	64.4	55.4	31	36.5	23.4	130.3%	73.2%
Spain	46	42.9	49.0	19	78.6	84.7	27	35.7	35.6	83.3%	72.7%
Myanmar	79	28.7	18.7	89	47.4	32.1	–10	18.7	13.4	65.2%	71.6%
Fiji	25	51.1	33.3	85	50.4	56.7	–60	–0.7	23.3	–1.4%	70.0%
Portugal	21	53.9	51.5	12	84.1	87.0	9	30.2	35.5	56.1%	69.0%
Lesotho	70	33.1	27.0	67	58.5	45.6	3	25.4	18.6	76.8%	68.8%
South Africa	14	58.9	39.4	45	65.1	65.2	–31	6.3	25.8	10.6%	65.6%
Burkina Faso	62	38.0	26.0	111	35.2	42.7	–49	–2.8	16.7	–7.3%	64.3%
Saudi Arabia	11	61.1	41.3	41	66.4	67.7	–30	5.3	26.4	8.6%	64.0%
Guinea	63	37.5	26.5	98	41.9	43.2	–35	4.4	16.7	11.7%	63.2%
Togo	66	36.1	30.0	87	50.1	48.9	–21	14.0	18.9	38.9%	63.1%
Congo, Rep.	52	40.8	28.6	37	68.5	46.6	15	27.7	18.0	67.8%	62.9%
Greece	20	54.3	49.4	32	72.4	80.3	–12	18.1	30.9	33.3%	62.7%
Ethiopia	84	27.2	22.9	115	25.1	36.7	–31	–2.1	13.8	–7.6%	60.0%
Bolivia	58	39.5	33.3	75	53.9	53.1	–17	14.4	19.9	36.6%	59.8%
Cote d'Ivoire	82	27.9	31.5	76	53.7	50.1	6	25.8	18.6	92.3%	59.3%
Australia	36	46.7	52.7	21	77.7	82.9	15	30.9	30.2	66.2%	57.3%
Austria	31	48.9	57.7	9	85.1	90.5	22	36.3	32.8	74.2%	56.8%
Germany	19	54.4	50.8	43	65.7	79.5	–24	11.3	28.7	20.8%	56.5%

Finland	33	47.8	54.9	8	85.8	85.9	25	38.0	31.0	79.6%	56.4%
Iceland	56	40.6	44.0	22	77.2	68.7	34	36.7	24.7	90.5%	56.2%
Brazil	59	39.5	38.3	82	51.6	59.8	–23	12.1	21.5	30.8%	56.0%
Sudan	111	16.3	20.5	113	28.1	31.7	–2	11.9	11.2	72.8%	54.8%
Chile	37	46.4	46.8	18	80.8	72.4	19	34.4	25.6	74.3%	54.7%
Costa Rica	47	42.8	40.6	54	62.4	62.0	–7	19.6	21.5	45.7%	53.0%
Jamaica	26	50.4	40.5	40	67.0	61.3	–14	16.7	20.8	33.1%	51.3%
Serbia	50	41.7	42.3	71	56.7	63.6	–21	15.1	21.3	36.2%	50.4%
New Zealand	39	45.5	52.6	15	82.1	78.8	24	36.7	26.3	80.6%	50.0%
Kuwait	18	56.1	47.0	42	66.0	70.5	–24	9.8	23.5	17.6%	49.9%
Mexico	60	38.9	40.7	56	61.6	60.8	4	22.7	20.1	58.2%	49.3%
Zambia	30	49.0	35.0	59	60.8	52.2	–29	11.8	17.2	24.1%	49.2%
Malta	9	64.1	51.5	4	91.8	76.0	5	27.7	24.4	43.1%	47.4%
Venezuela	67	35.2	35.1	94	43.4	51.6	–27	8.2	16.6	23.2%	47.2%
Tunisia	54	40.7	40.5	60	60.6	59.2	–6	19.9	18.7	49.0%	46.1%
Italy	27	49.7	55.4	35	70.3	80.3	–8	20.5	24.9	41.3%	45.0%
Guyana	45	42.9	34.7	46	65.0	50.3	–1	22.1	15.6	51.4%	44.8%
Singapore	2	84.4	61.4	1	96.7	88.6	1	12.3	27.3	14.6%	44.4%
Mauritania	38	46.4	32.1	48	64.8	45.6	–10	18.4	13.6	39.8%	42.3%
Algeria	51	41.0	34.8	104	39.7	49.3	–53	–1.3	14.6	–3.2%	41.9%
Israel	15	58.1	51.6	28	74.7	73.0	–13	16.6	21.5	28.6%	41.6%
Trinidad and Tobago	32	48.3	44.2	20	78.2	62.5	12	29.9	18.3	62.0%	41.4%
France	41	45.0	58.9	38	67.9	82.8	3	22.9	23.8	50.8%	40.5%
Switzerland	13	59.1	61.2	27	75.1	85.7	–14	16.0	24.6	27.0%	40.2%
Ireland	4	78.6	66.5	2	93.7	92.2	2	15.1	25.7	19.2%	38.7%
Uruguay	43	43.6	48.0	44	65.5	66.0	–1	21.8	18.1	50.0%	37.6%
Sweden	35	46.8	64.4	10	85.1	87.4	25	38.3	23.0	81.7%	35.8%

(continued)

Table 3.3 (continued)

		1970			2011			1970–2011		1970–2011	
	Rank (Econ. Dimension)	Econ. Dimension	Globaliz. Index	Rank	Econ. Dimension	Globaliz. Index	Δ Rank	Δ Econ. Dimension	Δ Globaliz. Index	%Δ Econ. Dimension	%Δ Globaliz. Index
Barbados	24	51.7	42.3	34	70.6	57.2	−10	18.9	14.9	36.6%	35.2%
Netherlands	5	69.9	67.9	5	91.2	91.3	0	21.3	23.4	30.5%	34.5%
Argentina	68	34.5	44.0	105	39.5	58.4	−37	5.0	14.4	14.6%	32.6%
Malawi	34	47.0	31.4	100	41.4	41.4	−66	−5.6	10.0	−11.9%	31.9%
Norway	17	57.4	63.9	29	74.6	82.8	−12	17.2	19.0	29.9%	29.7%
United Kingdom	23	53.5	64.6	33	72.3	83.7	−10	18.8	19.2	35.1%	29.7%
Panama	7	66.5	52.6	16	81.2	67.9	−9	14.7	15.3	22.2%	29.2%
Gabon	49	42.6	37.9	81	52.4	48.0	−32	9.8	10.1	23.1%	26.5%
Belgium	3	79.5	72.4	6	89.4	91.6	−3	10.0	19.2	12.5%	26.5%
United States	29	49.1	59.3	64	59.2	74.9	−35	10.1	15.7	20.7%	26.4%
Botswana	22	53.7	35.3	83	51.4	44.5	−61	−2.4	9.2	−4.4%	26.1%
Denmark	8	64.6	70.0	14	83.4	87.4	−6	18.8	17.5	29.0%	25.0%
Swaziland	16	57.6	39.8	57	61.6	48.7	−41	4.0	8.9	6.9%	22.3%
Canada	10	63.0	70.1	24	76.1	85.6	−14	13.1	15.5	20.8%	22.1%
Luxembourg	1	93.0	71.6	3	92.5	84.6	−2	−0.5	13.0	−0.5%	18.2%
Montenegro	6	69.5	63.4	23	76.9	67.3	−17	7.4	3.9	10.6%	6.1%
Group Average	.	72.05	37.26	.	93.98	60.96	.	21.60	23.69	70.6%	73.9%

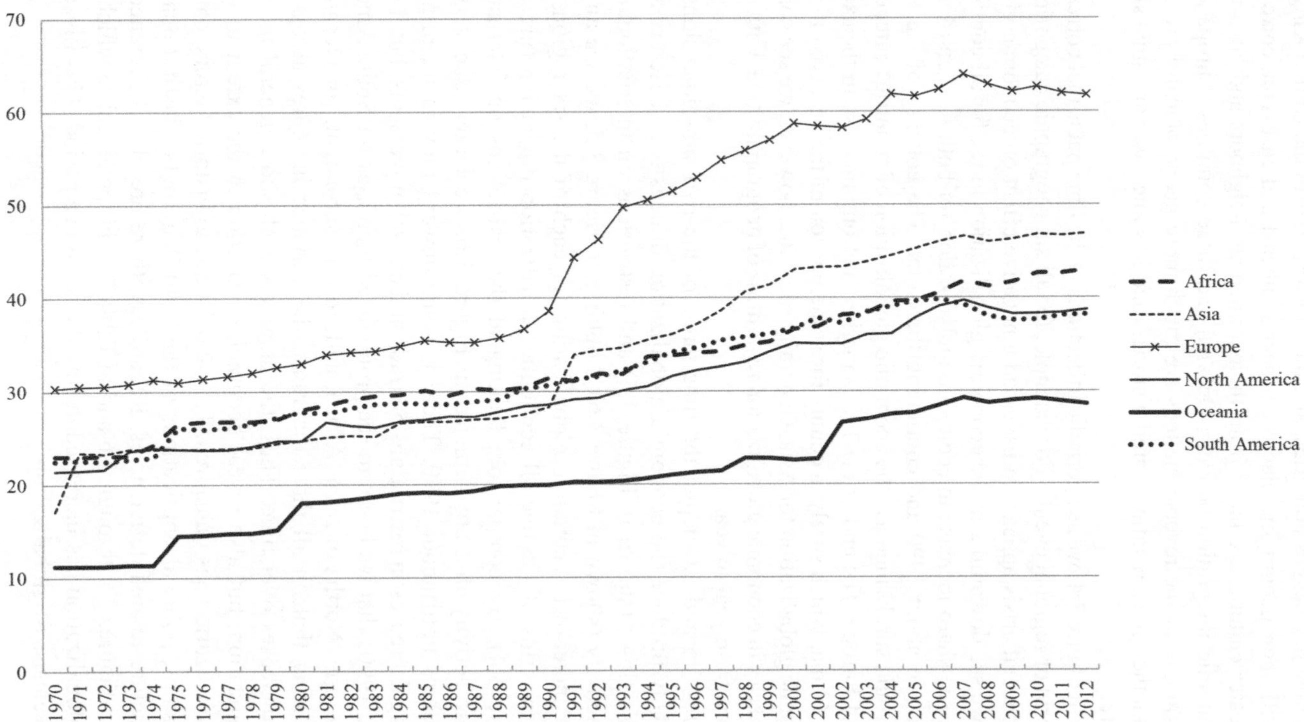

Figure 3.4 KOF economic globalization dimension, by continent, 1970–2012

in the middle. It is possible that economic remoteness has limited the abilities of Australia and New Zealand to integrate into the global economy, while geographic proximity has allowed the European nations to be more integrated internationally. Equally, it could be that the geographic remoteness of Australia and New Zealand, their relative newness as countries, and their historic ties to the United Kingdom, along with their geographic placement near southeast and east Asia, correspond with greater cultural distances from their immediate neighbors and, as a result, less economic integration between Oceania and these countries. Europe stands as an example of the reverse: nations are much more geographically proximate to one another, have lengthy shared histories, and in some cases are quite similar in culture.

Also in Figure 3.4, we see periodic inflections in the time paths that correspond with world or regional events. For example, for all six geographic categories, the 2008 financial crisis appears to have had a negative effect on economic globalization, we see downturns in the economic globalization index for all continents. We also see sharp increase in economic globalization for both Asia and Europe, beginning in about 1990 and continuing thereafter. The collapse of the Soviet Union would surely increase the economic globalization of countries categorized as part of Europe. The end of the 1980s marked a strong increase in the external trade of China, which surely accounts for some portion of the observed increase in economic globalization for Asia. Generally speaking, however, we see continuous increases in economic globalization regardless of geographic area, with minor deviations from year to year.

Figures 3.5 and 3.6 depict the time paths of the two sub-dimensions that collectively produce the economic globalization dimension. These are actual economic flows (shown in Figure 3.5) and restrictions on international economic activity (shown in Figure 3.6). Looking at Figure 3.5, we see an even stronger increase in economic globalization for each of the six regions than we see in terms of the overall economic globalization dimension (presented in Figure 3.4). By comparison, looking at the restrictions on international economic activity that are depicted in Figure 3.6, we largely see very flat relationships until about 1990. There is some upward movement, primarily reflecting decreases in restrictions on trade and capital movements, but it is not until the 1990s that we begin to see pronounced increases for South America, Asia, Europe, North America, Africa, and, to a lesser extent, for Oceania. It is interesting that, in all three diagrams, the variance in scores across continents increases over time. Thus, the diagrams each show general increases in globalization, but also reveal geographic variation in the extent to which more globalization has transpired. This may be due to historic factors, colonial relationships, political implications of the Cold War, and/or institutional and infrastructure-related deficiencies. Regardless, there are clear differences, as shown in Figures 3.4 through 3.6 and in Table 3.3, in the extent to which economic globalization has increased during the reference period. This illustrates the unevenness of globalization.

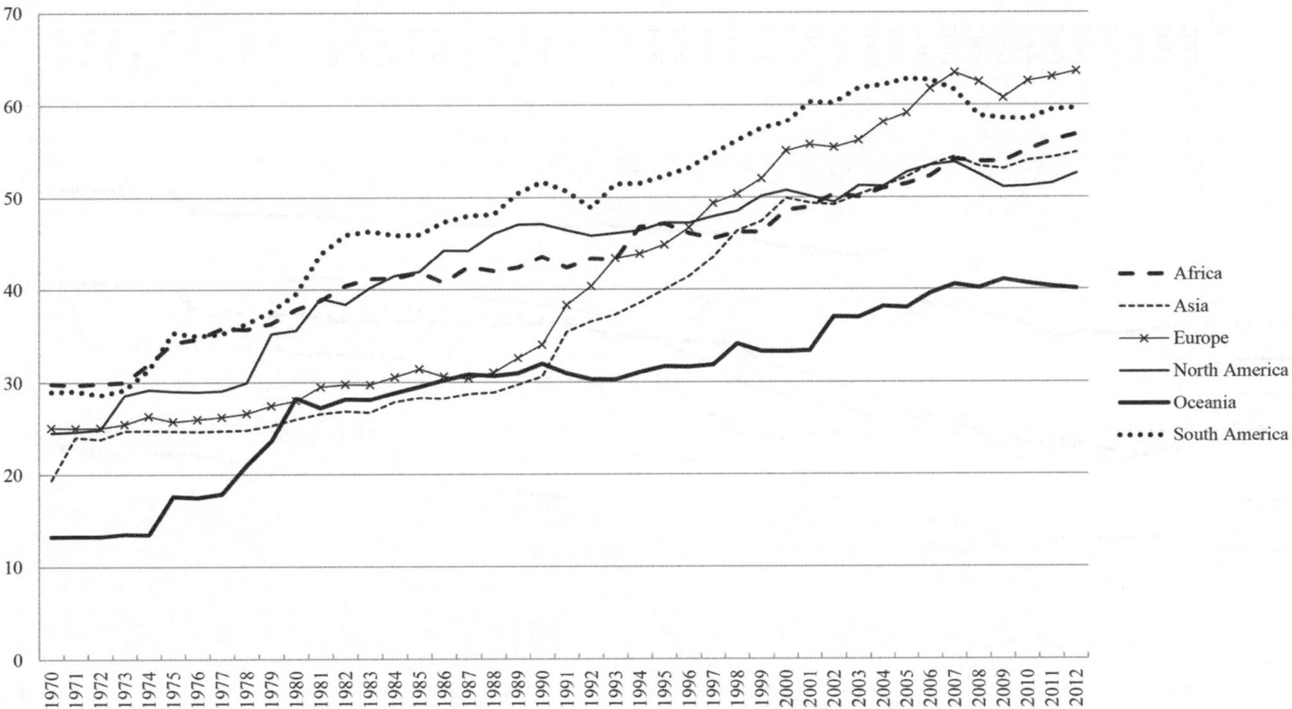

Figure 3.5 KOF economic globalization, actual flows sub-dimension by continent, 1970–2012

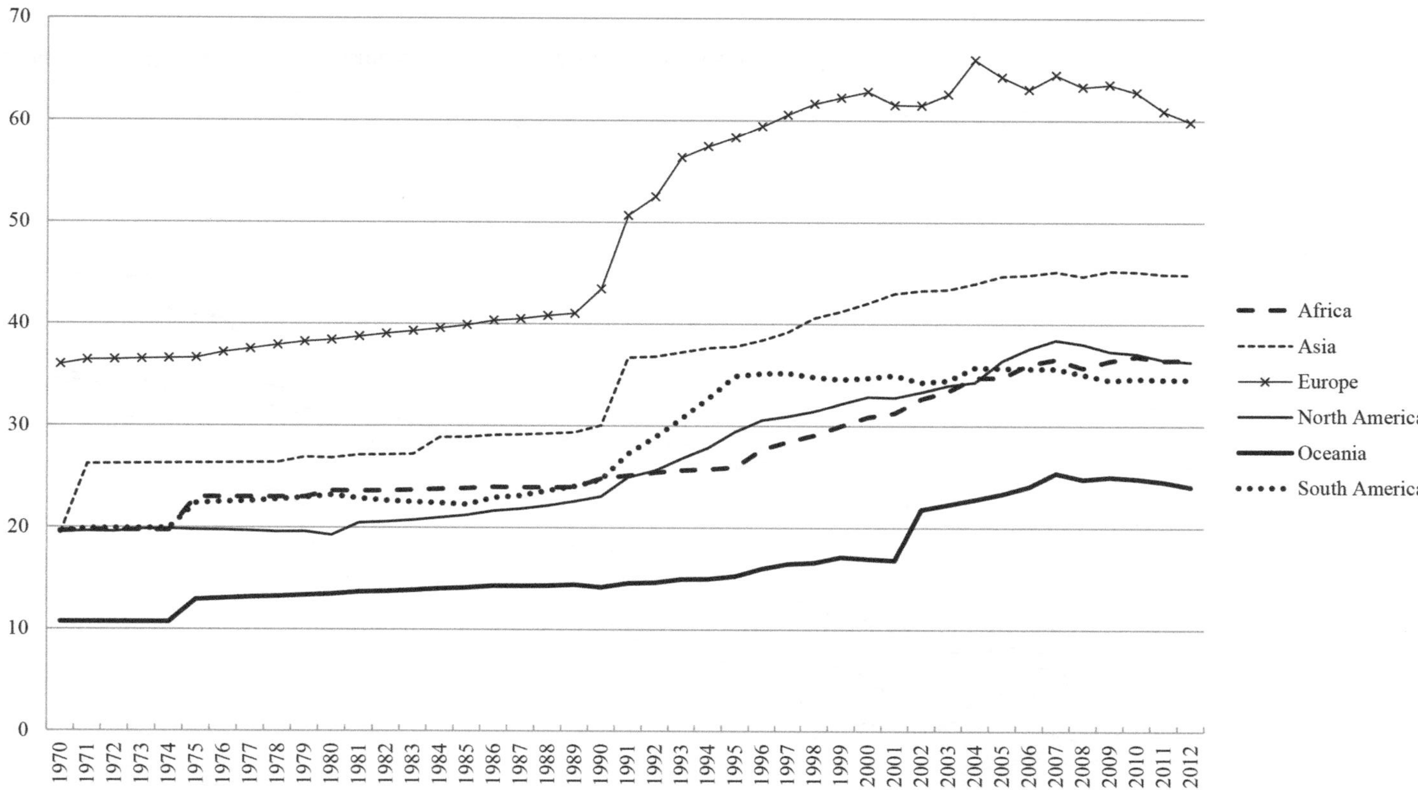

Figure 3.6 KOF economic globalization dimension, restrictions sub-dimension by continent, 1970–2012

Further evidence of the unevenness of globalization

Based on KOF Globalization Index values, Figure 3.1 depicts the extents to which countries are globalized at three points in time: 1970, 1990, and 2010. In doing so, the figure illustrates the variation in, and the unevenness of, globalization. The figure also illustrates the changes, especially considering Panel C relative to Panels A and B, in index values. These panels are discussed earlier in this chapter, but it is worth mentioning that a) there was considerable variation in the extent to which countries were globalized in 1970 and b) while all countries have become more globalized during the 1970–2010 period, considerable variation remains.

Extending from Figure 3.1, the values presented in Table 3.4 illustrate the initial unevenness of globalization, and the persistence of this unevenness, in greater detail. Further, the figure shows differences in the extent to which globalization has transpired across country cohorts that are defined based on World Bank income classifications (i.e., high income, upper middle income, lower middle income, and low income groupings). A reasonable *a priori* expectation would be that observed increases in the globalization index, over the period from 1970 to 2010, will generally be lower if the initial index value is higher. The rationale for this expectation is largely based on the observed increase in the international activities of developing countries and the inclusion of members of the former Soviet Union into the global trading system, financial networks, and political arena. In a sense,

Table 3.4 Beginning and ending KOF globalization dimension values, by World Bank income classification

	*Beginning of Period**	*End of Period (2011)*	*t statistics (inter-year Δ)*
All Countries	40.00	56.87	9.88
Standard Deviation	15.92	16.65	
Observations	182	182	
Minimum Index value	11.92	25.43	
Maximum Index value	84.12	92.17	
High Income Cohort	64.07	76.05	3.40
Standard Deviation	14.30	14.33	
Observations	33	33	
Minimum Index value	33.55	37.23	
Maximum Index value	84.12	92.17	
Upper Middle Income Cohort	42.29	61.21	6.45
Standard Deviation	8.04	14.52	
Observations	32	32	
Minimum Index value	23.54	40.06	
Maximum Index value	57.90	87.01	
Lower Middle Income Cohort	36.83	56.46	10.80
Standard Deviation	9.56	11.68	
Observations	69	69	

(continued)

Table 3.4 (continued)

	*Beginning of Period**	*End of Period (2011)*	*t statistics (inter-year Δ)*
Minimum Index value	14.08	26.20	
Maximum Index value	68.08	83.97	
Low Income Cohort	26.46	41.38	9.24
Standard Deviation	7.06	8.66	
Observations	48	48	
Minimum Index value	11.92	25.43	
Maximum Index value	45.30	60.50	
t statistics (intra-year differences)			
High relative to All	8.74	6.89	
Upper Middle relative to All	1.24	1.53	
Lower Middle relative to All	−1.92	−0.22	
Low relative to All	−8.68	−8.82	
High relative to Upper Middle	7.60	4.14	
High relative to Lower Middle	9.94	6.84	
High relative to Low	13.98	12.42	
Upper Middle relative to Lower Middle	2.99	1.62	
Upper Middle relative to Low	9.05	6.95	
Lower Middle relative to Low	6.74	8.01	

* Beginning of the period is 1987 for all countries unless noted below, parenthetically, otherwise.

High Income Cohort: Aruba, Australia, Austria, Bahamas, Bahrain, Belgium, Bermuda, Brunei Darussalam, Canada, Denmark, Finland, France, French Polynesia (1990), Germany, Iceland, Ireland, Israel, Italy, Japan, Kuwait, Luxembourg, Netherlands, New Zealand, Norway, Qatar, Saudi Arabia, Singapore, Spain, Sweden, Switzerland, United Arab Emirates, United Kingdom, and United States.

Upper Middle Income Cohort: Algeria, Antigua and Barbuda, Argentina, Barbados, Belarus (1991), Brazil, Cyprus, Estonia (1991), Gabon, Greece, Hungary, Iran, Iraq, Korea (Rep. of), Latvia (1991), Libya, Lithuania (1991), Macao, Malta, New Caledonia, Oman, Panama, Portugal, Romania, Russian Federation (1991), Seychelles, Slovenia (1992), St. Kitts and Nevis, Suriname, Trinidad and Tobago, Uruguay, and Venezuela.

Lower Middle Income Cohort: Albania (1990), Angola (1988), Armenia (1991), Azerbaijan (1991), Belize, Bolivia, Bosnia and Herzegovina (1992), Botswana, Bulgaria (1989), Cameroon, Cape Verde (1988), Chile, Colombia, Congo (Rep.), Costa Rica, Cote d'Ivoire, Croatia (1992), Cuba (1990), Czech Republic (1993), Djibouti (1990), Dominica, Dominican Republic, Ecuador, Egypt, El Salvador, Fiji, Georgia (1991), Grenada, Guatemala, Honduras, Jamaica, Jordan, Kazakhstan (1991), Kiribati, Kyrgyz Republic (1991), Lebanon, Macedonia FYR (1992), Malaysia, Mauritius, Mexico, Moldova (1991), Mongolia (1989), Morocco, Namibia (1990), Nicaragua, Papua New Guinea, Paraguay, Peru, Philippines, Poland, Samoa, Senegal, Slovak Republic (1993), South Africa, St. Lucia, St. Vincent and the Grenadines, Swaziland, Syrian Arab Republic, Tajikistan (1991), Thailand, Tunisia, Turkey, Turkmenistan (1991), Ukraine (1991), Uzbekistan (1991), Vanuatu, West Bank and Gaza (1994), Yemen, Rep., and Zimbabwe.

Low Income Cohort: Afghanistan, Bangladesh, Benin, Bhutan, Burkina Faso, Burundi, Cambodia, Central African Republic, Chad, China, Comoros, Congo (Dem. Rep.), Equatorial Guinea, Eritrea (1993), Ethiopia, Gambia, Ghana, Guinea, Guinea-Bissau, Guyana, Haiti, India, Indonesia, Kenya, Lao PDR, Lesotho, Liberia, Madagascar, Malawi, Maldives, Mali, Mauritania, Mozambique, Myanmar, Nepal, Niger, Nigeria, Pakistan, Rwanda, Sao Tome and Principe, Sierra Leone, Solomon Islands, Sudan, Tanzania, Togo, Uganda, Vietnam, and Zambia.

borrowing from the earlier discussion of the DHL Index, the countries that were less globalized as of 1970 have been able to engage internationally at a greater depth and breadth relative to those that were more globalized in 1970.

In Table 3.4, we see that the "beginning of the period" average KOF Globalization Index value is 40. Further, comparing across the cohorts, we can see that the average values follow the anticipated pattern, where members of the high income cohort are typically the most globalized and members of the low income cohort are, generally, the least. The corresponding mean index values for the high income and low income cohorts are 64.07 and 26.46 respectively. The mean values for the two middle income cohorts complete the expected pattern. The typical upper middle income country had an index value of 42.29, while the typical lower middle income country had a value of 36.83. Moreover, while the mean values follow the expected order in terms of magnitudes, as can be seen from the t-statistics presented at the bottom of the table, the mean value for each cohort is significantly different from those of the others.

Turning our attention to the 2011 (end of period) mean KOF Index values, we find that the overall mean value has increased from 40 (the beginning of the period mean value) to 56.87, and that this increase is statistically significant. While each of the cohort-specific mean values for 2011 are significantly higher than the corresponding beginning values, the mean values for the income classification cohorts follow the same pattern, in terms of magnitude, as was observed at the beginning of the period. Again, the differences in mean values across cohorts is significant, with the sole exception of the difference between the upper middle income cohort and the lower middle income cohort, which is marginally insignificant ($t = 1.62$). There are, however, decreases in the gaps between cohort-specific mean index values for 2011 relative to the gaps between the cohort averages at the beginning of the period. For example, the difference between mean index values for the high income and the low income country cohorts at the beginning of the period was 37.61; however, by 2011 this gap had decreased to 34.66. Even more striking, the gap between the mean value for the high income country cohort and the upper middle income and lower middle income cohorts declined from 21.78 to 14.83 and from 27.24 to 19.59, respectively.

In this chapter, we extend from the review of earlier periods of globalization that is introduced in Chapter 1 and more completely presented in Chapter 2. The goal has been to focus more intensively on the most recent wave of globalization and to garner a better understanding of the extent to which globalization has occurred. To accomplish these objectives, we have introduced several measures of economic globalization, compared and contrasted the dimensions and sub-indexes that underlie their constructions, and looked at the similarities and differences between the measures. We have also considered changes in the extent to which economic globalization has transpired in recent decades, as indicted by the measures we have introduced.

Thus, we can confirm the impression garnered from Figure 3.1 and say that, although countries are now, typically, more globalized than they were in 1970, there remains a significant unevenness across countries and country cohorts in the extent of globalization. We do see, however, a decline in the gaps between the mean values of the high income country cohort and the remaining income classifications. Effectively, lower income countries are, in general, catching up to the high income countries. Again, this is to be expected, as the time period we have looked at spans what can be considered (roughly) the middle of the second wave of globalization, and continues well into the current third wave.

While we have seen increases in the overall index values, as well as in the measures that comprise the economic dimension of the indexes, and as the increases are generally common in pattern across the measures of globalization, it stands to reason that the component facets that have been employed to generate the dimensions and, thus, the indexes, have also risen. This is not a surprise. In the initial chapter it was shown that, during the current wave of globalization, trade relative to GGP had risen, and FDI flows had increased as a share of total world output. Further, while more or less constant as a share of the world population, the international migrant stock has also increased during the reference period. The observed increases in various forms of international economic activity are represented by the globalization indexes.

Having introduced the measures of overall globalization and of economic globalization, and having discussed their constructions and the corresponding similarities (and differences) across measures, we can easily conclude that the globalization process is ongoing. We also see that the extent to which countries are currently globalized is linked to the countries' activities, with respect to engaging with the global economy, during earlier periods. The countries that were most active in earlier waves of globalization are typically among the most globalized countries today. Likewise, those countries that were less active, or inactive, during earlier waves are, today, less globalized. However, the pattern of globalization appears to mirror that of cultural (dis)similarities. To examine this relationship in greater detail, we now turn our focus to the measurement of cultural differences at the country (i.e., society) level.

Note

1 Information relating to the Ernst & Young Globalization Index is, unless otherwise noted, from E&Y (2015).

4 Dimensions of cross-societal cultural differences

To complement our general discussion of globalization and, more specifically, to augment the presentation of the economic dimension introduced in Chapter 3, in this chapter we discuss the construction of four composite measures of cultural differences (i.e., cultural distance), present their component dimensions, and introduce a number of variables that serve as proxies for cultural differences. It is these measures that we employ in later chapters to represent cultural differences when undertaking our econometric analysis. We also consider general differences in the extent to which countries are globalized across country cohorts, defined based on the countries' relative cultural (dis)similarities. In doing so, we bridge the topics of globalization and cultural differences and provide a foundation for the analysis that is presented in later chapters.

The first composite measure of cultural differences that we discuss is based on survey data collected as part of the first five waves of the World Values Survey (WVS) and, where applicable, the European Values Surveys (EVS) (WVSA, 2014 and Inglehart et al., 2004). We refer to this series as the Inglehart measure of cultural distance. Unlike all other measures of cultural differences employed here, the Ingelhart measure varies across time periods. The second and third composite measures, based largely on data collected during the late 1960s and the early 1970s with some updates, additions, and extensions made in recent years, is generated using Hofstede's cultural dimensions (Hofstede, 1980 and 2001). Accordingly, we refer to these measures as the Hofstede measures of cultural distance. The fourth composite measure, which we refer to as the GLOBE measure of cultural distance, is produced using data collected during the early 1990s as part of Project GLOBE (Global Leadership and Organizational Behavior Effectiveness) (House et al., 2004).

Extending from these composite measures of cultural distance, we also examine the potential influences of the corresponding component dimension on the facets of economic globalization. As noted, we also introduce a number of variables that serve as proxies for cultural differences. These measures include continuous variables such as indexes of linguistic differences/proximity and religious dissimilarity, as well as the genetic distance between populations. Additionally, we discuss a number of dichotomous variables that reflect linguistic commonality and serve as proxies for cultural differences. We conclude by comparing the extent to which economies are globalized in relation to their cultural characteristics and their attributes, as identified by the WVS/EVS data.

The four composite measures and corresponding component dimensions that we employ in our study have been well-received by researchers, and have been used in various empirical studies on many, many occasions. Likewise, the index measures, genetic distance and dichotomous linguistic commonality variables have been used, to varying extents, by prior researchers to reflect cultural (dis)similarities. Given the difficulty in defining culture and the even more trying task of quantifying culture with a degree of accuracy sufficient to be useful for empirical analysis, we employ each of the four composite measures, along with their component dimensions and the set of proxy variables, in turn, when undertaking the empirical analysis detailed in later chapters.

As noted, in the analysis that follows (specifically in Chapters 6 through 8 where we look at the relationships between cultural differences and international trade, foreign direct investment, and international migration, respectively), we employ multiple measures of cultural distance. As it is a near-certainty that no individual measure of cultural distance perfectly reflects cultural differences, a better case can be made that a meaningful relationship exists between cultural difference and the facets of international economic integration if our analysis results in findings that are consistent across the numerous alternative measures employed. Likewise, if the estimated relationships vary or are ambiguous then that meaningful relationship is called into question.

The Inglehart measure of cultural distance

We have defined culture in general terms, and we have, again generally, considered culture to be the representation of a society's shared habits, its traditions, and the collective learned beliefs of its residents. Accordingly, the measures of culture – that is, the cultural dimensions that we employ when generating our composite measures of cultural distance – need to reflect these attributes and characteristics. The first measure of cultural differences that we discuss is constructed using data from the World Value Surveys (WVS) and, where applicable, the European Values Surveys (EVS).[1] As the WVS/EVS data are drawn from representative national samples, we posit that the data represent the attitudes, values, behaviors, and norms of the societies in which the survey has been administered. Thus, differences across societies, as reflected by responses to the survey questionnaires, are indicative of cross-societal cultural differences.

The survey questions used to produce the cultural dimensions that are then used to generate the composite measures of Inglehart cultural distance elicit respondents' views on issues related to economics, politics, and technological advances, as well as topics such as gender roles, religion, sexual orientation, environmental issues, and family values (Inglehart et al., 2004). Two broad dimensions of culture – survival vs. self-expression values (SSE) and traditional vs. secular-rational authority (TSR) – are generated from the application of factor analysis to a subset of WVS/EVS questions. It is the data for these broad dimensions that are used to produce the composite cultural distance series. While distilling something as multifaceted and unique as culture into two dimensions may appear simplistic to the point of uselessness, it is important to note that these two dimensions explain more than 70 percent of the cross-cultural variance on scores for more specific values/questions.

A simple, yet illustrative, example holds that a survey respondent who firmly believes in the importance of a God, who holds views that are consistent with a nationalist perspective, and who indicates that they respect authority, would likely be categorized as being more traditional. If the other members of the society in which this individual lives commonly share these views and values, then the society would be identified as having a more traditional focus. A society comprised of individuals who hold views that are diametrically opposed to those described above would be categorized as being more secular-rational.

Looking more closely at the TSR cultural dimension, we can say that traditional societies tend to show greater deference to the authority of the nation, a God, or the family. In fact, such deference is viewed as important and is expected. It is common for members of more traditional societies to adhere to family or communal obligations, to express a high degree of national pride and/or to have a nationalistic outlook, and to show obedience to religious authority. Indeed, many characteristics of more traditional societies are closely linked to the importance of religion. For example, members of traditional societies typically have faith in the existence of a Heaven and a Hell, frequently attend religious services, believe good and evil are clearly defined, and garner strength and consolation from their faith. Thus, a country's historical religion can have a large, sustaining impact on the country's present national culture even if its inhabitants do not regularly attend religious services.

Since having a large number of children is viewed as desirable, large families are common in more traditional societies. Also, while parents are expected to always put their children's needs first, children are expected to respect and love their parents no matter what. Also, in accordance with the emphasis placed on family, pleasing one's parents is another common aspiration. Fertility rates in more traditional societies tend to be relatively high, and divorce, abortion, euthanasia and suicide are all viewed very negatively. Societies that are more secular-rational hold opposing views on these issues, often adhering to rational-legal norms and emphasizing economic accumulation and individual achievement.

Individuals in societies that are characterized as being more survival-oriented commonly emphasize hard work, self-denial, and the achievement of economic and physical security. Often, members of these societies consider foreigners and outsiders to be threats and, correspondingly, they hold negative opinions of ethnic diversity and cultural change. These views are consistent with an intolerance towards outgroups, such as homosexuals and ethnic minorities, and a strong adherence to traditional gender roles. For example, members of survival-oriented societies often believe that post-secondary education, jobs, and political activity are better suited for men than they are for women. Survey respondents who are categorized as being more survival-oriented often have an authoritarian political outlook. More specifically, members of such societies are often proponents of increased government or state ownership of businesses, and they are relatively more open to structures of government besides democracy. Individuals in societies that place greater emphasis on self-expression values commonly hold opposing views on these, and related, issues. The rationale is that when economic and physical security exist, cultural diversity begins to be appreciated and sought out. This leads to greater tolerance for deviation from traditional gender roles and sexual norms and to greater support for equal rights.

Based on the classification of respondents along the two cultural dimensions, country-specific SSE and TSR values are generated. The Inglehart measure of cultural distance is then generated by applying the Pythagorean theorem to the country-level SSE and TSR values. Specifically, $CDIST_{ij} = \sqrt{\left(SSE_i - SSE_j\right)^2 + \left(TSR_i - TSR_j\right)^2}$ (White, 2010). As the reference periods of our analyses span the period from 1981 through 2014, we employ SSE and TSR values for each of the first five waves of the World Values Survey.[2] Although we are unable to discern year-specific changes in the cultural distance measure, we do allow the measure to vary over time, according to the years covered by each of the WVS waves. Considering the length of our reference period, this seems not only reasonable but preferable as it allows us to best represent the extent of cross-societal cultural differences over time.

Table 4.1 lists all countries for which data for the TSR and SSE cultural dimensions are available from the first five waves of the WVS.[3] For example, the TSR value for the United States in wave 1 is equal to −0.83. This value largely remains

Table 4.1 Inglehart cultural dimensions, waves 1 through 5

	Wave 1 1981–1984 N = 23		*Wave 2 1990–1994 N = 41*		*Wave 3 1995–1998 N = 56*		*Wave 4 1999–2004 N = 70*		*Wave 5 2005–2009 N = 51*	
Country	*TSR*	*SSE*	*TSR*	*SSE*	*TSR*	*SSE*	*TSR*	*SSE*	*TSR*	*SSE*
Albania	.	.	.	.	0.52	−1.56	0.07	−1.14	.	.
Algeria	.	.	.	.	.	.	−1.48	−0.74	.	.
Andorra	.	.	.	.	.	.	.	.	0.8	1.62
Argentina	0	−0.3	−0.46	0.03	−0.6	0.71	−0.95	0.36	−0.66	0.38
Armenia	.	.	.	.	0.55	−1.31	.	.	.	.
Australia	−0.34	1.14	.	.	−0.18	1.96	.	.	0.21	1.75
Austria	.	.	0.23	0.8	.	.	0.25	1.43	.	.
Azerbaijan	.	.	.	.	−0.14	−1.38	.	.	.	.
Bangladesh	.	.	.	.	−1.24	−1.1	−1.21	−0.93	.	.
Belarus	.	.	0.93	−1.12	0.67	−1.72	0.89	−1.23	.	.
Belgium	0.09	0.08	0.4	0.77	.	.	0.5	1.13	.	.
Bosnia	.	.	.	.	0.09	−0.56	0.34	−0.65	.	.
Brazil	.	.	−0.95	−0.38	−1.29	0.02	.	.	−0.98	0.61
Bulgaria	.	.	1.28	−1.33	0.9	−1.23	1.15	−1.52	1.13	−1.01
Burkina Faso	.	.	.	.	.	.	.	.	−1.32	−0.49
Canada	−0.52	1.04	0.07	1.31	.	.	−0.16	1.72	−0.26	1.91

Chile	.	.	−1.1	−0.2	−0.81	−0.08	−0.87	0.12	−0.87	0
China	.	.	1.79	−1.13	0.79	−1.23	1.2	−0.93	0.8	−1.16
Colombia	.	.	.	.	−1.71	0.34	−1.67	0.68	−1.87	0.6
Croatia	.	.	.	.	0.72	−0.51	0.08	0.31	.	.
Cyprus	.	.	.	.	.	.	.	.	−0.56	0.13
Czech Rep.	.	.	1.24	−0.11	1.07	0.33	1.23	0.38	.	.
Denmark	1.6	1.44	1.25	1.2	.	.	1.16	1.87	.	.
Dominican Rep.	.	.	.	.	−1.05	0.33	.	.	.	.
Egypt	.	.	.	.	.	.	−1.61	−0.46	.	.
El Salvador	.	.	.	.	.	.	−2.06	0.53	.	.
Estonia	.	.	1.3	−0.88	1.27	−1.3	1.27	−1.19	.	.
Ethiopia	.	.	.	.	.	.	.	.	−0.65	−0.36
Finland	0.63	0.82	1.21	1.26	0.68	1.01	0.84	0.94	0.82	1.12
France	0.54	0.13	0.38	0.71	.	.	0.52	0.94	0.63	1.13
Georgia	.	.	.	.	−0.04	−1.31	.	.	.	.
Germany	0.83	−0.07	1.23	0.69	1.55	1.52	1.17	0.44	1.31	0.74
Ghana	.	.	.	.	−1.66	−0.05	.	.	−1.94	−0.29
Greece	.	.	.	.	.	.	0.77	0.55	.	.
Guatemala	.	.	.	.	.	.	−1.7	−0.17	.	.
Hong Kong	.	.	.	.	.	.	.	.	1.2	−0.98
Hungary	0.17	−1.07	0.46	−1.06	0.79	−0.77	0.4	−1.22	.	.
Iceland	0.01	0.83	0.27	1.12	.	.	0.44	1.63	.	.
India	.	.	−0.49	−0.91	−0.54	−0.69	−0.52	−0.6	−0.36	−0.21
Indonesia	.	.	.	.	.	.	−1.07	−0.5	−0.47	−0.8
Iran	.	.	.	.	−1.4	−0.34	−1.22	−0.45	.	.
Iraq	.	.	.	.	.	.	.	.	−0.4	−1.68
Ireland	−0.92	0.59	−1.1	1	.	.	−0.91	1.18	.	.
Israel	.	.	.	.	.	.	0.26	0.36	.	.
Italy	0.18	−0.6	0.11	0.53	.	.	0.19	0.85	0.13	0.6
Japan	1.41	−0.41	1.62	−0.12	1.79	0.37	1.91	0.54	1.96	−0.05
Jordan	.	.	.	.	−1.46	−0.97	−1.61	−1.05	.	.
Korea, Rep.	1.08	−0.74	1.11	−0.65	0.96	−0.64	1.13	−0.55	0.61	−1.37
Kyrgyz Rep.	.	.	.	.	.	.	−0.15	−0.91	.	.
Latvia	.	.	1.21	−0.6	1.33	−0.89	0.72	−1.27	.	.
Lithuania	.	.	0.68	−0.64	0.96	−1.45	0.98	−1	.	.
Luxembourg	.	.	.	.	.	.	0.42	1.13	.	.
Macedonia	.	.	.	.	0.31	−1.02	0.12	−0.72	.	.
Malaysia	.	.	.	.	.	.	.	.	−0.73	0.09
Mali	.	.	.	.	.	.	.	.	−1.25	−0.08
Malta	.	.	.	.	.	.	−1.53	−0.03	.	.
Mexico	−1.15	−0.26	−0.3	0.09	−0.81	0.3	−1.47	0.53	−1.47	1.03
Moldova	.	.	.	.	0.36	−1.91	0.46	−1.69	0.47	−1.28
Montenegro	.	.	.	.	0.58	−1.12	0.86	−1.24	.	.
Morocco	.	.	.	.	.	.	−1.64	−1.09	−1.32	−1.04
Netherlands	0.73	0.9	0.77	1.99	.	.	0.84	1.94	0.71	1.39

(continued)

Table 4.1 (continued)

	Wave 1 1981–1984 N = 23		*Wave 2 1990–1994 N = 41*		*Wave 3 1995–1998 N = 56*		*Wave 4 1999–2004 N = 70*		*Wave 5 2005–2009 N = 51*	
Country	*TSR*	*SSE*	*TSR*	*SSE*	*TSR*	*SSE*	*TSR*	*SSE*	*TSR*	*SSE*
New Zealand	.	.	.	.	0.2	1.78	.	.	0	1.86
Nigeria	.	.	−1.62	−0.68	−1.58	−0.68	−1.53	0.28	.	.
Norway	0.89	0.53	1.17	0.79	1.31	1.33	.	.	1.39	2.17
Pakistan	.	.	.	.	−1.39	−0.52	−1.42	−1.25	.	.
Peru	.	.	.	.	−1.26	−0.18	−1.36	0.03	.	.
Philippines	.	.	.	.	−1.38	−0.12	−1.21	−0.11	.	.
Poland	.	.	−0.81	−0.27	−0.47	−0.41	−0.43	−0.6	−0.78	−0.14
Portugal	.	.	−0.21	−0.43	.	.	−0.9	0.49	.	.
Romania	.	.	0.24	−1.18	0.36	−1.26	−0.28	−1.6	−0.39	−1.55
Russia	.	.	1.09	−1.34	0.87	−1.85	1.09	−1.88	0.49	−1.42
Rwanda	.	.	.	.	.	.	.	.	−1.57	−0.62
Saudi Arabia	.	.	.	.	.	.	−1.31	0.15	.	.
Serbia	.	.	.	.	0.84	−1.05	0.65	−1.03	0.35	−0.62
Singapore	.	.	.	.	.	.	−0.54	−0.28	.	.
Slovakia	.	.	0.75	−0.82	0.41	−0.27	0.67	−0.43	.	.
Slovenia	.	.	0.64	−0.62	0.69	−0.04	0.95	0.38	0.73	0.36
South Africa	−0.53	−0.4	−0.92	−0.46	−1.26	−0.46	−1.12	−0.1	−1.09	−0.1
Spain	−0.26	−0.52	−0.06	0.2	−0.37	0.47	0.12	0.51	0.09	0.54
Sweden	1.2	0.85	1.17	1.54	1.49	1.99	1.67	2.09	1.86	2.35
Switzerland	.	.	0.19	1.11	0.82	1.35	.	.	0.74	1.9
Taiwan	.	.	.	.	0.66	−0.81	.	.	1.16	−1.18
Tanzania	.	.	.	.	.	.	−1.84	−0.15	.	.
Thailand	.	.	.	.	.	.	.	.	−0.64	0.01
Trinidad and Tobago	.	.	.	.	.	.	.	.	−1.83	−0.26
Turkey	.	.	−0.89	−0.17	−1.13	0.28	−0.86	−0.34	−0.89	−0.33
Uganda	−1.42	−0.5	.	.	.	.	.	.	.	.
Ukraine	.	.	.	.	0.84	−1.83	0.9	−1.72	0.3	−0.83
United Kingdom	−0.25	0.95	0.08	1.13	0.08	1.24	0.29	1.31	0.06	1.68
United States	−0.83	0.68	−0.68	1.35	−0.89	1.62	−0.52	1.59	−0.81	1.76
Uruguay	.	.	.	.	−0.21	0.48	.	.	−0.37	0.99
Venezuela	.	.	.	.	−1.82	0.35	−1.6	0.43	.	.
Vietnam	.	.	.	.	.	.	−0.68	0.22	−0.3	−0.26
Zambia	.	.	.	.	.	.	.	.	−0.77	−0.62
Zimbabwe	.	.	.	.	.	.	−1.5	−1.36	.	.

stable across the five waves, increasing from the wave 1 value to −0.68 in wave 2, declining to −0.89 in wave 3, increasing again to −0.52 in wave 4, and then falling to −0.81 in wave 5. Thus, the TSR values for the United States are largely consistent across time, ranging from a high value of –0.52 to a low value of –0.89. To the contrary, again looking at the United States, we see that the SSE values range from a low of 0.68 to a high value of 1.76. This is somewhat misleading, however, and it is important to remember that in all cases the TSR and SSE values are constructed using survey data. Looking more closely at Table 4.1 for the United States, we see that the 0.68 value comes from the first wave of the WVS. The value for the second wave is 1.35. The third wave has a value of 1.62, and the fourth wave has a quite similar value of 1.59. Finally, the SSE value in the fifth wave is 1.76. Thus, other than the first wave, the value for the SSE dimension for the United States remains largely consistent, with a minimum wave of 1.35 and a maximum value of 1.76. Similar variations (and similarities) in values, across waves, are found for other countries in the table.

Figure 4.1 provides a "cultural map" of the world that is based on data from the fourth wave of the WVS (conducted between 1999 and 2004). The x axis

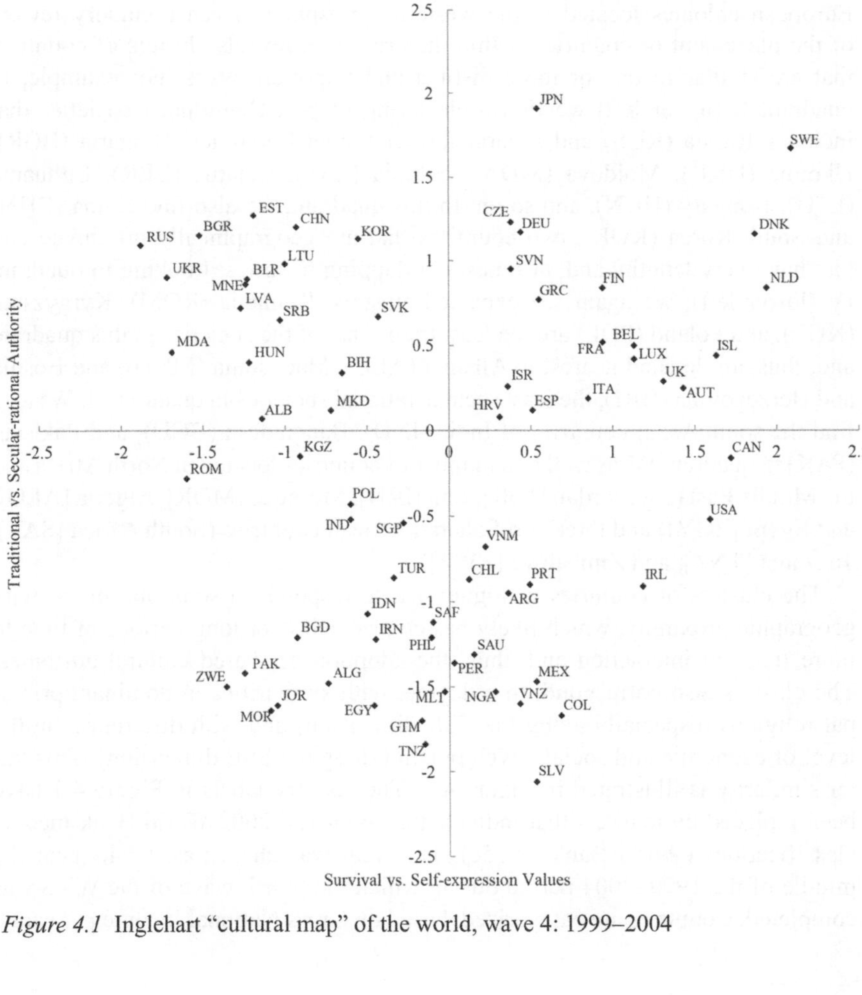

Figure 4.1 Inglehart "cultural map" of the world, wave 4: 1999–2004

in the figure identifies, for each country for which data are available, the value of the SSE dimension. Similarly, the y axis identifies countries according to the TSR dimension. The United States (denoted as USA), for example, is located in quadrant III (i.e., the lower right) of the cross-plot. It is noticeable that the United States is located near Canada (CAN) and Ireland (IRL). More specifically, using the values provided in Table 4.1, the estimated Inglehart cultural distances between the United States and Canada and Ireland are 0.3828 and 0.5659, respectively. Moving to quadrant I (upper right), we see the countries located nearest to the United States are Austria (AUT), the United Kingdom (UK), Italy (ITA), Luxembourg (LUX), and Iceland (ISL). Other countries located near the United States include Spain (ESP), France (FRA), Belgium (BEL), Finland (FIN), Greece (GRC), the Netherlands (NLD), and Denmark (DNK). Looking again at quadrant III, we see the United States is located near Portugal (PRT), Mexico (MEX), Argentina (ARG), Venezuela (VNZ), Colombia (COL), and so on.

Quite often, though not always, the societies that are nearest to the United States are European nations or countries that are, like the United States, former European colonies located in the western hemisphere. Even a cursory review of the placement of countries within the cross-plot reveals clusters of countries that are similar in one or more distinct and important ways. For example, in quadrant II (upper left) we find a clustering of post-Communist societies that includes Russia (RUS) and several former Soviet Republics: Bulgaria (BGR), Ukraine (UKR), Moldova (MDA), Estonia (EST), Belarus (BLR), Lithuania (LTU), Hungary (HUN), and so on. In this quadrant, we also find China (CHN) and South Korea (KOR), two countries that are geographically proximate and that have very lengthy and, at times, overlapping histories. Looking to quadrant IV (lower left), we again see expected clusters. Romania (ROM), Kyrgyzstan (KGZ), and Poland (POL) are the least traditional of the societies in this quadrant and, thus, are located nearest to Albania (ALB), Macedonia (MKD), and Bosnia and Herzegovina (BIH), the least secular-rational societies in quadrant II. We also find the south Asian countries of India (IND), Bangladesh (BGD), and Pakistan (PAK) in quadrant IV, as well as a number of countries located in North Africa and the Middle East (e.g., Jordan [JOR], Iran [IRN], Morocco [MOR], Algeria [ALG], and Egypt [EGY]) and three sub-Saharan African countries (South Africa [SAF], Tanzania [TNZ], and Zimbabwe [ZWE]).

The clusters of countries in Figure 4.1 correspond, in some instances, with geographic proximity, which likely has contributed over long periods of time to more frequent interaction and, thus, the adoption of shared cultural attributes. The clusters also correspond, to a degree, with similarities in dominant/principal religions (especially along the TSR dimension) and with differences in the level of economic and social development (along the SSE dimension). This latter similarity is illustrated in Figure 4.2. The country labels in Figure 4.1 have been replaced by markers that indicate the countries' 2002 World Bank income classifications (World Bank, 2015e). This year was chosen as it falls near the middle of the 1999–2004 period during which the fourth wave of the WVS was completed. Countries are categorized, based on Gross National Income per capita

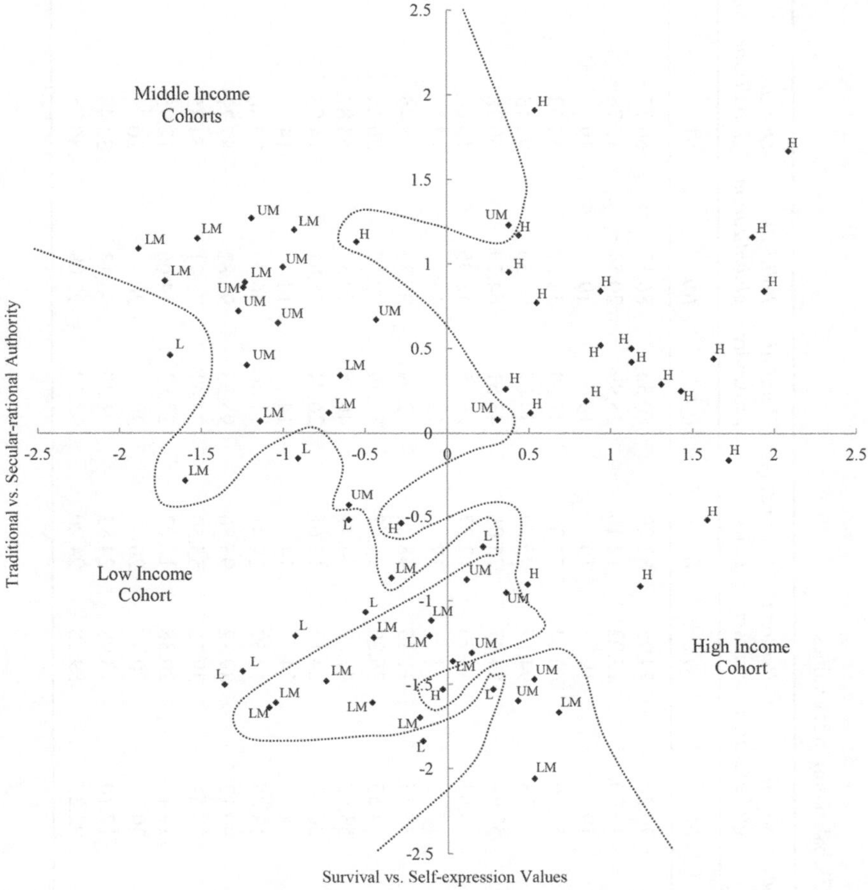

Figure 4.2 Income clusters within the Inglehart "cultural map", wave 4: 1999–2004

(GNIC), as being among the high income cohort (identified in Figure 4.2 by the "H" marker), the upper middle income cohort ("UM"), the lower middle income cohort ("LM"), or the low income cohort ("L").[4]

The income classification of each country is identified in Figure 4.2. We can easily see that the low income countries for which WVS data are available are typically located in quadrant IV. The high income countries occupy most of the right-hand side of the cross-plot and are particularly clustered in quadrant I. The middle income cohorts (i.e., upper middle and lower middle) occupy much of quadrant II as well as much of the more traditional segments of quadrants III and IV. Generally speaking, relative to the high income countries, the residents of the typical low income country are more survival-oriented and less focused on self-expression values, and they are more likely to hold traditional views. As the high income country cohort includes a large number of countries that also had relatively

Table 4.2 Inglehart cultural distance map and KOF Globalization Index values

		Economic globalization	*Actual flows*	*Restrictions*	*Social globalization*	*Personal contact*	*Information flows*	*Cultural proximity*	*Political globalization*	*Overall globalization index*
Quadrant		*(a)*	*(b)*	*(c)*	*(d)*	*(e)*	*(f)*	*(g)*	*(h)*	*(i)*
I	Mean	78.52	70.98	86.42	79.20	74.95	82.29	80.35	86.13	80.77
	Std. Dev.	13.56	15.53	16.94	13.20	15.92	12.10	28.99	20.54	12.76
	n	19	19	19	19	19	19	19	19	19
	min.	41.33	21.61	51.59	52.80	40.24	57.38	41.39	58.67	57.98
	max.	97.16	99.23	95.87	88.75	94.37	95.29	94.07	97.30	92.13
II	Mean	59.74	58.10	61.11	57.99	54.07	75.06	43.51	64.29	60.28
	Std. Dev.	13.32	15.26	13.87	10.83	14.76	12.37	25.95	18.95	10.04
	n	17	16	16	17	17	17	17	17	17
	min.	40.20	32.64	44.01	38.15	11.86	48.22	2.09	27.33	45.45
	max.	87.54	85.77	89.31	74.53	76.20	94.57	87.79	89.85	80.64
III	Mean	63.78	63.52	64.03	53.42	47.89	64.17	46.35	78.87	63.87
	Std. Dev.	13.61	15.65	19.63	20.47	24.12	18.61	26.74	15.01	14.03
	n	14	14	14	14	14	14	14	14	14
	min.	50.07	38.04	29.97	18.06	18.57	28.91	1.40	46.04	39.30
	max.	94.54	98.32	90.76	90.12	89.82	95.80	95.35	93.82	87.29
IV	Mean	51.33	52.47	50.41	43.61	39.36	55.50	34.61	75.71	54.85
	Std. Dev.	16.58	20.68	15.39	19.15	20.38	18.07	24.83	14.06	12.95
	n	20	20	20	20	20	20	20	20	20
	min.	25.15	19.69	24.38	17.10	13.98	24.82	1.30	43.13	32.46
	max.	93.39	97.72	89.06	92.27	89.28	94.20	97.19	92.09	86.75

T statistics	*(a)*	*(b)*	*(c)*	*(d)*	*(e)*	*(f)*	*(g)*	*(h)*	*(i)*
I v. II	4.19	2.47	4.86	5.29	4.08	1.77	4.02	3.32	5.38
I v. III	3.08	1.36	3.43	4.12	3.65	3.18	3.48	1.17	3.55
I v. IV	5.62	3.17	6.94	6.79	6.09	5.47	5.28	1.84	6.30
II v. III	–0.83	–0.96	–0.46	0.75	0.84	1.88	–0.30	–2.39	–0.80
II v. IV	1.71	0.94	2.19	2.86	2.54	3.89	1.06	–2.05	1.44
III v. IV	2.40	1.77	2.17	1.41	1.08	1.35	1.30	0.62	1.91

Quadrant I countries: Austria, Belgium, Croatia, Czech Rep., Denmark, Finland, France, Germany, Greece, Iceland, Israel, Italy, Japan, Luxembourg, Netherlands, Slovenia, Spain, Sweden, and the United Kingdom.

Quadrant II countries: Albania, Belarus, Bosnia, Bulgaria, China, Estonia, Hungary, Korea (Rep. of), Latvia, Lithuania, Macedonia, Moldova, Montenegro, Russia, Serbia, Slovakia, and Ukraine.

Quadrant III countries: Argentina, Chile, Colombia, El Salvador, Ireland, Mexico, Nigeria, Peru, Portugal, Saudi Arabia, United States, Venezuela, and Vietnam.

Quadrant IV countries: Algeria, Bangladesh, Canada, Egypt, Guatemala, India, Indonesia, Iran, Jordan, Kyrgyz Rep., Malta, Morocco, Pakistan, Philippines, Poland, Romania, Singapore, South Africa, Tanzania, Turkey, and Zimbabwe.

high average incomes in prior decades, these countries were more actively engaged in international economic integration than the middle and low income countries in the cross-plot, during the first and second waves of globalization. This suggests a correlation between cultural proximity and greater globalization – specifically, greater international economic integration.

Table 4.2 summarizes the relationship between quadrant location in the "cultural map" (Figure 4.1) and values from the 2002 overall KOF Globalization Index, including the component dimensions (economic globalization, social globalization and political globalization) and the corresponding sub-dimensions. Quadrant I is largely populated by high income countries. Specifically, 17 of the 19 countries in the quadrant are high income countries, and the other two are upper middle income. Similarly, the majority of countries in quadrant IV are low income or lower middle income countries. That is, seven of the 20 countries in the quadrant are classified as low income countries and another 10 are classified as lower middle income.

Comparing mean values for the overall KOF Globalization Index across quadrants, we see that quadrant I has the highest average value for both the overall KOF Globalization Index (80.77) and the economic globalization dimension (78.52). In fact, these mean values are significantly higher ($p < 0.01$) than the mean values for all three other quadrants. For both the overall KOF Index and the economic dimension (as well as the actual flows and the restrictions sub-dimensions), the mean values (listed from highest to lowest) follow the same ordering: quadrant I, quadrant III, quadrant II, and quadrant IV. It is notable that quadrant IV, which is comprised primarily of low income and lower middle income (i.e., developing) countries, has the lowest mean values and that quadrant I, where 17 of the 19 countries are high income and the other two are upper middle income, has the highest values. This is consistent with the notion, introduced in Chapter 3, that there is an unevenness in globalization that corresponds with the greater global engagement of higher-income economies during the first and second waves of globalization and the more recent engagement of many developing countries with the global economy.

Hofstede measures of cultural distance

Having provided a detailed description of the Inglehart measure of cultural distance, we can now turn our attention to the three other composite measures that are used in our empirical analysis. The second and third composite measures of cultural distance are from the Hofstede model of national culture.[5] In fact, using the Hofstede cultural dimensions data, we construct two related measures of cultural differences. In total, there are six cultural dimensions related to the Hofstede model, and the two Hofstede-based measures that we employ differ only in terms of the number of dimensions used to construct each measure. The first of these two measures, which we refer to as the Hofstede 4-factor measure of cultural distance, is constructed using four of the cultural dimensions. The second measure is constructed using data for all six dimensions and is referred to as the Hofstede

6-factor measure of cultural distance. Thus, the 4-factor measure is narrower in scope than the 6-factor measure, but it is representative of a greater number of countries. In this section, we discuss each dimension in turn and then focus our attention on the construction of the composite cultural distance measures.

Between 1967 and 1973, Geert Hofstede conducted two rounds of surveys to collect data from more than 116,000 employees of subsidiaries of IBM that worked/lived in 72 different countries. The surveys were intended to elicit information on differences, across countries, based on questions about employee values. The result was a set of country-specific values for four cultural dimensions that are labeled 1) the power distance index, 2) individualism vs. collectivism, 3) masculinity vs. femininity, and 4) the uncertainty avoidance index. Since the initial data collection period, the number of cultural dimensions has been expanded. However, before discussing the more recent additions, we will focus our attention on the initial four dimensions.

The power distance index (PDI) is described as "the degree to which the less powerful members of a society accept and expect that power is distributed unequally" (Hofstede, 2001, p. 79). The PDI is a reflection of how inequalities (perhaps in the forms of wealth, power, or general social status) within a society are viewed by its members. The PDI was constructed based on mean values, across respondents grouped by country, of responses to three survey questions which asked respondents to comment on subordinates' fear of disagreeing with their superiors, their preferences for the superiors' management style, and their superiors' actual/perceived management style. Members of societies for which the PDI score is higher tend to be more willing to accept a strict hierarchical order. Conversely, societies that wish to have a more equal distribution of power among its members, and/or that seek justifications for inequalities, have lower PDI values.

The second of Hofstede's cultural dimensions is individualism vs. collectivism (IDV). The measure "describes the relationship between the individual and the collectivity that prevails in a given society" (Hofstede, 2001, p. 209). In short, the measure is representative of how individuals live together, which has implications for behavior and values. Members of societies with high IDV scores (i.e., those that are more individual-oriented and less collectivist-minded) are self-oriented, more likely to formulate self-identities based on the individual rather than their role within a group, and more likely to believe that each person has a right to a private life. Such individuals are geared towards taking care of themselves and their immediate family and, accordingly, make decisions based largely on their needs and the needs of those closest to them. Those who are members of more collectivist-oriented societies share opposing views. While the individual is of importance, the group is considered to be more important. Thus, self-identity is based on the social system rather than the individual. It is expected that individuals will afford blind loyalty to the group and, accordingly, adhere to decisions that are made with the group's best interest in mind (even if the decision conflicts with the individual's best interest).

The third of Hofstede's cultural dimensions is masculinity vs. femininity (MAS). This dimension is focused on the implications of biological differences on the emotional and social roles of women and men. The distinction between genders in terms of this dimension is summarized by Hofstede as follows: "Masculinity stands for a society in which social gender roles are clearly distinct: men are supposed to be assertive, tough, and focused on material success; women are supposed to be more modest, tender, and concerned with the quality of life", while "[f]emininity stands for a society in which social gender roles overlap: both men and women are supposed to be modest, tender, and concerned with the quality of life" (Hofstede, 2001, p. 297).

Described by Hofstede as "a society's tolerance for uncertainty and ambiguity", the uncertainty avoidance index (UAI) is the last of the four initial Hofstede cultural dimensions. The UAI was constructed from mean response scores, across countries, to three questions that focus on rule orientation, stress, and employment stability. The index represents how comfortable members of a society are when they find themselves in unstructured situations. In short, the UAI is not a measure of risk-aversion or risk-avoidance but instead reflects how comfortable a society is when dealing with uncertainty. Members of societies that are characterized as having high levels of uncertainty avoidance tend to be more conservative with respect to social norms. They often have limited interest in political matters but favor more laws and safety/security measures and, in general, view citizen protests unfavorably. Such individuals adhere to traditional gender roles and believe that others should as well. In these regards, members of societies with high UAI values favor structured environments and seek to reduce the level of uncertainty that they experience or limit the amount of uncertainty they may face. Individuals in societies with low UAI values, being more comfortable with, and perhaps even welcoming of, uncertainty, hold opposing preferences. They may seek to minimize the number of rules or laws that govern daily life. They may also be more tolerant of diversity, maintain a strong interest in political matters, be more open to non-traditional gender roles, and generally more open to change.

Using data from the World Values Surveys, Hofstede et al. (2010) generate two additional cultural dimensions. The first of these two dimensions, labelled the pragmatic vs. normative (PRA) dimension, is an extension of a previously-added fifth dimension known as long-term orientation (or Confucian dynamism) (Hofstede and Bond, 1988). The extension from the long-term orientation dimension allows for more countries to be included in the data set. The second of these two dimensions is known as the indulgence vs. restraint (IND) dimension.

The PRA dimension represents how a society's past and present culture address the fact that much of what occurs in the world and what we experience as individuals appears unexplainable. Members of societies for which there is a higher PRA score (i.e., those societies described as having a pragmatic orientation) do not believe it is possible to understand all that happens in our lives. For these individuals, what is considered to be the truth is very much situation- and context-specific. This corresponds with a greater ability to accept apparent contradictions but also to quickly adapt when faced with changing circumstances. Individuals in societies that have more normative orientations seek to explain most or all of what we observe in the world and what we experience in our lives. Thus, establishing a known "truth" is an important concern among individuals in these societies. This corresponds with a desire for greater personal stability and more respect for social conventions and traditions. In a few words, those societies that have low scores in the PRA dimension are suspicious of societal change and instead exhibit a preference for time-honored traditions and norms. Those societies with high scores tend to hold opposing views.

The indulgence vs. restraint (IND) dimension is representative of the extent to which a society allows, or encourages, the satisfaction of desires and impulses that yield pleasure and happiness. "restraint" indicates the suppression of the gratification of wants and needs even if this is accomplished by the imposition of strict social norms and restrictions. Members of societies with high values for the IND dimension (i.e., societies that are more indulgent in nature) may be characterized as having limited control over their impulses or a lack of desire (or need) to control their impulses. To the contrary, individuals in societies that have low IND scores (i.e., that are more restraint-oriented) generally have more control over their impulses, or this may reflect a perceived greater need (or willingness) to exert (or adhere to) external controls that suppress impulses.

Table 4.3 presents country-specific scores for all six of Hofstede's cultural dimensions. The dimension scores range from 0 to 100. Comparing values for Albania and Angola, for illustrative purposes, we see that these two countries have similar scores for three of the six dimensions and quite dissimilar scores for the other three. Both Albania and Angola have high PDI scores, indicating that members of both societies are more willing, compared to members of societies with lower PDI scores, to accept a strict hierarchical order. Similarly, both countries have high UAI scores. A high score in this dimension represents, generally speaking, a preference for more structured situations. Albania and Angola also have near-identical scores for the IDV index; thus, members of the two societies are more collectivist-minded and, accordingly, are more group-focused and place greater emphasis on the social system. With respect to the three remaining cultural dimensions, Albania and Angola are quite dissimilar. Albania has a much higher score for the MAS dimension and a higher score for the PRA dimension. Albania also has a much lower score for the IND dimension. Thus, from these differences in scores, we can say, in very general terms, that relative to the culture of Angola, social roles of men and women are better defined in Albania. Residents of Albania often view the truth as dependent on the context or situation, and typically exhibit limited control over impulses, or simply a lack of interest in suppressing impulses, that lead to pleasure or happiness.

From the scores presented for the six cultural dimensions, we construct two composite measures of cultural distance using the Hofstede cultural dimensions data. As noted earlier, the 4-factor measure is narrower in scope than the 6-factor measure but is representative of a greater number of countries. More specifically, we employ the methodology of Kogut and Singh (1988) to generate the composite 4-factor measure of Hofstede cultural distance measure as $CD_{ij} = \sum_{k=1}^{4} \left[\frac{\left(I_{ik} - I_{jk}\right)^2}{V_k} \right] / 4$ where

Table 4.3 Hofstede cultural dimensions

		Power Distance Index	*Individualism vs. Collectivism*	*Masculinity vs. Femininity*	*Uncertainty Avoidance Index*	*Pragmatic vs. Normative*	*Indulgence vs. Restraint*
Country	*ISO3*	*PDI*	*IDV*	*MAS*	*UAI*	*PRA*	*IND*
Albania	ALB	90	20	80	70	61	15
Angola	AGO	83	18	20	60	15	83
Argentina	ARG	49	46	56	86	20	62
Australia	AUS	36	90	61	51	21	71
Austria	AUT	11	55	79	70	60	63
Bangladesh	BGD	80	20	55	60	47	20
Belgium	BEL	65	75	54	94	82	57
Bhutan	BTN	94	52	32	28	.	.
Brazil	BRA	69	38	49	76	44	59
Bulgaria	BGR	70	30	40	85	69	16
Burkina Faso	BFA	70	15	50	55	27	18
Canada	CAN	39	80	52	48	36	68
Cape Verde	CPV	75	20	15	40	12	83
Chile	CHL	63	23	28	86	31	68
China	CHN	80	20	66	30	87	24
Colombia	COL	67	13	64	80	13	83
Costa Rica	CRI	35	15	21	86	.	.
Croatia	HRV	73	33	40	80	58	33
Czech Rep.	CZE	57	58	57	74	70	29
Denmark	DNK	18	74	16	23	35	70
Dominican Rep.	DOM	65	30	65	45	13	54
Ecuador	ECU	78	8	63	67	.	.
Egypt	EGY	70	25	45	80	7	4
El Salvador	SLV	66	19	40	94	20	89
Estonia	EST	40	60	30	60	82	16
Ethiopia	ETH	70	20	65	55	.	.
Fiji	FJI	78	14	46	48	.	.
Finland	FIN	33	63	26	59	38	57
France	FRA	68	71	43	86	63	48
Germany	DEU	35	67	66	65	83	40
Ghana	GHA	80	15	40	65	4	72
Greece	GRC	60	35	57	100	45	50
Guatemala	GTM	95	6	37	99	.	.
Honduras	HND	80	20	40	50	.	.
Hong Kong	HKG	68	25	57	29	61	17
Hungary	HUN	46	80	88	82	58	31
Iceland	ISL	30	60	10	50	28	67
India	IND	77	48	56	40	51	26
Indonesia	IDN	78	14	46	48	62	38
Iran	IRN	58	41	43	59	14	40
Iraq	IRQ	95	30	70	85	25	17
Ireland	IRL	28	70	68	35	24	65
Israel	ISR	13	54	47	81	38	.

Italy	ITA	50	76	70	75	61	30
Jamaica	JAM	45	39	68	13	.	.
Japan	JPN	54	46	95	92	88	42
Jordan	JOR	70	30	45	65	16	43
Kenya	KEN	70	25	60	50	.	.
Korea, Rep. of	KOR	60	18	39	85	100	29
Kuwait	KWT	90	25	40	80	.	.
Latvia	LVA	44	70	9	63	69	13
Lebanon	LBN	75	40	65	50	14	25
Libya	LBY	80	38	52	68	23	34
Lithuania	LTU	42	60	19	65	82	16
Luxembourg	LUX	40	60	50	70	64	56
Malawi	MWI	70	30	40	50	.	.
Malaysia	MYS	100	26	50	36	41	57
Malta	MLT	56	59	47	96	47	66
Mexico	MEX	81	30	69	82	24	97
Morocco	MOR	70	46	53	68	14	25
Mozambique	MOZ	85	15	38	44	11	80
Namibia	NAM	65	30	40	45	35	.
Nepal	NPL	65	30	40	40	.	.
Netherlands	NLD	38	80	14	53	67	68
New Zealand	NZL	22	79	58	49	33	75
Nigeria	NGA	80	30	60	55	13	84
Norway	NOR	31	69	8	50	35	55
Pakistan	PAK	55	14	50	70	50	0
Panama	PAN	95	11	44	86	.	.
Peru	PER	64	16	42	87	25	46
Philippines	PHL	94	32	64	44	27	42
Poland	POL	68	60	64	93	38	29
Portugal	PRT	63	27	31	99	28	33
Romania	ROM	90	30	42	90	52	20
Russia	RUS	93	39	36	95	81	20
Saudi Arabia	SAU	95	25	60	80	36	52
Senegal	SEN	70	25	45	55	25	.
Serbia	SRB	86	25	43	92	52	28
Sierra Leone	SLE	70	20	40	50	.	.
Singapore	SGP	74	20	48	8	72	46
Slovakia	SVK	100	52	100	51	77	28
Slovenia	SVN	71	27	19	88	49	48
South Africa	SAF	49	65	63	49	34	63
Spain	ESP	57	51	42	86	48	44
Sri Lanka	LKA	80	35	10	45	45	.
Suriname	SUR	85	47	37	92	.	.
Sweden	SWE	31	71	5	29	53	78
Switzerland	CHE	34	68	70	58	74	66
Syria	SYR	80	35	52	60	30	.
Taiwan	TWN	58	17	45	69	93	49
Tanzania	TZA	70	25	40	50	34	38
Thailand	THA	64	20	34	64	32	45
Trinidad and Tobago	TTO	47	16	58	55	13	80
Turkey	TUR	66	37	45	85	46	49
United Arab Emirates	ARE	90	25	50	80	.	.
United Kingdom	GBR	35	89	66	35	51	69

(continued)

Table 4.3 (continued)

		Power Distance Index	*Individualism vs. Collectivism*	*Masculinity vs. Femininity*	*Uncertainty Avoidance Index*	*Pragmatic vs. Normative*	*Indulgence vs. Restraint*
Country	*ISO3*	*PDI*	*IDV*	*MAS*	*UAI*	*PRA*	*IND*
United States	USA	40	91	62	46	26	68
Uruguay	URY	61	36	38	99	26	53
Venezuela	VNZ	81	12	73	76	16	100
Vietnam	VNM	70	20	40	30	57	35
Zambia	ZMB	60	35	40	50	30	42
Group Average		64.0	39.0	47.6	63.9	43.1	47.7
Variance		429.8	486.1	344.3	454.7	549.6	535.3

Note: Variance calculations include only countries/observations for which data are available for all six cultural dimensions.

CD is the estimated cultural distance between countries i and j, *I* is the index value for the kth cultural dimension, and *V* is the variance of the index of the kth cultural dimension. The 6-factor Hofstede measure of cultural distance extends from this equation to include the PRA dimension and the measure of IND.

Panel A of Figure 4.3 presents the 6-factor Hofstede measures of cultural distance between 10 countries. The cultural distance values are calculated using the method described above and the corresponding cultural dimension scores and variances from Table 4.3. The dimension scores are reproduced, for these 10 countries, in Panel B of the figure. We see, for example, that the cultural distance between Australia and Canada is equal to 0.15. Likewise, the cultural distance between Australia and the United States is equal to 0.03, and the cultural distance between Canada and the United States is 0.12. In short, these three countries have similar cultures as represented by the 6-factor Hofstede measure. The upper left radar graph in Panel C of Figure 4.3 depicts the scores, across each of the six cultural dimensions, for Australia, Canada, and the United States. From the graph it is evident that the dimension scores are very similar – thus, the low cultural distance values.

The upper right radar graph is identical to the graph in the upper left portion of the page, with the single exception of China's inclusion. Here, we see a stark contrast in scores across all dimensions except for the MAS dimension and, to a lesser extent, the UAI. Returning to Panel A, we see that China's estimated cultural distances from Australia, Canada, and the United States are 4.61, 3.49, and 4.18, respectively. A look to Panel B reveals very dissimilar scores, as expected given the radar graph, for the PDI, IDV, PRA, and IND cultural dimensions. For example, the IDV dimension score for China is 20, whereas the score is 91 for the United States, 90 for Australia, and 80 for Canada. The four societies are more

Panel A: Cultural Distances

	ARG	AUS	CAN	CHN	IND	IRN	SGP	USA	VNM	ZMB
ARG	0.00	1.22	1.06	3.61	1.78	0.55	3.63	1.35	2.32	0.84
AUS	1.22	0.00	0.15	4.61	2.22	1.51	3.98	0.03	3.30	1.76
CAN	1.06	0.15	0.00	3.49	1.56	1.14	2.85	0.12	2.27	1.16
CHN	3.61	4.61	3.49	0.00	0.75	2.60	0.57	4.18	0.68	1.79
IND	1.78	2.22	1.56	0.75	0.00	0.85	0.94	1.93	0.48	0.54
IRN	0.55	1.51	1.14	2.60	0.85	0.00	2.25	1.51	1.09	0.13
SGP	3.63	3.98	2.85	0.57	0.94	2.25	0.00	3.59	0.32	1.37
USA	1.35	0.03	0.12	4.18	1.93	1.51	3.59	0.00	3.04	1.69
VNM	2.32	3.30	2.27	0.68	0.48	1.09	0.32	3.04	0.00	0.50
ZMB	0.84	1.76	1.16	1.79	0.54	0.13	1.37	1.69	0.50	0.00

Panel B: Cultural Dimensions

	PDI	IDV	MAS	UAI	PRA	IND
ARG	49	46	56	86	20	62
AUS	36	90	61	51	21	71
CAN	39	80	52	48	36	68
CHN	80	20	66	30	87	24
IND	77	48	56	40	51	26
IRN	58	41	43	59	14	40
SGP	74	20	48	8	72	46
USA	40	91	62	46	26	68
VNM	70	20	40	30	57	35
ZMB	60	35	40	50	30	42

Panel C: Radar Graphs

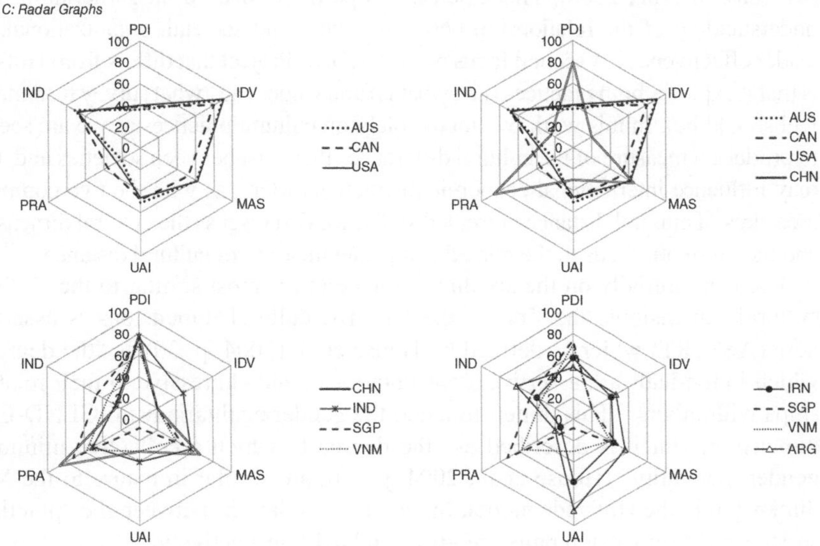

Figure 4.3 Hofstede 6-factor cultural distance measure, select country pairs

similar when viewed in terms of their UAI scores and are very similar along the MAS cultural dimension.

The remaining two radar graphs presented in Figure 4.3 further illustrate the differences in the estimated values of the 6-factor Hofstede measure of cultural distance. The graph positioned on the lower left side of the page includes China, as does the graph on the upper right, but replaces Australia, Canada, and the United States with India, Singapore, and Vietnam. Here, we see more similarity to China, particularly with respect to Singapore and Vietnam which have estimated cultural distances of 0.57 and 0.68, respectively. The estimated cultural distance between China and India, 0.75, is also much lower than that estimated between China and Australia, Canada, and the United States. The graph placed in the lower right corner of the page extends the comparisons further by replacing China and India with Iran and Argentina. In this graph, we see more clear similarities between Singapore and Vietnam (i.e., an estimated cultural distance value of 0.32) and between Argentina and Iran (i.e., a value of 0.55), as well as differences between Argentina and Singapore (3.63).

The GLOBE cultural distance measure

The GLOBE Project administered surveys in 62 societies to more than 17,300 middle managers who were members of 951 organizations.[6] The surveys were completed during the years 1991–1994. The GLOBE study produced data which allows the 62 participant societies in 58 countries to be scored along nine cultural dimensions. Six of these dimensions are similar to four of the Hofstede cultural dimensions. In that regard, the GLOBE Project can be thought of as an extension of Hofstede's research (Magnussen et al., 2008). This extension is partially focused on garnering a better understanding of the relationship between culture and societal, organizational, and leader effectiveness. A second focus of the GLOBE Project that differs from Hofstede is that it explores both practices (i.e., what is) and values (i.e., what survey respondents feel should be). In this work, we focus solely on cultural practices as we are seeking to produce a measure of the cultural differences that exist between societies and, thus, may influence international economic interactions. Here, as with the two composite measures of cultural distance presented so far, we first discuss the cultural dimensions and then turn our focus to the related composite measure of cultural distance.

Focusing initially on the six dimensions that are most similar to the Hofstede cultural dimensions, the first of the GLOBE cultural dimensions is assertiveness (ASSERT) which is defined by House et al. (2004, p. 30) as "the degree to which individuals are assertive, confrontational, and aggressive in their relationships with others." This dimension, and the gender egalitarianism (GEND-EGL) dimension, which is described as "the degree to which a collective minimizes gender inequality" (House et al., 2004, p. 30), are similar in nature to the MAS dimension in the Hofstede model. In fact the correlations between the "practices" series for the dimension pairs are –0.16 and 0.42, respectively.

A second Hofstede cultural dimension for which there are related GLOBE dimensions is IDV. The corresponding GLOBE dimensions are institutional collectivism (INST-COL) and in-group collectivism (INGP-COL). INST-COL is defined as "the degree to which organizational and societal institutional practices encourage and reward collective distribution of resources and collective action" (House et al., 2004, p. 30). The correlation between this GLOBE cultural dimension and Hofstede's IDV dimension is 0.15. INGP-COL is defined as "the degree to which individuals express pride, loyalty, and cohesiveness in their organizations or families" (House et al, 2004, p. 30). Here, there is a much stronger correlation (-0.82) between the GLOBE and Hofstede dimensions.

The remaining two GLOBE cultural dimensions that are related to the Hofstede dimensions are power distance and uncertainty avoidance. In fact, these two GLOBE and Hofstede dimensions are so closely related as to share the same names: Hofstede's dimensions are referred to as the power distance index (PDI) and the uncertainty avoidance index (UAI). The GLOBE dimension of power distance is a measure of "the degree to which members of a collective expect power to be distributed equally." (House et al., 2004, p. 12). By comparison, Hofstede's PDI is defined as "the degree to which the less powerful members of a society accept and expect that power is distributed unequally" (Hofstede, 2001, p. 79). The GLOBE uncertainty avoidance dimension reflects "the extent to which a society, organization, or group relies on social norms, rules, and procedures to alleviate the unpredictability of future events." (House et al., 2004, p. 13) Again, for the sake of comparison, the Hofstede UAI is defined as "a society's tolerance for uncertainty and ambiguity". Unsurprisingly, given the similarities in definitions, the correlations coefficient between the GLOBE power distance measure and Hofstede's PDI is equal to 0.61. The correlation between the GLOBE uncertainty avoidance measure and the UAI series is –0.61.

There are three additional cultural dimensions in the GLOBE data that are not clearly represented in the Hofstede data. These dimensions – future orientation, humane orientation, and performance orientation – are each connected to how behaviors are rewarded within a society. For example, future orientation is defined by House et al. (2004, p. 282) as "the degree to which a collectivity encourages and rewards future-oriented behaviors such as planning and delaying gratification." By contrast, humane orientation is "the degree to which an organization or society encourages and rewards individuals for being fair, altruistic, friendly, generous, caring, and kind to others" (House et al., 2004, p. 569). Lastly, performance orientation is defined as "the extent to which a community encourages and rewards innovation, high standards, excellence, and performance improvement" (House et al., 2004, p. 239). Table 4.4 presents the scores, for each country, across the nine GLOBE cultural dimensions.

The GLOBE cultural distance measure is constructed following the same methodology used to generate the Hofstede cultural distance measures. Specifically, using the nine cultural dimension scores, we employ the methodology of Kogut and Singh (1988) to generate the GLOBE composite measure of Hofstede cultural distance. Resulting values, for a sampling of countries, are presented in Figure 4.4. Similar to the 6-factor Hofstede measure of cultural distance presented in Figure 4.3, Panel A presents the GLOBE measures of cultural distance between seven countries. In Panel B, the corresponding cultural dimension scores are provided. Looking to a handful of cultural distance estimates as an example, we see that the cultural distance between Indonesia (IDN) and Japan (JPN) is equal to 15.74 and the distance between Indonesia and Ireland (IRL) is 13.35. Further, the estimated cultural distance between Japan and Ireland is 13.70. In short, these three countries have similar cultures as represented by the GLOBE cultural dimensions. These similarities are depicted by the upper left radar graph in Panel C. From the graph, it is evident that the dimension scores are very similar – thus, the low cultural distance values presented in Panel A and the similar cultural dimension scores provided in Panel B.

The upper right radar graph is nearly identical to the graph in the upper left of the figure. The sole change is the addition of Singapore (SGP). The cultural distances between Singapore and Indonesia, Ireland, and Japan are 31.09, 27.19, and 28.48, respectively. Thus, the culture of Singapore is quite different from the cultures of these three countries. Moreover, in the upper right radar graph, we see that while Singapore is similar to the three countries in terms of several dimensions, there are clear differences with respect to the uncertainty avoidance (UNC-AVD) and humane orientation (HUMANE) dimensions and, to a lesser extent, with respect to the power distance (POWDIST) and future orientation (FUTURE) dimensions.

Table 4.4 GLOBE cultural dimensions

	Assertiveness (ASSERT)	*Institutional Collectivism (INST-COL)*	*In-Group Collectivism (INGP-COL)*	*Future Orientation (FUTURE)*	*Gender Egalitarianism (GEND-EGL)*	*Humane Orientation (HUMANE)*	*Performance Orientation (PERFORM)*	*Power Distance (POWDIST)*	*Uncertainty Avoidance (UNC-AVD)*
Albania	4.57	4.28	5.51	3.69	3.48	4.40	4.57	4.44	4.45
Argentina	4.18	3.66	5.51	3.10	3.44	3.94	3.63	5.56	3.63
Australia	4.29	4.31	4.14	4.09	3.41	4.32	4.37	4.81	4.40
Austria	4.59	4.34	4.89	4.47	3.18	3.77	4.47	5.00	5.10
Bolivia	3.78	3.96	5.44	3.55	3.45	3.99	3.57	4.46	3.32
Brazil	4.25	3.94	5.16	3.90	3.44	3.76	4.11	5.24	3.74
Canada	4.09	4.36	4.22	4.40	3.66	4.51	4.46	4.85	4.54
China	3.77	4.67	5.86	3.68	3.03	4.29	4.37	5.02	4.81
Colombia	4.16	3.84	5.59	3.35	3.64	3.72	3.93	5.37	3.62
Costa Rica	3.83	3.95	5.26	3.64	3.56	4.38	4.10	4.70	3.84
Denmark	4.04	4.93	3.63	4.59	4.02	4.67	4.40	4.14	5.32
Ecuador	3.98	3.82	5.55	3.66	3.09	4.45	4.06	5.29	3.63
Egypt	3.91	4.36	5.49	3.80	2.90	4.60	4.15	4.76	3.97
El Salvador	4.49	3.74	5.22	3.73	3.23	3.69	3.72	5.56	3.69
England	4.23	4.31	4.08	4.31	3.67	3.74	4.16	5.26	4.70
Finland	4.05	4.77	4.23	4.39	3.55	4.19	4.02	5.08	5.11
France	4.44	4.20	4.66	3.74	3.81	3.60	4.43	5.68	4.66
Georgia	4.15	4.03	6.18	3.45	3.52	4.17	3.85	5.15	3.54
Germany	4.77	3.67	4.59	4.04	3.17	3.45	4.16	5.70	5.19
Greece	4.55	3.41	5.28	3.53	3.53	3.44	3.34	5.35	3.52
Guatemala	3.96	3.78	5.54	3.35	3.14	3.91	3.85	5.47	3.44
Hong Kong	4.53	4.03	5.33	3.88	3.26	3.72	4.69	4.94	4.17
Hungary	4.71	3.63	5.31	3.31	4.02	3.39	3.50	5.57	3.26
India	3.70	4.25	5.81	4.04	2.89	4.45	4.11	5.29	4.02
Indonesia	3.70	4.27	5.50	3.61	3.04	4.47	4.14	4.93	3.92
Ireland	3.93	4.57	5.12	3.93	3.19	4.96	4.30	5.13	4.25

Israel	4.19	4.40	4.63	3.82	3.21	4.07	4.03	4.71	3.97
Italy	4.12	3.75	4.99	3.34	3.30	3.66	3.66	5.45	3.85
Japan	3.69	5.23	4.72	4.29	3.17	4.34	4.22	5.23	4.07
Kazakhstan	4.51	4.38	5.50	3.72	3.87	4.44	3.72	5.40	3.76
Korea (South)	4.36	5.20	5.71	3.90	2.45	3.73	4.53	5.69	3.52
Kuwait	3.56	4.32	5.70	3.18	2.59	4.44	3.79	4.97	4.02
Malaysia	3.77	4.45	5.47	4.39	3.31	4.76	4.16	5.09	4.59
Mexico	4.31	3.95	5.62	3.75	3.50	3.84	3.97	5.07	4.06
Morocco	4.72	4.18	6.37	3.50	3.08	4.52	4.31	6.14	3.95
Namibia	3.81	4.02	4.39	3.32	3.69	3.83	3.52	5.29	4.09
Netherlands	4.46	4.62	3.79	4.72	3.62	4.02	4.46	4.32	4.81
New Zealand	3.47	4.96	3.58	3.46	3.18	4.43	4.86	5.12	4.86
Nigeria	4.53	4.00	5.34	3.95	3.04	3.96	3.79	5.32	4.14
Philippines	3.85	4.37	6.14	3.92	3.42	4.88	4.21	5.15	3.69
Poland	4.11	4.51	5.55	3.23	3.94	3.67	3.96	5.09	3.71
Portugal	3.75	4.02	5.64	3.77	3.69	3.96	3.65	5.50	3.96
Qatar	4.39	4.78	5.07	4.08	3.86	4.79	3.76	5.05	4.26
Russia	3.86	4.57	5.83	3.06	4.07	4.04	3.53	5.61	3.09
Singapore	4.06	4.77	5.66	4.88	3.52	3.29	4.81	4.92	5.16
Slovenia	4.01	4.09	5.49	3.56	3.84	3.75	3.62	5.32	3.76
Spain	4.39	3.87	5.53	3.52	3.06	3.29	4.00	5.53	3.95
Sweden	3.41	5.26	3.46	4.37	3.72	4.09	3.67	4.94	5.36
Switzerland	4.58	4.20	4.04	4.80	3.12	3.73	5.04	5.05	5.42
Taiwan	3.70	4.30	5.45	3.65	2.92	3.82	4.27	5.00	4.04
Thailand	3.58	3.88	5.72	3.27	3.26	4.87	3.84	5.62	3.79
Turkey	4.42	4.02	5.79	3.74	3.02	3.92	3.82	5.43	3.67
United States	4.50	4.21	4.22	4.13	3.36	4.18	4.45	4.92	4.15
Venezuela	4.25	3.96	5.41	3.43	3.60	4.19	3.41	5.22	3.55
Zambia	4.00	4.41	5.72	3.55	2.88	5.12	4.01	5.23	3.92
Zimbabwe	4.04	4.08	5.53	3.76	3.09	4.38	4.20	5.54	4.12

Panel A: Cultural Distances, Practices

	GRC	IDN	IRL	JPN	MEX	SGP	USA
GRC	0.00	31.83	35.16	38.94	17.26	38.87	28.15
IDN	31.83	0.00	13.35	15.74	17.38	31.09	19.29
IRL	35.16	13.35	0.00	13.70	20.18	27.19	17.93
JPN	38.94	15.74	13.70	0.00	25.40	28.48	20.98
MEX	17.26	17.38	20.18	25.40	0.00	25.99	15.47
SGP	38.87	31.09	27.19	28.48	25.99	0.00	25.15
USA	28.15	19.29	17.93	20.98	15.47	25.15	0.00

Panel B: Cultural Dimensions, Practices

	ASSERT	INST-COL	INGP-COL	FUTURE	GEND-EGL	HUMANE	PERFORM	POWDIST	UNC-AVD
GRC	4.55	3.41	5.28	3.53	3.53	3.44	5.35	3.34	3.52
IDN	3.7	4.27	5.5	3.61	3.04	4.47	4.93	4.14	3.92
IRL	3.93	4.57	5.12	3.93	3.19	4.96	5.13	4.3	4.25
JPN	3.69	5.23	4.72	4.29	3.17	4.34	5.23	4.22	4.07
MEX	4.31	3.95	5.62	3.75	3.5	3.84	5.07	3.97	4.06
SGP	4.06	4.77	5.66	4.88	3.52	3.29	4.92	4.81	5.16
USA	4.5	4.21	4.22	4.13	3.36	4.18	4.92	4.45	4.15

Panel C: Radar Graphs

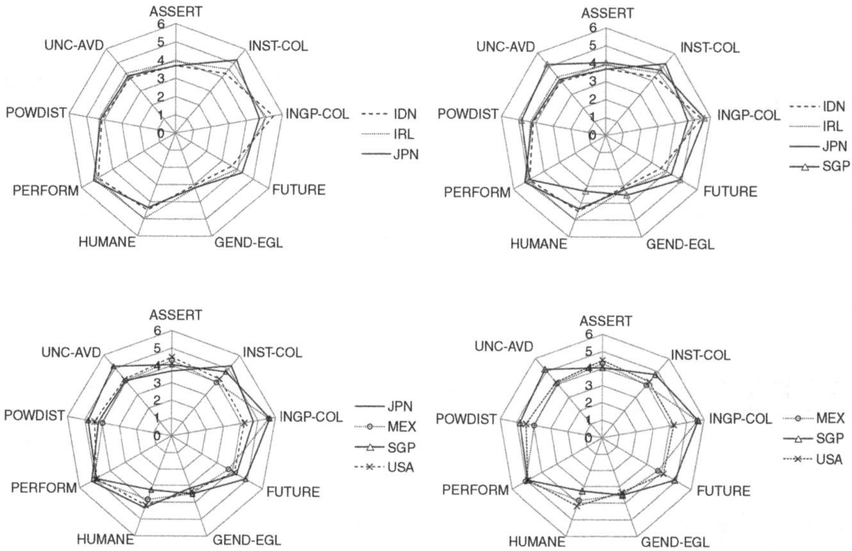

Figure 4.4 GLOBE dimension-based cultural distances, select country pairs

The two radar graphs that occupy the bottom of Figure 4.3 further illustrate the differences in estimated GLOBE cultural distance measures. The graph positioned on the lower left side of the page includes Japan and Singapore, as does the graph on the upper right, but this graph replaces Indonesia and Ireland with Mexico and the United States. Here, we see similarity between Mexico and the United States (i.e., a cultural distance value of 15.47) and the same similarity between Japan and Singapore as before, but the cultures of Japan and Mexico are different, as are the cultures of Singapore and the United States.

Comparing the Inglehart, Hofstede, and GLOBE cultural distance measures

Having now presented the four composite measures of cultural differences that are employed in this study, it is worthwhile to compare the measures statistically to gauge how similar the measures are. In Figure 4.5, there are three scatterplots. Each depicts the relationship between the Inglehart measure of cultural distance

Correlation with:	Hofstede, 4-factor	Hofstede, 6-factor	GLOBE
Inglehart Cultural Distance	0.4928	0.6707	0.3888
n pairs	946	903	465

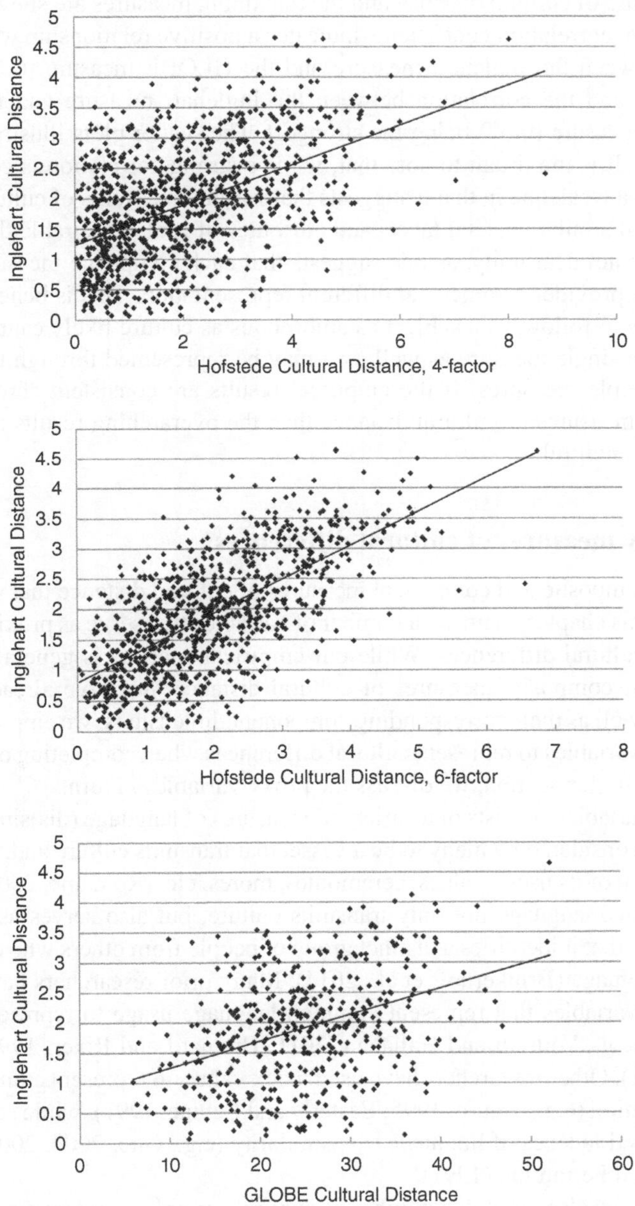

Figure 4.5 Correlation and scatterplots: Inglehart cultural distance and other composite measures

and one of the remaining three composite measures. We choose to compare the Hofstede measures and the GLOBE measure to the Inglehart measure as the latter possesses the attractive feature of varying over time and, thus, is emphasized somewhat more in subsequent chapters.

In addition to the scatter plots presented in Figure 4.5, the correlations between the Inglehart measure of cultural distance and the remaining measures are shown. Each of the pairwise correlation coefficients indicates a positive relationship with the correlation between the Inglehart measure and the GLOBE measure (0.39) being the weakest and the correlation between the Inglehart measure and the 6-factor Hofstede measure (0.67) being the strongest. The scatter plots illustrate these relationships. It is important to note that, while a strong correlation is certainly preferable to a weak one in that it suggests that varying measures of culture are representative of similar societal facets and attributes, it is also desirable that the correlations are not near unity, as this suggests that each composite measure of cultural distance provides a somewhat different representation. This is beneficial for the analysis to follow, as a subject as amorphous as culture likely cannot be represented by a single measure as well as it may be represented through the application of multiple measures. If the empirical results are consistent across multiple, different measures of cultural distance then the overarching results are that much more meaningful.

Additional proxy measures of cultural differences

In addition to the composite and component measures of cultural distance that we have presented in this chapter, there are a number of variables that serve as proxies for cross-societal cultural differences. While our empirical analysis is generally focused on the four composite measures of cultural distance that have already been presented, as well as their corresponding component dimensions, we employ a number of proxy variables to represent cultural differences when completing our empirical analysis. In this section, we discuss the proxy variables in turn.

The first set of variables consists of a variety of measures of language (dis)similarity. Language is considered by many to be a vessel that transmits culture and, as such, an embodiment of its users' values, ceremonies, mores, etc. (Romaine, 2000; Trudgill, 2000). Thus, language not only transmits culture, but also serves as a symbol of culture in that it identifies a distinct group of people from others who do not also use the language (Brinkerhoff et al., 2014). Many prior researchers have employed dummy variables that represent common language usage to represent cultural similarity (e.g., Vollrath and Hallahan, 2011; Brainard and Riker, 1997; and Veugelers, 1991). Other researchers have used index values to represent ethnolinguistic fragmentation (e.g., Mauro, 1995; Easterly and Levine, 1997), while still others have employed indexes of linguistic (dis)similarity (e.g., Guo, 2004, 2006, and 2012; Boisso and Ferrantino (1997).

In later chapters, we also employ a number of dummy variables, separately, as proxy variables for cultural distance. These dummy variables include two measures from the CEPII Gravity Database – the first of which is equal to one if the country pair shares a common language (and equal to zero otherwise) and the second measure which is equal to one if a language is spoken by nine percent or more of the populations in both countries (Mayer and Zignano, 2011). We also use three dummy variables from Melitz and Toubal (2012). The first is equal to one if a country pair has a common official language. The second is equal to one if the countries share a common spoken language, and the third is equal to one if the two countries have a common native language.

In addition to the dummy variables employed to represent language (i.e., cultural) similarity, we employ two related measures of linguistic proximity and two other measures of language distance. The measures of linguistic proximity are from Melitz and Toubal (2012). The first is an index of linguistic proximity that is based on the Automated Judgement Similarity Program (ASJP). The ASJP is a collaborative project that classifies languages by lexical similarity using lists of basic vocabulary words. The second measure of linguistic proximity is based on the *Ethnologue* classification of language family trees (Tree). As is noted by Melitz and Toubal (2012), the ASJP and Tree measures have a high correlation of 0.84. The measures of linguistic distance are from Belot and Ederveen (2012) and Dow (2015). The Belot and Ederveen measure is constructed from the joint probability that two individuals that are randomly selected from separate populations will speak the same language. The linguistic distance measure is equal to one minus the joint probability, weighted to adjust for differences across populations in the families of languages spoken. The Dow measure of language distance is constructed by employing factor analysis to data on distances between language categories and the incidence of country A's dominant language being spoken in country B and of country B's dominant language being spoken in A. Similar to the construction of their indexes of linguistic distance, both Belot and Ederveen and Dow also provide indexes of religious distance that we employ as proxy variables to represent cultural dissimilarities.

Our last proxy variables for cultural distance are two measures of the genetic distance between populations. Spolaore and Wacziarg (2011, p. 471) assert that genetic distance captures cross-societal divergence in "beliefs, customs, habits, biases, conventions, etc. that are transmitted across generations – biologically and/or culturally – with high persistence". Supporting this notion, Desmet et al. (2011) document a close relationship between genetic distance and an index of cultural differences computed from World Value Survey data (Inglehart et al., 2004). Genetic variation between populations can result from various factors, including genetic drift, isolation of populations from one another for a significant period of time, and selective pressures impacting genetic loci of populations.[7] The first measure of genetic distance that we employ is known as the Fixation Index (F_{ST}). The F_{ST} measure represents differences in the genetic structures of two populations. It is a measure of the extent to which heterozygosity exists, and it is constructed as $F_{ST} = \frac{\sigma_s^2}{p\left(1-\bar{p}\right)}$, where $\bar{p}$ is the average frequency of an allele in a population and σ_s^2 is the variance of the allele frequency between sub-populations. The lower the average frequency of allele observance, the higher is the F_{ST} value and, thus, the greater is the estimated genetic distance.

Our second measure of genetic distance comes from Nei (1972). The Nei measure is similar to the F_{ST}; however, the Nei measure allows for genetic mutations as well as genetic drift while the F_{ST} only allows for the former. The data for each of these two measures are from Spolaore and Wacziarg (2009). The Nei measure is calculated as $D = -\ln(I)$, where the genetic identity, I, across groups x and y, for any single locus with n alleles is calculated as $I = \frac{J_{xy}}{\sqrt{J_x J_y}}$ where $J_{xy} = \sum_{i=1}^{n} p_{ix} p_{iy}$, $J_x = \sum_{i=1}^{n} p_{ix}^2$, and $J_y = \sum_{i=1}^{n} p_{iy}^2$. The variables p_{ix} and p_{iy} represent the frequencies of the ith alleles for populations x and y, respectively. If x and y have identical allele frequencies, then I will be equal to 1, and if x and y share no alleles at all, then I will equal 0. Thus, the Nei measure of genetic distance, D, ranges in value from 0 (for identical populations) to infinity (for entirely dissimilar populations).

Notes

1 Unless otherwise noted, descriptive information in this section is from Inglehart and Baker (2000).

2 The first wave of the WVS was conducted between 1981 and 1984. Wave 2 was completed from 1990 to 1994. From 1995 to 1998, the third wave was completed. Wave 4 was conducted during the 1999–2004 period, and wave 5 spans the years from 2005 through 2009.

3 As is evident in the table, several countries have been surveyed multiple times. In Chapter 10, we explore the change in cultural distance values for the 17 countries for which data are available in both the first and the fifth waves of the WVS.

4 The World Bank income classifications, for the year 2002, are as follows: countries with GNIC values below $735 were classified as low income, those with GNIC values ranging from $736 to $2,935 were classified as lower middle income, countries with GNIC values ranging from $2,936 to $9,075 were classified as upper middle income, and all countries for which the GNIC value was above $9,075 were classified as high income.

5 Unless otherwise noted, the information provided in this section is from Hofstede (2012, 2001, and 1980).

6 Unless otherwise noted, the information presented in this section is from House et al. (2004).

7 Hedrick (2011) provides an excellent overview of genetic distance measures.

Part II

Do cultural differences hinder economic globalization?

In this portion of the book, we extend from the material presented in Chapters 1 through 4 to introduce the general analytic framework that guides us when conducting our empirical analyses. We also present the theoretical intuition that underlies our examinations, and we introduce the variables, our data and their sources, and the empirical models that are employed in our analyses. We follow with three chapters that provide detailed coverage of the observed relationships between cross-societal cultural differences and facets of economic globalization that we are interested in: international trade, foreign direct investment, and international migration.

In Chapter 6, we employ our four composite measures of cultural distance, along with their component dimensions and a set of variables that serve as proxies for cultural differences, to examine the influence of cultural distance on international trade flows. Our examination is generally focused on intensive margin effects; however, we also consider the influence of cultural distance on extensive margins of trade. We continue our analysis in Chapter 7, where we present results obtained from the examination of the relationships between cultural distance and both foreign direct investment inflows and FDI stocks. In Chapter 8, we complete our primary analysis by considering a potential influence of cultural distance on international migration flows.

Based on the information and rationale provided in Chapters 1 through 4, our expectation is that greater cultural differences correspond with higher transaction costs and that these higher costs raise the costs associated with engagement in international trade, foreign direct investment, and international migration. Further, since we expect to see reduced activity when related transaction costs rise, we anticipate that the measures of cultural distance that we employ in our analyses are negatively related to each of the three facets of economic globalization.

With these expectations in place, and the rationale for these general relationship having been put forth, we can now build on the initial chapters by addressing our research questions and, thus, by providing information that is necessary for a more complete understanding of the relationship between cross-societal cultural difference and facets of economic globalization. Briefly, the material presented in these chapters allows for a transition from the formulation of research questions and the corresponding descriptive analysis (both of which are provided in the opening chapters), to the examination of our posited empirical relationships, and then to the later chapters where we focus our attention on the broad implications that follow from the analysis presented here.

5 Expected relationships between cultural distance and facets of economic globalization

The expectation that cultural distance inhibits trade flows, foreign direct investment, and migration is based on the notion that, broadly defined and all else being equal, cultural differences correspond with higher transactions costs. As a result, greater cultural distance is thought to hinder cross-border interactions. This is, in a few words, the premise that we examine and for which results are presented in the following three chapters. Before proceeding to these results, in this chapter we bridge the material presented in Part 1 and the analyses presented in the remainder of Part 2. Accordingly, we provide additional details that are related to the anticipated relationships between cultural differences and our three facets of economic globalization.

Having already introduced a number of variables that represent cultural distance, along with measures of globalization in general and of economic globalization, and having provided descriptive overviews of these key concepts and a summary review of the three most recent waves of globalization, we now turn our attention to the empirical frameworks, the baseline estimation equations, and the data sets that are used to examine the potential influences of cultural distance on economic globalization. As noted, the results of our analyses are detailed in Chapters 6 through 8, along with discussions of the corresponding implications.

We look to the existing literature for guidance when developing a framework that allows examination of our research questions. In the cases of international trade flows and international migration, this leads us to employ the gravity model and related variants. This is likely unsurprising, as the gravity model is so commonly used that it has been referred to as the empirical workhorse for studies of international trade (Feenstra, 2004). To a much lesser extent, but with considerable success, the gravity model has also been employed in the analysis of international migration flows (e.g., Lewer and van den Berg, 2008; White, 2013; and White and Yamasaki, 2014) in addition to other topics. The frequency of the model's use, and its flexibility in terms of generating empirical specifications that correspond with our research questions, make the gravity model an excellent tool for our purposes. When examining the determinants of foreign direct investment flows and stocks, we utilize an empirical specification that is based on the work of Blonigen and Piger (2011), who use Bayesian statistical techniques to identify likely determinants of FDI flows.

Cultural distance and trade costs

The expected influences of cultural differences on the aspects of economic globalization we consider are intuitive. Greater differences are expected to correlate with higher transaction costs and, thus, limit or hinder cross-border economic activity. Though this relationship may be intuitive, there is scant statistical evidence of a relationship between cultural distance (i.e., differences) and the costs that are associated with economic activity. More specifically, there is some evidence of a direct, positive relationship between trade costs and cultural distance; however, evidence is lacking with respect to the influence of cultural distance on the costs associated with international migration and/or international investment activity.

Arvis et al., (2013) use data on trade flows and domestic production, along with the inverse form of the gravity model (Novy, 2013), to generate estimates of comprehensive bilateral trade costs. These estimated costs are available for the years 1995 through 2012 at the aggregate (total trade) level and, separately, for the agriculture and manufacturing sectors. The relationships between the Inglehart measure of cultural distance and the estimated total trade costs, as well as the costs associated

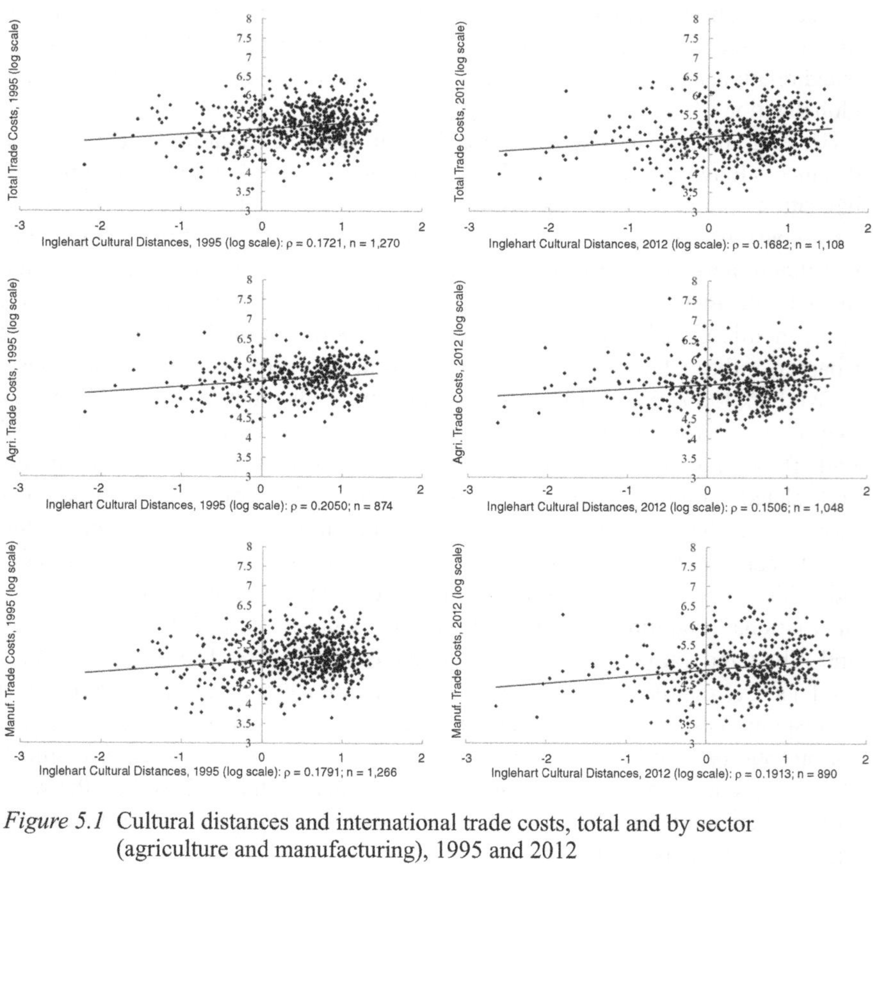

Figure 5.1 Cultural distances and international trade costs, total and by sector (agriculture and manufacturing), 1995 and 2012

with trade of agricultural products and manufactured goods, for the years 1995 and 2012, are illustrated in the six scatterplots that comprise Figure 5.1. Included with each figure is the correlation coefficient between the cultural distance measure and the corresponding measure of trade costs. The three scatterplots presented on the left side of the figure depict the correlations obtained when considering trade costs and cultural distance values for 1995. In all three instances, the correlations are positive and similar in magnitude, ranging from 0.1721 for total trade costs to 0.205 for agricultural trade costs. A similar pattern is found when the 2012 values are examined. Again, the Inglehart measure of cultural distance is positively correlated with total bilateral trade costs (0.1682), with costs related to trade in agricultural products (0.1506), and with costs associated with trade in manufactured goods (0.1913).

The bilateral trade cost estimates produced by Arvis et al. (2013) are comprehensive. Thus, these costs are composites, which potentially reflect all factors that increase the cost of trading. For example, transportation costs, tariffs and non-tariff barriers to trade, geographic impediments etc. are potentially represented by the estimates. In an attempt to isolate the specific relations between individual factors and the measures of bilateral trade costs, Tadesse and White (2015) estimate a series of empirical specifications using both a random effects approach and a fixed effects approach. The results are reproduced in Table 5.1.

Looking to the first row of the table, we see that, regardless of the estimation technique employed and the measure of trade costs considered, there is a positive and statistically significant relationship between bilateral trade costs and the Inglehart measure of cultural distance. More specifically, as the regression models have a double-log functional form, the results from the random effects estimations, presented in columns A through C, can be interpreted as elasticities. Thus, all else being constant, depending on the measure of trade costs considered, a one percent increase in the measure of cultural distance would increase the estimated trade cost value by 0.059 percent to 0.0896 percent. Results obtained from the fixed effects estimations presented in columns D through F of the table can be interpreted similarly. In response to a one percent increase in the cultural distance measure while all else is held constant, we would anticipate that bilateral trade costs increase by 0.142 to 0.165 percent, again depending on the measure of trade cost considered.

Focusing briefly on the remaining coefficients presented in Table 5.1, we generally see that greater geodesic distance between trading partners, greater economic remoteness of the importing country, and whether either partner is landlocked, all correspond with statistically significant increases in trade costs. More specifically, a one percent increase in geodesic distance, all else constant, increases estimated trade costs by 0.21 percent to 0.23 percent depending on the measure of trade costs considered. Similarly, trade costs are 33 to 41 percent higher if the exporting country is landlocked, and 26 to 43 percent higher if the importer is landlocked. On the contrary, being parties to a common trade agreement, sharing a common language, being adjacent (i.e., sharing a border), having (or having had) a colonial relationship, and the economic remoteness of the exporting country are all significantly related to decreases in trade costs.

The relationship documented by Tadesse and White (2015) is the first direct evidence of a positive and significant relationship between cultural distance and

Table 5.1 Determinants of international trade costs

	Panel Random Effects Estimates			*Panel Fixed Effects Estimates*		
	Total	*Manufactured Goods*	*Agricultural Goods*	*Total*	*Manufactured Goods*	*Agricultural Goods*
	(a)	*(b)*	*(c)*	*(d)*	*(e)*	*(f)*
ln Inglehart Cultural Distance$_{ijt}$	0.0590***	0.0665***	0.0896***	0.142***	0.151***	0.165***
	(0.0216)	(0.0231)	(0.0277)	(0.0309)	(0.0325)	(0.0371)
ln Economic Remoteness$_{it}$	0.0249	0.00611	−0.0533	−0.731*	−0.841*	−0.723**
	(0.0656)	(0.0657)	(0.0630)	(0.387)	(0.439)	(0.289)
ln Economic Remoteness$_{jt}$	0.150***	0.163***	0.0390	0.219***	0.237***	0.102***
	(0.0223)	(0.0228)	(0.0315)	(0.0263)	(0.0272)	(0.0370)
ln Geodesic Distance$_{ij}$	0.210***	0.222***	0.234***			
	(0.0217)	(0.0221)	(0.0252)			
Colonial Relationship$_{ij}$	−0.0751	−0.0768	−0.0989*			
	(0.0474)	(0.0499)	(0.0558)			
Common Border$_{ij}$	−0.342***	−0.333***	−0.370***			
	(0.0802)	(0.0844)	(0.0958)			
Common Language$_{ij}$	−0.241***	−0.247***	−0.223***			
	(0.0389)	(0.0410)	(0.0584)			
Common Trade Agreement$_{ijt}$	−0.0763**	−0.0808**	−0.0438	−0.289***	−0.304***	−0.283***
	(0.0317)	(0.0336)	(0.0385)	(0.0326)	(0.0337)	(0.0431)

$Landlocked_i$	0.412***	0.394***	0.332***			
	(0.103)	(0.102)	(0.0672)			
$Landlocked_j$	0.257***	0.260***	0.433***			
	(0.0295)	(0.0304)	(0.0393)			
Constant	1.728***	1.639***	3.505***	9.190***	9.906***	10.47***
	(0.560)	(0.572)	(0.577)	(3.107)	(3.532)	(2.272)
Observations	9,597	9,434	8,352	9,597	9,434	8,352
Pseudo R^2	0.446	0.438	0.374			
Wald χ^2	940.5	973	672			
R^2				0.248	0.256	0.122
F-Statistic				79.14***	84.90***	29.89***
Log-likelihood				–4,276	–4,721	–5,004
sigma_e	0.278	0.295	0.358	0.329	0.346	0.415
sigma_u	0.271	0.280	0.217	0.662	0.711	0.542
rho	0.487	0.475	0.269	0.802	0.809	0.630
corr				–0.689	–0.736	–0.753

Robust standard errors in parentheses. Number of source countries in each estimation is equal to 89. "***", "**", and "*" denote statistical significance from zero at the 1 percent, 5 percent, and 10 percent levels, respectively.

Source: Tadesse and White (2015).

trade costs. As such, it provides support for the intuitive link between cultural differences and trade-related transaction costs. Thus, these results provide support for the notion of an empirical link between cross-societal cultural differences and trade flows and, by extension, for the possible influences of cultural differences on foreign direct investment and international migration.

The gravity model

Originally applied to international trade flows, the gravity model has been extended and augmented and applied to a wide variety of relationships including, but not limited to, trade flows, migration flows (and stocks), and foreign direct investment flows (and stocks). Given the general finding of a positive relationship between cultural distance and estimated trade costs that is detailed in Section 5.1, our expectation is that there is a negative relationship between cross-societal cultural differences and bilateral trade flows. Intuitively, it seems reasonable that this negative relationship extends to foreign direct investment and international migration. We model the anticipated relationship for international trade flows while controlling for other factors that have been identified as likely determinants of trade, using the gravity model initially developed by Tinbergen (1962), Pöyhönen (1963a and 1963b), and Linnemann (1966) and later refined by Anderson (1979), Bergstrand (1985), Deardorff (1995), and Anderson and van Wincoop (2003) among others.

In its most basic form, the gravity model suggests that trade between two countries i and j during a given time period t, T_{ijt}, is positively related to the product of the trading partners' economic masses, Y_{it} and Y_{jt}, and negatively related to the physical distance, D_{ij}, between the two countries. In equation 5.1, Gross Domestic Product (GDP) represents economic mass and physical distance between trading partners (measured as geodesic distance) is a proxy variable that represents transportation costs. A is a constant that represents non-mass-related and non-distance-related determinants of trade flows. Equation 5.1 illustrates the suggested relationships.

$$T_{ijt} = A\frac{Y_{it}^{\beta_1} Y_{jt}^{\beta_2}}{D_{ij}^{\beta_3}} \tag{5.1}$$

Tinbergen's gravity equation, shown above, is an extension/application of Newtonian gravity to economics. In his *Principia* (1687), Isaac Newton proposed the famous relationship known as the law of universal gravitation. Expressed as an equation, the gravitational force between two objects, M_i and M_j, is positively related to the product of their physical masses and is negatively related to the distance, D_{ij}, between them. More precisely, to allow for comparison to equation 5.1, Newton's expression for physical gravity is provided as equation 5.2.

$$F_{ij} = G\frac{M_i M_j}{D_{ij}^2} \tag{5.2}$$

In equation 5.2, F_{ij} represents the gravitational force between objects, G is the universal gravitational constant, later to become known as the cosmological constant (Einstein, 1917), and M_i, M_j, and D_{ij} are as described above.

Note that, in equation 5.2, the superscripts on the physical mass variables are anticipated to equal one, and the exponent on the distance variable is expected to equal two. In equation 5.1, the values for β_1, β_2, and β_3 are unknown and, thus, are to be estimated. While this is the case, Head (2003) provides some information on the expected signs and magnitudes of the coefficients. Head and Celia Disdier conducted a meta-analysis of coefficient estimates from papers that employ the gravity model. They report an average coefficient value of –0.94 for the geodesic distance variable. Similarly, Head notes an observed range of 0.7 to 1.1 for the coefficients of the GDP variables. These values appear eminently reasonable. An increase in physical distance of one percent, signalling higher transportation costs, all else equal, would be expected to negatively affect trade flows. Increases in GDP indicate increases in output and in income. Thus, if output rises by one percent then we would expect an economy's capacity to export, and hence, the economy's observed level of exports, to rise by some near-proportional amount. Likewise, if income rises by a like one percent, then the ability to import increases by one percent; thus, it seems reasonable to expect observed imports to increase proportionally with income.

The baseline gravity model depicted as equation 5.1 can be augmented to include other trade-facilitating or trade-inhibiting variables. Trade-facilitating variables would be placed in the numerator on the right-hand side of equation 5.1 while trade-inhibiting variables would appear in the denominator. Continuous variables would enter as economic mass and geodesic distance have, while dichotomous explanatory variables would enter as exponentiated variables. For example, all else equal, a larger population (P_{it}) in country i, indicative of a larger potential market for exporters from country j to serve, has been found to facilitate trade flows. Likewise, being landlocked (lacking a sea port or coastal access) (L_i) results in higher transportation costs and, thus, has been shown to hinder trade flows. Equation 5.3 illustrates and equation 5.4 presents the log-transformed version of equation 5.3.

$$T_{ijt} = A\frac{Y_{it}^{\beta_1} Y_{jt}^{\beta_2} P_{it}^{\beta_4}}{D_{ij}^{\beta_3} e^{L_i^{\beta_5}}} \tag{5.3}$$

$$\ln T_{ijt} = \alpha_0 + \beta_1 \ln Y_{it} + \beta_2 \ln Y_{jt} - \beta_3 \ln D_{ij} + \beta_4 \ln P_{it} - \beta_5 L_i + \varepsilon_{ijt} \tag{5.4}$$

The log-transformation of equation 5.3 allows for the estimation of the regression model (i.e., equation 5.4) and, accordingly, the isolation of the respective effects of the explanatory variables on the dependent variable – that is, the imports of country i from country j during period t. In the regression model, ε_{ijt} is an assumed independent and identically-distributed error term.

International trade and cultural distance

Anderson (1979) was the first to provide an underlying theoretical foundation for the gravity model. This was followed by Bergstrand's (1985) contribution on the topic. More recently, Anderson and van Wincoop (2003) provide what has become known as the theoretical "gold standard" for gravity specifications. In Chapter 6, we explore the relationship between cultural distance and international trade flows using the Anderson and van Wincoop framework as our guide. We deviate, however, to varying degrees from their framework, in terms of our choice of explanatory variables and estimation methodology, to allow a more expansive analysis.

Beginning with the framework proposed by Anderson and van Wincoop (2003), we augment equation 5.1 such that our baseline estimation equation is given as equation 5.3, a log-transformation of an augmented variant of equation 5.1.

$$\begin{aligned} TRADE_{ijt} &= \alpha_0 + \beta_1 Y_{it} + \beta_2 Y_{jt} - \beta_3 GD_{ij} + \beta_4 REM_{it} + \beta_5 REM_{jt} \\ &+ \beta_6 CONTIG_{ij} - \beta_7 CD_{ijt} + \beta_\Omega \Omega_t + \beta_\Psi \Psi_i + \beta_\Theta \Theta_j + \varepsilon_{ijt} \end{aligned} \quad (5.5)$$

Our dependent variable series, $TRADE_{ijt}$, is the imports of country i from country j during year t. Bilateral trade data are from the UNCTAD database (UN, 2012). We choose to employ imports as the dependent variable series as we believe it is a more accurate measure of international trade flows than exports. Import values, as well as values for other variables expressed in nominal terms, have been converted to real values.

As in equation 5.1, Y_{it} and Y_{jt} represent the GDP values for countries i and j respectively, and GD_{ij} is a measure of the distance (calculated as weighted geodesic distance) between countries i and j. GDP data are from the World Bank (2014), and distance data are from the CEPII (2013). REM_{it} and REM_{jt} are measures of economic remoteness – i.e., a lack of outside trading opportunities. The remoteness variable for country i (and an analogous measure for country j) is constructed, per Head and Ries (1998), using GDP data from the World Bank (2014) and geodesic distance data from the CEPII (2013) as $REM_{it} = 1 / \sum_{k=1}^{K} \left[\left(Y_{kt} / Y_{wt} \right) / GD_{ik} \right]$, where Y_w represents gross global product and k identifies potential trading partners for country i other than country j. GD_{jk} is the geodesic distance between countries j and k.[1] To capture the expected trade-enhancing influence of a shared border, we include a dummy variable named $CONTIG_{ij}$ (CEPII, 2013). The vectors Ω, Ψ, and Φ control for year, exporting country, and importing country fixed effects, respectively. For the analysis presented in Chapter 6, equation 5.3 is estimated without any fixed effects terms and also controlling only for time (i.e., year) fixed effects, and simultaneously for time, exporter, and importer fixed effects.

To address our research topic, equation 5.3 contains a vector that includes several measures of cross-societal cultural differences, CD_{ijt}. More specifically, the vector includes the four composite measures of cultural distance that are presented in Chapter 4. The Inglehart measure is generated using data from the World Values Survey (WVS) and, where applicable, the European Values Survey (EVS)

(Inglehart and Welzel, 2005). Two other composite measures are constructed using survey data collected by Hofstede (1980 and 2001) and the fourth composite measure is generated from data collected as part of the GLOBE Project (House et al., 2004). The vector of cultural distance measures also includes the component dimensions on which the composite measures are based, and it includes a number of variables that serve as proxies for cultural differences between trading partners. This set of proxy variables includes measures of linguistic similarity and distance, religious distance, and genetic distance. We employ each of the cultural distance measures in turn when completing our analysis. Consistent results across empirical specifications, estimation methodologies, and measures of cultural distance will be taken as evidence of a robust relationship between cultural distance and international trade flows.

Table 5.2 presents descriptive statistics for the trade data set (i.e., the data used to conduct the analysis presented in Chapter 6). The reference period for our study is 1980–2011, and lists of countries for which data are available, depending on the measure of cultural distance employed, are provided in Tables 4.1, 4.3, and 4.4.[2] As we employ multiple measures of cultural distance, and the availability of data varies across the measures, Table 5.2 presents descriptive statistics that correspond to the estimations for which the Inglehart measure of cultural distance (presented in column A of the table), the 4-factor Hofstede measure of cultural distance (column B), the 6-factor Hofstede measure (column C), and the GLOBE measure of cultural distance (column D) are employed.

Focusing on the descriptive statistics presented in column A: that is, the sample used when the Inglehart measure of cultural distance is considered, we find that mean GDP values for exporting and importing countries are equal to \$708.3 billion and \$744.3 billion respectively, and that the average annual value of bilateral trade between the typical country pair is about \$1.9 billion. The average geodesic distance between the typical pair of trading partners is approximately 6,696 miles, and 4.3 percent of the country pairs in the data set share a common border. Further, the average value of the economic remoteness variable for exporters is quite similar to that of importers: 4,314 for exporting countries as compared to 4,234 for importing countries. The average value for the composite Inglehart measure of cultural distance is approximately 1.80, and the component dimensions have mean values of 1.15 and 1.17 for the SSE and TSR cultural distances, respectively.

International migration and cultural distance

The results from our examination of the potential relationship between cultural distance and international migration are not presented until Chapter 8. This follows our discussions of results related to cultural distance and international trade flows (in Chapter 6) and foreign direct investment (in Chapter 7). However, owing to the flexibility of the gravity model and our corresponding use of the model to examine both the determinants of international trade flows and those of international migration, we feel it is appropriate to discuss the related preliminaries here and save the topic of foreign direct investment until Section 5.3.

Table 5.2 Descriptive statistics, trade data set

Cultural Distance Estimations:	*Exp. Sign*	*Inglehart*	*Hofstede4*	*Hofstede6*	*GLOBE*
		$N = 55,921$	$N = 188,223$	$N = 127,253$	$N = 73,378$
		(a)	*(b)*	*(c)*	*(d)*
Real Imports$_{ijt}$ (millions of USD)	.	1,898.88	846.52	1,207.29	1,767.64
		(8,975.60)	(5,359.94)	(6,475.36)	(8,267.30)
Real GDP$_{it}$ (Exporter) (millions of USD)	+	708,299.61	442,300.10	523,291.54	669,505.80
		(1,716,500)	(1,301,197)	(1,408,959)	(1,592,570)
Real GDP$_{jt}$ (Importer) (millions of USD)	+	744,305.73	494,384.49	575,481.32	693,960.10
		(1,755,937)	(1,372,435)	(1,468,934)	(1,617,976)
Geodesic Distance$_{ij}$	–	6,695.67	7,686.98	7,480.69	8,066.53
		(4609.11)	(4,601.45)	(4,666.35)	(4,771.13)
Economic Remoteness$_{it}$ (Exporter)	+	4,314.37	5,052.42	4,770.89	4.685.07
		(2,519.26)	(2,612.24)	(2,671.48)	(2,662.85)
Economic Remoteness$_{jt}$ (Importer)	+	4,233.62	4,884.71	4,609.41	4,618.11
		(2,515.86)	(2,662.47)	2,686.43	(2,660.58)
Common Border$_{ij}$	+	0.0430	0.0278	0.0311	0.0340
		(0.2028)	(0.1645)	(0.1736)	(0.1812)
Inglehart Cultural Distance$_{ijt}$	–	1.7997	.	.	.
		(0.9029)	.	.	.
$\mid SSE_{it} - SSE_{jt} \mid$	–	1.1477	.	.	.
		(0.8257)	.	.	.
$\mid TSR_{it} - TSR_{jt} \mid$	–	1.1662	.	.	.
		(0.8338)	.	.	.
Hofstede 4-factor Cultural Distance$_{ij}$	–	.	2.1349	.	.
		.	(1.5634)	.	.
Hofstede 6-factor Cultural Distance$_{ij}$	–	.	.	2.0951	.
		.	.	(1.2008)	.
$\mid PDI_i - PDI_j \mid$	–	.	24.3357	23.4807	.
		.	(17.9937)	(17.2297)	.
$\mid IDV_i - IDV_j \mid$	–	.	27.0809	27.4629	.

		.	(20.0283)	(19.7511)	.
$\| MAS_i - MAS_j \|$	–	.	21.1473	21.9076	.
		.	(16.4074)	(16.9803)	.
$\| UAI_i - UAI_j \|$	–	.	24.3823	25.0716	.
		.	(17.6687)	(17.9755)	.
$\| PRA_i - PRA_j \|$	–	.	.	27.0218	.
		.	.	(19.4704)	.
$\| IND_i - IND_j \|$	–	.	.	25.9175	.
		.	.	(18.5877)	.
GLOBE Cultural $Distance_{ij}$	–	.	.	.	24.2030
		.	.	.	(8.5140)
$\| ASSERT_i - ASSERT_j \|$	–	.	.	.	0.4012
		.	.	.	(0.2808)
$\| INST\text{-}COL_i - INST\text{-}COL_j \|$	–	.	.	.	0.4804
		.	.	.	(0.3686)
$\| INGP\text{-}COL_i - INGP\text{-}COL_j \|$	–	.	.	.	0.7954
		.	.	.	(0.6395)
$\| FUTURE_i - FUTURE_j \|$	–	.	.	.	0.5056
		.	.	.	(0.3713)
$\| GEND\text{-}EGL_i - GEND\text{-}EGL_j \|$	–	.	.	.	0.3810
		.	.	.	(0.2859)
$\| HUMANE_i - HUMANE_j \|$	–	.	.	.	0.5137
		.	.	.	(0.3674)
$\| PERFORM_i - PERFORM_j \|$	–	.	.	.	0.4391
		.	.	.	(0.3196)
$\| POWDIST_i - POWDIST_j \|$	–	.	.	.	0.4252
		.	.	.	(0.3296)
$\| UNC\text{-}AVD_i - UNC\text{-}AVD_j \|$	–	.	.	.	0.6690
		.	.	.	(0.5085)

Standard deviations in parentheses. Values presented in column (a) correspond with data samples for which estimation results are presented in Table 6.2. Values presented in columns (b) and (c) correspond with estimation results presented in Table 6.5, and values presented in column (d) correspond with results presented in Table 6.6.

Due to various push and pull factors and the associated physical and monetary costs of moving from one country to another, international migration significantly parallels the underlying structure of international trade (Lewer and van den Berg, 2008; Cuaresma et al., 2013). In fact, these similarities allow for the application of the gravity model to international migration flows. The use of the gravity specification to examine bilateral migration is further motivated by Anderson (2011) and recent works that apply the model to international factor flows (e.g., Candau, 2013; Kleinert and Toubal, 2010). The basic gravity model of international trade assumes that trade flows are positively related to the trading partners' economic masses and negatively related to transportation costs, for which the physical distance between trading partners acts as proxy. Extending from this basic structure, we follow Lewer and van den Berg (2008) by modifying this basic structure to substitute the populations of the source and destination countries for the respective economic masses. We further augment the basic gravity specification to consider economic incentives, physical distance/direct migration costs, and interpersonal network effects as potential determinants of immigrant flows.

As Lewer and van den Berg (2008) note, there is evidence that indicates that immigrant flows from a particular country are stronger when the destination country's culture and language are similar to that of the source country. Accordingly, we consider the cultural distance between source and destination countries as a potential determinant of the immigrant flow between the source and destination countries. Equation 5.6 presents our baseline regression model.

$$
\begin{aligned}
IMMIG_{ijt} &= \alpha_0 - \beta_1 lnCD_{ijt} + \beta_2 lnSTOCK_{ijt-1} + \beta_3 \ln(POP_{it} \times POP_{jt}) \\
&- \beta_4 lnGDIST_{ij} + \beta_5 ln\frac{RGDPC_{it}}{RGDPC_{jt}} + \beta_6 UNEMP\,RATE_{it} \\
&- \beta_7 UNEMP\,RATE_{jt} + \beta_8 COLONY_{ij} + \beta_9 CONTIG_{ij} \\
&+ \beta_\Omega \Omega_t + \beta_\Psi \Psi_i + \beta_\Theta \Theta_j + \varepsilon_{ijt} \qquad (5.6)
\end{aligned}
$$

The dependent variable, $IMMIG_{ijt}$, is the flow of immigrants from source country i to destination country j during year t. We anticipate that greater cultural distance between source and destination countries increases the indirect costs associated with migration and thus results in lower immigrant inflows. We also expect that a larger existing immigrant stock (i.e., a higher number of immigrants from a given source country in a given destination country during the year prior), identified as $STOCK_{ijt-1}$, corresponds with a larger subsequent immigrant inflow. This expected relationship stems from the notion that a large immigrant stock encourages immigration by facilitating assimilation for the newcomers from the same source country (Lewer and van den Berg, 2008). In other words, later immigrants can more easily adapt to societal and legal changes by learning from the experiences of earlier immigrants, since both share the same cultural backgrounds. Furthermore, more recent immigrant arrivals can travel with less reticence, knowing they can find support among familiar faces. The data on immigrant flows and stocks that are used in this work are from the OECD (2015b).

The remaining explanatory variables in equation 5.6 include the product of source and destination countries' populations (POP_{it} x POP_{jt}). Larger populations, all else equal, are expected to be positively correlated with immigrant stocks. We also include the ratio of destination-to-source real GDP per capita values ($RGDPC_{it}/RGDPC_{jt}$). It is assumed that a higher destination country average income value, relative to the source country, will function as a strong pull factor and, thus, produce larger immigrant inflow values. Similarly, a higher unemployment rate ($UNEMP\ RATE_{it}$) in the source country is expected to induce more emigration, and a lower unemployment rate in the destination country is anticipated to attract immigrants. The source for the population, GDP per capita, and unemployment rate variables is the World Bank (2014).

To control for the anticipated migration-inhibiting influence of physical distance, and thus for direct migration costs, we include a measure of the geodesic distance ($GDIST_{ij}$) between each pair of source and destination countries. Mayda (2010) and Pedersen et al. (2008) control for a colonial link between the source and destination countries. Interestingly, the two studies find differing results. Mayda reports a negative relationship for the colonial link variable, while Pedersen et al. find the effects of a colonial link to be positive. We control for the influences of source-destination colonial links ($COLONY_{ij}$) and have the *a priori* expectation that such links will facilitate migration. For example, there may be, as a result of the colonial ties (past or present), a greater familiarity with the destination country among source country residents. Likewise, the destination country may afford entry preference to individuals from countries with which colonial relationships exist (or existed). In either instance, the colonial link would likely result in an increased level of immigrant inflows. To control for an additional geography-related determinant of immigrant inflows, we include a dummy variable that identifies country pairs that share a border ($CONTIG_{ij}$). The data source for the measure of geodesic distance, the colonial link dummy variable, and the common border dummy variable is the CEPII (2013).

Finally, in equation 5.6, the vectors Ω, Ψ, and Φ control for year, destination country, and source country fixed effects respectively. The destination and source country fixed effect terms control for time-invariant, location-specific factors such as geographic constraints on international migration and public policies governing emigration/immigration during the time period under consideration. By accounting for fixed effects, bias associated with the omission of unilateral variables (i.e. those pertaining only to country i or country j), as opposed to bilateral variables, can be removed (Lewer and van den Berg, 2008). Similarly, the time fixed effects term controls for any factors that facilitate (or hinder) migration and which are variable during the reference period but are source and destination country-invariant.

The descriptive statistics for the migration data set (i.e., the data set used to produce the results that are discussed in Chapter 8) are provided in Table 5.3. The reference period for our study is 1980–2014, and the countries for which complete

Table 5.3 Descriptive statistics, migration data set

Cultural Distance Estimations:	*Exp. Sign*	*Inglehart*	*Hofstede4*	*Hofstede6*	*GLOBE*
		N = 8,993	*N = 19,914*	*N = 16,513*	*N = 9,489*
		(a)	*(b)*	*(c)*	*(d)*
Immigrant $Flow_{ijt}$	.	3,597.442	2,294.462	2,618.647	3,714.571
		(11,856.23)	(8,682.27)	(9,363.93)	(11,976.33)
Inglehart Cultural $Distance_{ijt}$	–	1.9746	.	.	.
		(0.9623)	.	.	.
$\| SSE_{it} - SSE_{jt} \|$ [a]	–	1.4144	.	.	.
		(0.9206)	.	.	.
$\| TSR_{it} - TSR_{jt} \|$ [a]	–	1.1594	.	.	.
		(0.8125)	.	.	.
Hofstede 4-factor Cultural $Distance_{ij}$	–	.	2.7779	.	.
		.	(1.6692)	.	.
Hofstede 6-factor Cultural $Distance_{ij}$	–	.	.	2.3003	.
		.	.	(1.2910)	.
$\| PDI_{it} - PDI_{jt} \|$ [b,c]	–	.	30.2906	28.3198	.
		.	(18.8545)	(18.2833)	.
$\| IDV_{it} - IDV_{jt} \|$ [b,c]	–	.	33.3676	31.4895	.
		.	(20.4936)	(20.0664)	.
$\| MAS_{it} - MAS_{jt} \|$ [b,c]	–	.	28.0355	28.6123	.
		.	(18.8045)	(19.4064)	.
$\| UAI_{it} - UAI_{jt} \|$ [b,c]	–	.	23.8045	24.3960	.
		.	(16.8221)	(17.0599)	.
$\| PRA_{it} - PRA_{jt} \|$ [c]	–	.	.	24.2933	.

		.	.	(16.6316)	.
$\vert IND_t - IND_{jt}\vert$[c]	–	.	.	23.7767	.
		.	.	(16.5216)	.
Globe Cultural $Distance_{ij}$	–	.	.	.	25.8072
		.	.	.	(8.9788)
$\vert ASSERT_i - ASSERT_j\vert$[d]	–	.	.	.	0.4191
		.	.	.	(0.2963)
$\vert INST\text{-}COL_i - INST\text{-}COL_j\vert$[d]	–	.	.	.	0.5225
		.	.	.	(0.3794)
$\vert INGP\text{-}COL_i - INGP\text{-}COL_j\vert$[d]	–	.	.	.	1.0209
		.	.	.	(0.6461)
$\vert FUTURE_i - FUTURE_j\vert$[d]	–	.	.	.	0.5761
		.	.	.	(0.3712)
$\vert GEND\text{-}EGL_i - GEND\text{-}EGL_j\vert$[d]	–	.	.	.	0.3819
		.	.	.	(0.2758)
$\vert HUMANE_i - HUMANE_j\vert$[d]	–	.	.	.	0.486
		.	.	.	(0.3417)
$\vert PERFORM_i - PERFORM_j\vert$[d]	–	.	.	.	0.4334
		.	.	.	(0.3090)
$\vert POWDIST_i - POWDIST_j\vert$[d]	–	.	.	.	0.4696
		.	.	.	(0.3633)
$\vert UNC\text{-}AVD_i - UNC\text{-}AVD_j\vert$[d]	–	.	.	.	0.8034
		.	.	.	(0.5311)
Relative GDP per $capita_{ijt}$	+	16.1885	20.4828	14.6665	9.6397
		(30.4028)	(40.0194)	(26.5325)	(15.6477)
Geodesic $Distance_{ij}$	–	5,770.24	6,274.19	5,979.69	6,396.71
		(4,573.405)	(4,591.698)	(4,720.277)	(4,880.368)

(continued)

Table 5.3 (continued)

Cultural Distance Estimations:	*Exp. Sign*	*Inglehart*	*Hofstede4*	*Hofstede6*	*GLOBE*
		N = 8,993	*N = 19,914*	*N = 16,513*	*N = 9,489*
		(a)	*(b)*	*(c)*	*(d)*
$Population_{it}$ (Destination) (in millions)	+	49.4238	39.0558	40.0174	49.6601
		(80.0277)	(72.2917)	(72.8406)	(79.5869)
$Population_{jt}$ (Source) (in millions)	+	105.7026	74.7849	85.4726	106.0014
		(254.0115)	(205.6777)	(220.977)	(257.173)
Immigrant $Stock_{ijt-1}$	+	80,772.18	49,439.38	55,936.89	84,657.81
		(469,560.9)	(321,741.9)	(351,738.1)	(460,350.9)
$Colony_{ij}$	+	0.0655	0.0513	0.0524	0.0650
		(0.2474)	(0.2206)	(0.2228)	(0.2466)
Common $Border_{ij}$	+	0.0632	0.0491	0.0580	0.0571
		(0.2433)	(0.2161)	(0.2338)	(0.2321)
Unemployment $Rate_{jt}$ (Destination)	–	7.0214	6.8011	6.8540	7.3527
		(3.6545)	(3.6038)	(3.6686)	(3.6894)
Unemployment $Rate_{it}$ (Source)	+	8.5674	8.1636	8.3408	7.8359
		(5.5042)	(4.7688)	(4.7455)	(4.4528)

Standard deviations in parentheses. Values presented in column (a), (b), (c), and (d) correspond with data samples for which results are presented in column (a) of Table 8.5, in column (a) of Table 8.6 and in column (a) of Table 8.7, in column (b) of Table 8.6 and in column (b) of Table 8.7, and in Table 8.8, respectively. [a] N = 8,927. [b] N = 18,982 for values in column (b), and N = 15,439 for values in column (c). [d] N = 9,101.

data are available, for each of the composite measures of cultural distance, are listed in Tables 4.1, 4.3, and 4.4. As was the case for the trade data set, the descriptive statistics that are presented correspond to the estimations for which our four composite measures of cultural distance are used.

The descriptive statistics that correspond to the data sample that includes the 4-factor Hofstede measure of cultural distance are presented in column B of the table. Focusing primarily on this column, we see that the average annual flow of immigrants between the typical source and destination countries is equal to 2,294 persons. The average value of the annual immigrant stock, an expected pull factor, is equal to 49,439 persons. Looking to other expected pull factors, we find that the average ratio of destination country to source country real GDP per capita is equal to 20.48. About 4.9 percent of the country pairs in the data set share a common border, and 5.1 percent have (or had) a colonial relationship. Also, the average unemployment rate in the typical destination country is equal to 6.8 percent. Turning our focus to the anticipated push factors, we see the average unemployment rate in the typical source country is equal to nearly 8.2 percent. Additionally, the population in the average source country is considerably higher that of the typical destination country: 74.8 million persons compared to 39.1 million. The average geodesic distance between the typical pair of source and destination countries is approximately 6,274 miles.

The average value for the 4-factor Hofstede measure of cultural distance is approximately 2.78, while the average 6-factor Hofstede cultural distance value (presented in column C) is equal to 2.30. The mean values for the first four of Hofstede's component dimensions are similar across columns B and C (where the descriptive statistics for the 6-factor Hofstede cultural distance measure are presented), and mean values for the remaining two dimensions (PRA and IND) are presented in column C.

Foreign direct investment and cultural distance

The gravity framework, being empirically successful in the study of international trade flows and international migration, has also been applied to foreign direct investment flows. Similar, gravity-like (or gravity-inspired) specifications have been employed by researchers seeking to identify the determinants of FDI stocks (e.g., Kahouli and Maktouf, 2015; Bénassy-Quéré et al., 2005; and Bevan and Estrin, 2004). Unlike the trade literature, however, applications of *ad hoc* gravity specifications to the examination of FDI flows and FDI stocks have largely failed to produce results that identify a common set of determinants. As noted by Blonigen and Piger (2011, p. 1), "gravity variables may adequately capture "horizontal" motivations for FDI, where firms look to replicate their operations in other countries to be more proximate to consumers in those markets, additional controls are necessary to allow for "vertical" motivations of FDI, where firms look for low-cost locations for labor-intensive production." This has led to the development of theoretical models of international investment activity (e.g., Carr et al., 2001; Bergstrand and Egger, 2007; and Head and Ries, 2008). However, these efforts have also not resulted in a clearly-defined set of determinants for FDI flows or stocks.

As a clear theoretical foundation is lacking, we turn to the works of Blonigen (2005), Blonigen and Piger (2011), and Eicher et al. (2012) to generate our set of explanatory variables. Each of these works employs Bayesian Model Averaging (BMA) to determine the inclusion probability for each variable on a lengthy list of potential FDI determinants, based on the empirical specifications employed in earlier studies. Thus, the use of BMA allows for the identification of those variables for which there is both, at a minimum, an intuitive justification, and a statistical justification for the variables' inclusion when modelling the determinants of FDI. More specifically, we use those variables for which there is at least a 50 percent inclusion probability. The resulting set of explanatory variables is presented in equation 5.7.

$$\begin{aligned} ln\,FDI\,INFLOW_{ijt} = {} & \alpha_0 - \beta_1 lnCD_{ijt} + \beta_2 ln\left(\frac{K}{L}\right)_{jt} - \beta_3 lnCORP\ TAX_{jt} \\ & +\beta_4 lnREM_{jt} + \beta_5 lnHUM\ CAP_{it} + \beta_6 lnY_{jt} \\ & +\beta_7 lnY_{it} + \beta_8 ln\left(\frac{Y}{POP}\right)_{jt} + \beta_9 ln\left[\left(\frac{Y}{L}\right)_{it} - \left(\frac{Y}{L}\right)_{jt}\right]^2 \\ & +\beta_{10} ln\left(\frac{X+M}{Y}\right)_{jt} + \beta_{11} lnURB\ CON_{jt} \\ & +\beta_{12} COLONY_{ij} + \beta_{13} CUST\ UNION_{ijt} \\ & +\beta_{14} RTA_{ijt} + \beta_{\Omega}\Omega_t + \beta_{\Psi}\Psi_i + \beta_{\Theta}\Theta_j + \varepsilon_{ijt} \end{aligned} \tag{5.7}$$

The dependent variable, $FDI\ INFLOW_{ijt}$, is the net flow of foreign investment from parent country i to host country j during year t. In this work, we restrict our examination to those country pairs for which a net positive level of FDI is sent from the parent country to the host country. In other words, we do not examine the incidence of net disinvestment. We also substitute the FDI stock from country i in country j, $FDI\ STOCK_{ijt}$, to examine the relationship between cultural differences and FDI stocks. Our expectation, based on intuition and the results presented in Blonigen and Piger (2011), is that greater cultural differences between parent country i and host country j during a given year t, CD_{ijt}, will have a diminishing effect of FDI flows and, thus, on FDI stocks. The data for FDI flows and stocks are from the OECD (2015a) and have been converted to real US dollars.

Most of the remaining explanatory variables in equation 5.7 are thought to facilitate FDI flows (and, hence, FDI stocks). More specifically, FDI flows are expected to be greater, all else equal, if the parent country and the host country are members of a regional trade agreement (RTA_{ijt}), have (or had) a colonial relationship ($COLONY_{ij}$), or are members of a customs union ($CUST\ UNION_{ijt}$). The source for these variables is the CEPII (2013) with the exception of the regional trade agreement series for years since 2005, which is from the WTO (2015).. Similarly, a higher capital-labor ratio, $\left(\frac{K}{L}\right)_{jt}$, in the host country, greater host country economic remoteness (REM_{jt}), a higher index of per-person human capital ($HUM\ CAP_{it}$) in the parent country, greater values for real GDP in both the parent and host countries and a higher per capita income level in the host country, greater host country trade openness, $\left(\frac{X+M}{Y}\right)_{jt}$, a higher concentration of the host country's population in urban areas, and a greater difference between the parent and host countries in terms of real output per worker, $\left[\left(\frac{Y}{L}\right)_{it}-\left(\frac{Y}{L}\right)_{jt}\right]^2$, all are expected to correspond with higher FDI inflow values and, thus, greater FDI stocks. The data for these variables are from the World Bank (2014) with the exceptions of the capital-labor ratio and the difference in worker output levels (constructed using data from the Penn World Table [Feenstra et al., 2013] and the Conference Board [2014], respectively) and the measure of economic remoteness, for which the distance data are from the CEPII (2013). To the contrary, a higher corporate income tax rate in the host country is expected to correspond with reduced FDI flows and lower FDI stocks. Data on corporate tax rates are from the University of Michigan (2015) for years prior to 2003 and from KPMG (2011) for years after 2002. Finally, as with the regression equations used to isolate the determinants of international trade flows and of international migration, equation (5.7) includes the vectors Ω, Ψ, and Φ to control for year, destination country, and source country fixed effects, respectively.

Table 5.4 presents descriptive statistics for the FDI data set. The reference period for our study is 1985–2010. As we employ multiple measures of cultural distance, and data availability varies, the table provides multiple sets of descriptive statistics, each of which corresponds to a different composite measure of cultural distance. Columns D and H of the table present descriptive statistics that correspond to the estimations for which the GLOBE measure of cultural distance is employed to examine the determinants of FDI flows and FDI stocks, respectively.

Focusing on column D, we see that the average GLOBE cultural distance value between the typical parent and host country pair in our data is approximately 25.42. Across the nine GLOBE cultural dimensions, greater differences between parent and host countries are found across values for the in-group collectivism (INGP-COL) dimension (0.8527), the uncertainty avoidance (UNC-AVD) dimension (0.7044), the institutional collectivism (INST-COL) dimension (0.5570), and the humane orientation (HUMANE) dimension (0.5190). On average, parent and host countries are relatively more similar in terms of the future orientation (FUTURE) (0.4949), power distance (POWDIST) (0.4523), performance orientation (PERFORM) (0.4340), gender egalitarianism (GEND-EGL) (0.4265), and the assertiveness (ASSERT) (0.4113) dimensions of culture.

The average amount of FDI flowing, annually, from the typical parent country to the typical host country is \$714 million. A little more than 5 percent of

Table 5.4 Descriptive statistics, FDI data set

Cultural Distance Estimations:	*Exp. Sign*	*Inglehart*	*Hofstede4*	*Hofstede6*	*GLOBE*	*Inglehart*	*Hofstede4*	*Hofstede6*	*GLOBE*
		N = 12,310	*N = 24,447*	*N = 22,163*	*N = 14,688*	*N = 12,310*	*N = 25,867*	*N = 23,271*	*N = 14,061*
		(a)	*(b)*	*(c)*	*(d)*	*(e)*	*(f)*	*(g)*	*(h)*
Real FDI Flow_{ijt} (millions of USD)	.	786.5475	559.2198	615.86	714.4969	.	.	.	.
		(3,818.73)	(3,140.913)	(3,293.51)	(3,430.93)	.	.	.	.
Real FDI Stock_{ijt} (millions of USD)	.	.	.	.	.	6,176.925	4,073.26	4,516.09	5,913.04
		.	.	.	.	(23,996.54)	(18,369.86)	(19,315.33)	(22,393.78)
Inglehart Cultural Distance_{ijt}	–	1.7351	.	.	.	1.7348	.	.	.
		(0.8520)	.	.	.	(0.8734)	.	.	.
$\mid SSE_{it} - SSE_{jt} \mid$	–	1.1259	.	.	.	1.1494	.	.	.
		(0.8167)	.	.	.	(0.8395)	.	.	.
$\mid TSR_{it} - TSR_{jt}$	–	1.0963	.	.	.	1.0754	.	.	.
		(0.7746)	.	.	.	(0.7680)	.	.	.
Hofstede 4-factor Cultural	–	.	2.3692	.	.	.	2.3924	.	.
Distance_{ij}		.	(1.6548)	.	.	.	(1.6619)	.	.
Hofstede 6-factor Cultural	–	.	.	2.1757	.	.	.	2.1399	.
Distance_{ij}		.	.	(1.2713)	.	.	.	(1.2584)	.
$\mid PDI_i - PDI_j \mid$	–	.	24.5251	23.8566	.	.	25.1674	24.1292	.
		.	(17.7029)	(17.4492)	.	.	(18.4544)	(17.9318)	.
$\mid IDV_i - IDV_j \mid$	–	.	28.0791	27.3741	.	.	28.1641	27.3729	.

		.	(19.5025)	(19.2125)	.	.	(19.5414)	(19.3121)	.
$\lvert MAS_i - MAS_j \rvert$	–	.	25.3374	25.5702	.	.	25.5609	25.8283	.
		.	(18.7672)	(18.9446)	.	.	(19.0862)	(19.2769)	.
$\lvert UAI_i - UAI_j \rvert$	–	.	24.7043	25.0275	.	.	24.0184	24.2578	.
		.	(18.0216)	(18.1977)	.	.	(17.3520)	(17.5136)	.
$\lvert PRA_i - PRA_j \rvert$	–	.	.	27.4797	.	.	.	26.6653	.
		.	.	(19.6509)	.	.	.	(18.9723)	.
$\lvert IND_i - IND_j \rvert$	–	.	.	23.5826	.	.	.	22.7515	.
		.	.	(17.2886)	.	.	.	(16.7994)	.
Globe Cultural	–	.	.	.	25.4188	.	.	.	25.3702
$Distance_{ij}$		.	.	.	(8.6487)	.	.	.	(8.6327)
$\lvert ASSERT_i -$	–	.	.	.	0.4113	.	.	.	0.4147
$ASSERT_j \rvert$		.	.	.	(0.2888)	.	.	.	(0.2948)
$\lvert INST\text{-}COL_i -$	–	.	.	.	0.5570	.	.	.	0.5424
$INST\text{-}COL_j \rvert$		.	.	.	(0.4005)	.	.	.	(0.3952)
$\lvert INGP\text{-}COL_i -$	–	.	.	.	0.8527	.	.	.	0.8455
$INGP\text{-}COL_j \rvert$		.	.	.	(0.6264)	.	.	.	(0.6059)
$\lvert FUTURE_i -$	–	.	.	.	0.4949	.	.	.	0.5141
$FUTURE_j \rvert$		.	.	.	(0.3563)	.	.	.	(0.3669)
$\lvert GEND\text{-}EGL_i -$	–	.	.	.	0.4265	.	.	.	0.4213
$GEND\text{-}EGL_j \rvert$		.	.	.	(0.3209)	.	.	.	(0.3174)
$\lvert HUMANE_i -$ $HUMANE_j \rvert$	–	.	.	.	0.5190	.	.	.	0.5006
		.	.	.	(0.3704)	.	.	.	(0.3531)
$\lvert PERFORM_i -$	–	.	.	.	0.4340	.	.	.	0.4418
$PERFORM_j \rvert$		.	.	.	(0.3126)	.	.	.	(0.3153)
$\lvert POWDIST_i -$	–	.	.	.	0.4523	.	.	.	0.4492
$POWDIST_j \rvert$		.	.	.	(0.3519)	.	.	.	(0.3435)

(continued)

Table 5.4 (continued)

Cultural Distance Estimations:	*Exp. Sign*	*Inglehart*	*Hofstede4*	*Hofstede6*	*GLOBE*	*Inglehart*	*Hofstede4*	*Hofstede6*	*GLOBE*
		N = 12,310	*N = 24,447*	*N = 22,163*	*N = 14,688*	*N = 12,310*	*N = 25,867*	*N = 23,271*	*N = 14,061*
		(a)	*(b)*	*(c)*	*(d)*	*(e)*	*(f)*	*(g)*	*(h)*
$\mid UNC\text{-}AVD_i - UNC\text{-}AVD_j \mid$	–	.	.	.	0.7044	.	.	.	0.7118
		.	.	.	(0.5058)	.	.	.	(0.5053)
Capital-Labor $Ratio_{it}$ (Parent)	+	148,456.2	136,080.9	142,898.8	156,202.0	146,091.7	135,989.3	143,195.6	155,337.9
		(94,114.36)	(93,895.41)	(92,659.63)	(96,118.84)	(92,347.14)	(92,749.28)	(91,392.45)	(94,331.72)
Corporate Income Tax $Rate_{jt}$ (Host)	–	32.5763	31.5100	31.6684	32.7735	31.9047	30.5306	30.7315	31.8375
		(6.9395)	(7.8481)	(7.8140)	(7.6724)	(6.8566)	(7.2934)	(7.3606)	(7.3645)
Economic $Remoteness_{jt}$ (Host)	+	2,946.91	3,134.26	3,120.69	3,141.41	2,937.46	3,096.72	3,088.88	3,129.24
		(1937.98)	(2,337.65)	(2,318.46)	(2,324.62)	(1,977.48)	(2,303.54)	(2,301.30)	(2,331.69)
Index of Per-Person Human $Capital_{it}$ (Parent)	+	2.7402	2.6657	2.7008	2.7088	2.7555	2.6851	2.7220	2.7346
		(0.4484)	(0.4970)	(0.4785)	(0.4556)	(0.4501)	(0.4956)	(0.4755)	(0.4505)
Real GDP_{jt} (Host) (millions of USD)	+	1,404,703	1,185,556	1,192,351	1,405,635	1,539,847	1,236,279	1,263,751	1,527,927
		(2,359,632)	(2,159,014)	(2,170,475)	(2,332,652)	(2,584,990)	(2,345,628)	(2,362,375)	(2,538,986)
Real GDP_{it} (Parent) (millions of USD)	+	999,814	709,179	776,118	974,915	1,005,507	728,881	799,750	993,960
		(2,073,423)	(1,738,367)	(1,809,480)	(2,003,195)	(2,090,526)	(1,783,224)	(1,858,173)	(2,042,914)

Real GDP Per $Capita_{jt}$ (Host)	+	26,901.95	28,444.69	28,370.12	26,133.45	28,455.72	29,939.25	29,833.35	27,793.03
		(14,825.05)	(16,259.21)	(16,163.79)	(12,609.08)	(14,906.45)	(16,411.06)	(16,351.21)	(12,529.72)
Squared Difference in Output Per $Worker_{ijt}$ (millions of USD)	+	435.5763	483.7443	448.5743	407.7269	462.5143	512.5136	470.4761	433.9012
		(559.8009)	(594.2051)	(563.2237)	(521.1761)	597.6896	629.7554	(596.4522)	(555.1407)
Trade $Openness_{jt}$ (Host)	+	66.8677	75.5032	74.8980	64.5958	69.6696	79.6977	78.9356	67.0208
		(35.6981)	(47.3572)	(46.9343)	(32.1386)	(38.9688)	(50.2873)	(49.9296)	(32.8492)
Urban Concentration $Rate_{jt}$ (Host)	+	74.7969	75.2854	75.1038	74.1366	74.8812	75.2981	75.0791	74.4902
		(9.0145)	(9.9151)	(9.9248)	(8.9974)	(8.6518)	(9.6412)	(9.5531)	(8.6994)
Colonial $Relationship_{ijt}$	+	0.0573	0.0449	0.0458	0.0543	0.0539	0.0424	0.0438	0.0509
		(0.2324)	(0.2070)	(0.2090)	(0.2267)	(0.2259)	(0.2015)	(0.2046)	(0.2198)
Customs $Union_{ijt}$	+	0.187	0.1825	0.2013	0.2014	0.1753	0.1794	0.1994	0.2030
		(0.3899)	(0.3863)	(0.4010)	(0.4076)	(0.3803)	(0.3837)	(0.3996)	(0.4022)
Regional Trade $Agreement_{ijt}$	+	0.3981	0.3708	0.3937	0.3497	0.3771	0.3637	0.3858	0.3362
		(0.4895)	(0.4830)	(0.4886)	(0.4769)	(0.4847)	(0.4811)	(0.4868)	(0.4724)

Standard deviations in parentheses. Values presented in columns (a) through (d) correspond with data samples for which results are presented in column (a) of Tables 7.1, in columns (a) and (c) of Table 7.2, in columns (b) and (d) of Table 7.2, and in column (a) of Table 7.3, respectively. Values presented in columns (e) through (f) correspond with data samples for which results are presented in column (b) of Table 7.1, in column (c) of Table 7.2, in column (d) of Table 7.2, and in column (b) of Table 7.3, respectively.

parent-host country pairs have (or had) a colonial relationship, more than one fifth (20.14 percent) are members of a common customs union, and more than one third (34.97 percent) are members of at least one common trade agreement. The average annual real GDP value among parent countries is about 1.5 times the corresponding average value for host countries. However, the average income level in the typical host country is $26,133 during the typical year. The sum of FDI host countries exports and imports, on average, are equal to 64.6 percent of the country's real GDP. Almost three-fourths (74.1 percent) of the typical host country's population lives in urban areas, and the corporate tax rate in the typical host country during the typical year is 32.77 percent. The average capital-labor ratio among parent countries is 156,202, and the index of per-person human capital in the typical parent country is 2.71. Lastly, the squared value of the difference in the ratios of parent and home countries' productivity values is 407.73.

With our basic empirical frameworks in place and a cursory depiction of the data sets having been provided, we now turn our attention to the results obtained from our examinations of the relationships between measures of cross-societal cultural differences and the three facets of economic globalization in which we are interested. Chapter 6 presents the results of our examination of the relationship between cross-societal cultural differences and international trade flows. Findings relating to whether cultural distance is a significant determinant of FDI flows and/or FDI stocks are provided in Chapter 7, and Chapter 8 details the results obtained when we consider the potential influence of cultural distance on international migration.

Notes

1 When j=k, internal distance is calculated following Head and Mayer (2000) as $0.4 \times \sqrt{Land\ Mass_j}$. Data on land mass are from the World Bank (2014).

2 When proxy measures of cultural distance are employed in the analysis, the countries for which data are available differ from those presented in Tables 4.1, 4.3, and 4.4.

6 The influences of cultural distance on international trade

The existing literature on the topic of cultural distance and international trade is quite sparse. While there is a large literature examining the determinants of international trade flows, relatively few studies have considered the role of cultural distance as a potential determinant. Those studies that have allowed for a potential relationship between cultural distance and international trade flows have employed, as is done here, a number of measures to represent cultural differences. For example, Beugelsdijk et al. (2004) find that cultural distance, in addition to physical distance and institutional distance, is an important determinant of trade flows. Similarly, Boisso and Ferrantino (1997) employ an index measure of linguistic distance to represent cultural differences between trading partners. They find that greater cultural dissimilarity is negatively related to bilateral trade flows. Also focusing on language, Dunlevy (2006) uses a dummy variable to represent the commonality of official languages and, hence, to act as a proxy for cultural similarity. Considering the potential effect of cultural similarity on trade flows between the US and a number of immigrants' home countries, Dunlevy reports greater trade volumes among country pairs where either English or Spanish is an official language. Finally, Otten (2013) examines international factor movements and finds that linguistic distance reduces international trade and investment flows.

A number of more recent studies employ more direct measures to examine the relationship between Hofstede measures of cultural differences and international trade. For example, Lankhuizen and de Groot (2014) find a non-linear relationship when examining the relationship between cultural differences and trade. Tadesse and White (2008) and White and Tadesse (2008) employ the Inglehart measure of cultural distance that is described in earlier chapters, and find that US state-level exports decrease with a rise in cultural distance. In a related study, Tadesse and White (2010b) examine trade flows among nine OECD member host countries and 67 home countries and find that greater cultural distance imposes economically significant and statistically consistent negative effects on the intensive margins of trade both at aggregate and disaggregate levels. Operating under the assumption that "bilateral preferences" are a function of a country's cultural proximity, Disdier et al. (2010) use trade in cultural goods as a proxy variable for cultural similarity. Examining the corresponding effects on bilateral trade flows, the authors find that cultural similarity is positively related to overall trade volumes. Guiso et al. (2009)

employ genetic distance among European nations as a proxy for interpersonal trust, finding that greater genetic distance corresponds with a reduction in trust and, accordingly, a decrease in cross-border economic exchange.

Estimating the determinants of bilateral trade flows, composite and component measures of cultural distance

We begin the econometric analysis portion of the book by considering the influence of cultural distance on bilateral trade flows. While a small literature exists on this topic, the examination presented here goes beyond any existing study and, in doing so, offers new information on the topic. We consider a larger number of cultural distance measures, including some that are new to the literature (e.g., the GLOBE measure of cultural distance and its dimensions). We also examine trade at both the aggregate and disaggregate levels. This new information may be beneficial for any number of interested individuals (e.g., researchers, academicians, and policy makers). It may also serve to provide a greater understanding of the topic among the general public.

To facilitate a more complete understanding of our empirical strategy, we begin by reproducing equation 5.5. which serves as our baseline estimation equation.

$$
\begin{aligned}
ln\,TRADE_{ijt} &= \alpha_0 + \beta_1 Y_{it} + \beta_2 Y_{jt} - \beta_3 GD_{ij} + \beta_4 REM_{it} + \beta_5 REM_{jt} \\
&+ \beta_6 CONTIG_{ij} - \beta_7 CD_{ijt} + \beta_\Omega \Omega_t + \beta_\Psi \Psi_i \\
&+ \beta_\Theta \Theta_j + \varepsilon_{ijt} \qquad (6.1)
\end{aligned}
$$

In the regression model, our dependent variable series, $TRADE_{ijt}$, is the imports of country i from country j during year t. Our variable of primary interest, CD_{ijt}, is a vector that contains several measures of cultural distance between trading partners. Y_{it} and Y_{jt} represent the GDP values for countries i and j, respectively, and GD_{ij} is a measure of the geodesic distance between trading partners. REM_{it} and REM_{jt} are measures of economic remoteness that represent a lack of outside trading opportunities. To capture the expected trade-enhancing influence of a shared border, we include a dummy variable named $CONTIG_{ij}$ (CEPII, 2013). The vectors Ω, Ψ, and Φ control for year, exporting country, and importing country fixed effects respectively.

We begin our battery of estimations by replicating the general Anderson and van Wincoop (2003) regression specification. We estimate three versions of the specification. The first version does not include time or trading partner fixed effects terms. Thus, this is the most basic representation of the specification that is possible. Accordingly, there is no cultural distance variable in this estimation. We simply wish to see how the data conforms to the expectations that follow from Anderson and van Wincoop's treatment. Our second version of the regression specification includes time (i.e., year) fixed effects terms, but it does not include exporter or importer fixed effects terms. Here we begin to build the specification, and wish to see how the coefficient estimates change as additional controls are introduced. Continuing in this vein, our third version of the specification extends from the second version to include fixed effects terms for each exporter and importer in the sample.

Table 6.1 presents the results obtained when the three variants of the Anderson and van Wincoop (2003) specification are estimated.[1] In column A, we present results from the specification in which neither time nor country fixed effects terms are included. Results from the estimation of the baseline regression model with year fixed effects terms included (but without exporter or importer fixed effects terms) are presented in column B of the table. Finally, in column C, we report the results obtained when we control for year fixed effects as well as exporter and importer fixed effects. Our expectations are that the coefficients of the real GDP variables will be positive for both the exporter and importer measures, and that the coefficient of the geodesic distance variable will be negative. We also anticipate that the common border dummy variable will have a positive coefficient; however, we have no *a priori* expectations regarding the coefficients of the economic remoteness variables. Greater economic remoteness may entail more trade with specific partners; however, overall, more remote economies may be expected to engage less in external trade. The overall effect is, thus, indeterminable prior to estimation of the regression model.

Table 6.1 Baseline estimations, Anderson and van Wincoop (2003) specifications

	(a)	*(b)*	*(c)*
ln Real GDP$_{it}$ (Exporter)	1.1578***	1.165***	0.9968***
	(0.0019)	(0.0019)	(0.0269)
ln Real GDP$_{jt}$ (Importer)	0.9458***	0.9547***	1.2561***
	(0.002)	(0.0019)	(0.0326)
ln Economic Remoteness$_{it}$ (Exporter)	0.2692***	0.3051***	−0.2746***
	(0.0077)	(0.0075)	(0.0937)
ln Economic Remoteness$_{jt}$ (Importer)	−0.0852***	−0.0242***	−0.0243
	(0.0082)	(0.008)	(0.1048)
ln Geodesic Distance$_{ij}$	−1.2827***	−1.3197***	−1.6611***
	(0.0056)	(0.0055)	(0.0053)
Common Border$_{ij}$	1.0904***	0.9958***	0.6941***
	(0.0235)	(0.0237)	(0.0249)
Constant	−27.1194***	−26.8386***	−21.9083***
	(0.1352)	(0.1348)	(1.9076)
Time fixed effects?	No	Yes	Yes
Exporter fixed effects?	No	No	Yes
Destination fixed effects?	No	No	Yes
N	412,039	412,039	412,039
Pseudo R^2	0.6345	0.6477	0.7263

Standard errors in parentheses. Fixed effects coefficients not reported due to space constraints. "***", "**", and "*" denote statistical significance from zero at the 1 percent, 5 percent, and 10 percent levels, respectively.

Since the regression model presented as equation 6.1 has a double-log functional form, our coefficient estimates are interpreted as elasticities. More specifically, the coefficient on the exporter real GDP variable indicates, all else held constant, the estimated percent change in the predicted value of country i's aggregate exports to country j during the typical year in our reference period. With this in mind, looking to Table 6.1, we see that, regardless of the regression specification considered, the coefficient estimates of the exporter real GDP variable and the importer real GDP variable are positive and statistically significant from zero. Further, we can say that, dependent on the specification considered, a one percent increase in the real GDP of the exporting country will, all else held constant, increase that country's exports to country j by 1.0 percent to 1.17 percent. Similarly, a like one percent increase in the value of the importing country's real GDP corresponds, all else held constant, with an increase in the country's imports from country i equal to 0.95 percent to 1.26 percent depending on the specification considered.

Looking to the remaining variables listed in Table 6.1, we see that the estimated coefficient for the geodesic distance variable, our control for transportation costs, is negative and statistically significant in all three specifications. The coefficient value ranges from −1.28 when no time or country fixed effects are considered (column A) to −1.66 when year, exporter, and importer fixed effects terms are included in the specification (column C). We also find that the estimated coefficients on the common border dummy variable are positive and significant from zero. This finding, like the signs and statistical significance of the coefficients of the geodesic distance variables, is consistent with our expectations. Interpreting the coefficients on the common border variable, we can say that, all else held constant, if the exporting and importing countries shared a geographic border then trade between them will be 69.4 to 109 percent higher than if they do not share a common border. Finally, we did not have any prior expectations regarding the signs of the economic remoteness variables. Beginning with the exporter remoteness variable, looking across the specifications, we find that all three coefficient estimates are significant from zero. However, the coefficient sign changes from positive to negative once exporter and importer fixed effects are controlled for. Similarly, the importer remoteness variable is negative in columns A and B, but is not significantly different from zero in column C.

The next step in our estimation process is to augment the regression model to include each of the four composite measures of cultural distance in turn. We begin by adding the Inglehart cultural distance measure to equation 6.1 and estimating the regression model while controlling for year, exporter, and importer fixed effects. The results from this estimation are presented in column A of Table 6.2. The coefficient estimate of the Inglehart cultural distance measure is, as expected, negative and significantly different from zero. Specifically, we can interpret the coefficient as follows: all else held constant, a one percent increase in the cultural distance between countries i and j corresponds with a 0.0926 percent decrease in their bilateral trade value. Extrapolating, we can say that a ten percent increase in the cultural distance measure results in a 0.926 percent decrease in bilateral trade between the typical country pair. Evaluated as a one-standard deviation increase from the mean Inglehart cultural distance value (as shown to be equal to 0.9029 in Table 5.2), the estimated effect on bilateral trade flows is a decrease of 4.65 percent.

Extending from the use of the composite Inglehart measure of cultural distance, in column B of Table 6.2, we present the estimation results that are obtained when the Inglehart measure is replaced by its component dimensions: the differences between country i and country j in terms of the survival vs. self-expression values (SSE) dimension of culture and the traditional vs. secular-rational authority (TSR) dimension. The coefficient of the TSR dimension of culture is not statistically significant from zero. However, the coefficient of the SSE dimension of culture is negative and significantly different from zero. More specifically, while we observe no significant relationship between difference along the TSR cultural dimension and bilateral trade flows, we do find that, all else held constant, a one percent increase in the difference between country i and country j along the SSE dimension corresponds with an estimated decrease in bilateral trade of 0.0747 percent. The coefficients of the remaining variables for which

Table 6.2 Inglehart cultural distance and bilateral trade flows

	(a)	*(b)*
ln Inglehart Cultural Distance$_{ijt}$	−0.0926***	
	(0.0109)	
ln | SSE$_{it}$ − SSE$_{jt}$ |		−0.0747***
		(0.0063)
ln | TSR$_{it}$ − TSR$_{jt}$ |		0.0077
		(0.0063)
ln Real GDP$_{it}$ (Exporter)	1.1604***	1.1638***
	(0.0878)	(0.0877)
ln Real GDP$_{jt}$ (Importer)	1.6802***	1.6863***
	(0.0943)	(0.0943)
ln Economic Remoteness$_{it}$ (Exporter)	0.4343	0.4202
	(0.3201)	(0.3199)
ln Economic Remoteness$_{jt}$ (Importer)	1.6706***	1.6578***
	(0.3732)	(0.3735)
ln Geodesic Distance$_{ij}$	−1.3887***	−1.4044***
	(0.0111)	(0.0111)
Common Border$_{ij}$	0.4816***	0.4743***
	(0.0342)	(0.0344)
Constant	−61.5803***	−61.5036***
	(6.4751)	(6.47)
N	55,921	55,921
Pseudo R^2	0.8330	0.8331

All estimations include year, exporter, and importer country fixed effects. Corresponding coefficients not reported due to space limitations. Standard errors in parentheses. "***", "**", and "*" denote significance from zero at the 1 percent, 5 percent, and 10 percent levels, respectively.

results are presented in Table 6.2 are largely similar, in terms of their signs, magnitudes, and the patterns of statistical significance, to the results presented in Table 6.1 and discussed above.

An attractive aspect of the Inglehart measure of cultural distance is that, since the surveys that provide the data from which the measure is constructed have been repeated over time, the Inglehart measure is time-variant. This is beneficial since, especially when examining data that span time periods of considerable length, it is reasonable to expect that cultures change. To determine the period-specific relationships between the Inglehart measure of cultural distance and bilateral trade flows, we estimate equation 6.1 for each of the five World Values Survey waves for which data are available, and from which our time-varying Inglehart measure is constructed. We do this while using the composite Inglehart measure and when substituting the corresponding component dimensions of culture for the composite measure in our estimation equation. Results are presented in Table 6.3 and Table 6.4 respectively.

Focusing first on the coefficient estimates of the composite Inglehart measure, we find that they are negative across all five estimation periods and that they are significantly different from zero in four of the five instances. Moreover, comparing the coefficient estimates across waves of the WVS, we see they are largely consistent in terms of magnitude. Turning our attention to the component dimensions of the Inglehart cultural distance measure, we find a general pattern of coefficient sign and magnitudes as is reported in Table 6.2. Across the wave-specific estimations, for which results are presented in Table 6.4, we see that the coefficient of the variable that represents country pair differences over the SSE dimension are negative in all instances and significant from zero in four of the five cases. Somewhat similarly, the coefficient estimates of the variable that represents differences along the TSR dimension are negative in four of the five estimations but are significantly different from zero in only one instance. Surprisingly, the lone instance where the TSR coefficient is significant from zero is the single instance where the SSE coefficient is not statistically significant.

Another interesting facet of the results presented in Tables 6.3 and 6.4 is that the wave-specific coefficient estimates for the control variables can be compared to the corresponding coefficients from the time-pooled regression presented in Table 6.2. Both for the results presented in Table 6.3 (as compared to the results in column A of Table 6.2) and those that are presented in Table 6.4 (as compared to the results presented in column B of Table 6.2), we see that a large majority of coefficient estimates are of the same sign and statistical significance. More specifically, in both Table 6.3 and Table 6.4, 24 of the 30 coefficient estimates (80 percent) of the control variables (i.e., real GDP, geodesic distance, economic remoteness, and common border) have the same sign and statistical significance as is reported in Table 2. Moreover, the coefficient magnitudes are often quite similar. The consistency in results across estimations is meaningful, as it permits the case to be made that the time-varying aspect of the Inglehart measure of cultural distance and its component dimensions, while attractive, do not appear to be a requisite feature of cultural distance measures. This is to say that, since the results are largely consistent across

Table 6.3 Composite measure of Inglehart cultural distance, WVS wave-specific estimations

	Wave I	*Wave II*	*Wave III*	*Wave IV*	*Wave V*
	1981–1984	*1990–1994*	*1995–1998*	*1999–2004*	*2005–2009*
	(a)	*(b)*	*(c)*	*(d)*	*(e)*
ln Inglehart Cultural Distance$_{ij}$	−0.2205***	−0.0124	−0.2151***	−0.1287***	−0.2049***
	(0.0406)	(0.0236)	(0.0319)	(0.0181)	(0.0261)
ln Real GDP$_{it}$ (Exporter)	0.9457***	1.0804***	1.2891***	1.2193***	1.3441***
	(0.0218)	(0.0128)	(0.0106)	(0.0068)	(0.0112)
ln Real GDP$_{jt}$ (Importer)	0.9385***	1.0054***	1.0134***	1.0414***	1.0333***
	(0.0222)	(0.0135)	(0.0109)	(0.0064)	(0.0103)
ln Economic Remoteness$_{it}$ (Exporter)	0.077	0.1113***	0.6104***	0.2641***	0.5158***
	(0.054)	(0.0367)	(0.0371)	(0.0258)	(0.0318)
ln Economic Remoteness$_{jt}$ (Importer)	0.1102*	0.0201	0.39***	−0.0107	0.0808**
	(0.0587)	(0.0386)	(0.0362)	(0.0272)	(0.0381)
ln Geodesic Distance$_{ij}$	−0.8544***	−0.9171***	−1.4717***	−1.1682***	−0.9994***
	(0.036)	(0.0259)	(0.0273)	(0.0185)	(0.0296)
Common Border$_{ij}$	0.4448***	0.6848***	0.9573***	0.9037***	0.6887***
	(0.0788)	(0.0638)	(0.0805)	(0.0546)	(0.0945)
Constant	−24.1267***	−29.0306***	−37.1943***	−32.7209***	−39.8929***
	(1.1224)	(0.6936)	(0.5838)	(0.4227)	(0.6422)
N	1,727	5,220	8,516	24,986	10,652
Pseudo R^2	0.8035	0.7815	0.7396	0.7369	0.7530

All estimations include year, exporter, and importer country fixed effects. Corresponding coefficients not reported due to space limitations. Standard errors in parentheses. "***", "**", and "*" denote significance from zero at the 1 percent, 5 percent, and 10 percent levels, respectively.

Table 6.4 Component dimensions of Inglehart cultural distance measure, WVS wave-specific estimations

	Wave I	*Wave II*	*Wave III*	*Wave IV*	*Wave V*
	1981-1984	*1990-1994*	*1995-1998*	*1999-2004*	*2005-2009*
	(a)	*(b)*	*(c)*	*(d)*	*(e)*
ln $\mid SSE_i - SSE_j \mid$	−0.1427***	−0.0342**	−0.1311***	−0.0091	−0.1323***
	(0.0237)	(0.0153)	(0.0177)	(0.0106)	(0.0168)
ln $\mid TSR_{it} - TSR_{jt} \mid$	−0.0057	0.0165	−0.0266	−0.0574***	−0.0076
	(0.0361)	(0.0137)	(0.018)	(0.0105)	(0.0183)
ln Real GDP_{it} (Exporter)	0.9523***	1.082***	1.2904***	1.2209***	1.3478***
	(0.0218)	(0.0128)	(0.0105)	(0.0068)	(0.0113)
ln Real GDP_{jt} (Importer)	0.9402***	1.0082***	1.0157***	1.0423***	1.0381***
	(0.0218)	(0.0135)	(0.0109)	(0.0064)	(0.0103)
ln Economic $Remoteness_{it}$ (Exporter)	0.0822	0.1093***	0.6286***	0.2895***	0.5437***
	(0.0556)	(0.0368)	(0.0371)	(0.0256)	(0.0314)
ln Economic $Remoteness_{jt}$ (Importer)	0.1184**	0.0125	0.4174***	0.0132	0.1129***
	(0.0596)	(0.0389)	(0.0362)	(0.0272)	(0.0379)
ln Geodesic $Distance_{ij}$	−0.864***	−0.9185***	−1.4971***	−1.1732***	−1.0349***
	(0.0382)	(0.0259)	(0.0281)	(0.0187)	(0.0292)
Common $Border_{ij}$	0.4807***	0.6514***	0.9551***	0.9284***	0.6776***
	(0.0767)	(0.0653)	(0.0808)	(0.0554)	(0.0954)
Constant	−24.5016***	−29.0744***	−37.5815***	−33.2187***	−40.4211***
	(1.1328)	(0.6965)	(0.5827)	(0.4214)	(0.646)
N	1,727	5,196	8,469	24,838	10,604
Pseudo R^2	0.8047	0.7814	0.7402	0.7364	0.7528

All estimations include year, exporter, and importer country fixed effects. Corresponding coefficients not reported due to space limitations. Standard errors in parentheses. "***", "**", and "*" denote significance from zero at the 1 percent, 5 percent, and 10 percent levels, respectively.

time, the reference period examined is not sufficiently long that a time-invariant measure of cultural distance would be rendered less useful.

We have established at least a preliminary finding that cultural differences inhibit international trade flows, and we have documented that time-invariant measures of cultural distance, at least for the general time period covered in this work, are sufficient representations of cross-societal cultural differences. This allows us to examine the results obtained when we employ our two Hofstede composite measures of cultural distance and the GLOBE measure of cultural distance to consider the relationship between cultural differences and bilateral trade flows. As with the Inglehart measure of cultural distance, for both the Hofstede measures and the GLOBE measure, we employ the composite measures as well as the corresponding component dimensions and discuss the results in turn.

Columns A and B in Table 6.5 present the respective coefficient estimates of the 4-factor and 6-factor Hofstede measures of cultural distance. In both cases, we find a negative and statistically significant coefficient. Interpreting the coefficients, we can say that a one percent increase in the 4-factor Hofstede measure, all else constant, reduces bilateral trade flows between the typical country pair during the typical year in our reference period by 0.0245 percent. Similarly, a one percent increase in the 6-factor Hofstede measure is estimated to decrease, again all else held constant, bilateral trade between the typical country pair during the typical year by 0.0419 percent. To place these coefficient estimates into context, in response to one standard deviation increase above the means values of the Hofstede composite cultural distance measures, the estimated effects on bilateral trade flows are decreases of 1.79 percent when the 4-factor Hofstede measure is considered and of 2.4 percent when the 6-factor measure is considered.

When we replace the composite Hofstede measures of cultural distance in equation 6.1 with the variables that represent differences along the Hofstede component dimensions, we find varied results. Looking first at the coefficient estimates presented in column C of Table 6.5, we find that, while all four of the dimension-specific coefficient estimates are significantly different from zero, two of the coefficients are positive while the other two are negative. Specifically, the coefficient estimates of the variables which represent the differences between the exporting and importing nation in terms of the power distance index (PDI) and the individualism vs. collectivism (IDV) dimension are positive. To the contrary, the coefficient estimates of the variables that reflect country pair differences along the masculinity vs. femininity (MAS) dimension and in terms of the uncertainty avoidance index (UAI) are negative. The signs of the coefficients and their statistical significance are identical in column (d), where the results obtained when all six of the Hofstede cultural dimensions are employed. Further, the coefficients of the two additional dimensions that represent differences in terms of the pragmatic vs. normative (PRA) and the indulgence vs. restraint (IND) dimensions are both significant from zero but are positive and negative respectively.

Results generated when we examine the relationship between bilateral trade flows and our final composite measure of cultural distance are presented in Table 6.6. The GLOBE measure of cultural distance is constructed using data that represent nine

Table 6.5 Hofstede cultural distance and bilateral trade flows, composite and component measures

	(a)	*(b)*	*(c)*	*(d)*
ln Hofstede 4-factor Cultural Distance$_{ij}$	−0.0245***			
	(0.0055)			
ln Hofstede 6-factor Cultural Distance$_{ij}$		−0.0419***		
		(0.008)		
ln $\mid PDI_i - PDI_j \mid$			0.0084*	0.0131**
			(0.0049)	(0.0058)
ln $\mid IDV_i - IDV_j \mid$			0.065***	0.0568***
			(0.0046)	(0.0052)
ln $\mid MAS_i - MAS_j \mid$			−0.0462***	−0.083***
			(0.0048)	(0.0055)
ln $\mid UAI_i - UAI_j \mid$			−0.0513***	−0.0613***
			(0.0042)	(0.0047)
ln $\mid PRA_i - PRA_j \mid$				0.0739***
				(0.0051)
ln $\mid IND_i - IND_j \mid$				−0.0525***
				(0.0053)
ln Real GDP$_{it}$ (Exporter)	1.3505***	1.3779***	1.3552***	1.3873***
	(0.0426)	(0.0483)	(0.0426)	(0.0484)
ln Real GDP$_{jt}$ (Importer)	1.4436***	1.3687***	1.4452***	1.372***
	(0.0459)	(0.0508)	(0.0458)	(0.0508)
ln Economic Remoteness$_{it}$ (Exporter)	0.3006**	0.5214***	0.2955**	0.522***
	(0.1215)	(0.1308)	(0.1213)	(0.1306)
ln Economic Remoteness$_{jt}$ (Importer)	0.6732***	0.5526***	0.6655***	0.5513***
	(0.132)	(0.1422)	(0.1316)	(0.1424)
ln Geodesic Distance$_{ij}$	−1.4532***	−1.3338***	−1.4794***	−1.3785***
	(0.0069)	(0.0073)	(0.0069)	(0.0073)
Common Border$_{ij}$	0.2939***	0.3064***	0.2751***	0.2779***
	(0.0295)	(0.029)	(0.0294)	(0.0287)
Constant	−49.9793***	−50.6628***	−49.6818***	−50.3769***
	(2.8964)	(3.2005)	(2.8954)	(3.2034)
N	188,223	127,253	188,263	127,253
Pseudo R^2	0.7724	0.7902	0.7730	0.7916

All estimations include year, exporter, and importer country fixed effects. Corresponding coefficients not reported due to space limitations. Standard errors in parentheses. "***", "**", and "*" denote significance from zero at the 1 percent, 5 percent, and 10 percent levels, respectively.

Table 6.6 GLOBE cultural distance and bilateral trade flows, composite and component measures

	(a)	*(b)*
ln GLOBE Cultural Distance$_{ij}$	−0.1416***	
	(0.0181)	
ln | ASSERT$_i$ − ASSERT$_j$ |		−0.0089
		(0.0063)
ln | INST-COL$_i$ − INST-COL$_j$ |		−0.0862***
		(0.0070)
ln | INGP-COL$_i$ − INGP-COL$_j$ |		0.0873***
		(0.0061)
ln | FUTURE$_i$ − FUTURE$_j$ |		0.0192***
		(0.0068)
ln | GEND-EGL$_i$ − GEND-EGL$_j$ |		−0.0937***
		(0.0066)
ln | HUMANE$_i$ − HUMANE$_j$ |		−0.0182***
		(0.0059)
ln | PERFORM$_i$ − PERFORM$_j$ |		0.03383***
		(0.0063)
ln | POWDIST$_i$ − POWDIST$_j$ |		−0.0461***
		(0.0065)
ln | UNC-AVD$_i$ − UNC-AVD$_j$ |		−0.0056
		(0.0062)
ln Real GDP$_{it}$ (Exporter)	2.0102***	2.0001***
	(0.0541)	(0.0553)
ln Real GDP$_{jt}$ (Importer)	1.6073***	1.6179***
	(0.0602)	(0.0614)
ln Economic Remoteness$_{it}$ (Exporter)	1.5082***	1.4806***
	(0.1540)	(0.1582)
ln Economic Remoteness$_{jt}$ (Importer)	0.8340***	0.7950***
	(0.1607)	(0.1644)
ln Geodesic Distance$_{ij}$	−1.2615***	−1.2581***
	(0.0087)	(0.0089)
Common Border$_{ij}$	0.3630***	0.5007***
	(0.0358)	(0.0365)
Constant	−80.2914***	−80.3443***
	(3.3786)	(3.4570)
N	73,378	69,870
Pseudo R^2	0.8084	0.8109

All estimations include year, exporter, and importer country fixed effects. Corresponding coefficients not reported due to space limitations. Standard errors in parentheses. "***", "**", and "*" denote significance from zero at the 1 percent, 5 percent, and 10 percent levels, respectively.

cultural dimensions. In column A of the table, we present the results obtained when the composite measure is used in the regression model, and the resulting coefficient estimates from when we substitute our measures that represent differences across cultural dimensions for the composite measure (column B). Beginning with the coefficient on the composite GLOBE measure, we find that, as was the case for the Inglehart composite measure and the Hofstede composite measures, the coefficient estimate is negative and statistically significant from zero. More specifically, a one percent increase in the GLOBE cultural distance measure, all else held constant, corresponds with a 0.1416 percent decrease in the predicted value of bilateral trade between our typical country pair. Evaluated in relation to a one standard deviation increase in the measure of cultural distance (as indicated in Table 5.2) above its mean value, the corresponding effect on bilateral trade flows is an estimated decrease of 4.98 percent.

Turning our focus to the component dimensions of the GLOBE measure, results are presented in column B of Table 6.6. As with the results presented in Table 6.2 and Table 6.4 for the components of the Inglehart measure of cultural distance and in Table 6.5 for the components of the Hofstede measures, we find considerable variation in terms of coefficient signs and statistical significance across the GLOBE cultural dimensions. Specifically, of the nine coefficients of the cultural dimensions, three are positive and significant from zero, four are negative and statistically significant, and two are negative but insignificant from zero. This variation in coefficients is important as it indicates that certain cultural differences may enhance bilateral trade flows just as others may hinder them. In that regard, the coefficients collectively provide useful information.

Before moving ahead to discuss additional regression results, it is worthwhile to comment on the consistency of our results, both with respect to the composite measures and to the control variables included in the regression model. For all four composite measures of cultural distance, the regression analysis yields negative and statistically significant coefficients. Moreover, the estimated influences of one standard deviation change in the composite measures of cultural distance on bilateral trade flows range from decreases of 1.79 percent and 2.4 percent for the 4-factor and 6-factor Hofstede measures respectively, to a 4.65 percent decrease for the Inglehart measure and a 4.98 percent decrease for the GLOBE measure.

An additional measure of consistency is that the coefficients of the control variables in all estimations presented in Table 6.5 (for the regressions that involve the Hofstede measure) and in Table 6.6 (for the regressions involving the GLOBE measure) are of the same sign as the coefficients presented in Table 6.2 (when the Inglehart cultural distance measure is employed in the analysis). The only difference, other than variation in coefficient magnitudes, is that the coefficient of the exporter economic remoteness variable in Table 6.2, while positive, is not significantly different from zero while the corresponding coefficient estimates that are reported in Tables 6.5 and 6.6 are both positive and statistically significant.

Cultural distance and bilateral trade, employing proxy variables

As an additional means to examine the potential influence of cultural differences on bilateral trade flows, we estimate a series of alternative regression specifications in which each of a number of proxy variables represent cultural similarity, in some instances, or cultural differences. These proxy variables are discussed in greater detail in Chapter 5. Included in the set of proxy variables are index measures of linguistic proximity and language distance, religious distances, and genetic distances between populations. Additionally, the set of dummy variables also includes measures that identify different forms of common language use (e.g., common spoken language as compared to a common official language).

The logic for the use of these additional measures is similar to that which underlies the use of composite measures of cultural distance and their component dimensions. Since culture is difficult to define, cultural differences are, by extension, also difficult to define. As such, no single measure of cultural distance is likely sufficient to fully capture the vagaries of cultural differences. By examining the relationships between cultural difference and facets of economic globalization while using a broad set of related, yet distinct, measures of cultural (dis)similarity, we discern more information about the examined relationship while also hedging against the limitations and shortcomings of any single measure.

The results obtained when estimating equation 6.1 with our various proxy measures in place are presented in Tables 6.7 through 6.10. We begin with the results obtained when employing two measures of language distance and two measures of linguistic proximity as proxies for cultural distance. These results are presented in Table 6.7.

Corresponding with our expectations, the coefficient estimates of the Dow language distance variable and of the B-E linguistic distance variable are both negative and statistically significant from zero. As the functional form of our regression model continues to be double-log, we can interpret these coefficients as follows. First, all else held constant, a one percent increase in the Dow language distance variable corresponds with a 0.1348 percent decrease in bilateral trade between our typical country pair. Likewise, and again holding all other factors constant, a one percent increase in the B-E linguistic distance measure is estimated to reduce bilateral trade between the typical country pair by 0.311 percent. Extrapolating to ten percent increases in each measure, the corresponding decreases in bilateral trade flows are estimated to equal 1.348 percent and 3.11 percent respectively. Although different in sign, the coefficients on the M-T linguistic proximity variables are consistent with the results presented thus far in terms of their interpretations. Given one percent increases in the ASJP-based and Tree-based variables (i.e., the extent to which languages are similar), while holding all else constant, we find that the predicted amount of bilateral trade occurring between our typical country pair increases by 0.0659 percent and 0.1032 percent respectively.

Continuing with the theme of language commonality as a proxy variable for cultural similarity on bilateral trade flows, Table 6.8 presents regression results obtained from using each of five dummy variables when undertaking five estimations of equation 6.1. Each dummy variable indicates a different form of language commonality. For example, the CEPII common linguistic ethnography variable is equal to one if a language is spoken by at least nine percent of the populations

Table 6.7 Index measures of linguistic differences/similarities and bilateral trade flows

	(a)		*(c)*	*(d)*
ln B-E Linguistic Distance$_{ij}$	−0.311***			
	(0.0124)			
ln Dow Language Distance$_{ij}$		−0.1348***		
		(0.0042)		
ln M-T Linguistic Proximity$_{ij}$ (ASJP)			0.0659***	
			(0.0083)	
ln M-T Linguistic Proximity$_{ij}$ (Tree)				0.1032***
				(0.015)
ln Real GDP$_{it}$ (Exporter)	1.9062***	1.4712***	1.4342***	0.7701***
	(0.0737)	(0.0438)	(0.0358)	(0.0594)
ln Real GDP$_{jt}$ (Importer)	0.8703***	1.6254***	1.2642***	1.0160***
	(0.0844)	(0.0474)	(0.0388)	(0.0598)
ln Economic Remoteness$_{it}$ (Exporter)	4.4659***	0.4366***	0.6721***	0.6***
	(0.2976)	(0.1387)	(0.1124)	(0.1598)
ln Economic Remoteness$_{jt}$ (Importer)	0.1182	0.9212***	0.5106***	1.1018***
	(0.2964)	(0.146)	(0.1224)	(0.1847)
ln Geodesic Distance$_{ij}$	−1.0335***	−1.2815***	−1.58***	−1.5633***
	(0.0128)	(0.0088)	(0.0066)	(0.009)
Common Border$_{ij}$	0.1603***	0.2838***	0.5145***	0.4467***
	(0.0201)	(0.0467)	(0.0315)	(0.036)
Constant	−86.2246***	−61.9912***	−44.6279***	−30.2125***
	(6.3351)	(2.9551)	(2.3158)	(3.5049)
N	12,216	165,224	267,417	118,950
Pseudo R^2	0.9290	0.7517	0.7482	0.7817

All estimations include year, exporter, and importer country fixed effects. Corresponding coefficients not reported due to space limitations. Standard errors in parentheses. "***", "**", and "*" denote significance from zero at the 1 percent, 5 percent, and 10 percent levels, respectively.

Table 6.8 Dichotomous measures of language commonality and bilateral trade flows

	(a)	*(b)*	*(c)*	*(d)*	*(e)*
CEPII Common Linguistic $Ethnography_{ij}$	0.7782***				
	(0.0113)				
CEPII Common Official $Language_{ij}$		0.8746***			
		(0.0111)			
M-T Common Native $Language_{ij}$			1.4053***		
			(0.0229)		
M-T Common Official $Language_{ij}$				0.9512***	
				(0.0117)	
M-T Common Spoken $Language_{ij}$					1.1645***
					(0.0166)
ln Real GDP_{it} (Exporter)	0.9974***	0.9956***	1.1728***	1.17***	1.1653***
	(0.0267)	(0.0267)	(0.0288)	(0.0288)	(0.0288)
ln Real GDP_{jt} (Importer)	1.2551***	1.2603***	1.2823***	1.2842***	1.2779***
	(0.0323)	(0.0323)	(0.0333)	(0.0331)	(0.0332)
ln Economic $Remoteness_{it}$ (Exporter)	–0.2934***	–0.2828***	–0.236**	–0.2947***	–0.2155**
	(0.0931)	(0.093)	(0.0994)	(0.0987)	(0.0993)

(continued)

Table 6.8 (continued)

	(a)	*(b)*	*(c)*	*(d)*	*(e)*
ln Economic Remoteness$_{jt}$ (Importer)	−0.0367	−0.025	−0.098	−0.1369	−0.0842
	(0.1046)	(0.1047)	(0.1104)	(0.1104)	(0.1105)
ln Geodesic Distance$_{ij}$	−1.5645***	−1.5493***	−1.596***	−1.5821***	−1.5798***
	(0.0054)	(0.0054)	(0.0057)	(0.0055)	(0.0057)
Common Border$_{ij}$	0.5714***	0.5734***	0.5833***	0.5447***	0.5096***
	(0.025)	(0.0249)	(0.025)	(0.0247)	(0.0248)
Constant	−22.8976***	−23.1899***	−26.3717***	−25.5824***	−27.1311***
	(1.8977)	(1.8976)	(2.0047)	(1.998)	(2.0039)
N	412,039	412,039	378,649	378,649	378,649
Pseudo R^2	0.7296	0.7306	0.7289	0.7314	0.7298

All estimations include year, exporter, and importer country fixed effects. Corresponding coefficients not reported due to space limitations. Standard errors in parentheses. "***", "**", and "*" denote significance from zero at the 1 percent, 5 percent, and 10 percent levels, respectively.

in both country i and country j, and is otherwise equal to zero. The M-T common official language variable takes the value of one if both countries in a pair share an official language, and is otherwise equal to zero. We find that all five coefficients of the language commonality-related dummy variables are positive and all are statistically significant from zero. Thus, generally speaking, use of a common language corresponds with a higher level of bilateral trade flows. More specifically, the coefficient estimates indicate that, all else held constant, sharing a common language increases bilateral trade flows by 77.8 percent (if the countries have a common linguistic ethnography) to 140.5 percent (if they share a common native language). Since language is not merely representative of culture but also a means of transmitting culture, these findings are of particular interest. Stated differently, if two countries do not share a common language, we would observe a reduced volume of bilateral trade.

Religious distance is yet another measure that we employ as a proxy variable for cultural differences. Specifically, we employ two measures of religious distance, separately, when estimating modified versions of equation 6.1. The modifications are, of course, the replacement of the cultural distance variable in the regression model with each of the index measures of religious differences in turn. Results obtained from the estimations are presented in Table 6.9. For both

Table 6.9 Indexes of religious differences and bilateral trade flows

	(a)	*(b)*
ln B-E Religious Distance$_{ij}$	−0.233***	
	(0.0109)	
ln Dow Religious Distance$_{ij}$		−0.0445
		(0.0359)
ln Real GDP$_{it}$ (Exporter)	1.8124***	1.8569***
	(0.077)	(0.0548)
ln Real GDP$_{jt}$ (Importer)	0.8281***	1.8168***
	(0.0888)	(0.0609)
ln Economic Remoteness$_{it}$ (Exporter)	4.2626***	0.7088***
	(0.2989)	(0.1595)
ln Economic Remoteness$_{jt}$ (Importer)	0.1116	1.5647***
	(0.303)	(0.1707)
ln Geodesic Distance$_{ij}$	−0.9760***	−1.2078***
	(0.0140)	(0.0161)
Common Border$_{ij}$	0.2987***	−0.3855***
	(0.0203)	(0.0742)
Constant	−80.9816***	−83.3847
	(6.5192)	(3.6304)
N	13,478	94,313
Pseudo R^2	0.9292	0.7428

All estimations include year, exporter, and importer country fixed effects. Corresponding coefficients not reported due to space limitations. Standard errors in parentheses. "***", "**", and "*" denote significance from zero at the 1 percent, 5 percent, and 10 percent levels, respectively.

measures of religious distance, the coefficient estimates are negative; however, only in the case of the B-E measure of religious distance is the coefficient estimate also significantly different from zero. The corresponding interpretation is that a one percent increase in the religious distance between a given pair of trading partners, all else constant, results in a 0.233 percent decrease in bilateral trade between the country pair.

Our final proxy variable is perhaps the one measure most in need of extended explanation. We use the genetic distance between populations (i.e., countries) as a proxy for cultural distance based on the notion that genetic differences (i.e., observed heterozygosity) between societies occur over time due to a lack of interaction between members of the societies. For example, two populations that commonly interact will likely interbreed and, thus, have more similar genetic profiles relative to two populations that exist in isolation for extended periods of time. In addition to interbreeding, populations that come into contact with each other more frequently will interact in other ways that permit the transmission of culture. Thus, more genetically similar societies are also likely more similar in terms of their cultures.

In our analysis, we employ two measures of genetic distance. The first is the fixation index and the second is the Nei measure of genetic distance. The two measures are similar in that they each are constructed based on allele commonality. The measures differ, however, in that the Nei measure accounts for genetic mutations in addition to genetic drift while the fixation index only accounts for genetic drift. We again estimate equation 6.1, this time substituting each of the two measures of genetic distance as the cultural distance measure. The resulting coefficient estimates are presented in Table 6.10. In both instances, using either the fixation index or the Nei measure of genetic distance, we obtain negative and statistically significant coefficient estimates. More specifically, allowing for coefficient interpretation, we find that a one percent increase in the fixation index measure, all else held constant, reduces bilateral trade between our typical country pair by 0.1341 percent. Similarly, a like increase in the Nei measure of genetic distance corresponds with a decrease in bilateral trade of 0.1358 percent.

The influence of cultural distance on the intensive and extensive margins of bilateral trade flows

While the results presented so far indicate a clear negative relationship between the measures of cultural distance employed in the regression analysis and the level of bilateral trade flows, a separate, related question concerns whether cultural differences hinder the initiation of international trade. If cultural differences are sufficiently pronounced to heighten trade-related transaction costs to a level at which engaging in trade is prohibitive, and hence to a point where observed trade values are equal to zero, then the influences of cultural difference on bilateral trade are two-fold. They diminish the level of bilateral trade, conditional on trade occurring, and inhibit the negotiation and completion of cross-border trade deals. Accordingly, in this section we use the Tobit estimation technique and the McDonald and Moffitt

Table 6.10 Genetic distance and bilateral trade flows

	(c)	*(d)*
ln Fixation Index Genetic Distance (weighted)$_{ij}$	−0.1341***	
	(0.0067)	
ln Nei Standard Genetic Distance (weighted)$_{ij}$		−0.1358***
		(0.0065)
ln Real GDP$_{it}$ (Exporter)	−0.0211	−0.0212
	(0.0229)	(0.0229)
ln Real GDP$_{jt}$ (Importer)	0.6597***	0.6597***
	(0.0232)	(0.0232)
ln Economic Remoteness$_{it}$ (Exporter)	−1.0544***	−1.056***
	(0.1447)	(0.1447)
ln Economic Remoteness$_{jt}$ (Importer)	−1.6113***	−1.613***
	(0.1398)	(0.1398)
ln Geodesic Distance$_{ij}$	−1.8477***	−1.8458***
	(0.0106)	(0.0106)
Common Border$_{ij}$	0.7067***	0.7044***
	(0.0567)	(0.0567)
Constant	21.0925***	20.8809***
	(2.1184)	(2.1186)
N	897,912	897,912
Pseudo R^2	0.6107	0.6107

All estimations include year, exporter, and importer country fixed effects. Corresponding coefficients not reported due to space limitations. Standard errors in parentheses. "***", "**", and "*" denote significance from zero at the 1 percent, 5 percent, and 10 percent levels, respectively.

(1980) decomposition procedure to further explore the relationships between cultural differences and international trade. When completing our analysis, we limit our estimations to those variants of equation 6.1 where the Inglehart and Hofstede measures of cultural distance are employed. We do not pursue estimation of our regression model using the GLOBE cultural distance measure simply because there are few certain zero observations in the corresponding data. Estimation results, provided in Tables 6.11 and 6.12, are presented in the chapter appendix.

Tables 6.11a and 6.11b present the estimated Tobit coefficients. Included in the tables are the decomposed coefficients that represent, given a corresponding change in the explanatory variable series, the predicted changes in the level of bilateral trade (i.e., the intensive margin effect) and the predicted likelihoods that the level of bilateral trade will increase from the censored value (a value of no trade) to some positive level (the extensive margin effect).

Table 6.11a indicates that, conditional on bilateral trade between a given country pair being greater than zero (i.e., conditional on the pair already being engaged in trade), a one percent increase in the Inglehart measure of cultural distance, all else held constant, decreases the predicted level of bilateral trade between the countries by 0.9531 percent. Further, as the extensive margin coefficient is equal to −0.0055 and is significantly different from zero, we can say that an increase in the Inglehart cultural distance measure also reduces the likelihood that the country pair will engage in any trade at all. Looking to Table 6.11b, we find similar effects estimated for increases in the levels of the 6-factor Hofstede cultural distance measure. To the contrary, an increase in the 4-factor Hofstede cultural distance measure is estimated to have positive effects on bilateral trade at both the intensive and the extensive margins.

As we did earlier in this chapter, we now consider the relationships between bilateral trade flows and the component dimensions of the composite Inglehart measure of cultural distance and of the composite Hofstede cultural distance measures. The results obtained from the estimation of equation 6.1 using these component dimensions are presented in Tables 6.12a and 6.12b. Contrary to the results presented in Table 6.2, here the estimated coefficients on both the variable that represents differences along the SSE cultural dimension and that which represents differences along the TSR dimension are negative and statistically significant from zero. Thus, the results for both Inglehart dimensions are consistent with the results reported for the corresponding composite measure. The same is not true for the estimations that employ the component cultural dimensions of the Hofstede composite measure. As was the case in Table 6.5, when viewing the coefficients of the Hofstede cultural dimensions in Table 6.12b, we again see a mix of positive and negative signs and of scattered statistical significance.

The influence of cultural distance on disaggregate trade volumes

Our final set of estimations involves the estimation of a slightly modified version of equation 6.1. The slight modification is that, rather than employing aggregate trade measures as the dependent variable series, we now use data that represent bilateral trade flows at the SITC 1-digit sector-level of detail. The basis for these additional estimations is both to gain information that may afford a deeper understanding of the relationship between bilateral trade flows and cross-societal cultural differences, and to test the robustness of results that are reported in earlier sections of this chapter. Results obtained when representing cultural differences via the use of our four composite measures of cultural distance and their related component dimensions are reported in Tables 6.13a through 6.13d, and results from the estimations where the proxy measures of cultural distance are considered are presented in Tables 6.14a and 6.14b. Both sets of results are included in the chapter appendix.

Given that 10 estimations are performed (one for each SITC 1-digit sector classification) per measure of cultural distance, we restrict the presentation of results to the coefficient estimates of the cultural distance measures. We see that 37 of the 40 estimated coefficients (92.5 percent) of the composite measures of cultural distance presented in Table 6.13 are negative and significantly different from zero. Two coefficients (5 percent) are not significantly different from zero – one negative and the other positive – and a single coefficient (2.5 percent) is both positive and statistically significant. Thus, we feel comfortable in saying that the negative and statistically significant relationship between cultural distance and bilateral trade flows reported earlier in this chapter is supported by our sector-level analysis.

As anticipated, based on the findings reported earlier, the coefficient estimates of the individual cultural dimensions are varied in both sign and statistical significance. A summary of the coefficients is that, across the 10 sector classifications and 12 component dimension measures, 69.2 percent (83 of the 120 estimated coefficients) are negative and significantly different from zero, 17.5 percent (21 coefficients) are positive and significant from zero, and 13.3 percent (16 coefficients) are not significantly different from zero. Thus, while we see variation in the coefficient estimates, they are, generally speaking, in line with our overall finding that greater cultural differences hinder bilateral trade flows.

Finally, we perform the same accounting when reviewing the coefficient estimates of the set of variables that serve as proxies for cultural differences. Based on the coefficient estimates presented in Tables 6.14 and 6.14b, we see that 86.2 percent (112 of the 130 coefficient estimates) are of the anticipated sign and statistically significant from zero. Only 5.4 percent (7 coefficients) have an unexpected sign and are significant from zero, and the remaining 8.5 percent (11 coefficients) are not significantly different from zero. In a few words, we again see overwhelming evidence that supports the hypothesis that greater cross-societal cultural differences reduce bilateral trade flows.

A brief summary of findings

In an attempt to gain a deeper understanding of the relationship between measures of cross-societal cultural differences (i.e., cultural distance) and international trade flows, we have examined the relationship between cultural distance and trade for a group of culturally and economically heterogeneous countries. Our analysis extends the related literature, informs public and political discussions and, potentially, provides information beneficial in the formulation of public policy.

Our results indicate that, generally speaking, greater cultural differences correspond with reduced levels of bilateral trade and act to hinder the initiation of trade. The findings appear consistent across a considerable variety of cultural distance measures (e.g., composite measures, component dimensions, index measures of language (dis)similarity, religious distance, genetic distance, and a number of dummy variables that identify language commonality), across estimation procedures (i.e., feasible generalized least squares and Tobit estimation techniques), and across aggregate and disaggregate (i.e., SITC 1-digit sector classifications) trade values.

Appendix: Tobit estimation results and examination of SITC 1-digit sector classifications

The results obtained when estimating equation 6.1 using the Tobit technique and then applying the McDonald and Moffitt (1980) decomposition technique are presented here in Tables 6.11 and 6.12. Similarly, the estimation results produced when considering the relationships between cultural distance and bilateral trade flows at SITC 1-digit sector levels are provided in Tables 6.13 and 6.14. Sections 6.3 and 6.4, respectively, discuss these estimation results.

Note

1 In Chapters 6 and 7, due to panel-level heteroskedasticity and first-order serial correlation, unless otherwise noted, we employ the feasible generalized least squares estimation technique.

Table 6.11a Tobit estimations, Inglehart composite measure of cultural distance

	Tobit	*Intensive*	*Extensive*
ln Inglehart Cultural Distance$_{ijt}$	−1.0354***	−0.9531***	−0.0055***
	(0.0426)	(0.0392)	(0.0002)
ln Real GDP$_{it}$ (Exporter)	1.6031***	1.4757***	0.0085***
	(0.0151)	(0.0139)	(0.0001)
ln Real GDP$_{jt}$ (Importer)	1.786***	1.644***	0.0094***
	(0.0152)	(0.0139)	(0.0001)
ln Economic Remoteness$_{it}$ (Exporter)	0.4071***	0.3747***	0.0021***
	(0.0592)	(0.0545)	(0.0003)
ln Economic Remoteness$_{jt}$ (Importer)	−0.6785***	−0.6246***	−0.0036***
	(0.0592)	(0.0545)	(0.0003)
ln Geodesic Distance$_{ij}$	−0.871***	−0.8018***	−0.0046***
	(0.0423)	(0.039)	(0.0002)
Common Border$_{ij}$	0.6261***	0.5801***	0.003***
	(0.1464)	(0.1348)	(0.0008)
Constant	−60.2267***	−55.4397***	−0.3178***
	(1.0047)	(0.9249)	(0.0053)
_se	6.6275		
	(0.0209)		
N		66,136	
Pseudo R^2		0.0651	
Observations = 0 (lower limit)		10,215	
% Observations = 0		15.4%	

All estimations include year, exporter, and importer country fixed effects. Corresponding coefficients not reported due to space limitations. Standard errors in parentheses. "***", "**", and "*" denote significance from zero at the 1 percent, 5 percent, and 10 percent levels, respectively.

Table 6.11b Tobit estimations, Inglehart composite measure of cultural distance

	Tobit	*Intensive*	*Extensive*	*Tobit*	*Intensive*	*Extensive*
ln Hofstede 4-factor Cultural Distance$_{ij}$	0.3617***	0.2558***	0.008***			
	(0.0188)	(0.0133)	(0.0004)			
ln Hofstede 6-factor Cultural Distance$_{ij}$				−0.1514***	−0.1225***	−0.0021***
				(0.0294)	(0.0238)	(0.0004)
ln Real GDP$_{it}$ (Exporter)	2.0442***	1.4461***	0.0454***	1.847***	1.494***	0.0253***
	(0.0093)	(0.0066)	(0.0002)	(0.0113)	(0.0091)	(0.0002)
ln Real GDP$_{jt}$ (Importer)	2.361***	1.6702***	0.0524***	2.286***	1.8491***	0.0313***
	(0.0094)	(0.0066)	(0.0002)	(0.0113)	(0.0092)	(0.0002)
ln Economic Remoteness$_{it}$ (Exporter)	1.0939***	0.7739***	0.0243***	0.7359***	0.5953***	0.0101***
	(0.0352)	(0.0249)	(0.0008)	(0.0403)	(0.0326)	(0.0006)
ln Economic Remoteness$_{jt}$ (Importer)	−0.3835***	−0.2713***	−0.0085***	−0.6882***	−0.5567***	−0.0094***
	(0.035)	(0.0247)	(0.0008)	(0.0402)	(0.0325)	(0.0005)
ln Geodesic Distance$_{ij}$	−1.078***	−0.7626***	−0.0239***	−0.5335***	−0.4316***	−0.0073***
	(0.0258)	(0.0183)	(0.0006)	(0.0315)	(0.0255)	(0.0004)
Common Border$_{ij}$	1.0846***	0.7869***	0.0222***	1.2028***	0.9944***	0.0145***
	(0.1146)	(0.0811)	(0.0025)	(0.126)	(0.1019)	(0.0017)
Constant	−95.2315***	−67.3669***	−2.1137***	−87.5885***	−70.8487***	−1.1974***
	(0.6108)	(0.4321)	(0.0136)	(0.6916)	(0.5595)	(0.0095)
_se	8.0726			7.5824		
	(0.0143)			(0.0161)		
N		264,250			164,460	
Pseudo R^2		0.0834			0.0743	
Observations = 0 (lower limit)		76,027			37,207	
% Observations = 0		28.8%			22.6%	

All estimations include year, exporter, and importer country fixed effects. Corresponding coefficients not reported due to space limitations. Standard errors in parentheses. "***", "**", and "*" denote significance from zero at the 1 percent, 5 percent, and 10 percent levels, respectively.

Table 6.12a Tobit estimations, Inglehart component measures of cultural distance

	Tobit	*Intensive*	*Extensive*
ln | $SSE_{it} - SSE_{jt}$ |	−0.4261***	−0.3919***	−0.0023***
	(0.0255)	(0.0234)	(0.0001)
ln | $TSR_{it} - TSR_{jt}$ |	−0.1903***	−0.175***	−0.001***
	(0.0255)	(0.0235)	(0.0001)
ln Real GDP_{it} (Exporter)	1.6141***	1.4847***	0.0086***
	(0.0152)	(0.014)	(0.0001)
ln Real GDP_{jt} (Importer)	1.797***	1.6529***	0.0096***
	(0.0152)	(0.014)	(0.0001)
ln Economic $Remoteness_{it}$ (Exporter)	0.5484***	0.5044***	0.0029***
	(0.0588)	(0.0541)	(0.0003)
ln Economic $Remoteness_{jt}$ (Importer)	−0.536***	−0.493***	−0.0029***
	(0.0588)	(0.0541)	(0.0003)
ln Geodesic $Distance_{ij}$	−1.0045***	−0.924***	−0.0053***
	(0.0425)	(0.0391)	(0.0002)
Common $Border_{ij}$	0.6849***	0.6345***	0.0033***
	(0.1468)	(0.135)	(0.0008)
Constant	−63.2909***	−58.2178***	−0.3366***
	(0.9942)	(0.9145)	(0.0053)
_se	6.6412		
	(0.021)		
N		66,136	
Pseudo R^2		0.0645	
Observations = 0 (lower limit)		10,215	
% Observations = 0		15.4%	

All estimations include year, exporter, and importer country fixed effects. Corresponding coefficients not reported due to space limitations. Standard errors in parentheses. "***", "**", and "*" denote significance from zero at the 1 percent, 5 percent, and 10 percent levels, respectively.

Table 6.12b Tobit estimations, Inglehart component measures of cultural distance

	Tobit	*Intensive*	*Extensive*	*Tobit*	*Intensive*	*Extensive*
ln $\| PDI_i - PDI_j \|$	−0.1968***	−0.1393***	−0.0044***	−0.4308***	−0.3494***	−0.0058***
	(0.0167)	(0.0118)	(0.0004)	(0.0204)	(0.0165)	(0.0003)
ln $\| IDV_i - IDV_j \|$	0.4255***	0.3011***	0.0094***	0.419***	0.3398***	0.0057***
	(0.0169)	(0.0119)	(0.0004)	(0.0197)	(0.016)	(0.0003)
ln $\| MAS_i - MAS_j \|$	0.1472***	0.1041***	0.0033***	0.0171	0.0139	0.0002
	(0.0162)	(0.0115)	(0.0004)	(0.0192)	(0.0156)	(0.0003)
ln $\| UAI_i - UAI_j \|$	0.065***	0.046***	0.0014***	0.277***	0.2247***	0.0038***
	(0.0158)	(0.0112)	(0.0004)	(0.0189)	(0.0153)	(0.0003)
ln $\| PRA_i - PRA_j \|$				0.0631***	0.0511***	0.0009***
				(0.0192)	(0.0156)	(0.0003)
ln $\| IND_i - IND_j \|$				−0.4962***	−0.4025***	−0.0067***
				(0.0195)	(0.0158)	(0.0003)
ln Real GDP_{it} (Exporter)	2.0385***	1.4426***	0.0452***	1.8179***	1.4744***	0.0246***
	(0.0093)	(0.0066)	(0.0002)	(0.0113)	(0.0091)	(0.0002)
ln Real GDP_{jt} (Importer)	2.3536***	1.6656***	0.0522***	2.2558***	1.8296***	0.0306***
	(0.0094)	(0.0067)	(0.0002)	(0.0113)	(0.0092)	(0.0002)
ln Economic $Remoteness_{it}$ (Exporter)	1.0949***	0.7748***	0.0243***	0.9134***	0.7408***	0.0124***
	(0.0351)	(0.0248)	(0.0008)	(0.0401)	(0.0325)	(0.0005)
ln Economic $Remoteness_{jt}$ (Importer)	−0.3834***	−0.2713***	−0.0085***	−0.5058***	−0.4103***	−0.0069***
	(0.0348)	(0.0247)	(0.0008)	(0.04)	(0.0324)	(0.0005)

(continued)

Table 6.12b (continued)

	Tobit	*Intensive*	*Extensive*	*Tobit*	*Intensive*	*Extensive*
ln Geodesic Distance$_{ij}$	−1.1013***	−0.7794***	−0.0244***	−0.6636***	−0.5382***	−0.009***
	(0.0259)	(0.0183)	(0.0006)	(0.0312)	(0.0253)	(0.0004)
Common Border$_{ij}$	1.0828***	0.7859***	0.0221***	1.3109***	1.0886***	0.0155***
	(0.1146)	(0.0811)	(0.0025)	(0.1255)	(0.1018)	(0.0017)
Constant	−95.7996***	−67.7953***	−2.1253***	−87.6197***	−71.0649***	−1.1867***
	(0.6251)	(0.4424)	(0.0139)	(0.7163)	(0.5809)	(0.0097)
_se	8.0667			7.5428		
	(0.0143)			(0.016)		
N		264,312			164,460	
Pseudo R^2		0.0836			0.0758	
Observations = 0 (lower limit)		76,049			37,207	
% Observations = 0		28.8%			22.6%	

All estimations include year, exporter, and importer country fixed effects. Corresponding coefficients not reported due to space limitations. Standard errors in parentheses. "***", "**", and "*" denote significance from zero at the 1 percent, 5 percent, and 10 percent levels, respectively.

Table 6.13a Summary of estimated coefficients of composite and component cultural distance variables, SITC 1-digit sector-level estimations

	0: Food and Live Animals	*1: Beverages and Tobacco*	*2: Crude Materials, Inedible, Except Fuels*	*3: Mineral Fuels, Lubricants, and Related Materials*	*4: Animal and Vegetables Oils, Fats and Waxes*
ln Inglehart Cultural Distance$_{ijt}$	−0.0288**	−0.3738***	−0.0599***	0.0069	−0.1056***
	(0.0136)	(0.0192)	(0.0139)	(0.0261)	(0.0211)
ln | $SSE_{it} - SSE_{jt}$ |	−0.0853***	−0.2107***	−0.0603***	−0.1142***	−0.0759***
	(0.0077)	(0.0112)	(0.008)	(0.015)	(0.0125)
ln | $TSR_{it} - TSR_{jt}$ |	0.0634***	0.0081	−0.0037	0.1288***	0.0122
	(0.0081)	(0.0114)	(0.0081)	(0.0151)	(0.0129)
ln Hofstede 4-factor Cultural Distance$_{ij}$	−0.0115*	−0.2788***	−0.1893***	−0.184***	−0.0839***
	(0.0062)	(0.0086)	(0.0063)	(0.0121)	(0.0097)
ln | $PDI_i - PDI_j$ |	−0.0076	−0.0786***	−0.0413***	−0.0589***	0.015*
	(0.0056)	(0.0077)	(0.0055)	(0.0104)	(0.0089)
ln | $IDV_i - IDV_j$ |	0.1011***	−0.1322***	−0.068***	−0.0977***	−0.0195**
	(0.0054)	(0.0075)	(0.0053)	(0.0104)	(0.0088)
ln | $MAS_i - MAS_j$ |	−0.064***	−0.0563***	−0.0598***	−0.0843***	−0.112***
	(0.0055)	(0.0076)	(0.0056)	(0.0107)	(0.009)
ln | $UAI_i - UAI_j$ |	−0.0373***	−0.0411***	−0.0394***	0.0275***	−0.0643***
	(0.0047)	(0.0066)	(0.0049)	(0.0094)	(0.0079)
ln Hofstede 6-factor Cultural Distance$_{ij}$	0.0324***	−0.3665***	−0.1815***	−0.1094***	−0.0779***
	(0.0089)	(0.0122)	(0.0088)	(0.0165)	(0.0137)
ln | $PRA_i - PRA_j$ |	0.0545***	−0.0696***	−0.0387***	−0.0691***	0.0461***
	(0.0066)	(0.009)	(0.0064)	(0.0119)	(0.0101)
ln | $IND_i - IND_j$ |	0.0846***	−0.1216***	−0.0651***	−0.1043***	−0.0258***
	(0.006)	(0.0082)	(0.0059)	(0.0114)	(0.0094)
ln | $MAS_i - MAS_j$ |	−0.0808***	−0.0361***	−0.0804***	−0.0873***	−0.1338***
	(0.0062)	(0.0084)	(0.0063)	(0.0118)	(0.01)
ln | $UAI_i - UAI_j$ |	−0.0833***	−0.0415***	−0.0695***	−0.0087	−0.0726***
	(0.0054)	(0.0075)	(0.0055)	(0.0105)	(0.0086)
ln | $PRA_i - PRA_j$ |	0.0548***	−0.0131	0.0526***	0.1165***	−0.0093
	(0.0058)	(0.008)	(0.0059)	(0.0109)	(0.009)
ln | $IND_i - IND_j$ |	−0.0064	−0.0533***	−0.015**	0.029***	0.0174*
	(0.0061)	(0.0083)	(0.006)	(0.011)	(0.0095)

Standard errors in parentheses. "***", "**", and "*" denote statistical significance from zero at the 1 percent, 5 percent, and 10 percent levels, respectively.

Table 6.13b Summary of estimated coefficients of composite and component cultural distance variables, SITC 1-digit sector-level estimations

	0: Food and Live Animals	*1: Beverages and Tobacco*	*2: Crude Materials, Inedible, Except Fuels*	*3: Mineral Fuels, Lubricants, and Related Materials*	*4: Animal and Vegetables Oils, Fats and Waxes*
ln GLOBE Cultural Distance$_{ij}$	−0.0117	−0.3136***	−0.1555***	−0.3753***	−0.1099***
	(0.0229)	(0.0314)	(0.0231)	(0.0461)	(0.0380)
ln | ASSERT$_i$ – ASSERT$_j$ |	−0.021***	0.0401***	0.0398***	−0.0829***	0.0593***
	(0.0078)	(0.0104)	(0.0077)	(0.0149)	(0.0122)
ln | INST-COL$_i$ – INST-COL$_j$ |	−0.0516***	0.359	−0.0384***	−0.0464***	−0.0978***
	(0.0079)	(0.0111)	(0.008)	(0.0149)	(0.012)
ln | INGP-COL$_i$ – INGP-COL$_j$ |	0.0791***	−0.1139***	0.654	0.796	0.0761***
	(0.0073)	(0.0103)	(0.0072)	(0.0148)	(0.0114)
ln | FUTURE$_i$ – FUTURE$_j$ |	0.538	0.0279**	−0.0432***	−0.1312***	−0.0296**
	(0.0082)	(0.0109)	(0.0083)	(0.0159)	(0.0132)
ln | GEND-EGL$_i$ – GEND-EGL$_j$ |	−0.0178**	−0.0437***	−0.0697***	−0.1949***	0.165
	(0.0076)	(0.0106)	(0.0076)	(0.0139)	(0.0125)
ln | HUMANE$_i$ – HUMANE$_j$ |	0.776	0.033***	0.0337***	0.0459***	0.0711***
	(0.0074)	(0.0105)	(0.0076)	(0.0147)	(0.0126)
ln | PERFORM$_i$ – PERFORM$_j$ |	0.0157**	−0.0941***	−0.0261***	0.164	0.422
	(0.0081)	(0.0105)	(0.0079)	(0.0143)	(0.0122)
ln | POWDIST$_i$ – POWDIST$_j$ |	−0.1009***	−0.0551***	−0.0577***	0.0608***	−0.0399***
	(0.008)	(0.0109)	(0.0082)	(0.0154)	(0.0122)
ln | UNC-AVD$_i$ – UNC-AVD$_j$ |	0.0574***	0.0289***	0.173	0.726	−0.027**
	(0.0077)	(0.0108)	(0.0077)	(0.0152)	(0.0121)

Standard errors in parentheses. "***", "**", and "*" denote statistical significance from zero at the 1 percent, 5 percent, and 10 percent levels, respectively.

Table 6.13c Summary of estimated coefficients of composite and component cultural distance variables, SITC 1-digit sector-level estimations

	5: Chemicals and Related Products, n.e.s.	*6: Manufactured Goods Classified Chiefly by Material*	*7: Machinery and Transport Equipment*	*8: Miscellaneous Manufactured Articles*	*9: Commodities and Transactions Not Classified Elsewhere*
ln Inglehart Cultural $Distance_{ijt}$	−0.2661***	−0.1155***	−0.1692***	−0.0469***	−0.2341***
	(0.0124)	(0.0124)	(0.013)	(0.0119)	(0.0233)
$\ln \lvert SSE_{it} - SSE_{jt} \rvert$	−0.1159***	−0.0748***	−0.0698***	0.0313***	−0.2024***
	(0.0073)	(0.0071)	(0.0074)	(0.0067)	(0.013)
$\ln \lvert TSR_{it} - TSR_{jt} \rvert$	−0.043***	−0.0173**	−0.0283***	−0.0645***	0.0515***
	(0.0073)	(0.0071)	(0.0075)	(0.007)	(0.0133)
ln Hofstede 4-factor Cultural $Distance_{ij}$	−0.26***	−0.1513***	−0.1624***	−0.0867***	−0.2433***
	(0.006)	(0.0057)	(0.0058)	(0.0054)	(0.0094)
$\ln \lvert PDI_i - PDI_j \rvert$	−0.0787***	−0.0593***	−0.017***	0.0203***	−0.0721***
	(0.0054)	(0.005)	(0.0052)	(0.0048)	(0.0086)
$\ln \lvert IDV_i - IDV_j \rvert$	−0.0748***	0.0046	0.0021	0.0301***	−0.0331***
	(0.0052)	(0.0049)	(0.0049)	(0.0046)	(0.0082)
$\ln \lvert MAS_i - MAS_j \rvert$	−0.0423***	−0.0282***	−0.0454***	−0.0295***	−0.0826***
	(0.0053)	(0.0051)	(0.0052)	(0.0048)	(0.0087)
$\ln \lvert UAI_i - UAI_j \rvert$	−0.069***	−0.0529***	−0.1108***	−0.1092***	−0.1038***
	(0.0047)	(0.0045)	(0.0046)	(0.0043)	(0.0074)
ln Hofstede 6-factor Cultural $Distance_{ij}$	−0.2913***	−0.1225***	−0.1639***	−0.1018***	−0.2955***
	(0.0081)	(0.008)	(0.0081)	(0.0079)	(0.0134)
$\ln \lvert PRA_i - PRA_j \rvert$	−0.0806***	−0.0417***	0.0031	0.0204***	−0.053***
	(0.0062)	(0.0058)	(0.0061)	(0.0057)	(0.0102)
$\ln \lvert IND_i - IND_j \rvert$	−0.0315***	0.0271***	0.0366***	0.0708***	−0.024***
	(0.0056)	(0.0055)	(0.0054)	(0.0051)	(0.0092)
$\ln \lvert MAS_i - MAS_j \rvert$	−0.0414***	−0.0601***	−0.0529***	−0.0274***	−0.0924***
	(0.0059)	(0.0057)	(0.0058)	(0.0054)	(0.0099)
$\ln \lvert UAI_i - UAI_j \rvert$	−0.079***	−0.0651***	−0.111***	−0.1126***	−0.1117***
	(0.0052)	(0.005)	(0.0051)	(0.0048)	(0.0086)
$\ln \lvert PRA_i - PRA_j \rvert$	0.0054	0.0694***	0.0071	−0.0526***	0.0037
	(0.0055)	(0.0053)	(0.0055)	(0.0051)	(0.009)
$\ln \lvert IND_i - IND_j \rvert$	−0.0699***	−0.0227***	−0.0513***	−0.0001	−0.0771***
	(0.0057)	(0.0055)	(0.0054)	(0.0051)	(0.0091)

Standard errors in parentheses. "***", "**", and "*" denote statistical significance from zero at the 1 percent, 5 percent, and 10 percent levels, respectively.

Table 6.13d Summary of estimated coefficients of composite and component cultural distance variables, SITC 1-digit sector-level estimations

	5: Chemicals and Related Products, n.e.s.	*6: Manufactured Goods Classified Chiefly by Material*	*7: Machinery and Transport Equipment*	*8: Miscellaneous Manufactured Articles*	*9: Commodities and Transactions Not Classified Elsewhere*
ln GLOBE Cultural Distance$_{ij}$	–0.5320***	–0.3079***	–0.3524***	–0.1234***	–0.6477***
	(0.0210)	(0.0204)	(0.0210)	(0.0197)	(0.0374)
ln | ASSERT$_i$ – ASSERT$_j$ |	0.04***	0.314	0.0448***	0.0405***	0.0596***
	(0.0072)	(0.0068)	(0.0073)	(0.0068)	(0.0123)
ln | INST–COL$_i$ – INST–COL$_j$ |	–0.1273***	–0.1376***	–0.1241***	–0.173***	–0.043***
	(0.0073)	(0.0073)	(0.0077)	(0.007)	(0.0125)
ln | INGP–COL$_i$ – INGP–COL$_j$ |	–0.0403***	0.0393***	0.0423***	0.1178***	0.648
	(0.0067)	(0.0066)	(0.0069)	(0.0064)	(0.0112)
ln | FUTURE$_i$ – FUTURE$_j$ |	–0.045***	0.0125*	–0.0207***	0.894	–0.1074***
	(0.0076)	(0.0074)	(0.0075)	(0.0069)	(0.0131)
ln | GEND–EGL$_i$ – GEND–EGL$_j$ |	–0.0702***	–0.0587***	–0.0481***	–0.0235***	0.122
	(0.0074)	(0.0072)	(0.0073)	(0.0068)	(0.0129)
ln | HUMANE$_i$ – HUMANE$_j$ |	–0.0125*	0.0344***	0.0177***	0.048***	0.401
	(0.0072)	(0.0066)	(0.0069)	(0.0063)	(0.0119)
ln | PERFORM$_i$ – PERFORM$_j$ |	–0.0346***	0.511	–0.0545***	0.432	–0.1269***
	(0.007)	(0.0069)	(0.0073)	(0.0068)	(0.0129)
ln | POWDIST$_i$ – POWDIST$_j$ |	–0.0294***	–0.0464***	–0.0414***	–0.0276***	–0.0644***
	(0.0073)	(0.0072)	(0.0077)	(0.0068)	(0.0128)
ln | UNC–AVD$_i$ – UNC–AVD$_j$ |	–0.0547***	–0.0374***	–0.0303***	–0.0116*	–0.0982***
	(0.0071)	(0.0068)	(0.0073)	(0.0068)	(0.0125)

Standard errors in parentheses. "***", "**", and "*" denote statistical significance from zero at the 1 percent, 5 percent, and 10 percent levels, respectively.

Table 6.14a Summary of estimated coefficients on cultural distance variables: proxy variables, SITC 1-digit sector-level estimations

	0: Food and Live Animals	*1: Beverages and Tobacco*	*2: Crude Materials, Inedible, Except Fuels*	*3: Mineral Fuels, Lubricants, and Related Materials*	*4: Animal and Vegetables Oils, Fats and Waxes*
ln B-E Linguistic Distance$_{ij}$	−0.2083***	−0.19***	−0.3831***	−0.4684***	−0.6355***
	(0.02)	(0.0309)	(0.0213)	(0.0417)	(0.0371)
ln Dow Language Distance$_{ij}$	−0.074***	−0.0649***	−0.0796***	−0.0647***	−0.0116
	(0.005)	(0.0073)	(0.0054)	(0.0098)	(0.0087)
ln M-T Linguistic Proximity$_{ij}$ (ASJP)	0.0286***	0.1342***	−0.0224**	0.1783***	0.0665***
	(0.0101)	(0.0129)	(0.0105)	(0.0192)	(0.0164)
ln M-T Linguistic Proximity$_{ij}$ (Tree)	−0.0429**	0.0949***	0.0594***	0.2742***	0.1653***
	(0.0177)	(0.0208)	(0.0179)	(0.0312)	(0.0261)
CEPII Common Linguistic Ethnography$_{ij}$	0.7757***	0.758***	0.5364***	0.1058***	0.6307***
	(0.014)	(0.0195)	(0.0147)	(0.0281)	(0.0239)
CEPII Common Official Language$_{ij}$	0.8177***	0.8028***	0.5545***	0.0129	0.5669***
	(0.0141)	(0.0193)	(0.0147)	(0.0285)	(0.024)
M-T Common Native Language$_{ij}$	1.2478***	1.4744***	0.7544***	−0.2383***	1.0318***
	(0.0292)	(0.0366)	(0.0305)	(0.0573)	(0.0483)
M-T Common Official Language$_{ij}$	0.9022***	0.9102***	0.6282***	−0.0129	0.6383***
	(0.0147)	(0.0202)	(0.0155)	(0.0301)	(0.0254)
M-T Common Spoken Language$_{ij}$	1.0889***	1.5160***	0.9618***	0.2008***	0.9948***
	(0.0212)	(0.0274)	(0.0225)	(0.0425)	(0.0361)
ln B-E Religious Distance$_{ij}$	−0.3168***	−0.5036***	−0.3557***	−0.4811***	−0.5539***
	(0.0177)	(0.0255)	(0.02)	(0.039)	(0.0326)
ln Dow Religious Distance$_{ij}$	−0.3632***	−0.5232***	−0.0205	0.2594***	−0.4063***
	(0.0466)	(0.0723)	(0.042)	(0.087)	(0.0748)
ln Fixation Index Genetic Distance (weighted)$_{ij}$	0.0027	−0.1459***	0.0407***	−0.0331***	0.0145
	(0.006)	(0.0084)	(0.0062)	(0.0115)	(0.0104)
ln Nei Standard Genetic Distance (weighted)$_{ij}$	0.008	−0.1402***	0.0469***	−0.0412***	0.0128
	(0.0058)	(0.0081)	(0.0059)	(0.0111)	(0.0099)

Standard errors in parentheses. "***", "**", and "*" denote statistical significance from zero at the 1 percent, 5 percent, and 10 percent levels, respectively.

Table 6.14b Summary of estimated coefficients on cultural distance variables: proxy variables, SITC 1-digit sector-level estimations

	5: Chemicals and Related Products, n.e.s.	*6: Manufactured Goods Classified Chiefly by Material*	*7: Machinery and Transport Equipment*	*8: Miscellaneous Manufactured Articles*	*9: Commodities and Transactions Not Classified Elsewhere*
ln B-E Linguistic Distance$_{ij}$	−0.416***	−0.3217***	−0.5454***	−0.4086***	−0.5188***
	(0.0169)	(0.0163)	(0.0167)	(0.0176)	(0.0385)
ln Dow Language Distance$_{ij}$	−0.135***	−0.0795***	−0.0828***	−0.0547***	−0.0998***
	(0.0051)	(0.0047)	(0.0046)	(0.0043)	(0.0085)
ln M-T Linguistic Proximity$_{ij}$ (ASJP)	0.1539***	0.0451***	0.0222**	−0.0924***	0.0202
	(0.0102)	(0.0094)	(0.0097)	(0.0089)	(0.0146)
ln M-T Linguistic Proximity$_{ij}$ (Tree)	0.2191***	0.1627***	0.18***	0.0048	0.0824***
	(0.018)	(0.017)	(0.017)	(0.0157)	(0.0255)
CEPII Common Linguistic Ethnography$_{ij}$	0.6691***	0.7901***	0.7424***	0.9314***	0.6587***
	(0.0144)	(0.0133)	(0.0129)	(0.0121)	(0.0196)
CEPII Common Official Language$_{ij}$	0.7244***	0.8593***	0.8305***	1.0276***	0.6741***
	(0.0144)	(0.0133)	(0.0129)	(0.0121)	(0.0193)
M-T Common Native Language$_{ij}$	1.2697***	1.4550***	1.2868***	1.7422***	1.0558***
	(0.0279)	(0.0270)	(0.0265)	(0.0251)	(0.0425)
M-T Common Official Language$_{ij}$	0.8476***	0.9678***	0.9136***	1.1198***	0.7463***
	(0.0151)	(0.0140)	(0.0137)	(0.0127)	(0.0206)
M-T Common Spoken Language$_{ij}$	1.3634***	1.3373***	1.336***	1.4154***	1.1392***
	(0.0205)	(0.0194)	(0.0193)	(0.0177)	(0.0317)
ln B-E Religious Distance$_{ij}$	−0.3441***	−0.2176***	−0.3347***	−0.413***	−0.4813***
	(0.0153)	(0.0145)	(0.0151)	(0.0141)	(0.0362)
ln Dow Religious Distance$_{ij}$	−0.4757***	0.0185	−0.551***	−0.582***	−0.141**
	(0.0437)	(0.0403)	(0.0416)	(0.0401)	(0.063)
ln Fixation Index Genetic Distance (weighted)$_{ij}$	−0.1556***	−0.0516***	−0.1358***	−0.1391***	−0.0877***
	(0.0061)	(0.0058)	(0.0053)	(0.0051)	(0.0087)
ln Nei Standard Genetic Distance (weighted)$_{ij}$	−0.1486***	−0.0482***	−0.1214***	−0.1246***	−0.0821***
	(0.0059)	(0.0055)	(0.0051)	(0.0049)	(0.0084)

Standard errors in parentheses. "***", "**", and "*" denote statistical significance from zero at the 1 percent, 5 percent, and 10 percent levels, respectively.

7 The link between cultural distance and foreign direct investment

As is noted in Chapter 5, while there is a considerable literature that seeks to identify the determinants of foreign direct investment, a clear theoretical foundation is lacking. Similarly, there is no consensus on what factors determine the levels of FDI flows and stocks. Several prior researchers have employed the gravity model when examining FDI flows; however, each of these works has its limitations and shortcomings. An alternative approach is followed by Blonigen (2005), Blonigen and Piger (2011), and Eicher et al. (2012), who seek to isolate the determinants of FDI flows and stocks by employing Bayesian Model Averaging (BMA). BMA is used to estimate the probability that each of a series of variables should be included among the set of explanatory variables.

In this chapter, we employ an empirical specification based on the work of Blonigen and Piger (2011), who considered a lengthy list of variables, drawn from the existing empirical literature on FDI flows, for inclusion in the regression model as potential determinants of FDI. As a result, we can assert that the use of BMA leads to the identification of a set of explanatory variables that share two desirable characteristics. First, the variables all have at least an intuitive theoretical justification for their inclusion in the regression model. Second, the variables each have, due to the application of BMA, a statistical justification for their inclusion. Equation 7.1, which is a restatement of equation 5.7, illustrates.

$$\begin{aligned} \ln FDI\,INFLOW_{ijt} = {} & \alpha_0 - \beta_1 lnCD_{ijt} + \beta_2 ln\left(\frac{K}{L}\right)_{jt} - \beta_3 lnCORP\,TAX_{jt} \\ & + \beta_4 lnREM_{jt} + \beta_5 lnHUM\,CAP_{it} + \beta_6 lnY_{jt} \\ & + \beta_7 lnY_{it} + \beta_8 ln\left(\frac{Y}{POP}\right)_{jt} \\ & + \beta_9 ln\left[\left(\frac{Y}{L}\right)_{it} - \left(\frac{Y}{L}\right)_{jt}\right]^2 + \beta_{10} ln\left(\frac{X+M}{Y}\right)_{jt} \\ & + \beta_{11} lnURB\,CON_{jt} + \beta_{12} COLONY_{ij} \\ & + \beta_{13} CUST\,UNION_{ijt} + \beta_{14} RTA_{ijt} + \beta_\Omega \Omega_t \\ & + \beta_\Psi \Psi_i + \beta_\Theta \Theta_j + \varepsilon_{ijt} \end{aligned} \tag{7.1}$$

The dependent variable, $FDI\ INFLOW_{ijt}$, is the net flow of foreign investment from parent country i to host country j during year t. We also employ the FDI stock from country i in country j, $FDI\ STOCK_{ijt}$, as the dependent variable series in equation 7.1 to examine the relationship between cultural differences and FDI stocks.

Blonigen and Piger (2011) identify cultural (dis)similarity as a potential determinant of FDI flows. Accordingly, given the focus of this work, our variables of primary interest are the measure of cultural differences, CD_{ijt}, which are defined in detail in Chapters 4 and 5. The remaining explanatory variables in equation 7.1 include the real GDP values of both the parent country (Y_{jt}) and the host country (Y_{it}) and the parent-host country difference in output per worker, $\left[\left(\frac{Y}{L}\right)_{it} - \left(\frac{Y}{L}\right)_{jt}\right]^2$. The regression model also includes an index of per-person human capital ($HUM\ CAP_{it}$) in the parent country and three dummy variables that indicate whether the parent country and the host country are members of a common regional trade agreement (RTA_{ijt}), whether they have (or had) a colonial relationship ($COLONY_{ij}$), and whether they are members of a common customs union ($CUST\ UNION_{ijt}$). We also include several host country-specific variables in equation 7.1, including the host country capital-labor ratio $\left(\frac{K}{L}\right)_{jt}$, a measure of host country economic remoteness (REM_{jt}), its GDP per capita $\left(\frac{Y}{POP}\right)_{jt}$, a measure of trade openness $\left(\frac{X+M}{Y}\right)_{jt}$, the host country urban concentration rate $URB\ CON_{jt}$, and the country's highest corporate income tax rate, $CORP\ TAX_{jt}$. Finally, as in Chapter 6, the vectors Ω, Ψ, and Φ control for year, parent country, and host country fixed effects respectively.

We begin our analysis by estimating equation 7.1 with FDI inflows employed as the dependent variable series. In the latter portion of this chapter, we detail the findings obtained when we replace our measure of FDI flows between the parent and host countries with a measure of the FDI stock in the host country. Further, we follow the structure of the analysis presented in Chapter 6 by first examining the relationships between our composite measures of cultural distance and the related component dimensions on FDI flows. Subsequent sections detail the results obtained when we employ our series of variables that serve as proxies for cultural differences.

Composite measures of cultural distance, component dimensions, and FDI flows

Table 7.1 presents results obtained when regressing our dependent variable series on the Inglehart measure of cultural distance (column A) and the corresponding component cultural dimensions (column B) along with the set of control variables identified by Blonigen and Piger (2011). As anticipated, the coefficient of the Inglehart cultural distance variable is negative and statistically significant from zero. As the estimation equation has a double-log functional form, we can interpret the coefficient as follows. All else held constant, a one percent increase in the Inglehart cultural distance between the typical parent and host country pair

Table 7.1 Inglehart composite and component measures of cultural distance and FDI inflows

	(a)	*(b)*
ln Inglehart Cultural Distance$_{ijt}$	–0.5514***	
	(0.0575)	
ln | SSE_{it} – SSE_{jt} |		–0.1213***
		(0.0339)
ln | TSR_{it} – TSR_{jt} |		–0.2451***
		(0.0327)
ln Capital-Labor Ratio$_{it}$ (Parent)	1.0389**	0.9744**
	(0.4075)	(0.4072)
ln Corporate Income Tax Rate$_{jt}$ (Host)	–1.7635***	–1.7933***
	(0.2355)	(0.2356)
ln Economic Remoteness$_{jt}$ (Host)	0.0481	–0.0389
	(2.3186)	(2.3269)
ln Index of Per-Person Human Capital$_{it}$ (Parent)	4.1001***	4.0935***
	(1.0282)	(1.0279)
ln Real GDP$_{jt}$ (Host)	–1.8765	–2.2483
	(1.5478)	(1.549)
ln Real GDP$_{it}$ (Parent)	0.8786**	0.9003**
	(0.4087)	(0.4087)
ln Real GDP Per Capita$_{jt}$ (Host)	4.8211***	5.2141***
	(1.2923)	(1.2904)
ln Squared Difference in Output Per Worker$_{ijt}$	0.0557***	0.0357**
	(0.0169)	(0.0167)
ln Trade Openness$_{jt}$ (Host)	–0.4113	–0.3821
	(0.3995)	(0.3991)
ln Urban Concentration Rate$_{jt}$ (Host)	–3.0096*	–2.7813*
	(1.5924)	(1.5992)
Colonial Relationship$_{ijt}$	2.6212***	2.6808***
	(0.145)	(0.1445)
Customs Union$_{ijt}$	0.2556**	0.2994**
	(0.1286)	(0.1289)
Regional Trade Agreement$_{ijt}$	2.3193***	2.348***
	(0.1208)	(0.121)
Constant	–23.6659	–17.5913
	(49.4588)	(49.5953)
N	12,310	12,310
Pseudo R^2	0.6941	0.6937

All estimations include year, parent, and host country fixed effects. Corresponding coefficients not reported due to space limitations. Standard errors in parentheses "***", "**", and "*" denote significance from zero at the 1 percent, 5 percent, and 10 percent levels, respectively.

corresponds with a 0.5514 percent decrease in FDI flows from the parent country to the host country. To provide a contextualized interpretation of the coefficient, if we allow for a one standard deviation change in the level of Inglehart cultural distance (as identified in Table 5.4), all else constant, the predicted level of FDI flows between the parent and host countries would decrease by 49.1 percent.

In column B of Table 7.1, we present the results obtained when the Inglehart measure is replaced by its two component dimensions. In both instances, for the coefficients of the measure that reflects differences along the survival vs. self-expression (SSE) dimension and of the measure that represents differences along the traditional vs. secular-rational (TSR) cultural dimension, the estimated coefficient values are negative and significantly different from zero. Accordingly, we can say that, all else constant, a one percent increase in the extent to which the parent and host countries differ along the SSE cultural dimension corresponds with a 0.1213 percent decrease in FDI flows. Similarly, a like one percent increase in parent-host country differences along the TSR dimension results in a 0.2451 percent decline in FDI flows.

Turning our attention to the coefficients on the remaining (control) variables in Table 7.1, we see that most coefficient estimates are statistically significant. The three exceptions are all related to the host country: specifically, the coefficients of the economic remoteness variable, the real GDP variable, and the trade openness measure are not significant from zero in either column A or column B. All else equal, a higher urban concentration ratio in the host country and higher corporate income tax rates significantly decrease FDI flows from the parent country. To the contrary, a higher level of host country GDP per capita corresponds with higher FDI inflows. A number of parent country attributes are found to result in higher FDI inflows. Specifically, increases in the parent country's real GDP, their capital-labor ratio, and in the per-person human capital index value all correspond with a higher level of FDI flows from the parent country to the host country. Similarly, FDI flows are higher between parent and host country pairs that share a colonial relationship (past or present), that are members of a common customs union, or that are members of a common regional trade agreement. Lastly, a higher value for the squared difference in parent-to-host output per worker is correlated with higher parent-to-host FDI flows.

Further examining the relationship between cultural differences and FDI flows, we replace the Inglehart measure of cultural distance in equation 7.1, in turn, with the 4-factor and 6-factor Hofstede measures of cultural distance. We subsequently employ the Hofstede cultural components in place of the composite Hofstede measures. Results are presented in Table 7.2. Consistent with the coefficient of the Inglehart cultural distance measure presented in Table 7.1, here we see that the estimated coefficients of both the 4-factor Hofstede measure of cultural distance and the 6-factor Hofstede measure are significantly different from zero. More specifically, we can say that, all else held constant, a one percent increase in the 4-factor Hofstede measure of cultural distance between the typical parent and host country pair results in a 0.4591 percent decrease in FDI flows. Similarly, a like one percent increase in the 6-factor Hofstede measure results in a 0.7679

Table 7.2 Hofstede composite and component measures of cultural distance and FDI inflows

	(a)	*(b)*	*(c)*	*(d)*
ln Hofstede 4-factor Cultural Distance$_{ijt}$	–0.4591***			
	(0.0308)			
ln Hofstede 6-factor Cultural Distance$_{ijt}$		–0.7679***		
		(0.0388)		
ln $\| PDI_{it} - PDI_{jt} \|$			0.0042	0.0276
			(0.0289)	(0.0312)
ln $\| IDV_{it} - IDV_{jt} \|$			–0.1404***	–0.1303***
			(0.0272)	(0.0286)
ln $\| MAS_{it} - MAS_{jt} \|$			–0.2796***	–0.2718***
			(0.0276)	(0.0293)
ln $\| UAI_{it} - UAI_{jt} \|$			–0.1479***	–0.1005***
			(0.0251)	(0.0277)
ln $\| PRA_{it} - PRA_{jt} \|$				–0.1941***
				(0.0288)
ln $\| IND_{it} - IND_{jt} \|$				–0.3015***
				(0.0281)
ln Capital-Labor Ratio$_{it}$ (Parent)	0.4454**	0.5404**	0.4551**	0.5427**
	(0.2137)	(0.2253)	(0.214)	(0.2256)
ln Corporate Income Tax Rate$_{jt}$ (Host)	–1.936***	–2.0044***	–1.9371***	–2.0084***
	(0.1713)	(0.1778)	(0.1716)	(0.178)
ln Economic Remoteness$_{jt}$ (Host)	7.9952***	6.7945***	8.4721***	7.7374***
	(1.6224)	(1.6931)	(1.6243)	(1.6969)
ln Index of Per-Person Human Capital$_{it}$ (Parent)	1.4798*	0.7399	1.5901**	1.0286
	(0.797)	(0.8116)	(0.7993)	(0.8123)

(continued)

Table 7.2 (continued)

	(a)	*(b)*	*(c)*	*(d)*
ln Real GDP_{jt} (Host)	0.9	0.0561	1.0958	0.3427
	(1.0727)	(1.1061)	(1.0697)	(1.1037)
ln Real GDP_{it} (Parent)	1.9332***	2.0014***	1.9779***	2.0644***
	(0.2453)	(0.2532)	(0.2457)	(0.2538)
ln Real GDP Per $Capita_{jt}$ (Host)	3.0891***	3.9292***	2.9745***	3.7713***
	(0.9749)	(1.0011)	(0.9699)	(0.9951)
ln Squared Difference in Output Per $Worker_{ijt}$	0.0433***	0.0637***	0.0148	0.0429***
	(0.013)	(0.0131)	(0.0133)	(0.0135)
ln Trade $Openness_{jt}$ (Host)	0.2048	0.0758	0.2953	0.1387
	(0.3012)	(0.3122)	(0.3011)	(0.3122)
ln Urban Concentration $Rate_{jt}$ (Host)	3.6522***	2.7544**	3.8968***	3.007***
	(1.1378)	(1.1582)	(1.1402)	(1.1619)
Colonial $Relationship_{ijt}$	2.91***	2.7727***	2.972***	2.8486***
	(0.12)	(0.121)	(0.1201)	(0.1228)
Customs $Union_{ijt}$	1.126***	1.0677***	1.1126***	1.0322***
	(0.0989)	(0.1009)	(0.0993)	(0.1012)
Regional Trade $Agreement_{ijt}$	2.2633***	2.2037***	2.2555***	2.2309***
	(0.0933)	(0.0971)	(0.0943)	(0.098)
Constant	−198.4043***	−170.3172***	−207.7564***	−185.4529***
	(33.6997)	(35.0289)	(33.6883)	(35.0605)
N	24,447	22,163	24,447	22,163
Pseudo R^2	0.6878	0.6802	0.6874	0.6800

All estimations include year, parent, and host country fixed effects. Corresponding coefficients not reported due to space limitations. Standard errors in parentheses "***", "**", and "*" denote significance from zero at the 1 percent, 5 percent, and 10 percent levels, respectively.

percent decline in FDI from the typical parent country to the typical host country. If we again allow for a one standard deviation change in the respective cultural distance measures (as identified in Table 5.4), all else constant, the corresponding estimated decreases in the levels of FDI flows are 32.1 percent (based on the coefficient of the 4-factor Hofstede measure) and 44.9 percent (based on the 6-factor Hofstede measure).

The coefficients obtained when employing the variables that represent differences between parent and host countries across the Hofstede cultural dimensions are presented in columns C and D of Table 7.2. Consistently, across the two estimations and the individual component dimensions, we find coefficients that are negative and statistically significant from zero. Only in the case of the power distance index (PDI) dimension is the corresponding coefficient not significantly different from zero. Tang (2012) also examines the relationships between Hofstede's component cultural dimensions and FDI flows and finds that differences in terms of the PDI, uncertainty avoidance index (UAI) and masculinity vs. femininity (MAS) dimensions are significantly related to FDI flows.

Our final composite measure of cultural distance is the GLOBE measure. As with the Inglehart measure and the Hofstede measures, we estimate equation 7.1 while using both the composite measure and the corresponding cultural dimensions. Results are presented in Table 7.3. Consistent with results from the initial estimations in this chapter, we again find a negative and statistically significant relationship between the GLOBE cultural distance measure and FDI flows. Specifically, the coefficient indicates that, given a one percent increase in the GLOBE measure, all else constant, the predicted level of FDI flows between the typical parent and host country pair will decrease by -1.1598 percent. For the sake of comparison, we once more estimate the effects on FDI flows of a one standard deviation increase above the mean value for the measure of cultural distance. For the GLOBE measure, the corresponding decrease in the predicted level of FDI flows is 39.5 percent.

In addition to the similarities in coefficient signs and statistical significance across our four composite measures of cultural distance, looking at the component dimensions of the GLOBE measure we generally see negative and statistically significant coefficients. This is consistent with the results reported in Tables 7.1 and 7.2 for the coefficients on the cultural dimensions that are related to the Inglehart and Hofstede composite measures, respectively. Of the nine GLOBE cultural dimensions, six are negative and significant from zero, two are insignificant from zero, and one is both positive and statistically significant from zero. Thus, with respect to both the composite measures of cultural differences and their component dimensions, the results generally suggest a significant negative influence of cross-societal cultural differences on bilateral FDI flows.

While our focus has been on the coefficient estimates for the composite measures of cultural distance and the associated component dimensions, it is important to note that, across estimations involving different cultural distance measures, the signs and statistical significance of the coefficients of the control variables have been quite consistent. Comparing the coefficients of the control variables from

Table 7.3 GLOBE composite and component measures of cultural distance and FDI inflows

	(a)	*(b)*
ln GLOBE Cultural Distance$_{ijt}$	−1.1598***	
	(0.1105)	
ln | $ASSERT_i$ − $ASSERT_j$ |		0.0794**
		(0.0374)
ln | $INST\text{-}COL_i$ − $INST\text{-}COL_j$ |		−0.1285***
		(0.0363)
ln | $INGP\text{-}COL_i$ − $INGP\text{-}COL_j$ |		−0.1568***
		(0.0343)
ln | $FUTURE_i$ − $FUTURE_j$ |		−0.1125***
		(0.0361)
ln | $GEND\text{-}EGL_i$ − $GEND\text{-}EGL_j$ |		−0.1002***
		(0.0353)
ln | $HUMANE_i$ − $HUMANE_j$ |		−0.1451***
		(0.0364)
ln | $PERFORM_i$ − $PERFORM_j$ |		−0.0114
		(0.0341)
ln | $POWDIST_i$ − $POWDIST_j$ |		−0.0438
		(0.0355)
ln | $UNC\text{-}AVD_i$ − $UNC\text{-}AVD_j$ |		−0.1016***
		(0.0348)
ln Capital-Labor Ratio$_{it}$ (Parent)	−0.14	−0.0767
	(0.3111)	(0.2911)
ln Corporate Income Tax Rate$_{jt}$ (Host)	−2.21***	−2.2011***
	(0.1941)	(0.205)
ln Economic Remoteness$_{jt}$ (Host)	9.9004***	10.2712***
	(1.8558)	(1.9891)
ln Index of Per-Person Human Capital$_{it}$ (Parent)	3.8353***	3.6109***
	(0.8815)	(0.9835)
ln Real GDP$_{jt}$ (Host)	3.3261***	2.5191**
	(1.227)	(1.235)
ln Real GDP$_{it}$ (Parent)	2.4072***	2.4667***
	(0.3049)	(0.2768)
ln Real GDP Per Capita$_{jt}$ (Host)	1.4855	2.2618**
	(1.1011)	(1.0772)
ln Squared Difference in Output Per Worker$_{ijt}$	0.0842***	0.0981***
	(0.0155)	(0.0178)
ln Trade Openness$_{jt}$ (Host)	1.128***	0.9869***
	(0.3555)	(0.3523)
ln Urban Concentration Rate$_{jt}$ (Host)	3.5007***	3.6179***
	(1.2158)	(1.3697)
Colonial Relationship$_{ijt}$	2.9051***	2.8105***
	(0.1269)	(0.1504)
Customs Union$_{ijt}$	0.6803***	0.6407***
	(0.1233)	(0.1326)
Regional Trade Agreement$_{ijt}$	2.418***	2.6199***
	(0.1173)	(0.1213)
Constant	−269.7061***	−265.8396***
	(38.5087)	(39.9204)
N	14,688	14,061
Pseudo R^2	0.6872	0.685

All estimations include year, parent, and host country fixed effects. Corresponding coefficients not reported due to space limitations. Standard errors in parentheses "***", "**", and "*" denote significance from zero at the 1 percent, 5 percent, and 10 percent levels, respectively.

the results presented thus far, we find that 56 of the 78 coefficients (71.8 percent) presented in Tables 7.2 and 7.3 collectively have the same sign and statistical significance as are presented in Table 7.1. In fact, the differences are largely clustered around two variables. In Table 7.1 the coefficients of the host country economic remoteness variable are not significantly different from zero. However, in all six later regressions (i.e., those for which results are reported in Tables 7.2 and 7.3), the coefficients are positive and statistically significant. Similarly, the coefficients of the host country urban concentration rate are negative and significant in Table 7.1, but the six coefficients from the later regressions are all positive and significantly different from zero. If the coefficient signs and statistical significance for these two variables were the same across all three tables, then 87.2 percent (68 of the 78 regression coefficients) presented in Tables 7.2 and 7.3 would match, in terms of sign and statistical significance, the values presented in Table 7.1.

FDI flows and variables that act as proxies for cultural differences

Continuing our examination of the relationship between cultural differences and FDI flows, we estimate equation 7.1 while employing our series of variables that serve as proxies for cultural differences. We begin by considering four index measures, two of which represent linguistic similarity and two others that measure language dissimilarity. The results are presented in Table 7.4. Consistent with the general finding from Section 7.1 that cultural distance is negatively related to FDI flows, we find that the two coefficient estimates for the linguistic proximity variables are positive and significant from zero. Also consistent with the results presented so far, the coefficient estimates for the two measures of language distance are negative and significantly different from zero.

In a few words, greater language similarity (a proxy for cultural similarity) corresponds, all else equal, with higher levels of FDI flows, and greater dissimilarity in terms of language (and, hence, culture) is negatively related to the level of FDI flows. Discussed in greater detail, we can say that, given a one percent increase in the ASJP linguistic proximity variable, all else constant, FDI flows between the typical parent country and the typical host country would decrease by 0.5299 percent. A like increase in the Tree linguistic proximity variable is estimated to result in a 0.5933 percent decrease in bilateral FDI flows. A one percent increase in the B-E language distance variable is estimated to correlate with FDI flows that are 1.473 percent lower, and the same increase in the Dow linguistic distance variables would cause FDI flows to fall by 0.26 percent.

As an alternative to indexes of linguistic proximity and language distance, in Table 7.5 we present results obtained when employing five dummy variables, separately, to represent commonality of language. The measures are similar in that they each represent commonality of language usage, official languages, native languages, etc. Each measure is, however, distinct. The estimated coefficients indicate that FDI flows between parent and host countries are positively affected by common language usage. For example, if the parent and host country share

Table 7.4 Index measures of linguistic differences and similarities and FDI inflows

	(a)	*(b)*	*(c)*	*(d)*
ln Adj. Value of Linguistic Proximity$_{ij}$ (ASJP)	0.5299***			
	(0.0509)			
ln Adj. Value of Linguistic Proximity$_{ij}$ (Tree)		0.5933***		
		(0.0799)		
ln B-E Linguistic Distance$_{ijt}$			−1.473***	
			(0.0685)	
ln Dow Linguistic Distance$_{ijt}$				−0.26***
				(0.0256)
ln Capital-Labor Ratio$_{it}$ (Parent)	0.2209	0.8306**	0.5068	0.1702
	(0.2086)	(0.3597)	(0.6343)	(0.2001)
ln Corporate Income Tax Rate$_{jt}$ (Host)	−1.9686***	−2.162***	−2.5622***	−1.9491***
	(0.1793)	(0.2166)	(0.2231)	(0.2176)
ln Economic Remoteness$_{jt}$ (Host)	30.0537***	33.2188***	24.8546***	4.7027***
	(2.4002)	(3.1358)	(3.2769)	(1.8349)
ln Index of Per-Person Human Capital$_{it}$ (Parent)	0.8398	0.1639	1.2507	1.0745
	(0.8243)	(0.9537)	(1.0339)	(0.9137)
ln Real GDP$_{jt}$ (Host)	8.0044***	8.4711***	3.5063*	1.0737
	(1.2432)	(1.6418)	(1.9755)	(1.2453)
ln Real GDP$_{it}$ (Parent)	1.0775***	1.0476***	4.8074***	1.4403***
	(0.2284)	(0.3217)	(0.6331)	(0.2224)
ln Real GDP Per Capita$_{jt}$ (Host)	−4.4357***	−5.7114***	1.565	2.1619*
	(1.1482)	(1.5138)	(2.1611)	(1.1309)
ln Squared Difference in Output Per Worker$_{ijt}$	0.0087	0.0221	0.0123	0.0583***

	(0.0131)	(0.0168)	(0.0223)	(0.0145)
ln Trade Openness$_{jt}$ (Host)	−0.7039**	−1.7644***	−3.3596***	0.1437
	(0.3301)	(0.4451)	(0.627)	(0.3279)
ln Urban Concentration Rate$_{jt}$ (Host)	0.3249	−2.8001*	−8.995***	4.291***
	(1.2033)	(1.4745)	(1.6597)	(1.3441)
Colonial Relationship$_{ijt}$	2.3084***	1.829***	1.7674***	2.4056***
	(0.1481)	(0.1918)	(0.1881)	(0.1995)
Customs Union$_{ijt}$	1.4328***	1.5177***	0.673***	1.2772***
	(0.1058)	(0.1269)	(0.1687)	(0.1095)
Regional Trade Agreement$_{ijt}$	1.6028***	1.4415***	2.7831***	1.748***
	(0.1)	(0.1255)	(0.206)	(0.1092)
Constant	−476.205***	−494.1064***	−413.1817***	−155.3222***
	(42.1164)	(55.5234)	(61.2874)	(38.1069)
N	22,126	13,120	5,493	20,206
Pseudo R^2	0.6992	0.7203	0.6606	0.6752

All estimations include year, parent, and host country fixed effects. Corresponding coefficients not reported due to space limitations. Standard errors in parentheses "***", "**", and "*" denote significance from zero at the 1 percent, 5 percent, and 10 percent levels, respectively.

Table 7.5 Dichotomous measures of language commonality and FDI inflows

	(a)	*(b)*	*(c)*	*(d)*	*(e)*
CEPII Common Language used by $\geq$ 9% of Populations$_{ij}$	2.1964***				
	(0.0947)				
CEPII Common Official or Primary Language$_{ij}$		2.0022***			
		(0.1035)			
M-T Common Native Language$_{ij}$			4.8819***		
			(0.1839)		
M-T Common Official Language$_{ij}$				2.5738***	
				(0.118)	
M-T Common Spoken Language$_{ij}$					4.5571***
					(0.1454)
ln Capital-Labor Ratio$_{it}$ (Parent)	0.2666	0.275	0.3289*	0.2711	0.2909*
	(0.1679)	(0.168)	(0.1695)	(0.1696)	(0.1685)
ln Corporate Income Tax Rate$_{jt}$ (Host)	−1.8834***	−1.8879***	−1.8651***	−1.818***	−1.9596***
	(0.1617)	(0.1619)	(0.1671)	(0.1674)	(0.166)
ln Economic Remoteness$_{jt}$ (Host)	6.5692***	6.6397***	7.4624***	7.1192***	8.5432***
	(1.4882)	(1.4901)	(1.5422)	(1.5453)	(1.5404)
ln Index of Per-Person Human Capital$_{it}$ (Parent)	0.8181	0.7768	1.2378*	1.3444*	1.7096**
	(0.7355)	(0.7376)	(0.746)	(0.7468)	(0.7464)
ln Real GDP$_{jt}$ (Host)	−0.0841	−0.1892	0.84	0.1574	0.7683
	(0.9883)	(0.9915)	(1.0297)	(1.0302)	(1.0322)
ln Real GDP$_{it}$ (Parent)	1.2501***	1.2697***	1.1625***	1.1978***	1.1936***
	(0.1887)	(0.1888)	(0.1904)	(0.191)	(0.1891)

ln Real GDP Per Capita$_{jt}$ (Host)	3.5598***	3.661***	2.7747***	3.3002***	2.9444***
	(0.8974)	(0.9041)	(0.9212)	(0.9242)	(0.9248)
ln Squared Difference in Output Per Worker$_{ijt}$	0.0014	0.0112	0.0187	0.0183	0.099***
	(0.012)	(0.0121)	(0.0125)	(0.0125)	(0.0127)
ln Trade Openness$_{jt}$ (Host)	0.309	0.2926	0.3401	0.4035	0.0563
	(0.2768)	(0.2779)	(0.2802)	(0.2806)	(0.2805)
ln Urban Concentration Rate$_{jt}$ (Host)	5.1208***	5.0765***	4.8305***	4.9461***	4.1255***
	(1.0878)	(1.0861)	(1.0964)	(1.0976)	(1.1012)
Colonial Relationship$_{ijt}$	2.1875***	2.1933***	2.2014***	1.8967***	2.0342***
	(0.119)	(0.1214)	(0.1251)	(0.1277)	(0.1186)
Customs Union$_{ijt}$	1.2203***	1.242***	1.451***	1.4158***	1.284***
	(0.0966)	(0.097)	(0.1007)	(0.1006)	(0.0996)
Regional Trade Agreement$_{ijt}$	1.8759***	1.9834***	1.8911***	1.8688***	1.762***
	(0.0899)	(0.0895)	(0.0889)	(0.0909)	(0.0895)
Constant	−153.5088***	−152.6686***	−176.7142***	−161.9559***	−184.625***
	(30.7)	(30.7162)	(32.1052)	(32.1123)	(32.1098)
N	29,086	29,086	27,389	27,389	27,389
Pseudo R^2	0.7022	0.7004	0.6996	0.6978	0.7031

All estimations include year, parent, and host country fixed effects. Corresponding coefficients not reported due to space limitations. Standard errors in parentheses "***", "**", and "*" denote significance from zero at the 1 percent, 5 percent, and 10 percent levels, respectively.

speak the same language, all else the same, FDI flows are estimated to be 4.55 times higher than if they do not share a language. The coefficient of the M-T common native language variable is similar in magnitude, while the three other common language dummy variables have coefficient estimates that are lower and that, as a result, appear more reasonable from an intuitive perspective.

Religion is a potential marker of cultural similarity between societies. Two societies that share a common religion or that adhere to the same dominant religion are likely more culturally similar than are two societies that adhere to different religious beliefs. Similar to language, which acts as a representation of culture and a means by which culture can be transmitted, to the extent that religious views align with or influence broader attitudes, norms, expectations, and mores, it can be viewed as a vessel that allows culture to be communicated across peoples and time periods. Accordingly, we employ two measures of religious distance between parent and host countries as a potential proxy variable for cultural differences. Results obtained from these estimations are presented in Table 7.6.

In both instances, when the B-E measure of religious distance is used and when the Dow measure is employed, the resulting coefficient estimates are negative and statistically significant from zero. The corresponding interpretations are that, all else constant, a one percent increase in the B-E measure of religious distance results in a 1.1833 percent decrease in FDI flows between the typical parent country and the typical host country. Additionally, a like increase in the Dow measure of religious distance corresponds with a 1.8424 percent decrease in the level of bilateral FDI flows.

Our final proxy variable is the genetic distance between populations (i.e., countries). As explained in greater detail in Chapters 5 and 6, genetic distance serves as a proxy for cultural distance based on the notion that genetic differences (i.e., observed heterozygosity) between societies is the result of interaction between the populations. We employ two measures of genetic distance: the fixation index measure of cultural distance and the Nei measure. Estimating equation 7.1 with each of the two genetic distance measures substituting as the cultural distance measure results in the coefficient estimates presented in Table 7.7. The coefficient estimates of the fixation index measure and the Nei measure are negative

Table 7.6 Indexes of religious differences and FDI inflows

	(a)	*(b)*
ln B-E Religious Distance$_{ijt}$	−1.1833***	
	(0.0711)	
ln Dow Religious Distance$_{ijt}$		−1.8424***
		(0.3779)
ln Capital-Labor Ratio$_{it}$ (Parent)	0.1365	0.4053
	(0.6282)	(0.2599)
ln Corporate Income Tax Rate$_{jt}$ (Host)	−2.5849***	−1.0367***
	(0.2073)	(0.3374)
ln Economic Remoteness$_{jt}$ (Host)	23.0958***	1.5546
	(3.0993)	(3.2407)

ln Index of Per-Person Human Capital$_{it}$ (Parent)	2.162**	4.5124***
	(0.9605)	(1.6655)
ln Real GDP$_{jt}$ (Host)	3.3534*	−1.877
	(1.819)	(1.925)
ln Real GDP$_{it}$ (Parent)	4.8588***	2.7616***
	(0.5959)	(0.3586)
ln Real GDP Per Capita$_{jt}$ (Host)	1.3906	5.2141***
	(1.9596)	(1.7266)
ln Squared Difference in Output Per Worker$_{ijt}$	0.0214	−0.0146
	(0.0199)	(0.0311)
ln Trade Openness$_{jt}$ (Host)	−2.5216***	0.9337*
	(0.5437)	(0.531)
ln Urban Concentration Rate$_{jt}$ (Host)	−7.7638***	6.6983***
	(1.4056)	(2.2717)
Colonial Relationship$_{ijt}$	1.7227***	2.572***
	(0.1376)	(0.3837)
Customs Union$_{ijt}$	0.4429***	2.2018***
	(0.1564)	(0.3171)
Regional Trade Agreement$_{ijt}$	3.0067***	1.1291***
	(0.1881)	(0.2009)
Constant	−395.8287***	−130.366**
	(57.5299)	(63.7981)
N	6,237	7,616
Pseudo R^2	0.6631	0.6189

All estimations include year, parent, and host country fixed effects. Corresponding coefficients not reported due to space limitations. Standard errors in parentheses "***", "**", and "*" denote significance from zero at the 1 percent, 5 percent, and 10 percent levels, respectively.

Table 7.7 Genetic distance and FDI inflows

	(a)	*(b)*
ln Fixation Index Genetic Distance (weighted)$_{ij}$	−0.197***	
	(0.0317)	
ln Nei Standard Genetic Distance (weighted)$_{ij}$		−0.1659***
		(0.0302)
ln Capital-Labor Ratio$_{it}$ (Parent)	0.325*	0.3238*
	(0.1693)	(0.1693)
ln Corporate Income Tax Rate$_{jt}$ (Host)	−1.8825***	−1.8785***
	(0.1641)	(0.1641)
ln Economic Remoteness$_{jt}$ (Host)	7.9368***	7.8938***
	(1.5191)	(1.5189)
ln Index of Per-Person Human Capital$_{it}$ (Parent)	1.3772*	1.3724*
	(0.7572)	(0.7573)
ln Real GDP$_{jt}$ (Host)	−0.0275	−0.0251
	(1.0176)	(1.0173)
ln Real GDP$_{it}$ (Parent)	1.2102***	1.2105***
	(0.19)	(0.1901)

(continued)

Table 7.7 (continued)

	(a)	*(b)*
ln Real GDP Per Capita$_{jt}$ (Host)	3.8482***	3.8366***
	(0.9276)	(0.9272)
ln Squared Difference in Output Per Worker$_{ijt}$	0.0037	0.0024
	(0.0124)	(0.0124)
ln Trade Openness$_{jt}$ (Host)	0.3268	0.3315
	(0.2832)	(0.2831)
ln Urban Concentration Rate$_{jt}$ (Host)	5.0634***	5.0623***
	(1.0923)	(1.0923)
Colonial Relationship$_{ijt}$	3.1572***	3.1585***
	(0.117)	(0.117)
Customs Union$_{ijt}$	1.1717***	1.1774***
	(0.0979)	(0.0979)
Regional Trade Agreement$_{ijt}$	2.095***	2.1077***
	(0.0929)	(0.093)
Constant	−169.1144***	−169.1174***
	(31.4652)	(31.4603)
N	28,837	28,837
Pseudo R^2	0.6955	0.6954

All estimations include year, parent, and host country fixed effects. Corresponding coefficients not reported due to space limitations. Standard errors in parentheses "***", "**", and "*" denote significance from zero at the 1 percent, 5 percent, and 10 percent levels, respectively.

and statistically significant from zero. More specifically, allowing for coefficient interpretation, a one percent increase in the fixation index measure of genetic distance, all else held constant, reduces FDI flows between the typical pair of parent and host countries by 0.197 percent. A similar increase in the Nei measure results in a 0.1659 percent decrease in bilateral FDI flows.

FDI stocks, FDI flows and stocks relative to GDP, and cultural distance

The results presented in Tables 7.1 through 7.7 are consistent with the notion that greater cross-societal cultural differences correspond with reduced bilateral FDI flows. This finding supports the premise that cultural differences increase the costs associated with international economic activity and, hence, lead to reductions in such activities. Extending from the documented negative influence of cultural distance on the levels of parent country-to-host country FDI flows, as a form of robustness check, in this section we replicate the analysis presented thus far in this chapter with the sole difference being that we employ a different dependent variable series. Rather than examining the determinants of bilateral FDI flows, we instead examine the determinants of parent countries' FDI stocks in the corresponding host countries.

Table 7.8 Summary of coefficients, cultural distance measures and FDI stocks

Cultural Distance Measure	*Coefficient (Std. Error)*	*Consistent with Expectations (Sign and Significance)?*
ln Inglehart Cultural Distance$_{ijt}$	−0.4423*** (0.0571)	Yes
ln | $SSE_{it} - SSE_{jt}$ |	−0.0606** (0.0308)	Yes
ln | $TSR_{it} - TSR_{jt}$ |	−0.1671*** (0.0317)	Yes
ln Hofstede 4-factor Cultural Distance$_{ijt}$	−0.4653*** (0.0308)	Yes
ln | $PDI_{it} - PDI_{jt}$ |	−0.1249*** (0.0292)	Yes
ln | $IDV_{it} - IDV_{jt}$ |	−0.0179 (0.0261)	Yes (sign); No (significance)
ln | $MAS_{it} - MAS_{jt}$ |	−0.243*** (0.0279)	Yes
ln | $UAI_{it} - UAI_{jt}$ |	−0.1797*** (0.0246)	Yes
ln Hofstede 6-factor Cultural Distance$_{ijt}$	−0.7993*** (0.037)	Yes
ln | $PDI_{it} - PDI_{jt}$ |	−0.1153*** (0.0308)	Yes
ln | $IDV_{it} - IDV_{jt}$ |	−0.018 (0.0271)	Yes (sign); No (significance)
ln | $MAS_{it} - MAS_{jt}$ |	−0.2314*** (0.0296)	Yes
ln | $UAI_{it} - UAI_{jt}$ |	−0.1015*** (0.0269)	Yes
ln | $PRA_{it} - PRA_{jt}$ |	−0.1516*** (0.0266)	Yes
ln | $IND_{it} - IND_{jt}$ |	−0.3601*** (0.0266)	Yes
ln GLOBE Cultural Distance$_{ijt}$	−1.0547*** (0.0953)	Yes
ln | $ASSERT_{i} - ASSERT_{j}$ |	0.1088*** (0.033)	No
ln | $INST\text{-}COL_{i} - INST\text{-}COL_{j}$ |	−0.1333*** (0.0331)	Yes
ln | $INGP\text{-}COL_{i} - INGP\text{-}COL_{j}$ |	−0.0617** (0.0311)	Yes

(continued)

Table 7.8 (continued)

Cultural Distance Measure	*Coefficient (Std. Error)*	*Consistent with Expectations (Sign and Significance)?*
ln | $FUTURE_i$ – $FUTURE_j$ |	−0.1922*** (0.0323)	Yes
ln | $GEND\text{-}EGL_i$ – $GEND\text{-}EGL_j$ |	−0.1544*** (0.0322)	Yes
ln | $HUMANE_i$ – $HUMANE_j$ |	−0.0269 (0.032)	Yes (sign); No (significance)
ln | $PERFORM_i$ – $PERFORM_j$ |	0.0007 (0.0304)	No
ln | $POWDIST_i$ – $POWDIST_j$ |	0.0314 (0.0318)	No
ln | $UNC\text{-}AVD_i$ – $UNC\text{-}AVD_j$ |	−0.2096*** (0.0308)	Yes
ln Adj. Value of Linguistic Proximity_{ij} (ASJP)	0.6326*** (0.0469)	Yes
ln Adj. Value of Linguistic Proximity_{ij} (Tree)	0.5618*** (0.0693)	Yes
ln B-E Linguistic Distance_{ijt}	−1.2607*** (0.055)	Yes
ln Dow Linguistic Distance_{ijt}	−0.4113*** (0.0244)	Yes
CEPII Common Language used by ≥ 9% of Populations_{ij}	1.9803*** (0.0912)	Yes
CEPII Common Official or Primary Language_{ij}	1.8611*** (0.0948)	Yes
M&T Common Native Language_{ij}	4.8817*** (0.1877)	Yes
M&T Common Official Language_{ij}	2.2071*** (0.1097)	Yes
M&T Common Spoken Language_{ij}	4.9889*** (0.1622)	Yes
ln B-E Religious Distance_{ijt}	−1.1772*** (0.0652)	Yes
ln Dow Religious Distance_{ijt}	−1.2971*** (0.3635)	Yes
ln Fixation Index Genetic Distance $(\text{weighted})_{ij}$	−0.1293*** (0.03)	Yes
ln Nei Standard Genetic Distance $(\text{weighted})_{ij}$	−0.1039***	Yes

Complete regression results from which the coefficients presented here have been culled are presented in the chapter appendix. "***", "**", and "*" denote significance from zero at the 1 percent, 5 percent, and 10 percent levels, respectively.

The results obtained from the estimation of equation 7.1 when using FDI stocks as the dependent variable measure are reported in the chapter appendix. A summary of the coefficients of the composite cultural distance measures, the corresponding component dimensions of culture, and the variables that are employed as proxies for cultural differences is presented in Table 7.8. Beginning with the coefficients of our four composite measures of cultural distance, in each instance we see that the estimated coefficient is negative and statistically significant from zero. While it is interesting to interpret the proportional influence of a change in each measure, since the measures are scaled without respect to any common metric or to each other, comparing coefficient values across the four estimations is of limited practical use.

As an alternative, as we have done in Chapter 6 and earlier in this chapter when considering the effects of changes in the composite cultural distance measures, we calculate the predicted decrease in FDI stocks given a one standard deviation increase above the mean value for each of the composite cultural distance measures. The calculations indicate that a one standard deviation increase in the Inglehart measure of cultural distance would correspond with a 22.3 percent decrease in the predicted FDI stock value. An increase of one standard deviation in the 4-factor Hofstede cultural distance measure would be expected to lower the typical host country's FDI stock value by 32.3 percent, and a similar increase in the 6-factor Hofstede measure would result in a 47 percent decline in the FDI stock value. Lastly, again given a one standard deviation increase, this time in the GLOBE measure of cultural distance, we anticipate the FDI stock value to be 35.9 percent lower.

Looking to the coefficient estimates of the component dimensions of our composite cultural distance measures, we find a general pattern of negative and statistically significant values. In nearly three quarters of the cases (71.4 percent), we see that the coefficient estimates are consistent with our expectations. It should be noted as well that three of the six coefficients that do not entirely conform to expectations are negative (i.e., of the expected sign) but lack statistical significance. The other three coefficients are positive in sign; however, only in one case is the coefficient also significant from zero.

The remaining coefficient estimates reported in Table 7.8 correspond to our set of variables that serve as proxies for cultural differences. In all 13 cases, the coefficient estimates are of the anticipated sign and are statistically significant from zero. Thus, we can say that, with respect to the relationship between cultural differences and FDI stock values, the results are overwhelmingly supportive of the notion that cultural differences hinder foreign direct investment. Setting aside the coefficient estimates for the component dimensions of cultural distance, we see that in 17 of 17 instances the estimated coefficients in Table 7.8 are consistent with expectations both in terms of sign and statistical significance. As FDI flow values are more volatile than stock values due, possibly, to random variation across time, the results presented in Table 7.8 are arguably more indicative of a significant influence of cultural dissimilarity on bilateral FDI. Speaking more generally, if we revisit Tables 7.1 through 7.7, focusing only on the coefficients of the cultural distance measures and again excluding those for the component dimensions of the composite measures, we see again that all 17 coefficient estimates are of the anticipated sign and are statistically significant from zero.

An additional series of estimations, undertaken as a robustness check of sorts, involves yet more changes in the dependent variable series. We first repeat our series of estimations in which we employ our four composite cultural distance measures, the related component dimensions of culture, and the set of variables that serve as proxies for cultural differences; however, we now use parent-to-host country FDI flows as a share of host country GDP as the dependent variable series. A second set of alternative estimations follows this same basic framework with the exception that we employ parent country FDI stocks in the host country as a share of the host country's GDP as the dependent variable series. Results are presented in Table 7.9.

Summarizing the coefficients from this set of alternative estimations, while again focusing on whether the coefficients are consistent with expectations in terms of sign and statistical significance, we find some support for the general negative relationship of cultural differences to FDI when viewing the results of the estimations that employ FDI flows as a share of GDP as the dependent variable series. Much to the contrary, we find abundant support for our anticipated general relationship when we look to the results of estimations where FDI stocks as a share of GDP is the dependent variable series. More specifically, only 20 of the 38 estimated coefficients (52.6 percent) from the series of estimations that employ the level of FDI flows as a share of GDP as the dependent variable are both of the expected sign and statistically significant from zero. A much higher percentage (84.2 percent) of the coefficient estimates obtained from regressing the FDI stock level as a share of GDP on our measures of cultural distance and additional control variables are consistent with our expectations and the general findings presented in this chapter.

Summarizing our results

Extending from the examination of cultural distance and international trade flows that is presented as Chapter 6, here we have examined the potential relationship between cross-societal cultural differences and foreign direct investment. Again, our data includes a group of culturally and economically heterogeneous countries. Our empirical framework is motivated by the results of Blonigen and Piger's (2011) application of BMA to a set of potential determinants of FDI flows. Our findings extend the related literature, offering new information that may be of value to members of the general public and that may be of value to policy makers.

Our results appear robust to our choice of cultural distance measure. Further, they appear to be robust to changes in the dependent variable series, notably to the choice of FDI flows or FDI stocks both in levels and as a proportion of the host country's GDP level. We conclude that greater cultural dissimilarities do, indeed, correspond with reduced levels of bilateral FDI flows and stocks.

Appendix: results from ancillary estimations

In this appendix we present the complete set of regression results from our estimations that employ parent country FDI stocks in the host country. A summary of the estimated coefficients of the cultural distance measures employed in these estimations is provided in the chapter as Table 7.8 and is discussed in Section 7.3.

Table 7.9 Summary of coefficients on cultural distance measures, alternative estimations

Dependent Variable: Cultural Distance Measure	*ln FDI Flow$_{ijt}$/ GDP$_{jt}$*		*ln FDI Stock$_{ijt}$/ GDP$_{jt}$*	
	Coefficient (Std. Error)	*Consistent with Expectations?*	*Coefficient (Std. Error)*	*Consistent with Expectations?*
ln Inglehart Cultural Distance$_{ijt}$	−0.0015** (0.0008)	Yes	−0.0036*** (0.0004)	Yes
ln $\mid SSE_{it} - SSE_{jt} \mid$	−0.0004* (0.0002)	Yes	−0.0016*** (0.0002)	Yes
ln $\mid TSR_{it} - TSR_{jt} \mid$	−0.0004* (0.0002)	Yes	−0.0006*** (0.0002)	Yes
ln Hofstede 4-factor Cultural Distance$_{ij}$	−0.0001 (0.0001)	Yes (sign); No (significance)	−0.0035*** (0.0002)	Yes
ln $\mid PDI_{it} - PDI_{jt} \mid$	−0.0015*** (0.0005)	Yes	−0.0009*** (0.0002)	Yes
ln $\mid IDV_{it} - IDV_{jt} \mid$	0.0008*** (0.0003)	No	−0.0009*** (0.0002)	Yes
ln $\mid MAS_{it} - MAS_{jt} \mid$	0.0004** (0.0002)	No	−0.0005*** (0.0001)	Yes
ln $\mid UAI_{it} - UAI_{jt} \mid$	0.0004*** (0.0002)	No	−0.0011*** (0.0001)	Yes
ln Hofstede 6-factor Cultural Distance$_{ij}$	−0.0003** (0.0001)	Yes	−0.0051*** (0.0003)	Yes

(continued)

Table 7.9 (continued)

Dependent Variable: Cultural Distance Measure	*ln FDI Flow$_{ijt}$/ GDP$_{jt}$*		*ln FDI Stock$_{ijt}$/ GDP$_{jt}$*	
	Coefficient (Std. Error)	*Consistent with Expectations?*	*Coefficient (Std. Error)*	*Consistent with Expectations?*
ln $\vert PDI_{it} - PDI_{jt} \vert$	−0.0018*** (0.0006)	Yes	−0.0006*** (0.0002)	Yes
ln $\vert IDV_{it} - IDV_{jt} \vert$	0.0009*** (0.0003)	No	−0.0008*** (0.0002)	Yes
ln $\vert MAS_{it} - MAS_{jt} \vert$	0.0004** (0.0002)	No	−0.0006*** (0.0002)	Yes
ln $\vert UAI_{it} - UAI_{jt} \vert$	0.0006*** (0.0002)	No	−0.001*** (0.0001)	Yes
ln $\vert PRA_{it} - PRA_{jt} \vert$	−0.0004** (0.0002)	Yes	−0.0006*** (0.0001)	Yes
ln $\vert IND_{it} - IND_{jt} \vert$	0.0003* (0.0002)	No	−0.0017*** (0.0002)	Yes
ln GLOBE Cultural Distance$_{ijt}$	−0.6944*** (0.0605)	Yes	−1.0547*** (0.0953)	Yes
ln $\vert ASSERT_i - ASSERT_j \vert$	0.0470** (0.0214)	No	0.1088*** (0.0315)	No
ln $\vert INST\text{-}COL_i - INST\text{-}COL_j \vert$	−0.0379* (0.0196)	Yes	−0.1333*** (0.0324)	Yes
ln $\vert INGP\text{-}COL_i - INGP\text{-}COL_j \vert$	−0.0387** (0.0186)	Yes	−0.0617** (0.0301)	Yes
ln $\vert FUTURE_i - FUTURE_j \vert$	−0.0627*** (0.0213)	Yes	−0.1922*** (0.0311)	Yes
ln $\vert GEND\text{-}EGL_i - GEND\text{-}EGL_j \vert$	−0.0334* (0.0200)	Yes	−0.1544*** (0.0328)	Yes

ln | $HUMANE_i$ – $HUMANE_j$ |	–0.1533***	Yes	–0.0269	Yes (sign); No (significance)
	(0.0204)		(0.0301)	
ln | $PERFORM_i$ – $PERFORM_j$ |	0.0258	No	0.0007	No
	(0.0184)		(0.0303)	
ln | $POWDIST_i$ – $POWDIST_j$ |	–0.0689***	Yes	0.0314	No
	(0.0193)		(0.0322)	
ln | $UNC\text{-}AVD_i$ – $UNC\text{-}AVD_j$ |	–0.1641***	Yes	–0.2096***	Yes
	(0.0192)		(0.0300)	
ln B-E Linguistic $Distance_{ijt}$	–0.0006***	Yes	–0.0078***	Yes
	(0.0002)		(0.0006)	
ln Dow Linguistic $Distance_{ijt}$	–0.0001***	Yes	–0.0005***	Yes
	(0.00004)		(0.0001)	
ln M-T Linguistic $Proximity_{ij}$ (ASJP)	0.0001	Yes (sign); No (significance)	–0.0001	No
	(0.0001)		(0.0003)	
ln M-T Linguistic $Proximity_{ij}$ (Tree)	0.0002	Yes (sign); No (significance)	–0.001**	No
	(0.0002)		(0.0004)	
ln B-E Religious $Distance_{ijt}$	0.001	No	–0.0051***	Yes
	(0.0009)		(0.0009)	
ln Dow Religious $Distance_{ijt}$	–0.00003	Yes (sign); No (significance)	–0.0012***	Yes
	(0.0001)		(0.0004)	

(continued)

Table 7.9 (continued)

Dependent Variable: Cultural Distance Measure	*ln FDI Flow$_{ijt}$/ GDP$_{jt}$*		*ln FDI Stock$_{ijt}$/ GDP$_{jt}$*	
	Coefficient (Std. Error)	*Consistent with Expectations?*	*Coefficient (Std. Error)*	*Consistent with Expectations?*
CEPII Common Language used by ≥ 9% of Populations$_{ij}$	–0.0011** (0.0005)	No	0.0042*** (0.0006)	Yes
CEPII Common Official or Primary Language$_{ij}$	0.0004 (0.0011)	Yes (sign); No (significance)	0.0118*** (0.0012)	Yes
M-T Common Native Language$_{ij}$	0.0004 (0.0003)	Yes (sign); No (significance)	0.0175*** (0.0015)	Yes
M-T Common Official Language$_{ij}$	0.0002 (0.0002)	Yes (sign); No (significance)	0.0065*** (0.0006)	Yes
M-T Common Spoken Language$_{ij}$	0.0004*** (0.0002)	Yes	0.0114*** (0.0009)	Yes
ln Fixation Index Genetic Distance (weighted)$_{ij}$	–0.0008*** (0.0002)	Yes	–0.0023*** (0.0002)	Yes
ln Nei Standard Genetic Distance (weighted)$_{ij}$	–0.0007*** (0.0001)	Yes	–0.0022*** (0.0002)	Yes

"***", "**", and "*" denote significance from zero at the 1 percent, 5 percent, and 10 percent levels, respectively.

Table 7.10 Inglehart composite and component measures of cultural distance and FDI stocks

	(a)	*(b)*
ln Inglehart Cultural Distance$_{ijt}$	−0.4423***	
	(0.0571)	
ln | SSE$_{it}$ − SSE$_{jt}$ |		−0.0606**
		(0.0308)
ln | TSR$_{it}$ − TSR$_{jt}$ |		−0.1671***
		(0.0317)
ln Capital-Labor Ratio$_{it}$ (Parent)	1.7699***	1.6819***
	(0.4207)	(0.4209)
ln Corporate Income Tax Rate$_{jt}$ (Host)	0.4098*	0.3844*
	(0.2155)	(0.2159)
ln Economic Remoteness$_{jt}$ (Host)	1.5607	1.6356
	(2.779)	(2.7902)
ln Index of Per-Person Human Capital$_{it}$ (Parent)	4.0109***	4.175***
	(0.9748)	(0.9788)
ln Real GDP$_{jt}$ (Host)	−0.2162	−0.4816
	(1.8462)	(1.8522)
ln Real GDP$_{it}$ (Parent)	−0.0482	0.0075
	(0.4433)	(0.4443)
ln Real GDP Per Capita$_{jt}$ (Host)	3.5157**	3.8207***
	(1.4568)	(1.4599)
ln Squared Difference in Output Per Worker$_{ijt}$	0.0769***	0.0515***
	(0.0168)	(0.0168)
ln Trade Openness$_{jt}$ (Host)	−0.3097	−0.2891
	(0.3541)	(0.3552)
ln Urban Concentration Rate$_{jt}$ (Host)	11.97***	12.2888***
	(1.4813)	(1.4869)
Colonial Relationship$_{ijt}$	2.7385***	2.7919***
	(0.1301)	(0.1292)
Customs Union$_{ijt}$	0.0413	0.0766
	(0.1184)	(0.1186)
Regional Trade Agreement$_{ijt}$	2.4582***	2.4896***
	(0.119)	(0.1191)
Constant	−131.7511**	−129.9747**
	(60.0193)	(60.2589)
N	12,809	12,809
Pseudo R^2	0.7573	0.7568

All estimations include year, parent, and host country fixed effects. Corresponding coefficients not reported due to space limitations. Standard errors in parentheses "***", "**", and "*" denote significance from zero at the 1 percent, 5 percent, and 10 percent levels, respectively.

Table 7.11 Hofstede composite and component measures of cultural distance and FDI stocks

	(a)	*(b)*	*(c)*	*(d)*
ln Hofstede 4-factor Cultural Distance$_{ijt}$	−0.4653***			
	(0.0308)			
ln Hofstede 6-factor Cultural Distance$_{ijt}$		−0.7993***		
		(0.037)		
ln $\mid PDI_{it} - PDI_{jt} \mid$			−0.1249***	−0.1153***
			(0.0292)	(0.0308)
ln $\mid IDV_{it} - IDV_{jt} \mid$			−0.0179	−0.018
			(0.0261)	(0.0271)
ln $\mid MAS_{it} - MAS_{jt} \mid$			−0.243***	−0.2314***
			(0.0279)	(0.0296)
ln $\mid UAI_{it} - UAI_{jt} \mid$			−0.1797***	−0.1015***
			(0.0246)	(0.0269)
ln $\mid PRA_{it} - PRA_{jt} \mid$				−0.1516***
				(0.0266)
ln $\mid IND_{it} - IND_{jt} \mid$				−0.3601***
				(0.0266)
ln Capital-Labor Ratio$_{it}$ (Parent)	1.3266***	1.363***	1.325***	1.3285***
	(0.2294)	(0.2404)	(0.2287)	(0.239)
ln Corporate Income Tax Rate$_{jt}$ (Host)	0.9703***	0.9553***	0.9799***	0.9594***
	(0.1574)	(0.1613)	(0.1574)	(0.161)
ln Economic Remoteness$_{jt}$ (Host)	3.6095**	3.8773**	4.0649**	4.4812***
	(1.6466)	(1.7405)	(1.6522)	(1.7473)
ln Index of Per-Person Human Capital$_{it}$ (Parent)	0.349	−0.9798	0.5359	−0.7649
	(0.8094)	(0.8206)	(0.8056)	(0.8152)

ln Real GDP$_{jt}$ (Host)	−3.423***	−3.5402***	−3.457***	−3.3483***
	(1.0886)	(1.1409)	(1.0912)	(1.1439)
ln Real GDP$_{it}$ (Parent)	0.2867	0.4534*	0.3306	0.547**
	(0.259)	(0.2661)	(0.2591)	(0.2656)
ln Real GDP Per Capita$_{jt}$ (Host)	6.5753***	6.8934***	6.7246***	6.947***
	(1.001)	(1.0373)	(1.0032)	(1.0397)
ln Squared Difference in Output Per Worker$_{ijt}$	0.0708***	0.0861***	0.0453***	0.0738***
	(0.0124)	(0.0126)	(0.0126)	(0.0128)
ln Trade Openness$_{jt}$ (Host)	0.7872***	0.6872**	0.808***	0.6866**
	(0.2687)	(0.276)	(0.2692)	(0.2768)
ln Urban Concentration Rate$_{jt}$ (Host)	14.7276***	13.1501***	15.0903***	13.5873***
	(1.1475)	(1.1657)	(1.1517)	(1.171)
Colonial Relationship$_{ijt}$	3.2573***	3.0308***	3.3297***	3.125***
	(0.1097)	(0.1114)	(0.1099)	(0.1127)
Customs Union$_{ijt}$	1.1913***	1.1305***	1.1751***	1.1065***
	(0.0925)	(0.0939)	(0.0928)	(0.0937)
Regional Trade Agreement$_{ijt}$	2.3832***	2.326***	2.4239***	2.4187***
	(0.0911)	(0.0957)	(0.0921)	(0.0965)
Constant	−112.0686***	−109.9032***	−118.1114***	−122.4993***
	(33.3655)	(35.2974)	(33.4377)	(35.3865)
N	25,867	23,271	25,867	23,271
Pseudo R^2	0.7603	0.7523	0.7600	0.7523

All estimations include year, parent, and host country fixed effects. Corresponding coefficients not reported due to space limitations. Standard errors in parentheses "***", "**", and "*" denote significance from zero at the 1 percent, 5 percent, and 10 percent levels, respectively.

Table 7.12 GLOBE composite and component measures of cultural distance and FDI stocks

	(a)	*(b)*
ln GLOBE Cultural Distance$_{ijt}$	−1.0547*** (0.0953)	
ln | ASSERT$_i$ − ASSERT$_j$ |		0.1088*** (0.033)
ln | INST-COL$_i$ − INST-COL$_j$ |		−0.1333*** (0.0331)
ln | INGP-COL$_i$ − INGP-COL$_j$ |		−0.0617** (0.0311)
ln | FUTURE$_i$ − FUTURE$_j$ |		−0.1922*** (0.0323)
ln | GEND-EGL$_i$ − GEND-EGL$_j$ |		−0.1544*** (0.0322)
ln | HUMANE$_i$ − HUMANE$_j$ |		−0.0269 (0.032)
ln | PERFORM$_i$ − PERFORM$_j$ |		0.0007 (0.0304)
ln | POWDIST$_i$ − POWDIST$_j$ |		0.0314 (0.0318)
ln | UNC-AVD$_i$ − UNC-AVD$_j$ |		−0.2096*** (0.0308)
ln Capital-Labor Ratio$_{it}$ (Parent)	0.9605*** (0.3016)	1.0193*** (0.2743)
ln Corporate Income Tax Rate$_{jt}$ (Host)	0.9166*** (0.1663)	1.0067*** (0.1999)
ln Economic Remoteness$_{jt}$ (Host)	22.7468*** (2.2094)	22.4307*** (2.2801)
ln Index of Per-Person Human Capital$_{it}$ (Parent)	2.4271*** (0.8524)	2.4125** (0.9516)
ln Real GDP$_{jt}$ (Host)	10.4066*** (1.4922)	9.2806*** (1.4983)
ln Real GDP$_{it}$ (Parent)	0.6887** (0.3122)	0.7888*** (0.2532)
ln Real GDP Per Capita$_{jt}$ (Host)	−2.0513* (1.2271)	−1.3581 (1.2121)
ln Squared Difference in Output Per Worker$_{ijt}$	0.1214*** (0.0146)	0.1656*** (0.0165)
ln Trade Openness$_{jt}$ (Host)	1.6032*** (0.3058)	1.5784*** (0.3072)
ln Urban Concentration Rate$_{jt}$ (Host)	10.0963*** (1.1928)	10.1494*** (1.397)
Colonial Relationship$_{ijt}$	2.8476*** (0.1171)	2.6067*** (0.1388)
Customs Union$_{ijt}$	0.5704*** (0.1117)	0.5494*** (0.1233)
Regional Trade Agreement$_{ijt}$	2.6759*** (0.1119)	2.8954*** (0.1126)
Constant	−558.3895*** (47.6904)	−540.6097*** (48.1009)
N	15,311	14,678
Pseudo R^2	0.7614	0.7580

All estimations include year, parent, and host country fixed effects. Corresponding coefficients not reported due to space limitations. Standard errors in parentheses "***", "**", and "*" denote significance from zero at the 1 percent, 5 percent, and 10 percent levels, respectively.

Table 7.13 Index measures of linguistic differences and similarities and FDI stocks

	(a)	*(b)*	*(c)*	*(d)*
ln Adj. Value of Linguistic Proximity$_{ij}$ (ASJP)	0.6326***			
	(0.0469)			
ln Adj. Value of Linguistic Proximity$_{ij}$ (Tree)		0.5618***		
		(0.0693)		
ln B-E Linguistic Distance$_{ijt}$			−1.2607***	
			(0.055)	
ln Dow Linguistic Distance$_{ijt}$				−0.4113***
				(0.0244)
ln Capital-Labor Ratio$_{it}$ (Parent)	0.8706***	1.7071***	0.9312*	0.6277***
	(0.2302)	(0.3863)	(0.5323)	(0.2152)
ln Corporate Income Tax Rate$_{jt}$ (Host)	0.6963***	0.3835**	0.1948	0.9338***
	(0.167)	(0.1954)	(0.155)	(0.2086)
ln Economic Remoteness$_{jt}$ (Host)	34.0078***	26.2896***	6.3041*	4.9163***
	(2.3634)	(3.0919)	(3.3424)	(1.8262)
ln Index of Per-Person Human Capital$_{it}$ (Parent)	−0.5675	0.0558	0.9946	−3.776***
	(0.8106)	(0.901)	(0.6966)	(1.0217)
ln Real GDP$_{jt}$ (Host)	9.6025***	6.1857***	−6.2072***	−0.8208
	(1.3777)	(1.8522)	(2.0802)	(1.2471)
ln Real GDP$_{it}$ (Parent)	0.167	−0.1189	3.0621***	0.2745
	(0.2386)	(0.3347)	(0.5116)	(0.2418)
ln Real GDP Per Capita$_{jt}$ (Host)	−4.9307***	−2.6958	7.0466***	4.3959***
	(1.2091)	(1.6488)	(1.8025)	(1.1626)

(continued)

Table 7.13 (continued)

	(a)	*(b)*	*(c)*	*(d)*
ln Squared Difference in Output Per Worker$_{ijt}$	0.0485***	0.0128	−0.044***	0.126***
	(0.0124)	(0.0159)	(0.0154)	(0.014)
ln Trade Openness$_{jt}$ (Host)	0.1184	−0.0352	−0.7134	0.6761**
	(0.288)	(0.4008)	(0.457)	(0.3026)
ln Urban Concentration Rate$_{jt}$ (Host)	12.4676***	10.4607***	5.8812***	14.1984***
	(1.1912)	(1.4763)	(1.6442)	(1.3584)
Colonial Relationship$_{ijt}$	3.0058***	2.1971***	1.5184***	3.2951***
	(0.1416)	(0.1712)	(0.1331)	(0.1969)
Customs Union$_{ijt}$	1.5151***	1.5147***	0.7012***	1.1549***
	(0.0979)	(0.1156)	(0.1265)	(0.1025)
Regional Trade Agreement$_{ijt}$	1.9934***	1.8642***	2.8732***	1.9779***
	(0.0969)	(0.1218)	(0.1707)	(0.1093)
Constant	−603.29***	−457.1854***	−78.4438	−157.4452***
	(45.1587)	(59.4244)	(69.3086)	(37.5182)
N	23,767	14,305	5,960	20,896
Pseudo R^2	0.7658	0.7802	0.7112	0.7501

All estimations include year, parent, and host country fixed effects. Corresponding coefficients not reported due to space limitations. Standard errors in parentheses "***", "**", and "*" denote significance from zero at the 1 percent, 5 percent, and 10 percent levels, respectively.

Table 7.14 Dichotomous measures of language commonality and FDI stocks

	(a)	*(b)*	*(c)*	*(d)*	*(e)*
CEPII Common Language used by ≥ 9% of Populations$_{ij}$	1.9803***				
	(0.0912)				
CEPII Common Official or Primary Language$_{ij}$		1.8611***			
		(0.0948)			
M&T Common Native Language$_{ij}$			4.8817***		
			(0.1877)		
M&T Common Official Language$_{ij}$				2.2071***	
				(0.1097)	
M&T Common Spoken Language$_{ij}$					4.9889***
					(0.1622)
ln Capital-Labor Ratio$_{it}$ (Parent)	1.1111***	1.0966***	1.0916***	1.0662***	1.0797***
	(0.1806)	(0.1809)	(0.1865)	(0.1856)	(0.185)
ln Corporate Income Tax Rate$_{jt}$ (Host)	0.784***	0.7847***	1.0583***	1.0169***	0.9637***
	(0.1537)	(0.1548)	(0.158)	(0.1593)	(0.156)
ln Economic Remoteness$_{jt}$ (Host)	3.902***	3.9681***	13.0731***	13.6348***	13.8513***
	(1.4733)	(1.4695)	(1.7402)	(1.7421)	(1.7321)
ln Index of Per-Person Human Capital$_{it}$ (Parent)	−1.4639*	−1.5767**	−1.2479	−1.0894	−0.9419
	(0.7513)	(0.7504)	(0.7646)	(0.7621)	(0.7602)
ln Real GDP$_{jt}$ (Host)	−3.1645***	−3.2567***	3.8202***	3.8102***	4.473***
	(0.983)	(0.9772)	(1.1944)	(1.1992)	(1.1856)
ln Real GDP$_{it}$ (Parent)	−0.042	−0.0132	0.2166	0.2569	0.2137
	(0.1968)	(0.1972)	(0.2051)	(0.2051)	(0.2025)
ln Real GDP Per Capita$_{jt}$ (Host)	6.2087***	6.3248***	1.6488	1.7846*	1.2527
	(0.9173)	(0.917)	(1.0154)	(1.0238)	(1.0116)

(continued)

Table 7.14 (continued)

	(a)	*(b)*	*(c)*	*(d)*	*(e)*
ln Squared Difference in Output Per Worker$_{ijt}$	0.0272**	0.0365***	0.0649***	0.0607***	0.1487***
	(0.0116)	(0.0116)	(0.0119)	(0.0119)	(0.0123)
ln Trade Openness$_{jt}$ (Host)	0.508**	0.5253**	1.2102***	1.2395***	1.0658***
	(0.253)	(0.2532)	(0.2616)	(0.263)	(0.2609)
ln Urban Concentration Rate$_{jt}$ (Host)	16.4072***	16.4498***	16.212***	16.279***	16.6122***
	(1.1057)	(1.1038)	(1.1018)	(1.1027)	(1.1163)
Colonial Relationship$_{ijt}$	2.7526***	2.7193***	2.8259***	2.5831***	2.6023***
	(0.1129)	(0.1149)	(0.1195)	(0.1249)	(0.113)
Customs Union$_{ijt}$	1.2819***	1.3116***	1.4806***	1.3811***	1.3117***
	(0.0913)	(0.0915)	(0.0948)	(0.0945)	(0.0928)
Regional Trade Agreement$_{ijt}$	1.9608***	2.0276***	2.0595***	2.0447***	1.9632***
	(0.0886)	(0.0882)	(0.0884)	(0.0908)	(0.089)
Constant	−112.719***	−112.7433***	−347.0359***	−354.3923***	−370.6487***
	(29.7458)	(29.5541)	(37.5381)	(37.5829)	(37.1999)
N	30,930	30,930	28,878	28,878	28,878
Pseudo R^2	0.7716	0.7708	0.7666	0.7648	0.7704

All estimations include year, parent, and host country fixed effects. Corresponding coefficients not reported due to space limitations. Standard errors in parentheses "***", "**", and "*" denote significance from zero at the 1 percent, 5 percent, and 10 percent levels, respectively.

Table 7.15 Indexes of religious differences and FDI stocks

	(a)	*(b)*
ln B-E Religious Distance$_{ijt}$	−1.1772***	
	(0.0652)	
ln Dow Religious Distance$_{ijt}$		−1.2971***
		(0.3635)
ln Capital-Labor Ratio$_{it}$ (Parent)	0.5855	1.092***
	(0.505)	(0.2646)
ln Corporate Income Tax Rate$_{jt}$ (Host)	0.1359	1.1981***
	(0.1386)	(0.3368)
ln Economic Remoteness$_{jt}$ (Host)	6.5981**	10.4942***
	(3.1521)	(3.0679)
ln Index of Per-Person Human Capital$_{it}$ (Parent)	1.8388***	−1.1791
	(0.6407)	(1.7019)
ln Real GDP$_{jt}$ (Host)	−6.3556***	0.0412
	(1.9179)	(1.9259)
ln Real GDP$_{it}$ (Parent)	2.9033***	1.8651***
	(0.4906)	(0.3476)
ln Real GDP Per Capita$_{jt}$ (Host)	7.9603***	5.9972***
	(1.5796)	(1.8992)
ln Squared Difference in Output Per Worker$_{ijt}$	−0.0281**	0.0922***
	(0.0135)	(0.031)
ln Trade Openness$_{jt}$ (Host)	−0.5193	1.0253**
	(0.4099)	(0.5037)
ln Urban Concentration Rate$_{jt}$ (Host)	5.5285***	21.0386***
	(1.5577)	(2.2007)
Colonial Relationship$_{ijt}$	1.7537***	3.6673***
	(0.0947)	(0.2848)
Customs Union$_{ijt}$	0.551***	2.7605***
	(0.1172)	(0.3267)
Regional Trade Agreement$_{ijt}$	3.0955***	1.9928***
	(0.1662)	(0.1919)
Constant	−76.5372	−327.2455***
	(64.823)	(59.4326)
N	6,758	7,933
Pseudo R^2	0.7192	0.7391

All estimations include year, parent, and host country fixed effects. Corresponding coefficients not reported due to space limitations. Standard errors in parentheses "***", "**", and "*" denote significance from zero at the 1 percent, 5 percent, and 10 percent levels, respectively.

Table 7.16 Genetic distance and FDI stocks

	(a)	*(b)*
ln Fixation Index Genetic Distance (weighted)$_{ij}$	−0.1293***	
	(0.03)	
ln Nei Standard Genetic Distance (weighted)$_{ij}$		−0.1039***
		(0.0287)
ln Capital-Labor Ratio$_{it}$ (Parent)	1.1461***	1.1437***
	(0.182)	(0.182)
ln Corporate Income Tax Rate$_{jt}$ (Host)	0.8152***	0.8184***
	(0.155)	(0.1549)
ln Economic Remoteness$_{jt}$ (Host)	4.0797***	4.057***
	(1.4952)	(1.4952)
ln Index of Per-Person Human Capital$_{it}$ (Parent)	−0.1928	−0.1876
	(0.7664)	(0.7665)
ln Real GDP$_{jt}$ (Host)	−3.3487***	−3.3475***
	(1.0004)	(1.0004)
ln Real GDP$_{it}$ (Parent)	−0.0832	−0.0814
	(0.1985)	(0.1986)
ln Real GDP Per Capita$_{jt}$ (Host)	6.5234***	6.5211***
	(0.9375)	(0.9374)
ln Squared Difference in Output Per Worker$_{ijt}$	0.0228*	0.0218*
	(0.0119)	(0.0119)
ln Trade Openness$_{jt}$ (Host)	0.5307**	0.5322**
	(0.2571)	(0.2571)
ln Urban Concentration Rate$_{jt}$ (Host)	16.6069***	16.6027***
	(1.1112)	(1.1107)
Colonial Relationship$_{ijt}$	3.615***	3.617***
	(0.1111)	(0.1111)
Customs Union$_{ijt}$	1.292***	1.2955***
	(0.0921)	(0.0922)
Regional Trade Agreement$_{ijt}$	2.1879***	2.1991***
	(0.0921)	(0.0922)
Constant	−113.0349***	−113.1546***
	(30.1741)	(30.1778)
N	30,677	30,677
Pseudo R^2	0.7674	0.7673

All estimations include year, parent, and host country fixed effects. Corresponding coefficients not reported due to space limitations. Standard errors in parentheses "***", "**", and "*" denote significance from zero at the 1 percent, 5 percent, and 10 percent levels, respectively.

8 Origin-destination cultural distance and international migration

While there is a considerable literature that examines the determinants of international migration, it is only recently that researchers have begun to consider the cultural differences between immigrants' source and destination countries as a possible determinant of international migration flows.[1] Because migration policy has been, and remains, a prominent and often contentious social and political issue in many countries, the lack of focus on the potential influence of cultural differences on international migration flows is somewhat surprising. In 2010, more than three percent of the world's population (about 215 million individuals) lived outside of their country of birth (UN, 2012). This emphasizes the importance of a more complete understanding of the factors that determine immigrant inflows and, thus, immigrant stocks. Also, in a great many instances, considerable differences exist between the cultures of migrants' source and destination countries. For example, two thirds or more of all international migrants originate in the global South; however, the majority of all migrants reside in the North (IOM, 2013).

In this chapter, we extend the related literature by following the leads of Lewer and van den Berg (2008) and Cuaresma et al. (2013) by applying the gravity model to examine the potential effect of cultural distance on international migration flows. We employ a number of composite measures of cultural distance, and their related composite cultural dimensions, as well as several variables that serve as proxies for cultural differences. We complete the analysis by applying the zero-inflated negative binomial (ZINB) regression technique when estimating our baseline regression model and its variants. The ZINB technique generates two separate models and then combines them. First, a logit model is estimated for the "certain zero" cases. Then, a negative binomial model is estimated to predict the counts for those observations that are not certain zeroes. Our choice of the ZINB technique is based on two factors. First, our dependent variable, the annual immigrant inflow, is count data and, second, the results of Vuong and Zip tests indicate that the ZINB technique is the appropriate estimation technique. More specifically, for all estimations, the Vuong test indicates that the ZINB technique is preferable to the ordinary negative binomial technique, and the Zip test statistics indicate the appropriateness of the ZINB technique rather than the zero-inflated Poisson technique.

We have posited in earlier chapters that cross-societal cultural differences, to the extent that they exist and are not easily overcome, represent a cost that is potentially quite large but, as noted, has largely not been accounted for in prior empirical studies of the determinants of international migration. In this chapter, we examine whether greater cultural differences (i.e., cultural distance) between immigrants' source and destination countries have a significant effect on bilateral immigrant inflows. Moreover, by incorporating cultural distance as a potential determinant of immigrant inflow levels, we are able to determine if international migration is influenced by source-destination country differences in religion, gender roles, political views, social norms, etc.

A few recent studies have considered the influence of diasporas on bilateral migration flows. Beine et al. (2011), for example, examine migration from 195 source countries to 30 OECD member nations during the years 1990 and 2000. The authors find that diasporas lower migration costs and, thus, increase migration while lowering the skill/human capital composition of immigrant inflows. Beine et al. (2010) report similar findings, but also examine the concentration of immigrant stocks and find that larger diasporas increase the concentration of unskilled immigrants relative to skilled immigrants. Beine and Salomone (2013) stress the influence of networks (i.e., existing immigrant stocks or diasporas) as a key determinant of bilateral migration flows, noting that existing immigrant stocks explain a large share of the observed variation in stocks.

Although limited attention has been paid by prior researchers to the potential influence of cultural differences on bilateral migration, Belot and Ederveen (2012), Sprenger (2013), and Caragliu et al. (2013) are noteworthy exceptions. Collectively, these studies employ multiple measures of cultural distance (e.g., linguistic distance, religious distance, institutional distance, Hofstede's cultural dimensions, a measure based on World Values Surveys data, etc.). Belot and Ederveen (2012) examine flows between 22 OECD member countries during the period from 1990 through 2003 and report that cultural differences correspond with lower migration flows. Additionally, the measures of cultural distance the authors employ (i.e., religious distance, linguistic distance, and survey-based measures of cultural distance) are found to do a better job of explaining migration than several more traditional economic variables such as average incomes and unemployment rates.

Caragliu et al. (2013) include measures of source-destination country differences in values and institutions in an effort to represent different dimensions of cultural differences. Employing a gravity model to examine data for the years 2002–2007, the authors report negative relationships between migration flows and measures of trust and both financial and institutional distances between source countries and EU member destination countries. They also find that their results are sensitive to the distance indicator used. Finally, Sprenger (2013) considers migration between 21 members of the EU and the OECD during the years 2000–2009. While a positive relationship is found between common language and migration flows, the author reports that cultural proximity appears unrelated to migration flows. Thus, the disparities in findings between Belot and Ederveen (2012), Caragliu et al. (2013), and Sprenger (2013) suggest that the relationship between cultural difference and international migration remains an open empirical question.

Migration and the composite and component measures of cultural distance

As indicated, we employ the zero-inflated negative binomial (ZINB) technique when estimating equation 5.6 and its variants to examine the potential influences of cultural differences on international migration. Equation 5.6 is reproduced below as equation 8.1.

$$\begin{aligned} IMMIG_{ijt} &= \alpha_0 - \beta_1 lnCD_{ijt} + \beta_2 lnSTOCK_{ijt-1} + \beta_3 \ln(POP_{it} \times POP_{jt}) \\ &- \beta_4 lnGDIST_{ij} + \beta_5 ln\frac{RGDPC_{it}}{RGDPC_{jt}} + \beta_6 UNEMP\,RATE_{it} \\ &- \beta_7 UNEMP\,RATE_{jt} + \beta_8 COLONY_{ij} + \beta_9 CONTIG_{ij} \\ &+ \beta_\Omega \Omega_t + \beta_\Psi \Psi_i + \beta_\Theta \Theta_j + \varepsilon_{ijt} \end{aligned} \qquad (8.1)$$

The dependent variable, $IMMIG_{ijt}$, is the flow of immigrants from source country i to destination country j during year t. CD_{ijt} is a vector comprised of composite measures of cross-societal cultural differences, related component dimensions, and a number of other variables that serve as proxies for cultural distance. The existing immigrant stock from country i in country j during the prior year is identified by the $STOCK_{ijt-1}$ variable. The product of source and destination countries' populations, POP_{it} x POP_{jt}, is a measure of the countries' combined population mass. The measure of the source-destination geodesic distance, $GDIST_{ij}$, controls for direct costs of migrating from the source country to the destination country. The ratio of destination-to-source real GDP per capita values, $RGDPC_{it}/RGDPC_{jt}$, serves to capture economic motivations for migration. To further control for economic motivations, we include the unemployment rates in the source country, $UNEMP\ RATE_{it}$, and the destination country, $UNEMP\ RATE_{jt}$. The regression model also includes a pair of dummy variables. To control for the influences of source-destination colonial links, we have added the $COLONY_{ij}$ variable to equation 8.1, and the $CONTIG_{ij}$ variable is included to identify country pairs that share a border. The vectors Ω, Ψ, and Φ control for year, destination country, and source country fixed effects, respectively.

We begin by estimating equation 8.1 without controlling for either time (i.e., year) fixed effects, source country fixed effects, or destination country fixed effects (column A). We then augment the regression model to include time fixed effects terms (column B). We see that the estimated negative binomial coefficient of the Inglehart measure of cultural distance ranges from -0.0408 to -0.0361 and that both coefficients are significantly different from zero. Exponentiation of the coefficients produces the corresponding changes in the dependent variable series which are equal to 0.96 and 0.965 respectively. More precisely, all else constant, a one percent increase in the Inglehart cultural distance measure is estimated to decrease the rate for the immigrant inflow variable by a factor of approximately 0.96. Neither of the logit coefficients for the Inglehart cultural distance measure, reported in columns A and B of Table 8.1, are significantly different from zero.

All other negative binomial coefficients presented in Table 8.1 are of the anticipated signs and all are significantly different from zero with the exceptions of the coefficients for the common border variable, which, while statistically significant,

Table 8.1 Inglehart composite measure of cultural distance, without/with time fixed effects

	Neg. Bin.	*Logit*	*Neg. Bin.*	*Logit*
	(a)		*(b)*	
ln Inglehart Cultural Distance$_{ijt}$	−0.0408**	−0.0235	−0.0361**	−0.0226
	(0.0177)	(0.0672)	(0.0172)	(0.0671)
ln Geodesic Distance$_{ij}$	−0.3928***	−0.3254***	−0.3739***	−0.3198***
	(0.0122)	(0.0516)	(0.0122)	(0.0513)
ln Immigrant Stock$_{ijt-1}$	0.6826***	−0.4275***	0.6889***	−0.4268***
	(0.0056)	(0.0227)	(0.0057)	(0.0226)
ln (Population$_{it}$ x Population$_{jt}$)	0.2368***	0.3589***	0.2223***	0.3548***
	(0.0062)	(0.0273)	(0.0064)	(0.0271)
ln Relative GDP per capita$_{ijt}$	0.0148**	−0.2703***	0.0232***	−0.2672***
	(0.0072)	(0.0277)	(0.0071)	(0.0275)
Unemployment Rate$_{jt}$ (Destination)	−0.0149***	−0.0175	−0.0057**	−0.0172
	(0.0025)	(0.0107)	(0.0026)	(0.0106)
Unemployment Rate$_{it}$ (Source)	0.0116***	0.0162**	0.0105***	0.0155**
	(0.0019)	(0.0071)	(0.0019)	(0.0071)
Colony$_{ij}$	0.5353***	0.3024*	0.5042***	0.2997*
	(0.04)	(0.1796)	(0.0395)	(0.1795)
Common Border$_{ij}$	−0.3017***	0.6532***	−0.2932***	0.6589***
	(0.0447)	(0.1607)	(0.0439)	(0.1605)
Constant	−4.2747***	−7.9823***	−4.6165***	−7.8884***
	(0.1628)	(0.7008)	(0.5978)	(0.6964)
ln alpha	−0.387***		−0.4239***	
	(0.0151)		(0.015)	
alpha	0.6791		0.6545	
	(0.0102)		(0.0098)	
Time Fixed Effects?	No		Yes	
Source Country Fixed Effects?	No		No	
Destination Country Fixed Effects?	No		No	
Vuong test (ZINB vs. NB)	22.40***		23.28***	
LR test of alpha = 0 (ZINB vs. ZIP)	1.8E+07***		1.7E+07***	
N	8,993		8,993	
Immigrant flow > 0	8,090		8,090	
LR χ^2	16,168***		16,502***	
Log-likelihood	−63,124		−62,956	

Standard errors in parentheses. "***", "**", and "*" denote significance from zero at the 1 percent, 5 percent, and 10 percent levels, respectively.

has signs that are contrary to our expectations. We see that larger existing immigrant stocks (i.e., higher lagged immigrant stock values) correspond with larger immigrant inflows in the present period. Likewise, there tends to be more migration between source and destination country pairs that have larger populations than between pairs with smaller populations. Higher destination-to-source GDP per capita ratios also correlate with larger immigrant inflows, as does a higher unemployment rate in the source country. Also, a current or prior colonial relationship between the source and destination countries corresponds with a higher immigrant inflow. Greater geodesic distance between the source and destination countries is negatively related with immigrant inflows, as is a higher destination country unemployment rate and, as previously mentioned, contrary to expectations, the sharing of a geographic border.

As noted, the logit coefficients reported in Table 8.1 for the Inglehart measure of source-destination cultural distance indicate no significant relationship with immigrant inflows. However, larger existing immigrant stocks in a given destination country, higher relative destination-to-source GDP per capita values, and greater geodesic distance between source and destination countries are all significant determinants of whether immigrants from a typical source country migrate to a given destination country. For example, all else equal, an increase of one percent in the existing immigrant stock decreases the odds that no immigrants will migrate from the corresponding source country to the destination country by a factor of 0.6521. To the contrary, source and destination countries with larger populations, a higher unemployment rate in the source country, a colonial link (past or present) between the source country and the destination country, and a shared geographic border are estimated to have increased odds that the immigrant inflow value will be equal to zero. These results are somewhat contrary to expectations and may be due to the lack of controls for source country and destination country fixed effects in these initial estimations.

Before presenting results that are obtained when we augment our regression model with a complete set of fixed effects terms, we discuss the negative binomial and logit coefficients from the estimation of equation 8.1, when the remaining composite measures of cultural distance are substituted, in turn, for the composite Inglehart measure. The results obtained when the 4-factor and 6-factor Hofstede measures of cultural distance are used in place of the Inglehart measure are presented in Tables 8.2 and 8.3 respectively. Results obtained when the Inglehart measure is replaced by the GLOBE measure of cultural distance are presented in Table 8.4.

In Tables 8.2 and 8.3, where the two composite Hofstede measures of cultural distance are considered, we see results that are quite similar to those presented in Table 8.1. Exclusive of the coefficients of the cultural distance variables, 31 of the 32 negative binomial coefficients in the two tables (96.9 percent) are of the same sign and statistical significance as the corresponding coefficients reported in Table 8.1. Similarly, 27 of the 32 logit coefficients (84.4 percent) are of the same significance and sign as those presented in Table 8.1. While the data samples differ in terms of the countries included and, of course, the cultural distance measure employed, the results remain largely consistent.

Table 8.2 Hofstede 4-factor composite measure of cultural distance, without/with time fixed effects

	Neg. Bin.	*Logit*	*Neg. Bin.*	*Logit*
	(a)		*(b)*	
ln Hofstede 4-factor Cultural Distance$_{ij}$	−0.1361***	−0.0023	−0.1338***	−0.0005
	(0.008)	(0.0314)	(0.0078)	(0.0313)
ln Geodesic Distance$_{ij}$	−0.3994***	−0.1565***	−0.3842***	−0.1463***
	(0.0087)	(0.0339)	(0.0086)	(0.0335)
ln Immigrant Stock$_{ijt-1}$	0.7166***	−0.2883***	0.7133***	−0.2893***
	(0.0039)	(0.0156)	(0.0039)	(0.0155)
ln (Population$_{it}$ x Population$_{jt}$)	0.2166***	0.2092***	0.2054***	0.2016***
	(0.0042)	(0.0179)	(0.0042)	(0.0177)
ln Relative GDP per capita$_{ijt}$	0.0208***	−0.2262***	0.023***	−0.2221***
	(0.0046)	(0.0186)	(0.0046)	(0.0183)
Unemployment Rate$_{jt}$ (Destination)	−0.0208***	0.0406***	−0.012***	0.0408***
	(0.0019)	(0.0067)	(0.002)	(0.0066)
Unemployment Rate$_{it}$ (Source)	0.0026*	0.0095*	0.0043***	0.0089
	(0.0014)	(0.0056)	(0.0014)	(0.0055)
Colony$_{ij}$	0.6196***	0.3465***	0.5753***	0.3425***
	(0.0314)	(0.1233)	(0.031)	(0.1232)
Common Border$_{ij}$	−0.3944***	0.5039***	−0.3736***	0.5207***
	(0.035)	(0.1217)	(0.0343)	(0.1215)
Constant	−3.6785***	−5.783***	−2.9156***	−5.5979***
	(0.1141)	(0.4852)	(0.3955)	(0.4808)
ln alpha	−0.2904***		−0.3301***	
	(0.0105)		(0.0104)	
alpha	0.748		0.7188	
	(0.0078)		(0.0075)	
Time Fixed Effects?	No		Yes	
Source Country Fixed Effects?	No		No	
Destination Country Fixed Effects?	No		No	
Vuong test (ZINB vs. NB)	30.15***		29.52***	
LR test of alpha = 0 (ZINB vs. ZIP)	2.8E+07***		2.7E+07***	
N	19,914		19,914	
Immigrant flow > 0	17,639		17,639	
LR χ^2	35,677***		36,366***	
Log-likelihood	−126,740		−126,395	

Standard errors in parentheses. "***", "**", and "*" denote significance from zero at the 1 percent, 5 percent, and 10 percent levels, respectively.

Looking to the coefficients on the Hofstede measures, we see that the negative binomial coefficients are negative and significantly different from zero for both the 4-factor and the 6-factor measures. More specifically, we can say that, all

Table 8.3 Hofstede 6-factor composite measure of cultural distance, without/with time fixed effects

	Neg. Bin.	*Logit*	*Neg. Bin.*	*Logit*
	(a)		*(b)*	
ln Hofstede 6-factor Cultural Distance$_{ij}$	−0.0894***	0.0247	−0.0905***	0.0237
	(0.0102)	(0.0413)	(0.01)	(0.0412)
ln Geodesic Distance$_{ij}$	−0.4082***	−0.1269***	−0.3933***	−0.1208***
	(0.0089)	(0.0361)	(0.0088)	(0.0358)
ln Immigrant Stock$_{ijt-1}$	0.7095***	−0.2817***	0.7057***	−0.2828***
	(0.0041)	(0.0172)	(0.0042)	(0.0171)
ln (Population$_{it}$ x Population$_{jt}$)	0.2195***	0.204***	0.2091***	0.1991***
	(0.0043)	(0.0194)	(0.0044)	(0.0192)
ln Relative GDP per capita$_{ijt}$	0.0099*	−0.2396***	0.0112**	−0.2361***
	(0.0053)	(0.0215)	(0.0053)	(0.0214)
Unemployment Rate$_{jt}$ (Destination)	−0.0233***	0.0538***	−0.0141***	0.0539***
	(0.002)	(0.007)	(0.0021)	(0.007)
Unemployment Rate$_{it}$ (Source)	0.0058***	0.0127**	0.0081***	0.0121**
	(0.0015)	(0.0061)	(0.0015)	(0.0061)
Colony$_{ij}$	0.5711***	0.2404*	0.5312***	0.2389*
	(0.0326)	(0.1402)	(0.0321)	(0.1401)
Common Border$_{ij}$	−0.3684***	0.4469***	−0.3497***	0.4557***
	(0.0344)	(0.1308)	(0.0336)	(0.1306)
Constant	−3.6509***	−6.0834***	−2.8812***	−5.9526***
	(0.1151)	(0.5182)	(0.3829)	(0.5144)
ln alpha	−0.3583***		−0.4019***	
	(0.0112)		(0.0112)	
alpha	0.6989		0.6691	
	(0.0078)		(0.0075)	
Time Fixed Effects?	No		Yes	
Source Country Fixed Effects?	No		No	
Destination Country Fixed Effects?	No		No	
Vuong test (ZINB vs. NB)	30.33***		30.37***	
LR test of alpha = 0 (ZINB vs. ZIP)	2.5E+07***		2.4E+07***	
N	16,513		16,513	
Immigrant flow > 0	14,832		14,832	
LR χ^2	29,862***		30,544***	
Log-likelihood	−110,089		−109,749	

Standard errors in parentheses. "***", "**", and "*" denote significance from zero at the 1 percent, 5 percent, and 10 percent levels, respectively.

else constant, a one percent increase in the 4-factor measure of cultural distance would reduce the level of the immigrant inflow by a factor of about 0.87. A like one percent increase in the 6-factor measure is estimated to reduce the level of

Table 8.4 GLOBE composite measure of cultural distance, without/with time fixed effects

	Neg. Bin.	*Logit*	*Neg. Bin.*	*Logit*
	(a)		*(b)*	
ln GLOBE Cultural Distance$_{ij}$	−0.0214	−0.5638***	0.0133	−0.5633***
	(0.0265)	(0.0975)	(0.026)	(0.0972)
ln Geodesic Distance$_{ij}$	−0.3961***	−0.1577***	−0.3741***	−0.1533***
	(0.0111)	(0.0445)	(0.0111)	(0.0443)
ln Immigrant Stock$_{ijt-1}$	0.6797***	−0.3086***	0.6819***	−0.3091***
	(0.0052)	(0.0216)	(0.0053)	(0.0215)
ln (Population$_{it}$ x Population$_{jt}$)	0.2918***	0.1489***	0.2702***	0.1445***
	(0.0061)	(0.0261)	(0.0062)	(0.026)
ln Relative GDP per capita$_{ijt}$	−0.0001	−0.2209***	0.0034	−0.2185***
	(0.0069)	(0.0278)	(0.0069)	(0.0277)
Unemployment Rate$_{jt}$ (Destination)	−0.0166***	0.0191**	−0.0067***	0.0193**
	(0.0025)	(0.0093)	(0.0026)	(0.0093)
Unemployment Rate$_{it}$ (Source)	−0.002	−0.0113	−0.0005	−0.0113
	(0.0022)	(0.0088)	(0.0022)	(0.0087)
Colony$_{ij}$	0.9528***	−0.05	0.8907***	−0.0524
	(0.0392)	(0.1789)	(0.0388)	(0.1788)
Common Border$_{ij}$	−0.3957***	0.4332***	−0.3571***	0.439***
	(0.0451)	(0.1689)	(0.0441)	(0.1688)
Constant	−5.9648***	−1.449*	−5.0108***	−1.3343
	(0.2261)	(0.8696)	(0.4222)	(0.8663)
ln alpha	−0.3903***		−0.4347***	
	(0.0145)		(0.0145)	
alpha	0.6769		0.6475	
	(0.0098)		(0.0094)	
Time Fixed Effects?	No		Yes	
Source Country Fixed Effects?	No		No	
Destination Country Fixed Effects?	No		No	
Vuong test (ZINB vs. NB)	25.23***		24.67***	
LR test of alpha = 0 (ZINB vs. ZIP)	2.1E+07***		2.1E+07***	
N	9,489		9,489	
Immigrant flow > 0	8,519		8,519	
LR χ^2	16,793***		17,202***	
Log-likelihood	−67,356		−67,152	

Standard errors in parentheses. "***", "**", and "*" denote significance from zero at the 1 percent, 5 percent, and 10 percent levels, respectively.

the immigrant inflow by a factor of roughly 0.91. As is reported in Table 8.1, the logit coefficients on the Hofstede cultural distance measures are not significantly different from zero.

Comparing the results presented in Table 8.4 (where the GLOBE measure of cultural distance is employed in the regression model) to the results presented in Table 8.1, we find considerable differences. First, with respect to the coefficients (negative binomial and logit) on the control variables, we find that only 26 of the 32 coefficient estimates (81.25 percent) are the same in terms of sign and level of statistical significance. The negative binomial coefficients of the GLOBE cultural distance measure are both insignificant from zero; however, the corresponding logit coefficients are negative and significant in both column A and column B. The magnitudes of the coefficient estimates suggest that, all else equal, an increase of one percent in the GLOBE cultural distance measure decreases the odds that no immigrants will migrate from the corresponding source country to the destination country by a factor of 0.57.

While the results presented thus far are informative, the lack of controls for source country and destination country fixed effects gives pause to leaning too heavily on the findings. Further, the results that have been presented only involve the use of our composite measures of cultural distance. To fully augment our regression model, we now include the country fixed effects terms. Additionally, we extend from the use of our composite measure of cultural distance to include the related component dimensions. Doing so may provide a more comprehensive understanding of the relationship between cultural differences and international migration flows.

Beginning with Table 8.5, we find a negative and statistically significant coefficient for the Inglehart cultural distance variable in column A. As before, the corresponding logit coefficient is not significantly different from zero. The same pattern is found when reviewing the results presented in column B. Neither of the logit coefficients on the variables that represent differences across countries in the SSE and TSR cultural dimensions is significantly different from zero. However, the negative binomial coefficients are both negative and statistically significant. Thus, it appears that greater cultural distance, whether represented by the composite Inglehart measure or by the two corresponding component dimensions, is negatively related to the level of immigrant inflows. Specifically, the results suggest that a one percent increase in the composite measure results in a decrease in the immigrant inflow level by a factor of roughly 0.85. Similar individual increases, along the SSE and TSR dimensions, with all else held constant, is estimated to decrease the level of immigrant inflows by factors of 0.98 and 0.95 respectively.

Table 8.6 reports the coefficient estimates obtained when the 4-factor Hofstede measure of cultural distance is considered (column A) and when the 6-factor measure is used (column B). In Table 8.7, the coefficients for the Hofstede cultural dimensions are presented. Focusing first on the negative binomial coefficients, we see that both are negative and statistically significant. The coefficients suggest that, in response to a one percent increase in the 4-factor Hofstede measure of cultural distance and the 6-factor Hofstede measure, the expected levels of the immigrant inflow, all else constant, are estimated to decrease by factors of 0.92 and 0.85, respectively. Turning our attention to the logit coefficients, which

Table 8.5 Inglehart composite and component measures of cultural distance and international migration

	Neg. Bin.	*Logit*	*Neg. Bin.*	*Logit*
	(a)		*(b)*	
ln Inglehart Cultural Distance$_{ijt}$	−0.1663***	−0.0823		
	(0.0198)	(0.0808)		
ln | SSE$_{it}$ − SSE$_{jt}$ |			−0.0242**	−0.0768
			(0.0111)	(0.049)
ln | TSR$_{it}$ − TSR$_{jt}$ |			−0.0465***	0.0499
			(0.0096)	(0.0476)
ln Geodesic Distance$_{ij}$	−0.3641***	−0.5995***	−0.3834***	−0.8484***
	(0.0188)	(0.0661)	(0.0186)	(0.0715)
ln Immigrant Stock$_{ijt-1}$	0.5976***	−0.6342***	0.6184***	−0.7011***
	(0.0079)	(0.0296)	(0.0077)	(0.0318)
ln (Population$_{it}$ x Population$_{jt}$)	−0.0241	0.7915***	−0.0245	0.8854***
	(0.1917)	(0.0381)	(0.1888)	(0.0416)
ln Relative GDP per capita$_{ijt}$	−0.1696**	−0.2672***	−0.1901***	−0.2506***
	(0.0706)	(0.0306)	(0.0694)	(0.0315)
Unemployment Rate$_{jt}$ (Destination)	−0.0542***	−0.1306***	−0.0543***	−0.1424***
	(0.0044)	(0.0149)	(0.0043)	(0.0152)
Unemployment Rate$_{it}$ (Source)	0.0072*	0.0271***	0.0042	0.0272***
	(0.0038)	(0.0087)	(0.0037)	(0.009)
Colony$_{ij}$	0.3677***	0.5202**	0.3699***	0.6834***
	(0.0374)	(0.2077)	(0.037)	(0.2101)
Common Border$_{ij}$	−0.0099	0.6351***	−0.0652	0.281
	(0.0414)	(0.1909)	(0.041)	(0.1975)
Constant	7.3698	−18.448***	7.3713	−19.0766***
	(6.101)	(0.9458)	(6.0079)	(0.9933)
ln alpha	−0.8317***		−0.858***	
	(0.0167)		(0.0166)	
alpha	0.4353		0.424	
	(0.0073)		(0.007)	
Vuong test (ZINB vs. NB)	16.28***		16.60***	
LR test of alpha = 0 (ZINB vs. ZIP)	8.1E+06***		8.0E+06***	
N	8,993		8,927	
Immigrant flow > 0	8,090		8,032	
LR χ^2	20,829***		20,809***	
Log-likelihood	−60,793		−60,228	

All estimations include year, source, and destination country fixed effects. Corresponding coefficients not reported due to space limitations. Standard errors in parentheses. "***", "**", and "*" denote significance from zero at the 1 percent, 5 percent, and 10 percent levels, respectively.

in these cases are positive and significantly different from zero, all else equal, an increase of one percent in the 4-factor Hofstede measure of cultural distance increases the odds that no immigrants will migrate from the corresponding source

Table 8.6 Hofstede composite measures of cultural distance and international migration

	Neg. Bin.	*Logit*	*Neg. Bin.*	*Logit*
	(a)		*(b)*	
ln Hofstede 4-factor	−0.0788***	0.0621*		
Cultural Distance$_{ij}$	(0.0087)	(0.0332)		
ln Hofstede 6-factor			−0.1677***	0.0928**
Cultural Distance$_{ij}$			(0.0114)	(0.0447)
ln Geodesic Distance$_{ij}$	−0.4107***	−0.1174***	−0.4015***	−0.0292
	(0.0128)	(0.034)	(0.013)	(0.0387)
ln Immigrant Stock$_{ijt-1}$	0.7651***	−0.2316***	0.6346***	−0.3527***
	(0.0053)	(0.0163)	(0.0058)	(0.0178)
ln (Population$_{it}$ x	−0.6541***	0.1466***	−0.0271	0.3819***
Population$_{jt}$)	(0.0853)	(0.0186)	(0.1037)	(0.0212)
ln Relative GDP per	0.1912***	−0.1874***	−0.2602***	−0.2742***
capita$_{ijt}$	(0.0509)	(0.0188)	(0.0534)	(0.0215)
Unemployment Rate$_{jt}$	−0.0388***	0.0438***	−0.0559***	0.0426***
(Destination)	(0.0032)	(0.0069)	(0.0033)	(0.0074)
Unemployment Rate$_{it}$	0.0213***	0.0059	0.02***	0.0283***
(Source)	(0.0026)	(0.0057)	(0.0027)	(0.0062)
Colony$_{ij}$	0.3205***	0.2189*	0.4155***	0.1252
	(0.0296)	(0.1288)	(0.0306)	(0.1504)
Common Border$_{ij}$	−0.3293***	0.4945***	−0.1278***	0.8434***
	(0.032)	(0.1256)	(0.0316)	(0.1396)
Constant	23.375***	−4.5816***	7.0125**	−12.4181***
	(2.819)	(0.5034)	(3.4475)	(0.5873)
ln alpha	−0.7454***		−0.7933***	
	(0.0108)		(0.0122)	
alpha	0.4745		0.4524	
	(0.0051)		(0.0055)	
Vuong test	23.03***		20.31***	
(ZINB vs. NB)				
LR test of alpha = 0	1.4E+07***		1.2E+07***	
(ZINB vs. ZIP)				
N	19,914		16,513	
Immigrant flow > 0	17,639		14,832	
LR χ^2	44,657***		37,049***	
Log-likelihood	−122,250		−106,496	

All estimations include year, source, and destination country fixed effects. Corresponding coefficients not reported due to space limitations. Standard errors in parentheses. "***", "**", and "*" denote significance from zero at the 1 percent, 5 percent, and 10 percent levels, respectively.

country to the destination country by a factor of 1.06. Likewise, a one percent increase in the 6-factor Hofstede measure of cultural distance is estimated to increase the odds that there will be no immigration between the corresponding source and destination countries by a factor of 1.10.

Table 8.7 Hofstede component measures of cultural distance and international migration

	Neg. Bin.	Logit	Neg. Bin.	Logit
	(a)		(b)	
ln | $PDI_{it} - PDI_{jt}$ |	−0.0213**	0.8662	−0.0161	1.3096***
	(0.0106)	(0.9846)	(0.0106)	(0.2346)
ln | $IDV_{it} - IDV_{jt}$ |	−0.1365***	0.3092***	−0.1128***	0.3389
	(0.0115)	(0.0802)	(0.0108)	(0.6021)
ln | $MAS_{it} - MAS_{jt}$ |	−0.1226***	1.0192***	−0.114***	1.5405***
	(0.0077)	(0.2706)	(0.0079)	(0.1759)
ln | $UAI_{it} - UAI_{jt}$ |	−0.0597***	0.8426	−0.054***	1.0266***
	(0.0071)	(0.6206)	(0.0073)	(0.0463)
ln | $PRA_{it} - PRA_{jt}$ |			0.0103	0.9228***
			(0.0072)	(0.0692)
ln | $IND_{t} - IND_{jt}$ |			−0.0067	0.1726
			(0.0081)	(0.5714)
ln Geodesic $Distance_{ij}$	−0.3278***	1.4292***	−0.3806***	2.0291***
	(0.0137)	(0.6216)	(0.0135)	(0.1718)
ln Immigrant $Stock_{ijt-1}$	0.5891***	0.6835	0.6244***	1.0426***
	(0.0059)	(0.8476)	(0.006)	(0.1158)
ln ($Population_{it}$ x $Population_{jt}$)	−0.0201	0.3785*	−0.023	0.6029
	(0.091)	(0.2034)	(0.1048)	(0.8256)
ln Relative GDP per $capita_{ijt}$	−0.1658***	−0.0067	-0.2546***	−0.1286
	(0.0545)	(0.3981)	(0.0544)	(0.4772)
Unemployment $Rate_{jt}$ (Destination)	−0.0541***	0.2261	−0.0544***	0.3299**
	(0.0033)	(0.8309)	(0.0033)	(0.1602)
Unemployment $Rate_{it}$ (Source)	0.0117***	0.1039	0.0184***	0.1676
	(0.0027)	(0.105)	(0.0028)	(0.9264)
$Colony_{ij}$	0.5149***	507.5337***	0.3281***	175.671***
	(0.0329)	(0.836)	(0.0321)	(0.6438)
Common $Border_{ij}$	0.0561	115.41***	0.0059	189.7408***
	(0.0347)	(0.8704)	(0.0338)	(0.9252)
Constant	7.2101**	39.6513***	7.1985**	45.535***
	(3.0096)	(0.6105)	(3.4845)	(0.2093)
ln alpha	−0.6782***		−0.8413***	
	(0.0119)		(0.0125)	
alpha	0.5075		0.4311	
	(0.006)		(0.0054)	
Vuong test (ZINB vs. NB)	40.65***		40.87***	
LR test of alpha = 0 (ZINB vs. ZIP)	1.5E+08***		1.7E+07***	

N	18,982	15,439
Immigrant flow > 0	16,845	13,871
LR χ^2	43,363***	36,984***
Log-likelihood	−111,995	−94,386

All estimations include year, source, and destination country fixed effects. Corresponding coefficients not reported due to space limitations. Standard errors in parentheses. "***", "**", and "*" denote significance from zero at the 1 percent, 5 percent, and 10 percent levels, respectively.

While the findings from the use of our composite Hofstede measures of cultural distance are informative, by considering the relationships between international migration and the component dimensions of our composite measures we are able to discern a more complete understanding of the relationship. Table 8.7 presented results obtained when the individual Hofstede cultural dimensions are substituted in our regression model (equation 1) for the 4-factor and 6-factor Hofstede composite measures.

Beginning with the results presented in column A, we see that the negative binomial coefficients of all four cultural dimension variables are negative and significantly different from zero. The negative binomial coefficients presented in column B are somewhat similar. The main differences are that the coefficient estimate of the variable that represents the source-destination country difference in the power distance index (PDI) dimension is no longer significantly different from zero, and the coefficient estimates of the two additional dimensions (i.e., the difference in the pragmatic vs. normative (PRA) and indulgence vs. restraint (IND) dimensions) are not significantly different from zero. There is more variation in the logit coefficient estimates across the two estimations. In the estimation that involves the 4-factor Hofstede cultural distance measure, the logit coefficients for the IDV (individualism vs. collectivism) and MAS (masculinity vs. femininity) dimensions are positive and significant – indicating that greater differences along these dimensions are correlated with higher odds that the immigrant inflow level is equal to zero – while the remaining two coefficients are not statistically significant. With respect to the component dimensions of cultural distance, in column B we find four of six logit coefficients that are positive and significant from zero. Even so, there is limited consistency across the two sets of results in this regard.

Our last set of estimates that relate to the composite measures of cultural distance or the associated component measures are presented in Table 8.8. Here, results obtained using the GLOBE measure of cultural distance are presented (column A). Additionally, in column B we present results from the estimation of equation 8.1 when the nine component dimensions of the GLOBE measure are used in the regression model. We find that a one percent increase in the GLOBE measure of cultural distance corresponds with a decrease in the level of the immigrant inflow equal to a factor of 0.89 and decrease in the odds that there will be no immigration between the corresponding source and destination countries by a factor of 0.60. Considerable variation is found when individual components are considered. Greater differences in the institutional collectivism (INST-COL), in-group collectivism (INGP-COL), humane orientation (HUMANE), and

Table 8.8 GLOBE composite and component measures of cultural distance and international migration

	Neg. Bin.	*Logit*	*Neg. Bin.*	*Logit*
	(a)		*(b)*	
ln GLOBE Cultural Distance$_{ij}$	−0.1138***	−0.5051***		
	(0.0281)	(0.0992)		
$\ln \lvert ASSERT_i - ASSERT_j \rvert$			−0.0080	−0.1404***
			(0.0090)	(0.0367)
$\ln \lvert INST\text{-}COL_i - INST\text{-}COL_j \rvert$			−0.0359***	−0.0835**
			(0.0102)	(0.0410)
$\ln \lvert INGP\text{-}COL_i - INGP\text{-}COL_j \rvert$			−0.0490***	0.0293
			(0.0100)	(0.0405)
$\ln \lvert FUTURE_i - FUTURE_j \rvert$			0.0243**	−0.0774*
			(0.0103)	(0.0413)
$\ln \lvert GEND\text{-}EGL_i - GEND\text{-}EGL_j \rvert$			0.0543***	−0.1026***
			(0.0089)	(0.0371)
$\ln \lvert HUMANE_i - HUMANE_j \rvert$			−0.0253***	0.0200
			(0.0096)	(0.0408)
$\ln \lvert PERFORM_i - PERFORM_j \rvert$			−0.0041	0.1794***
			(0.0083)	(0.0411)
$\ln \lvert POWDIST_i - POWDIST_j \rvert$			0.0051	−0.1299***
			(0.0095)	(0.0374)
$\ln \lvert UNC\text{-}AVD_i - UNC\text{-}AVD_j \rvert$			−0.0353***	−0.0046
			(0.0096)	(0.0428)
ln Geodesic Distance$_{ij}$	−0.3972***	−0.1189***	−0.4134***	−0.1426***
	(0.0155)	(0.0445)	(0.0165)	(0.0465)
ln Immigrant Stock$_{ijt\text{-}1}$	0.7349***	−0.2597***	0.7252***	−0.2624***

	(0.0073)	(0.0224)	(0.0075)	(0.0237)
ln ($Population_{it}$ x $Population_{jt}$)	−0.4028***	0.0814***	−0.3408***	0.1129***
	(0.1197)	(0.0270)	(0.1225)	(0.0280)
ln Relative GDP per $capita_{ijt}$	0.1576**	−0.1771***	0.1898***	−0.2029***
	(0.0644)	(0.0283)	(0.0674)	(0.0299)
Unemployment $Rate_{jt}$ (Destination)	−0.0293***	0.0249***	−0.0285***	0.0223**
	(0.0040)	(0.0094)	(0.0041)	(0.0098)
Unemployment $Rate_{it}$ (Source)	0.0187***	−0.0153*	0.0174***	−0.0131
	(0.0034)	(0.0089)	(0.0034)	(0.0091)
$Colony_{ij}$	0.4473***	−0.1488	0.3309***	0.1256
	(0.0361)	(0.1847)	(0.0393)	(0.1915)
Common $Border_{ij}$	−0.3281***	0.4378**	−0.2853***	−0.0596
	(0.0394)	(0.1716)	(0.0427)	(0.2022)
Constant	15.155***	−0.1582	−2.9702***	
	(3.7489)	(0.8916)	(0.8030)	
ln alpha	−0.8973***		−0.8945***	
	(0.0150)		(0.0153)	
alpha	0.4077		0.4088	
	(0.0061)		(0.0063)	
Vuong test (ZINB vs. NB)	19.54***		19.13***	
LR test of alpha = 0 (ZINB vs. ZIP)	1.0E+07***		8.7E+06***	
N	9,489		9,101	
Immigrant flow > 0	8,519		8,178	
LR χ^2	21,695***		20,769***	
Log-likelihood	−64,905		−61,949	

All estimations include year, source, and destination country fixed effects. Corresponding coefficients not reported due to space limitations. Standard errors in parentheses. "***", "**", and "*" denote significance from zero at the 1 percent, 5 percent, and 10 percent levels, respectively.

uncertainty avoidance (UNC-AVD) dimensions correspond with reduce immigrant inflow levels. To the contrary, more pronounced differences along the future orientation (FUTURE) and gender-egalitarianism (GEND-EGL) dimensions correspond with higher levels of immigrant inflows. The coefficients for the remaining three cultural dimensions are not significantly different from zero, and considerable variation is found, in terms of coefficient signs and statistical significance, for the logit estimation.

Migration and proxy measures of cultural distance

The results presented so far suggest a generally negative relationship between cross-societal cultural differences and international migration. For all composite measures of cultural distance, we find negative and statistically significant coefficients when estimating equation 8.1 while including controls for time, source country, and destination country fixed effects. Even when not controlling for source and destination country fixed effects, we see that coefficients are negative and significantly different from zero in a majority (i.e., 6 of 8 coefficients) of instances.

Extending from the analysis presented to this point, we now present results obtained from a series of estimations employing variables that serve as proxies for cultural distance. This set of proxy variables is detailed in Chapters 4 and 5. Tables 8.9 and 8.10 present estimation results obtained from the use of index and dummy variables that represent language dissimilarity and similarity respectively.

Column A of Table 8.9 indicates that a one percent increase in the B-E measure of linguistic distance, all else held constant, decreases the level of the immigrant inflow by a factor of 0.80. Similarly, a like increase in the Dow linguistic distance measure is estimated to decrease the immigrant inflow level by a factor of 0.965. These findings, to the extent that linguistic dissimilarity is representative of cultural differences, are consistent with the results obtained when examining the composite measures of cultural distance. Looking to the logit coefficients, we find conflicting results. The coefficient of the B-E linguistic distance measure is negative, while the coefficient of the Dow measure is positive. Both are statistically significant from zero. The B-E coefficient suggests that a one percent increase in the B-E linguistic distance measure will decrease the odds that there will be no immigration between the corresponding source and destination countries by a factor of 0.73. A like increase in the Dow measure of linguistic distance suggests the opposite – an increase in the odds, by a factor of 1.20, that there will be no immigration between the corresponding source and destination countries.

Table 8.10 presents coefficients for four different dichotomous measures of language commonality. In all cases, the negative binomial regression coefficients are, as expected, positive and statistically significant. Again, this is consistent with the notion that cultural differences are significant determinants of international migration. We do see, however, continued variation in the signs of the logit coefficients.

Table 8.9 Index measures of linguistic differences/similarities and international migration

	Neg. Bin.	*Logit*	*Neg. Bin.*	*Logit*
	(a)		*(b)*	
ln B-E Linguistic Distance$_{ijt}$	−0.2229***	−0.3161**		
	(0.0217)	(0.1285)		
ln Dow Linguistic Distance$_{ijt}$			−0.0355***	0.1824***
			(0.0058)	(0.0264)
ln Geodesic Distance$_{ij}$	−0.3821***	−0.1904**	−0.4552***	−0.1019**
	(0.0189)	(0.0812)	(0.0171)	(0.042)
ln Immigrant Stock$_{ijt-1}$	0.6715***	−0.1731***	0.7101***	−0.2511***
	(0.0096)	(0.0606)	(0.0064)	(0.0193)
ln (Population$_{it}$ x Population$_{jt}$)	0.4418*	0.0252	−0.649***	0.1947***
	(0.2294)	(0.0577)	(0.0887)	(0.0225)
ln Relative GDP per capita$_{ijt}$	1.4602***	−0.433**	0.1447***	−0.2695***
	(0.1733)	(0.1985)	(0.0535)	(0.0215)
Unemployment Rate$_{jt}$ (Destination)	−0.0284***	0.0631***	−0.0376***	0.0283***
	(0.0045)	(0.019)	(0.0038)	(0.0083)
Unemployment Rate$_{it}$ (Source)	0.0147***	0.0008	0.0203***	0.0012
	(0.0038)	(0.0216)	(0.0027)	(0.0068)
Colony$_{ij}$	0.0933**	−2.1965**	−0.1125**	0.9216***
	(0.0448)	(1.0112)	(0.0555)	(0.2138)
Common Border$_{ij}$	−0.2206***	0.3156	−0.0593	−0.162
	(0.0314)	(0.2336)	(0.0518)	(0.2307)
Constant	−10.6704	−1.4079	24.9728***	−5.6597***
	(7.6352)	(1.3851)	(2.9817)	(0.6263)
ln alpha	−1.4499***		−0.7712***	
	(0.022)		(0.0126)	
alpha	0.2346		0.4624	
	(0.0052)		(0.0058)	
Vuong test (ZINB vs. NB)	40.65***		16.60***	
LR test of alpha = 0 (ZINB vs. ZIP)	1.5E+08***		8.0E+06***	
N	18,982		8,927	
Immigrant flow > 0	16,845		8,032	
LR χ^2	43,363***		20,809***	
Log-likelihood	−111,995		−60,228	

All estimations include year, source, and destination country fixed effects. Corresponding coefficients not reported due to space limitations. Standard errors in parentheses. "***", "**", and "*" denote significance from zero at the 1 percent, 5 percent, and 10 percent levels, respectively.

Similar to the index measures of linguistic distance, in Table 8.11 we present findings obtained when the B-E measure of religious distance (column A) and the Dow measure of religious distance (column B) are employed. Again, we find the familiar negative and statistically significant negative binomial regression

Table 8.10 Dichotomous measures of language commonality and international migration

	(a) Neg. Bin.	(a) Logit	(b) Neg. Bin.	(b) Logit	(c) Neg. Bin.	(c) Logit	(d) Neg. Bin.	(d) Logit
CEPII Common Language used by ≥ 9 percent of $Populations_{ij}$	0.4792***	0.1707**						
	(0.0218)	(0.08)						
M-T Common Native $Language_{ij}$			0.6537***	−0.6994***				
			(0.0494)	(0.2265)				
M-T Common Official $Language_{ij}$					0.5012***	0.1896*		
					(0.0255)	(0.1016)		
M-T Common Spoken $Language_{ij}$							0.7666***	−0.9155***
							(0.04)	(0.1236)
ln Geodesic $Distance_{ij}$	−0.3691***	0.2289***	−0.4302***	−0.1489***	−0.4147***	−0.1764***	−0.4133***	−0.1718***
	(0.0119)	(0.0306)	(0.0125)	(0.0314)	(0.0123)	(0.0316)	(0.0125)	(0.0316)
ln Immigrant $Stock_{ijt-1}$	0.723***	−0.2126***	0.7482***	−0.2323***	0.7431***	−0.2429***	0.7432***	−0.1997***
	(0.0045)	(0.0134)	(0.0047)	(0.0138)	(0.0047)	(0.0139)	(0.0047)	(0.0144)
ln ($Population_{it}$ x $Population_{jt}$)	−0.032	0.0889***	−0.2866***	0.127***	−0.301***	0.1336***	−0.2993***	0.0815***
	(0.0748)	(0.0154)	(0.078)	(0.0166)	(0.0776)	(0.0165)	(0.078)	(0.0174)
ln Relative GDP per $capita_{ijt}$	−0.1033***	−0.1659***	0.5207***	−0.1361***	0.5108***	−0.1353***	0.5128***	−0.1858***
	(0.0399)	(0.0144)	(0.0429)	(0.0151)	(0.0427)	(0.0151)	(0.0426)	(0.0165)
Unemployment $Rate_{jt}$ (Destination)	−0.0423***	0.0459***	−0.0387***	0.031***	−0.0384***	0.03***	−0.038***	0.0254***
	(0.0029)	(0.006)	(0.003)	(0.0063)	(0.003)	(0.0062)	(0.003)	(0.0063)
Unemployment $Rate_{it}$ (Source)	0.0205***	0.0124***	0.0175***	0.003	0.0179***	0.0031	0.0182***	−0.0033
	(0.0023)	(0.0038)	(0.0025)	(0.0042)	(0.0025)	(0.0042)	(0.0025)	(0.0043)
$Colony_{ij}$	0.2656***	0.2468**	0.2849***	0.5882***	0.1493***	0.3398***	0.1657***	0.6813***
	(0.0296)	(0.1107)	(0.0316)	(0.1176)	(0.0326)	(0.1218)	(0.0322)	(0.1145)

Common $Border_{ij}$	−0.2572***	1.1059***	−0.3636***	0.4407***	−0.3479***	0.3695***	−0.3764***	0.4216***
	(0.0315)	(0.1197)	(0.0343)	(0.1248)	(0.0341)	(0.124)	(0.0342)	(0.1252)
Constant	6.5347***	−5.7345***	10.6402***	−3.4771***	10.9624***	−3.3958***	11.0141***	−1.6555***
	(2.5351)	(0.449)	(2.5962)	(0.4644)	(2.5832)	(0.4618)	(2.5958)	(0.5116)
ln alpha	−0.6499***		−0.635***		−0.6459***		−0.6452***	
	(0.0098)		(0.01)		(0.0099)		(0.01)	
alpha	0.5221		0.5299		0.5242		0.5246	
	(0.0051)		(0.0053)		(0.0052)		(0.0052)	
Vuong test (ZINB vs. NB)	23.48***		22.86***		22.94***		22.85***	
LR test of alpha = 0 (ZINB vs. ZIP)	1.2E+06***		1.5E+06***		1.8E+06***		1.6E+06***	
N	29,597		27,047		27,047		27,047	
Immigrant flow > 0	24,677		22,732		22,732		22,732	
LR χ^2	63,664.64***		58,288.73***		58,490.31***		58,523.87***	
Log-likelihood	−160,582.70		−148,932.20		−148,831.40		−148,814.70	

All estimations include year, source, and destination country fixed effects. Corresponding coefficients not reported due to space limitations. Standard errors in parentheses. "***", "**", and "*" denote significance from zero at the 1 percent, 5 percent, and 10 percent levels, respectively.

Table 8.11 Indexes of religious differences and international migration

	Neg. Bin.	*Logit*	*Neg. Bin.*	*Logit*
	(a)		*(b)*	
ln B-E Religious Distance$_{ijt}$	−0.0581***	0.0142		
	(0.0163)	(0.1014)		
ln Dow Religious Distance$_{ijt}$			−0.6998***	−1.4948***
			(0.1208)	(0.1889)
ln Geodesic Distance$_{ij}$	−0.3218***	−0.3118***	−0.232***	−1.0033***
	(0.0185)	(0.0721)	(0.0374)	(0.0998)
ln Immigrant Stock$_{ijt-1}$	0.7122***	−0.0592	0.6056***	−0.4252***
	(0.0102)	(0.0558)	(0.0107)	(0.029)
ln (Population$_{it}$	0.2827	0.051	−0.0237	0.3123***
x Population$_{jt}$)	(0.2292)	(0.0572)	(0.1401)	(0.0351)
ln Relative GDP per capita$_{ijt}$	1.0852***	−0.465**	−0.2891***	−0.2989***
	(0.175)	(0.1933)	(0.0762)	(0.0339)
Unemployment Rate$_{jt}$	−0.0353***	0.042**	−0.0286***	−0.0338**
(Destination)	(0.0045)	(0.0186)	(0.0059)	(0.0145)
Unemployment Rate$_{it}$	0.0149***	−0.0269	0.0069	−0.0158
(Source)	(0.0038)	(0.0214)	(0.0049)	(0.0104)
Colony$_{ij}$	0.2317***	−1.2224***	0.2206**	1.6601***
	(0.0396)	(0.4626)	(0.088)	(0.2376)
Common Border$_{ij}$	−0.1902***	−0.1009	−1.1097	3.668***
	(0.0325)	(0.2088)	(0.7468)	(1.0495)
Constant	−6.04	−1.6031	7.0286	−0.16
	(7.634)	(1.4292)	(4.9017)	(1.1141)
ln alpha	−1.3343***		−0.7302***	
	(0.0205)		(0.0205)	
alpha	0.2634		0.4818	
	(0.0054)		(0.0099)	
Vuong test (ZINB vs. NB)	15.87***		9.91***	
LR test of alpha = 0 (ZINB vs. ZIP)	1.9E+06***		2.3E+07***	
N	5,051		6,776	
Immigrant flow > 0	4,681		5,806	
LR χ^2	12,530.73***		15,124.28***	
Log-likelihood	−34,327.68		−39,949.92	

All estimations include year, source, and destination country fixed effects. Corresponding coefficients not reported due to space limitations. Standard errors in parentheses. "***", "**", and "*" denote significance from zero at the 1 percent, 5 percent, and 10 percent levels, respectively.

coefficient; however, the coefficient magnitudes are dissimilar. A one percent increase in the B-E religious distance measure will decrease the level of the immigrant inflow by a factor of 0.94. A like increase in the Dow measure of religious distance is estimated to decrease the inflow by a factor of only 0.50.

Table 8.12 Genetic distance and international migration

	Neg. Bin.	*Logit*	*Neg. Bin.*	*Logit*
	(a)		*(b)*	
ln Fixation Index Genetic Distance (weighted)$_{ij}$	−0.1507***	0.0589***		
	(0.009)	(0.0219)		
ln Nei Standard Genetic Distance (weighted)$_{ij}$			−0.1534***	0.033
			(0.0086)	(0.0222)
ln Geodesic Distance$_{ij}$	−0.3478***	0.2387***	−0.3399***	0.2493***
	(0.0123)	(0.0322)	(0.0122)	(0.0325)
ln Immigrant Stock$_{ijt-1}$	0.7266***	−0.1888***	0.7092***	−0.1979***
	(0.0045)	(0.0135)	(0.0045)	(0.0133)
ln (Population$_{it}$ x Population$_{jt}$)	−0.0249	0.0571***	−0.0254	0.0504***
	(0.0747)	(0.0156)	(0.0747)	(0.0154)
ln Relative GDP per capita$_{ijt}$	−0.0929**	−0.1733***	−0.0951**	−0.1675***
	(0.0426)	(0.0152)	(0.0426)	(0.0153)
Unemployment Rate$_{jt}$ (Destination)	−0.0451***	0.0474***	−0.0474***	0.0488***
	(0.0029)	(0.0062)	(0.0029)	(0.0061)
Unemployment Rate$_{it}$ (Source)	0.0196***	0.0111***	0.0174***	0.0102***
	(0.0023)	(0.0039)	(0.0023)	(0.0039)
Colony$_{ij}$	0.5558***	0.287***	0.5928***	0.309***
	(0.0284)	(0.1065)	(0.0285)	(0.1064)
Common Border$_{ij}$	−0.1835***	1.1674***	−0.1462***	1.1779***
	(0.0314)	(0.1199)	(0.0314)	(0.1195)
Constant	6.7641***	-5.2717***	6.7503***	-4.859***
	(2.5204)	(0.4504)	(2.5195)	(0.451)
ln alpha	−0.6547***		−0.6512***	
	(0.0099)		(0.0099)	
alpha	0.5196		0.5214	
	(0.0051)		(0.0051)	
Vuong test (ZINB vs. NB)	22.86***		22.75***	
LR test of alpha = 0 (ZINB vs. ZIP)	1.6E+07***		1.6E+07***	
N	28,951		28,951	
Immigrant flow > 0	24,266		24,266	
LR χ^2	62,332.23***		62,197.79***	
Log-likelihood	−158,158.70		−158,230.00	

All estimations include year, source, and destination country fixed effects. Corresponding coefficients not reported due to space limitations. Standard errors in parentheses. "***", "**", and "*" denote significance from zero at the 1 percent, 5 percent, and 10 percent levels, respectively.

As one final alternative to our composite measures of cultural distance, we employ the genetic distance between populations to represent cultural distance. Two separate measures are employed. The first is the fixation index, and the second is the Nei standard genetic distance. The coefficient estimates suggest that, in response to a one percent increase in the fixation index or the Nei distance, the expected level of the immigrant inflow, all else constant, will decrease by factors of approximately 0.86. Turning our attention to the logit coefficients, we see that the fixation index logit coefficient is positive and significantly different from zero, while the Nei distance logit coefficient is insignificant from zero. Thus, the results indicate that, all else equal, an increase of one percent in the fixation index value increases the odds that no immigrants will migrate from the corresponding source country to the destination country by a factor of 1.06.

Concluding thoughts

We have employed the ZINB technique to consider whether greater cultural differences (i.e., cultural distance) between a source and a destination country correspond with a reduced immigrant inflow level. The results obtained when employing our composite measures of cultural distance indicate that greater source-destination cultural distance corresponds with lower immigrant inflow values. Examination of the relationship, while substituting the component dimensions of the composite cultural distance variables for the composite measures, reveals several instances of statistically significant relationships; however, the signs and magnitudes of the coefficient values very considerably. Employing a series of proxy measures to represent cultural similarity or difference, we again find consistent evidence of a negative relationship between cultural differences and immigrant inflow values.

Note

1 Ruyssen (2013), Grogger and Hanson (2011), Bodvarsson and van den Berg (2009), and Hatton and Williamson (2002) provide surveys of the literature.

Part III

Interpreting a cultural distance-economic globalization nexus

We have examined the potential relationships between cross-societal cultural differences and three facets of economic globalization. Results presented in Chapter 6 provide abundant evidence that greater cultural distance has a diminishing effect on bilateral trade flows and that it hinders the initiation and completion of trade deals. We also find from the results provided in Chapter 7 that greater cultural distance between parent and host countries is associated with both lower foreign direct investment (FDI) inflows and lower FDI stocks. Additionally, the results presented in Chapter 8 indicate a significant negative relationship when we examine the influence of cultural differences on international migration. In short, if the various measures of cultural distance we have used in our analysis are representative of cultural differences across societies, then we can say that greater cultural differences are consistently and significantly related to lower levels of international economic interaction (i.e., economic globalization).

The remainder of this book consists of two final chapters. Having identified a negative relationship between cultural differences and the varying aspects of economic globalization, in Chapter 9 we extend our analysis by exploring the potential influence of international economic integration on cultural differences, effectively examining the notion that economic globalization results in cultural homogenization. It may be the case that repeated interaction by individuals who reside in two culturally-distinct societies results in some degree of acculturation by one or both individuals (or societies). However, it also may be that culture is sufficiently resilient to not change in any discernible way or to any meaningful extent in response to the potential pressures of economic globalization. We follow, in Chapter 10, by first taking stock of the material presented thus far. A detailed summary is provided of the analyses that we have undertaken and the findings presented in earlier chapters. These findings are synthesized to inform our conclusions. We then present estimates of the proportional effects of increased levels of cultural distance on bilateral trade flows and FDI. In a final section, we close with concluding thoughts.

9 Economic globalization and the potential for cultural homogenization

The results presented in the preceding three chapters suggest a robust, negative relationship between cross-societal cultural differences and the three facets of economic globalization we have examined. In the empirical models that have been estimated so far, we have consistently regressed dependent variable series that represent specific aspects of economic globalization on a variety of cultural distance measures and appropriate sets of control variables. The empirical models are constructed based on the prior literature and, thus, on the related theoretical intuition. Accordingly, there is an assumed direction of causality that runs from the cultural distance variables, and the other explanatory variables, to the measures of economic globalization. A separate strand of the literature, which has gained considerable attention in recent years, introduces the possible influence of economic globalization on cross-societal cultural differences.

The basis for the study of a possible influence of increased international economic integration on the degree to which involved populations are culturally (dis)similar is that, as the process of globalization is ongoing, repeated interactions between different groups may diminish cultural differences. For example, Cyrus (2012) employs a time-varying measure of cultural distance that is constructed using WVS responses and finds that exports are a significant determinant of cultural distance. Fatehi and Sanchez (2012) argue that lower transaction costs lead to more cross-border economic activity and, ultimately, an increase in the degree of cultural sameness. This is to say that more frequent interaction may lead to cultural homogenization. Accordingly, the authors posit that lower transaction costs that are related to economic globalization should be viewed as a warning sign. The notion that increased interaction between countries acts to reduce cultural distances between engaged parties is a common presumption across studies that focus on the influences of globalization on cultural diversity. Since we depict cross-societal cultural differences as having the potential to increase costs associated with trade, foreign direct investment and migration, our assumption that greater cultural dissimilarity corresponds with higher transactions costs is consistent, in a manner, with the assertion of Fatehi and Sanchez. Even so, if we are to view repeated interaction as a process by which higher related transaction costs can be ameliorated without the sacrifice of cultural uniqueness – that is, if we envision a scenario under which culture is sufficiently resilient to withstand the influences of repeated economic interaction with culturally-dissimilar partners – then we may find that there is no evidence of cultural homogenization in the short run or in the long run.

Some argue that the true relationship between globalization and culture is not as straightforward as one may be led to believe. Cowen (2002), for example, claims that globalization may both increase and decrease bilateral cultural distances. Increased trade between two populations may result in greater cultural similarity. However, the availability of new products, as resources are shifted away from import-competing production and towards the production of goods and services for which the trading partners hold comparative advantage, can lead to greater cultural diversity within and between populations. To the contrary, Van Krieken et al. (2006) suggest that local homogeneity is replaced by a sort of global diversity rather than being replaced by something akin to global homogeneity. Seabrook (1998) suggests that societies internalize global culture in different ways, offering religion as an aspect of culture that is resistant, to a considerable degree, to globalization-induced change. Thus, there is no reason to expect that globalization will diminish cultural diversity. Lechner (2001) goes so far as to say that globalization might even result in greater cultural diversity across societies.

Given the perceived threat that globalization either leads to, or will result in, a loss of cultural uniqueness, it is not surprising that some have suggested the adoption of policies aimed at the protection of culture. For example, Barlow (2002) proposes the establishment of an international committee to recognize and maintain the importance of cultural diversity. Mitterand (1993) shares this notion and defends the adoption of such policies.

While considerable attention has been paid to the topic of economic globalization and the potential for cultural homogenization, there is little empirical evidence that supports or refutes the notion. Thus, the relationship, it would seem, remains an open empirical question. In this chapter, we address the possible influence of increased economic globalization on cross-societal cultural differences. More specifically, we use globalization index scores and the Inglehart composite measure of cultural distance to consider the potential relationship. We also consider country-specific changes in the KOF economic globalization dimension as compared to changes in the countries' values for the KOF cultural proximity sub-dimension.

It should be noted that the KOF cultural proximity sub-dimension, as described in Chapter 4, is based on a number of factors that, on the surface, may raise questions about its validity as an empirical tool. The sub-dimension is constructed, at the country level, using data on the number of McDonald's restaurant locations per capita, the number of IKEA store locations, again per capita, and the total amount of trade in books as a share of the country's GDP. While the components of the cultural proximity sub-dimension may appear poorly-suited to represent culture and, hence, to provide information about country-level differences in culture, it is important to remember that the relevant feature of the variable is that it should provide a representation of culture rather than serving as a measurement of culture. Accordingly, while we acknowledge that, in general, the available data are far from ideal and, thus, that our examination may accordingly be hindered and limited, we proceed cautiously with the shortcomings of our data in mind.

Temporal changes in globalization index values and in the Inglehart measure of cultural distance

Beginning with the Inglehart measure of cultural distance, there are 17 countries for which the World Values Survey was completed in both the first WVS wave (1981–1984) and in the fifth WVS wave (2005–2009). We first check our six globalization indexes to see if these 17 countries had become more globally-integrated over the quarter century period. Table 9.1 lists the 17 countries as well as KOF Globalization Index values for the years 1983 and 2007 and CSGR Index values for 1983 and 2004. The table also presents each country's index rank (in parentheses) for all six of the globalization indexes. For all indexes other than the KOF Index and the CSGR Index, presented values are from the most recent year for which data are available.

Perhaps what is first noticed when looking at Table 9.1 is that both the KOF Index values and the CSGR Index values increased for all 17 countries during the noted intervals. Thus, based on these metrics, we can say that each listed country is more globalized now compared to their respective degree of global integration in 1983. Further, looking to the KOF Index and CSGR Index rankings that are provided parenthetically, we find that, notwithstanding the 1983 KOF Index ranking of South Korea, the countries are all in the top halves of the rankings. Looking to the 2007 KOF Index rankings, we see that South Korea's ranking increased to the extent that it is now solidly in the top half. These index values and rankings suggest that the typical member of this cohort of 17 countries is generally more integrated into the global economy than other countries and that the extent of their integration, as noted above, has increased over time.

Further examining the 17 countries for which Inglehart cultural distance measures can be constructed at the two points in time, the cultural dimension scores for the first and fifth survey waves are listed in Table 9.2. The rightmost two columns in the table present the changes for each country over each of the two Inglehart component cultural dimensions. While there are near-equal numbers of countries for which the TSR cultural dimension value increased or decreased, all but one of the countries (South Korea) realized an increase in their SSE dimension score over the period. Thinking of the placement of the typical member of this cohort of countries in the Inglehart "cultural map" of the world (initially presented in Chapter 4) the group average values for the TSR and SSE dimensions (0.11 and 0.78, respectively) suggest that the typical cohort member moved slightly upward within the cultural map and, to a more pronounced extent, from left to right during the time period.

The bottom portion of the table summarizes the placement of the countries in the Inglehart cultural map – that is, the location of the countries in x, y space where the survival vs. self-expression Values (SSE) dimension of culture occupies the x axis and the traditional vs. secular-rational authority (TSR) dimension is located along the y axis.

Table 9.1 Globalization index scores and rankings, various indexes

		KOF		*CSGR*		*DHL*	*E&Y*	*FP/ATK*	*MGI*
Country	*ISO3*	*(1983)*	*(2007)*	*(1983)*	*(2004)*	*(2007)*	*(2007)*	*(2007)*	*(2008)*
Argentina	ARG	46.96 (44)	59.75 (73)	.	0.384 (37)	42 (70)	3.08 (51)	. (34)	49.12 (56)
Australia	AUS	68.41 (14)	81.98 (23)	0.251 (12)	0.627 (16)	55 (35)	4.34 (21)	. (13)	58.67 (37)
Canada	CAN	79.50 (2)	86.19 (14)	0.397 (3)	0.895 (3)	55 (36)	4.51 (15)	. (8)	61.34 (28)
Finland	FIN	62.09 (18)	86.45 (11)	0.266 (11)	0.656 (15)	70 (13)	4.60 (12)	. (18)	61.09 (29)
France	FRA	71.65 (13)	84.51 (18)	0.418 (2)	0.819 (9)	73 (11)	4.39 (19)	. (25)	68.60 (9)
Germany	DEU	61.59 (19)	82.77 (20)	.	0.750 (12)	77 (8)	4.61 (10)	. (22)	68.97 (8)
Italy	ITA	58.28 (21)	81.71 (24)	0.328 (9)	0.672 (13)	62 (24)	4.09 (28)	. (34)	65.25 (17)
Japan	JPN	42.90 (56)	65.35 (52)	0.221 (15)	0.568 (21)	53 (39)	3.45 (42)	. (28)	59.25 (36)
Korea, Rep. of	KOR	35.42 (92)	62.52 (63)	0.132 (28)	0.578 (20)	59 (31)	3.81 (34)	. (32)	63.93 (21)
Mexico	MEX	44.20 (52)	58.52 (77)	0.137 (26)	0.263 (61)	35 (92)	3.6 (37)	. (45)	46.98 (63)
Netherlands	NLD	83.90 (1)	91.86 (2)	0.333 (8)	0.617 (17)	89 (1)	5.12 (6)	. (3)	78.72 (1)
Norway	NOR	75.72 (8)	82.56 (21)	0.219 (16)	0.516 (26)	71 (12)	4.34 (22)	. (17)	67.77 (11)
South Africa	SAF	40.72 (61)	64.96 (53)	.	0.340 (48)	53 (42)	3.26 (48)	. (49)	51.25 (51)
Spain	ESP	62.56 (17)	85.37 (17)	0.212 (18)	0.524 (22)	62 (25)	4.42 (17)	. (29)	66.41 (13)
Sweden	SWE	77.43 (6)	88.71 (5)	0.321 (10)	0.838 (7)	78 (7)	4.94 (7)	. (11)	69.49 (7)
United Kingdom	UK	75.68 (9)	85.87 (16)	0.394 (4)	0.874 (4)	77 (9)	4.61 (11)	. (12)	71.18 (5)
United States	USA	63.80 (15)	77.49 (29)	0.360 (7)	0.870 (5)	61 (27)	4.35 (20)	. (7)	61.41 (27)
Cohort Average		61.8 (26.4)	78.0 (30.5)	0.285 (12.1)	0.666 (17.1)[a]	63.1 (28.4)	4.2 (23.5)	. (22.8)	62.9 (24.6)
N Countries Ranked		163	187	39	103	140	60	72	117

[a] To permit comparison to 1983 values, the 2004 cohort average values are calculated using only the values for countries for which there is a 1983 value. Rank values in parentheses. Measures employed: KOF Globalization Index; CSGR (Centre for the Study of Globalisation and Regionalisation) Globalization Index; DHL Global Connectedness Score; E&Y (Ernst & Young) Globalization Index; FP/ATK (Foreign Policy-AT Kearney) Globalization Index; and MGI (Maastricht Globalization Index).

Table 9.2 Inglehart cultural dimensions, waves 1 and 5

	Wave 1		*Wave 5*			
	1981–1984		*2005–2009*		*Change*	
Country	*TSR*	*SSE*	*TSR*	*SSE*	*ΔTSR*	*ΔSSE*
Argentina*	0.00	−0.30	−0.66	0.38	−0.66	0.68
Australia*	−0.34	1.14	0.21	1.75	0.55	0.61
Canada	−0.52	1.04	−0.26	1.91	0.26	0.87
Finland	0.63	0.82	0.82	1.12	0.19	0.30
France	0.54	0.13	0.63	1.13	0.09	1.00
Germany*	0.83	−0.07	1.31	0.74	0.48	0.81
Italy*	0.18	−0.60	0.13	0.60	−0.05	1.20
Japan	1.41	−0.41	1.96	−0.05	0.55	0.36
Korea, Rep.	1.08	−0.74	0.61	−1.37	−0.47	−0.63
Mexico*	−1.15	−0.26	−1.47	1.03	−0.32	1.29
Netherlands	0.73	0.90	0.71	1.39	−0.02	0.49
Norway	0.89	0.53	1.39	2.17	0.50	1.64
South Africa	−0.53	−0.40	−1.09	−0.10	−0.56	0.30
Spain*	−0.26	−0.52	0.09	0.54	0.35	1.06
Sweden	1.20	0.85	1.86	2.35	0.66	1.50
United Kingdom*	−0.25	0.95	0.06	1.68	0.31	0.73
United States	−0.83	0.68	−0.81	1.76	0.02	1.08
Group Average	0.21	0.22	0.32	1.00	0.11	0.78
Group Standard Deviation	0.54	0.44	0.92	0.86	0.18	0.31
Orientations…	1981–1984		2005–2009		N changed	
Survival Values (i.e., left of y axis)	8		3		−5	
Self-expression Values (i.e., right of y axis)	9		14		5	
Traditional Authority (i.e., below x axis)	7		5		−2	
Secular-rational Authority (i.e., above y axis)	10		12		2	
Quadrant locations…						
Quadrant I (i.e., upper right)	5		10		5	
Quadrant II (i.e., upper left)	5		2		−3	
Quadrant III (i.e., lower right)	3		1		−2	
Quadrant IV (i.e., lower left)	4		4		0	

* Indicates that the country changed from one orientation to another during the period.

During the first wave of the WVS, the 17 countries listed in Table 9.2 were almost evenly split between being more oriented towards survival values (eight of the 17 countries) or more towards a self-expression values orientation

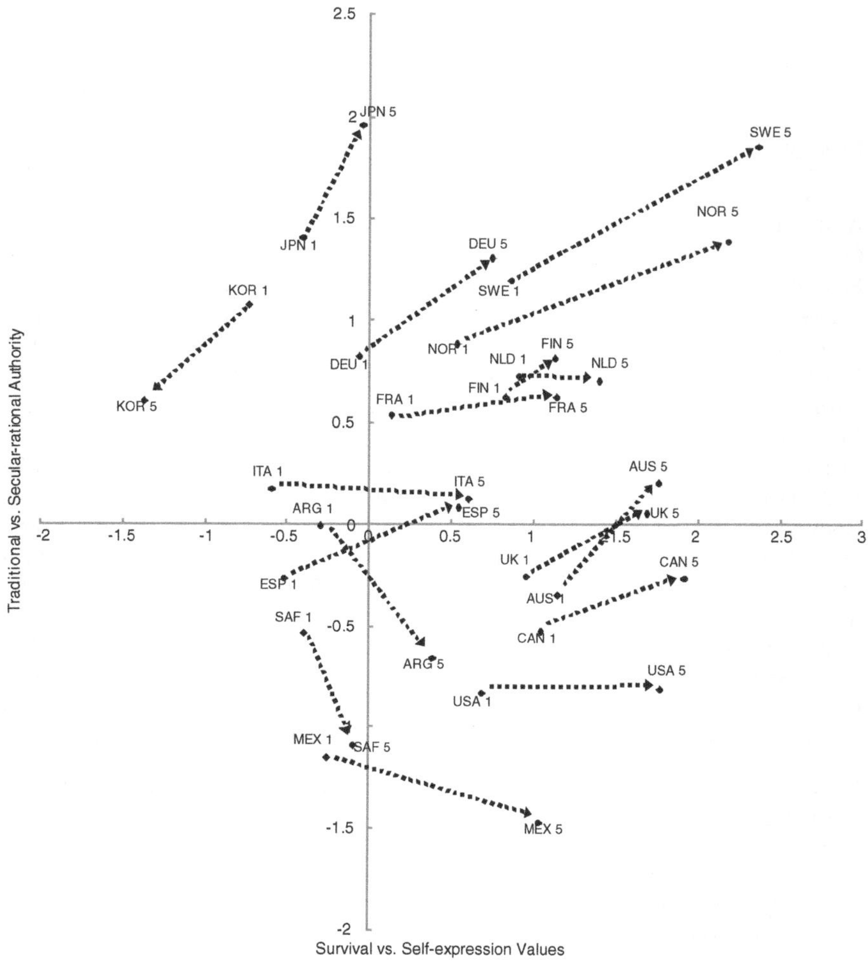

Figure 9.1 Changes in Inglehart cultural distances, "cultural map", waves 1 and 5

(the remaining nine countries). Likewise, the countries were also fairly evenly split between being more traditional (seven countries) or placing greater focus on secular-rational authority (10 countries). Accordingly, in terms of quadrant placement within our cross-plot, during the first WVS wave, these 17 countries were quite dispersed. Five countries were located in quadrant I (upper right, indicating an emphasis on self-expression values and secular-rational authority), another five were in quadrant II (upper left, where survival values and secular-rational authority are emphasized), four were located in quadrant III (lower right, a mix of self-expression values and traditional orientation), and the remaining three were located in quadrant IV (lower left, a combination of survival values and traditional orientation).

A near-quarter century later, the vast majority of countries (14 of the 17 listed) emphasize self-expression values, and 12 of the 17 countries are more focused on secular-rational authority. As a result, 10 countries are now in the upper right quadrant (an increase of five countries). The lower left quadrant still contains four countries as it did in 1983. However, there are now only two countries in the upper left quadrant (a decrease of three) and only one in the lower right quadrant (decrease of two). Thus, we have witnessed considerable changes in the cultural orientations of these countries over a relatively brief period of time. Further, during this time period, as is noted earlier and in Table 9.1, all of the involved countries have increased their degree of global integration.

The changes in orientation that are detailed in Table 9.2 are also illustrated in Figure 9.1. A cursory review of the figure indicates the considerable left-to-right movement over time that is identified in Table 9.2. Again, left-to-right movements are found for all countries in the cohort with the single exception of South Korea (KOR). We also see that there are some upward and some downward movements in the figure, as has been noted. Returning to Table 9.2 and looking to the change in the group average values for the TSR and SSE cultural dimensions, we see that the average change over the TSR dimension is equal to 0.11. A t-test of the difference in TSR dimension mean values between wave 5 and wave 1 yields a test statistic of 0.43 ($p = 0.3367$), which falls short of the critical value that is necessary to say that the change is significantly different from zero. In other words, there has been no significant change in the average TSR value over the time period. We also see that the average change over the SSE dimension during the period is equal to 0.78. There are two things to note here. First, the difference in SSE mean values is significantly different from zero ($t = 3.34$). Second, the change is positive, meaning there has been, generally speaking, rightward movement in the cross-plot (i.e., movement away from an emphasis on survival and towards self-expression).

Panels A and B of Table 9.3 present the country pair-specific cultural distance values from the first and fifth waves of the WVS respectively. These values are calculated using the mean values, at the country level, of the TSR and SSE dimensions presented in Table 9.2. Comparing the differences in the country pair-specific cultural distance over the two survey periods, we see that the average change in pairwise cultural distance is positive for all 17 countries, ranging from as low as 0.01 for Australia to 1.11 for South Korea. That is to say that, between the first and fifth waves of the WVS, each of the 17 countries listed in the table became more culturally distant compared to the typical country in this cohort.

More striking are the findings that, of the 272 country pair-specific changes in cultural distance presented in Table 9.4, 210 of the changes in cultural distances (i.e., 77.2 percent) are positive and only 62 changes are negative. Checking the number of cultural distance values that increased or decreased, by country, over the period, reveals some impressive differences. Four of the 17 countries (Japan, South Korea, South Africa and Sweden) have seen increases in their cultural distances from all other 16 countries in the cohort. Another two countries – Argentina and Norway – have seen increases in their cultural distance values for 15 of the 16 other countries in the cohort, while Mexico has seen its cultural distance increase for 14 of the 16 countries. While there are no countries for which we see more decreased

Table 9.3 Inglehart cultural distances, waves 1 and 5

Panel A: Cultural Distances, wave 1 (1981–1984)

	ARG	*AUS*	*CAN*	*FIN*	*FRA*	*DEU*	*ITA*	*JPN*	*KOR*	*MEX*	*NLD*	*NOR*	*SAF*	*ESP*	*SWE*	*UK*	*USA*
ARG	0.00	1.48	1.44	1.29	0.69	0.86	0.35	1.41	1.17	1.15	1.40	1.22	0.54	0.34	1.66	1.27	1.28
AUS	1.48	0.00	0.21	1.02	1.34	1.68	1.82	2.34	2.36	1.62	1.10	1.37	1.55	1.66	1.57	0.21	0.67
CAN	1.44	0.21	0.00	1.17	1.40	1.75	1.78	2.41	2.39	1.44	1.26	1.50	1.44	1.58	1.73	0.28	0.48
FIN	1.29	1.02	1.17	0.00	0.70	0.91	1.49	1.46	1.62	2.08	0.13	0.39	1.68	1.61	0.57	0.89	1.47
FRA	0.69	1.34	1.40	0.70	0.00	0.35	0.81	1.02	1.02	1.73	0.79	0.53	1.19	1.03	0.98	1.14	1.48
DEU	0.86	1.68	1.75	0.91	0.35	0.00	0.84	0.67	0.72	1.99	0.98	0.60	1.40	1.18	0.99	1.49	1.82
ITA	0.35	1.82	1.78	1.49	0.81	0.84	0.00	1.24	0.91	1.37	1.60	1.33	0.74	0.45	1.77	1.61	1.63
JPN	1.41	2.34	2.41	1.46	1.02	0.67	1.24	0.00	0.47	2.56	1.48	1.07	1.94	1.67	1.28	2.15	2.49
KOR	1.17	2.36	2.39	1.62	1.02	0.72	0.91	0.47	0.00	2.28	1.68	1.28	1.65	1.36	1.59	2.15	2.38
MEX	1.15	1.62	1.44	2.08	1.73	1.99	1.37	2.56	2.28	0.00	2.21	2.19	0.64	0.93	2.60	1.51	0.99
NLD	1.40	1.10	1.26	0.13	0.79	0.98	1.60	1.48	1.68	2.21	0.00	0.40	1.81	1.73	0.47	0.98	1.58
NOR	1.22	1.37	1.50	0.39	0.53	0.60	1.33	1.07	1.28	2.19	0.40	0.00	1.70	1.56	0.45	1.21	1.73
SAF	0.54	1.55	1.44	1.68	1.19	1.40	0.74	1.94	1.65	0.64	1.81	1.70	0.00	0.30	2.13	1.38	1.12
ESP	0.34	1.66	1.58	1.61	1.03	1.18	0.45	1.67	1.36	0.93	1.73	1.56	0.30	0.00	2.00	1.47	1.33
SWE	1.66	1.57	1.73	0.57	0.98	0.99	1.77	1.28	1.59	2.60	0.47	0.45	2.13	2.00	0.00	1.45	2.04
UK	1.27	0.21	0.28	0.89	1.14	1.49	1.61	2.15	2.15	1.51	0.98	1.21	1.38	1.47	1.45	0.00	0.64
USA	1.28	0.67	0.48	1.47	1.48	1.82	1.63	2.49	2.38	0.99	1.58	1.73	1.12	1.33	2.04	0.64	0.00
Avg.	1.03	1.29	1.31	1.09	0.95	1.07	1.16	1.51	1.47	1.61	1.15	1.09	1.25	1.19	1.37	1.17	1.36
Std. Dev.	0.48	0.69	0.70	0.59	0.43	0.55	0.56	0.74	0.71	0.71	0.63	0.60	0.61	0.59	0.70	0.61	0.67

Panel B: Cultural Distances, wave 5 (2005–2009)

	ARG	*AUS*	*CAN*	*FIN*	*FRA*	*DEU*	*ITA*	*JPN*	*KOR*	*MEX*	*NLD*	*NOR*	*SAF*	*ESP*	*SWE*	*UK*	*USA*
ARG	0.00	1.62	1.58	1.65	1.49	2.00	0.82	2.66	2.16	1.04	1.70	2.72	0.64	0.77	3.20	1.49	1.39
AUS	1.62	0.00	0.50	0.88	0.75	1.49	1.15	2.51	3.15	1.83	0.62	1.25	2.26	1.22	1.76	0.17	1.02
CAN	1.58	0.50	0.00	1.34	1.18	1.96	1.37	2.96	3.39	1.50	1.10	1.67	2.17	1.41	2.17	0.39	0.57
FIN	1.65	0.88	1.34	0.00	0.19	0.62	0.86	1.63	2.50	2.29	0.29	1.19	2.27	0.93	1.61	0.94	1.75
FRA	1.49	0.75	1.18	0.19	0.00	0.78	0.73	1.78	2.50	2.10	0.27	1.29	2.11	0.80	1.73	0.79	1.57
DEU	2.00	1.49	1.96	0.62	0.78	0.00	1.19	1.02	2.22	2.80	0.88	1.43	2.54	1.24	1.70	1.56	2.35
ITA	0.82	1.15	1.37	0.86	0.73	1.19	0.00	1.94	2.03	1.66	0.98	2.01	1.41	0.07	2.46	1.08	1.49
JPN	2.66	2.51	2.96	1.63	1.78	1.02	1.94	0.00	1.89	3.60	1.91	2.29	3.05	1.96	2.40	2.57	3.31
KOR	2.16	3.15	3.39	2.50	2.50	2.22	2.03	1.89	0.00	3.18	2.76	3.62	2.12	1.98	3.92	3.10	3.44
MEX	1.04	1.83	1.50	2.29	2.10	2.80	1.66	3.60	3.18	0.00	2.21	3.08	1.19	1.64	3.58	1.66	0.98
NLD	1.70	0.62	1.10	0.29	0.27	0.88	0.98	1.91	2.76	2.21	0.00	1.03	2.34	1.05	1.50	0.71	1.56
NOR	2.72	1.25	1.67	1.19	1.29	1.43	2.01	2.29	3.62	3.08	1.03	0.00	3.36	2.08	0.50	1.42	2.24
SAF	0.64	2.26	2.17	2.27	2.11	2.54	1.41	3.05	2.12	1.19	2.34	3.36	0.00	1.34	3.83	2.12	1.88
ESP	0.77	1.22	1.41	0.93	0.80	1.24	0.07	1.96	1.98	1.64	1.05	2.08	1.34	0.00	2.53	1.14	1.52
SWE	3.20	1.76	2.17	1.61	1.73	1.70	2.46	2.40	3.92	3.58	1.50	0.50	3.83	2.53	0.00	1.92	2.73
UK	1.49	0.17	0.39	0.94	0.79	1.56	1.08	2.57	3.10	1.66	0.71	1.42	2.12	1.14	1.92	0.00	0.87
USA	1.39	1.02	0.57	1.75	1.57	2.35	1.49	3.31	3.44	0.98	1.56	2.24	1.88	1.52	2.73	0.87	0.00
Avg.	1.58	1.30	1.49	1.23	1.18	1.52	1.25	2.20	2.59	2.02	1.23	1.84	2.04	1.28	2.21	1.29	1.69
Std. Dev.	0.81	0.83	0.88	0.74	0.73	0.74	0.66	0.87	0.92	0.99	0.78	0.99	0.94	0.67	1.07	0.83	0.92

Table 9.4 Changes in Inglehart cultural distances, wave 5 cultural distance less wave 1 cultural distance

	ARG	*AUS*	*CAN*	*FIN*	*FRA*	*DEU*	*ITA*	*JPN*	*KOR*	*MEX*	*NLD*	*NOR*	*SAF*	*ESP*	*SWE*	*UK*	*USA*
ARG	0.00	0.14	0.14	0.37	0.80	1.14	0.47	1.24	1.00	−0.11	0.30	1.50	0.11	0.43	1.54	0.21	0.10
AUS	0.14	0.00	0.29	−0.14	−0.59	−0.19	−0.66	0.17	0.79	0.21	−0.48	−0.12	0.71	−0.45	0.19	−0.04	0.35
CAN	0.14	0.29	0.00	0.17	−0.21	0.21	−0.42	0.55	1.00	0.05	−0.16	0.17	0.73	−0.17	0.43	0.11	0.10
FIN	0.37	−0.14	0.17	0.00	−0.51	−0.29	−0.63	0.18	0.88	0.21	0.16	0.81	0.58	−0.68	1.04	0.05	0.28
FRA	0.80	−0.59	−0.21	−0.51	0.00	0.43	−0.09	0.75	1.48	0.37	−0.52	0.76	0.92	−0.23	0.76	−0.35	0.10
DEU	1.14	−0.19	0.21	−0.29	0.43	0.00	0.35	0.35	1.51	0.81	−0.09	0.83	1.14	0.06	0.71	0.08	0.53
ITA	0.47	−0.66	−0.42	−0.63	-0.09	0.35	0.00	0.70	1.12	0.28	−0.62	0.68	0.67	−0.38	0.69	−0.53	−0.14
JPN	1.24	0.17	0.55	0.18	0.75	0.35	0.70	0.00	1.42	1.03	0.43	1.22	1.11	0.29	1.12	0.42	0.82
KOR	1.00	0.79	1.00	0.88	1.48	1.51	1.12	1.42	0.00	0.89	1.08	2.34	0.48	0.62	2.33	0.95	1.06
MEX	−0.11	0.21	0.05	0.21	0.37	0.81	0.28	1.03	0.89	0.00	0.00	0.89	0.56	0.71	0.98	0.15	−0.01
NLD	0.30	−0.48	−0.16	0.16	−0.52	−0.09	−0.62	0.43	1.08	0.00	0.00	0.63	0.53	−0.68	1.03	−0.27	−0.01
NOR	1.50	−0.12	0.17	0.81	0.76	0.83	0.68	1.22	2.34	0.89	0.63	0.00	1.66	0.53	0.06	0.20	0.51
SAF	0.11	0.71	0.73	0.58	0.92	1.14	0.67	1.11	0.48	0.56	0.53	1.66	0.00	1.05	1.70	0.74	0.76
ESP	0.43	−0.45	−0.17	−0.68	−0.23	0.06	−0.38	0.29	0.62	0.71	-0.68	0.53	1.05	0.00	0.53	−0.33	0.19
SWE	1.54	0.19	0.43	1.04	0.76	0.71	0.69	1.12	2.33	0.98	1.03	0.06	1.70	0.53	0.00	0.47	0.70
UK	0.21	−0.04	0.11	0.05	−0.35	0.08	−0.53	0.42	0.95	0.15	−0.27	0.20	0.74	−0.33	0.47	0.00	0.23
USA	0.10	0.35	0.10	0.28	0.10	0.53	−0.14	0.82	1.06	−0.01	−0.01	0.51	0.76	0.19	0.70	0.23	0.00
Avg.	0.55	0.01	0.18	0.15	0.23	0.45	0.09	0.69	1.11	0.41	0.08	0.75	0.79	0.09	0.84	0.12	0.33
Std. Dev.	0.54	0.41	0.35	0.50	0.61	0.52	0.57	0.44	0.59	0.40	0.53	0.65	0.45	0.51	0.60	0.38	0.35
N incr.	15	8	12	11	9	13	8	16	16	14	8	15	16	9	16	11	13
N decr.	1	8	4	5	7	3	8	0	0	2	8	1	0	7	0	5	3

cultural distance values than increased values, three countries (Australia, Italy, and the Netherlands) have equal numbers of increases and decreases.

Representative of the general extent to which cultural distances between the countries in this cohort have increased, the average number of increased cultural distances is equal to 12.35 and the average number of decreased cultural distances is only 3.65. To demonstrate the extent to which cultural distances among this cohort of countries changed during the reference period, Figure 9.2 illustrates the changes in cultural distances, from the largest decrease (on the left side of the x axis) to the largest increase. Because the overwhelming majority of instances indicate increased cultural distance values, it is clear that the average change in cultural distance is positive.

The fact that cultural distances among these countries have largely increased is, in itself, an interesting development. When coupled with the fact (as is shown in Table 9.1) that every one of these 17 countries saw their KOF Globalization Index values increase over the 1983 to 2007 period, and that their CSGR Globalization Index values also increased from 1983 to 2004, the increasing cultural distances become both even more interesting and, perhaps, more informative. While this analysis is purely descriptive, it would appear that this cohort of countries has increased their individual levels of integration into the global economy while becoming more culturally distant from the other members of the cohort. While this does not definitively refute the notion that globalization leads to cultural homogeneity, it clearly contradicts the notion and, thus, does not support the cultural homogenization hypothesis.

Changes in the KOF economic globalization index and cultural proximity measures

Given the shortcomings of only being able to compare cultural distances over time for 17 countries and not being able to isolate pairwise increases in economic integration, in this section we pursue a different approach. We still hope to provide information that may help to answer the question of whether economic globalization leads to cultural homogeneity. The difference in the approach employed here is that we now compare annual changes in country-specific KOF economic globalization dimension values, over the years from 1980 through 2010, with the corresponding annual changes in country-specific KOF cultural proximity sub-dimension values for the same period. Additionally, we compare the annual changes in the values of the cultural proximity sub-dimension to the KOF actual flows and restrictions sub-dimensions. In a few words, the actual flows and restrictions sub-dimensions collectively form the economic globalization dimension, and the cultural proximity sub-dimension is a component of the social globalization dimension. Thus, by examining the relationships at multiple levels of detail, we increase the amount of information to be garnered from the analysis and, thus, the likelihood that we may attain evidence that supports an answer to our question. Finally, we undertake a variation on this approach. Since annual changes may be too frequent for us to observe any significant changes in

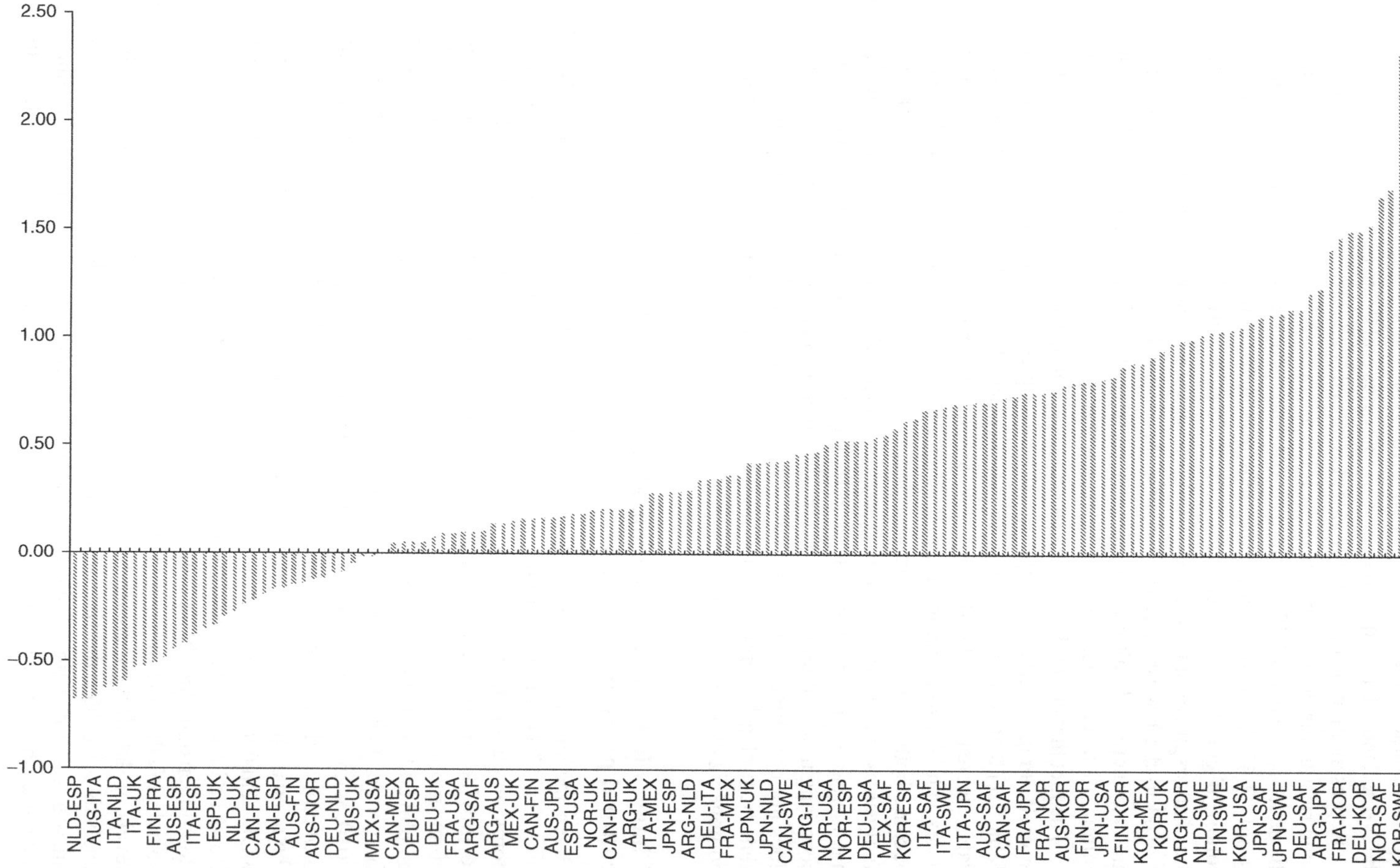

Figure 9.2 Country pair-specific changes in Inglehart cultural distance measure, waves 1 to 5

the relationships, as indicated by the correlation coefficient values, we also calculate the pairwise correlation coefficients for the difference in 2010 series values relative to their 1980 levels.

Table 9.5 presents the correlation coefficients, calculated for each of the series comparisons, and for each pairing of the cultural proximity sub-dimension and the series that are related to the economic globalization dimension. Panel A reports the correlation coefficients when the annual (year-to-year) changes are compared. We see that, across the economic globalization dimension series and the values of the actual flows and restrictions sub-dimensions, the correlation coefficient values are practically zero. In fact, t-tests of the significance of the correlation coefficients indicate that none of the three coefficients presented in Panel A are significant from zero. Scatter plots of these series are provided as Figure 9.3.

In Panel B of Table 9.5, we present the correlation coefficients obtained when comparing the changes, from 1980 to 2010, in the cultural proximity sub-dimension and the series that related to the economic globalization dimension. Unlike the results presented in Panel A, in this case we do observe statistical significance. More specifically, the correlation coefficient of the cultural proximity-economic globalization dimension pairing is equal to 0.1683 and it is significant from zero. Likewise, the cultural proximity-actual flows correlation coefficient is 0.1793 and also significantly different from zero. As before, the correlation coefficient for the pairing of changes in the cultural proximity series and the restrictions dimension is not significant from zero. Corresponding scatter plots are presented in Figure 9.4.

Table 9.5 Correlation coefficients, changes in KOF cultural proximity and economic globalization dimension values

Panel A: Annual Changes

	Economic Globalization Index	*Actual Flows Dimension*	*Restrictions Dimension*
Cultural Proximity Sub-dimension	0.0233	0.0071	0.0243
n	4,293	5,000	4,004
t statistic	1.5267	0.502	1.5377

Panel B: Change from 1980 to 2010

	Economic Globalization Index	*Actual Flows Dimension*	*Restrictions Dimension*
Cultural Proximity Sub-dimension	0.1683*	0.1793**	–0.0029
n	131	150	122
t statistic	1.9392	2.2172	0.0318

"***", "**", and "*" indicate statistical significance from zero at the 1 percent, 5 percent, and 10 percent levels, respectively.

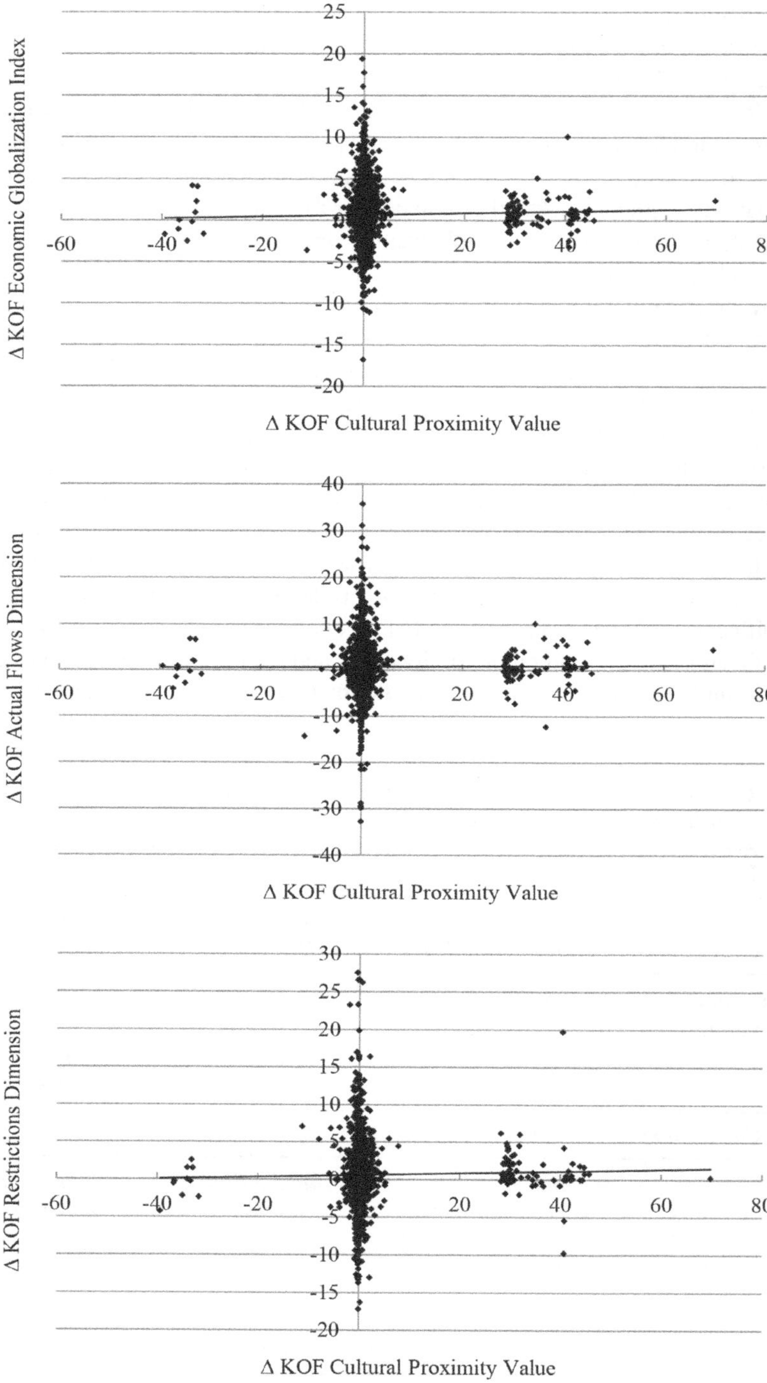

Figure 9.3 Scatterplots: annual changes in KOF cultural proximity and economic globalization dimension values, 1980–2010

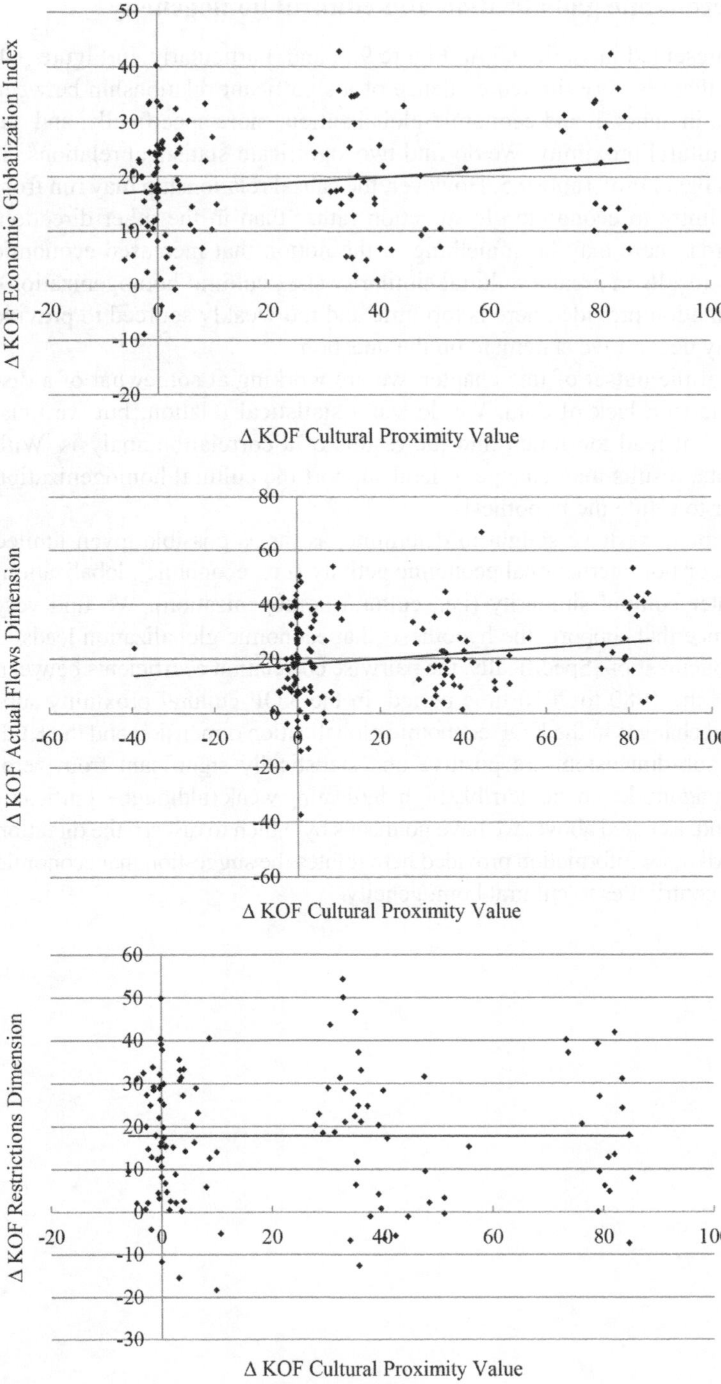

Figure 9.4 Scatterplots: change in KOF cultural proximity and economic globalization dimension values, 1980 and 2010

Increased economic globalization and cultural homogeneity

The results presented in Table 9.5, in Figure 9.3, and, particularly, in Figure 9.4, indicate that there is very limited evidence of a significant relationship between globalization, in general, and economic globalization, more specifically, and our measure of cultural proximity. We do find two significant statistical relations, as is reported in Panel B of Table 9.5. However, the causal relationship may run from cultural proximity to economic globalization rather than in the other direction. In a few words, there may be something to the notion that increased economic globalization results in greater cultural similarity (i.e., cultural homogenization), but the information provided here is too little and too weakly sourced to provide a basis for any declarative statement on the question.

As noted at the outset of this chapter, we are working at somewhat of a disadvantage due to a lack of data. We do see a statistical relation, but we must be careful to not read too much into the results of a correlation analysis. With additional data, results may change to lend support the cultural homogenization hypothesis or to refute the hypothesis.

In this chapter, we have sought to determine, as far as possible given limited data, whether or not international economic activity (i.e., economic globalization) leads to greater cultural similarity (i.e., cultural homogenization). We find very limited evidence that supports the hypothesis that economic globalization leads to cultural homogenization. Specifically, the pairwise correlation coefficients between changes, over the 1980 to 2010 time period, in the KOF cultural proximity sub-dimension and changes in the KOF economic globalization dimension and the KOF actual flows sub-dimension, are positive and statistically significant from zero. Even so, the magnitudes are not terribly high, indicating weak (although significant) correlations and, as noted above, we have no means by which to discern the direction of causality. All other information provided here refutes the suggestion that economic globalization contributes to cultural homogeneity.

10 The implications of being culturally distant

The goal of this book has been to provide information on the relationship between cross-societal cultural differences and economic globalization – specifically, through the potential influence of cultural differences on the transaction costs that may affect international trade flows, foreign direct investment, and international migration. A second, related topic that we have explored is the common criticism that repeated economic interaction and intensified international economic integration (i.e., economic globalization) diminish cultural differences and, thus, result in a loss of cultural diversity and in greater cultural homogeneity. Developing a better understanding of the relationship between cross-societal cultural differences and the facets of economic globalization we have examined in this work provides a more complete understanding of international economic integration and, more generally, the process of globalization.

We began by producing working definitions for the terms "culture" and "globalization". Our working definition of culture has been "the totality of behavior, beliefs, arts, institutions, and all other avenues by which a population, community, or a class collectively expresses its values and attitudes." (White, 2010). To describe globalization, we have leaned on two, related terms and the definitions provided for each by Scholte (2002). These terms are "internationalization", defined as "a growth of transactions and interdependence between countries (2002, p. 54). From this perspective, a more global world is one where more messages, ideas, merchandise, money, investments and people cross borders between national-state-territorial units" and "liberalization", which Scholte defines as "a process of removing officially imposed restrictions on movements of resources between countries in order to form an 'open' and 'borderless' world economy. On this understanding, globalization occurs as authorities reduce or abolish regulatory measures like trade barriers, foreign-exchange restrictions, capital controls, and visa requirements" (2002, p. 56).

To provide an appropriate background understanding of recent globalization, we detailed the three waves of globalization that have occurred over the past 150 years or so. Focusing on the past few decades, we introduced multiple measures of globalization, in the form of indexes, and compared the indexes and their component sub-dimensions to one another. Although varied in their construction and coverage, the indexes are largely consistent with each other. This is to be expected as they are frequently constructed using the same or similar data series. To link recent periods of globalization and the corresponding index measures to the topic of cultural differences, we also introduced a number of variables that have been used throughout the book to produce measures of cross-societal cultural distance. This set of variables includes four composite measures of cultural distance as well as the corresponding component dimensions of culture that underlie the composite measures. Also included in the set are a number of index variables that represent linguistic proximity, language distance, religious distance, and even genetic distance between populations. These index variables are included as they serve as proxies for cultural differences. Additionally, and with a similar motive in mind, five dichotomous measures of language commonality are included among this set of variables. The data on cultural differences (i.e., cultural distance) and the measures of globalization are presented in separate chapters; however, the discussions are not entirely separate. Each topic overlaps, from time to time, with the other, and parallels are drawn.

To facilitate our empirical analysis and, thus, to allow the primary and secondary research questions to be addressed, we employed both descriptive analysis and rigorously applied appropriate econometric techniques. The theoretical bases for our examinations and the corresponding empirical specifications are detailed in Chapter 5. Our data, which are also largely detailed in that chapter, represent a large number of culturally and economically heterogeneous countries and, while the reference periods for our analyses vary based on the facet of economic globalization considered, we have generally examined annual data covering the period from the early 1980s through to the recent past. For example, our analysis of the potential influence of cultural distance on FDI is completed using data for the years 1985 through 2010, while our examination of the effects of cultural distance on international migration spans the period from 1981 through 2014.

The intuition behind our primary research question is that greater cultural differences are anticipated to increase the transaction costs associated with cross-border economic transactions. Intuitively, these higher costs, to the extent that they cannot be overcome, would inhibit the bilateral trade flows and possibly the successful completion of new trade deals. Such differences may also make FDI less likely to occur, and they could make international migration more costly and, hence, a less common occurrence. For all three facets of economic globalization, the expected relationship is generally the same: cultural differences lead to increased transaction costs which, in turn, result in less intensive and less frequent cross-border interactions.

Our general finding is that, controlling for other factors that determine trade flows, FDI flows and stocks and international migration flows, greater cultural distance between countries corresponds with reduced cross-border activity. Specifically, our estimation results indicate that country pairs that are more culturally distant trade less intensively and are less likely to initiate new trade deals. Bilateral FDI levels are lower among country pairs that are more culturally-distant from one another. As a result, FDI stocks are lower among culturally-distant country pairs. Also, source and destination countries that are more culturally dissimilar are found to have reduced levels of international migration between them. With respect to the potential for economic globalization to result in cultural homogeneity, a lack of data limits our ability to say anything definitive. While there is no strong evidence to indicate that greater economic globalization corresponds with cultural homogenization, we do see some very limited evidence in the form of pairwise correlation coefficients that supports the notion of a statistical relationship between economic globalization and cultural homogeneity. The findings presented here extend the related literature, inform public and political discussions, and, potentially, provide information beneficial for the formulation of public policy.

In the next section, we present the estimated effects of greater cultural distance on bilateral trade flows, FDI flows and stocks, and international migration. This is followed by some final, ending thoughts.

A summary of results

In our analysis, to represent cultural differences, we have employed a large number of variables, including four composite measures of cultural distance. These composite measures have been constructed using data from the first five waves of the World Values Surveys, from Hofstede's cultural dimensions data, and by using data from the GLOBE Project. We have also employed variables that represent the component dimensions of culture from which the composite cultural distance measures are constructed. Lastly, we use a set of variables that serve as proxies for cultural differences. These measures include indexes of linguistic similarity, language differences, religious distances, genetic distances between populations, and a group of dummy variables that represent language commonality. By using such a large and varied set of cultural distance measures, we hedge against the shortcomings of any one measure. The logic behind this approach is that if consistent results are obtained from a series of estimations that employ related, yet distinct, measures of cultural differences, then a much stronger case can be made that the documented relationship is meaningful.

We now discuss our findings, somewhat briefly, with respect to each of the facets of economic globalization we have examined, and in terms of the cultural homogenization hypothesis.

International trade

We began our econometric examination seeking to develop a more complete understanding of the relationship between cross-societal cultural differences (i.e., cultural distance) and international trade. The results are presented and discussed in Chapter 6. They indicate that, generally speaking, greater cultural differences correspond with reduced levels of bilateral trade. For example, all else equal, a one percent increase in the Inglehart measure of cultural distance is found to reduce bilateral trade flows by 0.0926 percent. As the Inglehart measure varies over time, separate estimations were performed for each of the first five waves of the WVS. The results confirm that the statistically significant negative influence of cultural differences on bilateral trade is generally consistent across time. Results obtained when employing the other three composite measures of cultural distance when estimating our regression model tell a similar story. All three measures have coefficient estimates that are negative and statistically significant. A summary of the coefficient estimates of the composite cultural distance measures is provided in Table 10.1. Column A of the table presents the results from the estimations that involve bilateral trade flows.

When our battery of empirical specifications is estimated using each of the variables in our set of proxy measures for cultural distance in turn, we find a consistent pattern of statistical significance across the estimated coefficients. More specifically, in 11 of 12 instances, we find that the estimated coefficient is of the anticipated sign and is statistically significant from zero. The results are much more mixed when the component dimensions that correspond to the composite cultural distance measures are considered as determinants of trade flows. Of the 21 coefficients of the component dimension measures, only 10 were negative, as expected, and statistically significant. Another eight coefficients were significant from zero but positive in sign, and three others were not significantly different from zero. Thus, the frequency of commonality in coefficient sign and statistical significance observed between the coefficients of the composite measures of cultural distance and the set of proxy variables lends considerable credence to the assumed relationship between cultural differences and international trade flows. However, the "mixed bag" of coefficients found for the component dimensions weakens this support to some degree.

To determine whether cultural differences inhibit trade at the extensive margin, a series of estimations were conducted using the Tobit regression technique and the McDonald and Moffitt (1980) decomposition procedure. Again, looking to the composite measures of cultural distance, we see that the coefficients of the Inglehart measure and of the 6-factor Hofstede measure are negative and statistically significant, indicating that greater cultural distance does correspond with a reduced likelihood that trade will occur. The coefficient of the 4-factor Hofstede measure, however, is unexpectedly positive and significant from zero. Checking the coefficients of the component cultural dimensions, we again find a mix of positive and negative coefficient values.

Finally, as a form of robustness check, we repeat our series of estimations with 1-digit SITC sector-level bilateral trade values employed as the dependent variable series rather than the aggregate bilateral trade values employed earlier. The results, obtained when estimating the specifications with our composite cultural distance measures, with the component dimensions of cultural distance, and with our set of proxy variables, are quite consistent. Specifically, we find that 280 of the 380 estimated coefficients (73.7 percent) are of the expected sign and are statistically significant from zero. Of the remaining 100 coefficients, 55 (14.5 percent) are significantly different from zero but are of the unexpected sign and the remaining 45 (11.8 percent) are not significantly different from zero.

Generally speaking, the empirical findings are largely consistent across the broad set of cultural distance measures employed. Moreover, the results are

Table 10.1 Summary of estimated coefficients, composite cultural distance measures and proxy variables

Cultural Distance Measure . . .	*Economic Globalization Facet . . .*				
	Trade	*FDI Flows*	*FDI Stocks*	*Migration*	
				NB Coef.	*Logit Coef.*
	(a)	*(b)*	*(c)*	*(d)*	*(e)*
ln Inglehart Cultural Distance$_{ijt}$	−0.0926***	−0.5514***	−0.4423***	−0.1663***	−0.0823
	(0.0109)	(0.0575)	(0.0571)	(0.0198)	(0.0808)
ln Hofstede 4-factor Cultural Distance$_{ij}$	−0.0245***	−0.4591***	−0.4653***	−0.0788***	0.0621*
	(0.0055)	(0.0308)	(0.0308)	(0.0087)	(0.0332)
ln Hofstede 6-factor Cultural Distance$_{ij}$	−0.0419***	−0.7679***	−0.7993***	−0.1677***	0.0928**
	(0.008)	(0.0388)	(0.037)	(0.0114)	(0.0447)
ln GLOBE Cultural Distance$_{ij}$	−0.1416***	−1.1598***	−1.0547***	−0.1138***	−0.5051***
	(0.0181)	(0.1105)	(0.0953)	(0.0281)	(0.0992)

"***", "**", and "*" denote statistical significance form zero at the 1 percent, 5 percent, and 10 percent levels, respectively.

consistent across estimation procedures (i.e., feasible generalized least squares and Tobit estimation techniques) and across aggregate and disaggregate (i.e., SITC 1-digit sector classifications) trade values. Moreover, the results are consistent with prior studies of the relationship. Thus, we conclude that, generally speaking, greater cross-societal cultural differences are negatively related to bilateral trade flows in that such differences both reduce the volume of trade occurring between trading partners (have a negative effect on the intensive margin of trade) and diminish the likelihood that trade will begin to occur (have a negative influence on the extensive margin of trade).

Foreign direct investment

The second facet of economic globalization we have examined is foreign direct investment flows and stocks. Different from the analysis of international trade flows and that of international migration, which both used variants of the gravity model, the empirical framework used for this portion of the book is motivated by the results of Blonigen and Piger's (2011) application of Bayesian Model Averaging (BMA) to a set of potential determinants of FDI flows. The decision to use the set of determinants proposed by Blonigen and Piger is based, in part, on the lack of a strong alternative estimation framework. Prior studies of the determinants of FDI have employed a wide variety of possible empirical specifications. The set of variables identified by Blonigen and Piger are drawn from the existing empirical literature on FDI flows. This leads to the second rationale for using the set of proposed variables. Because the use of BMA identified each of the variables as having at least a 50 percent inclusion probability, and because the initial set of potential variables was drawn from the FDI literature, it can be argued that the variables each have a theoretical justification for their inclusion in the regression model as well as a statistical justification.

Again beginning our summary by focusing on the coefficients of our composite measures of cultural distance, we find that all four are negative and significantly different from zero when the FDI inflow variable is used as the dependent variable series. An example is provided by the coefficient of the 4-factor Hofstede measure of cultural distance. Given a one percent increase in the measure, all else held constant, the level of FDI flows from the typical parent country to the typical host is expected to decrease by 0.4591 percent. A similar result is obtained when the FDI stock variable is used in place of FDI inflows as the dependent variable series. Looking again at the coefficient of the 4-factor Hofstede measure, we see that, again with all else held constant, a one percent increase in cultural distance is estimated to decrease the parent country's FDI stock level in the host country by 0.4653 percent. These coefficient estimates, as well as those obtained when using the other composite cultural distance measures, are reported in columns B and C, respectively, of Table 10.1.

As with the examination of bilateral trade flows, the relationship between the measures of cultural distance employed in this study and the variables that represent FDI appears to be remarkably consistent across estimations. More specifically, we estimate our full complement of regression specifications using the FDI inflow variable, the FDI stock variable, and two other modest transformations of these variables: the level of FDI inflow as a share of the host country's GDP value and the FDI stock level, also as a share of the host country GDP value. When the two FDI inflow variables (the FDI inflow value, by itself, or the FDI inflow value as a share of the host country's GDP value) are employed as the dependent variable series, we find that 26 of the 34 coefficient estimates (76.5 percent) of the cultural distance variables are of the expected sign and are statistically significant from zero. Even more striking is that, when either of the FDI stock variables (i.e., the level of the FDI stock or the FDI stock value relative to the host country's GDP) are employed, we see that 32 of the 34 coefficient estimates (94.1 percent) are statistically significant and of the anticipated sign.

In summary, our results appear robust to our choice of cultural distance measure. Further, they seem to be robust to changes in the dependent variable series, with respect to both FDI flows and stocks and, notably, to the choice of FDI flows or stocks both in levels and as a proportion of the host country's GDP level. Given the results obtained from the battery of estimations and the general consistency and robustness of the coefficient estimates, we conclude that greater cultural dissimilarities do, indeed, correspond with reduced levels of bilateral FDI flows and of FDI stocks.

International migration

The empirical specification used to estimate the relationship between cultural differences and international migration is a variant of the gravity model of international trade. Since the dependent variable series is count data, to consider whether greater cultural differences (i.e., cultural distance) between a source and a destination country correspond with reduced migration flows, we estimate our now-familiar battery of regression specifications using the zero-inflated negative binomial technique. The results obtained when employing our four composite measures of cultural distance indicate that greater source-destination cultural distance corresponds with lower immigrant inflow values. The negative binomial coefficient of the Inglehart cultural distance variable is statistically significant and equal to -0.1663. The corresponding negative binomial coefficients of the remaining composite measures of cultural distance are also negative and statistically significant. These values are presented in column D of Table 10.1.

Examination of the relationship between cultural distance and international migration, while substituting the variables that represent differences along the component cultural dimensions for the composite cultural distance measures, reveals that, in most instances, the coefficient estimates confirm, in terms of sign and statistical significance, with those reported for the composite cultural distance measures. More specifically, of the coefficients estimated for the component dimensions, nine of 17 (52.9 percent) are negative and statistically significant. Only two coefficients (11.8 percent) are positive and significant from zero, while the remaining six coefficients (35.3 percent) are not significantly different from zero. It is notable, however, that four of the six statistically insignificant coefficient estimates are negative in sign.

When we employ the series of proxy measures to represent cultural similarity or differences, we find abundant evidence of a negative relationship between cultural differences and immigrant inflow values. The coefficients of both measures of linguistic distance between the source and destination countries are negative and significantly different from zero. The same can be said of the coefficients of the two measures of religious distance, and for those of the two measures of genetic distance. Similarly, the coefficients of the four dummy variables that represent various forms of language commonality are all positive and significantly different from zero. Thus, all coefficients that correspond with our set of proxy variables are of the expected signs and are statistically significant from zero. Thus, we can conclude that this facet of economic globalization is, like bilateral trade flows and foreign direct investment flows and stocks, negatively influenced by cultural differences.

Economic globalization and cultural homogeneity

From the results presented in Chapters 6 through 8 and summarized in the earlier portions of this chapter, we know that there is a robust, negative relationship between cultural distance and the three facets of economic globalization that we have considered. In all three instances, the direction of causality is assumed to run from the measure of cultural distance to the dependent variable series (i.e., from cross-societal cultural differences to economic globalization). It is possible, however, that through repeated interactions over time, cultures may begin to converge. It may also be possible, for example, that economic interactions are simply not powerful enough to change culture in any meaningful way. As the literature lacks a clear answer to this, the topic very much remains an open empirical question. Thus, we have attempted to determine whether economic globalization corresponds with cultural homogenization.

Before proceeding, it is important to make clear that the available data is largely insufficient to address this topic adequately, if "adequately" means reaching a strongly-supported conclusion. What data are available permit a descriptive analysis involving the comparison of changes in bilateral cultural distances among a cohort of 17 countries for which Inglehart cultural distance data are available in both the 1981–1984 period and the 2005–2009 period to changes in the countries' KOF economic globalization index values. As is turns out, all 17 countries had become more globalized during the period for which data are available. Thus, there would be support for the cultural homogenization hypothesis if a number (or perhaps the majority) of the countries either realized decreases in their average cultural distance values, across the 17 country cohort, or observed more decreases than increases in their bilateral cultural distance values over the period.

In all 17 cases, we found that the average cultural distance value increased. Further, in a vast majority of cases (14 of 17) there was a greater incidence of increased bilateral cultural distance values relative to the number of decreased values. The remaining three countries had equal numbers of increases and decreases in their bilateral cultural distance values. Overall, the average country in the group realized increases in more than three quarters (12.35 of 16) of its cultural distance values. Moreover, four of the 17 countries realized increases in bilateral cultural distance with all 16 other countries in the cohort, and two others realized increases in bilateral cultural distance with 15 of the 16.

Thus, based on this metric, there was no evidence found that would support the notion that greater economic globalization leads to cultural homogeneity. In fact, the results suggest the opposite – either that greater cultural distance facilitates increased economic globalization, or that higher degrees of economic globalization produce more cultural heterogeneity. Of course, the data employed in this portion is limited to 17 countries and, although the measure of cultural distance is bilateral, the globalization index values are constructed based on each country's interactions with the rest of the world (i.e., are multilateral).

A second approach was also considered. This time, the correlation coefficients for the annual change in the KOF cultural proximity sub-dimension over the period from 1980 through 2010 and the corresponding annual changes in the KOF series related to economic globalization (i.e., the economic globalization index, the actual flows dimension, and the restrictions dimension) were calculated. Additionally, recognizing that annual changes may be too frequent for a meaningful relationship to be observed, the change in each data series from 1980 to 2010 – that is, over the entire 31 year period – was calculated and compared. As with the first approach, here we are again using data that are constructed based on multilateral interactions; however, we gain coverage for a few additional years and, perhaps more importantly, we are able to include a much larger number of countries in the analysis.

The second approach did yield some evidence that affords limited support for the notion that economic globalization results in cultural homogeneity. Specifically, the pairwise correlation coefficient for the cultural proximity sub-dimension and the economic globalization index is equal to 0.1683. Similarly, the correlation coefficient for the cultural proximity sub-dimension and the actual flows dimension is equal to 0.1793. Thus, the two series move in the same direction and it could be said that increased economic globalization corresponds with greater cultural proximity and, thus, less cultural distinctiveness. Of course, these are correlation coefficients, so it could also be stated that countries that are culturally more proximate to others in a general sense are more apt to engage in activities such as trade, FDI, and migration. In other words, while we find some evidence that may support the hypothesis, there is also a good amount of evidence that refutes it. Accordingly, more work is needed before any firm conclusions can be drawn.

Estimated effects of changes in composite cultural distance measures on facets of economic globalization

We have established a significant negative relationship between cultural distance (a measure of the extent of cross-border cultural differences) and the three facets of economic globalization considered in this work. Extending from this conclusion, to gain a sense of the estimated influences of cultural differences on each facet considered, for trade, FDI, and migration, we calculate the corresponding effects of changes in each measure of cultural distance. More specifically, for the bilateral trade and FDI inflow and stock series, we estimate the proportional effect of a one standard deviation increase above the mean in each of the composite cultural distance measures. For example, we calculate the proportional increase that corresponds with an assumed increase in the relevant cultural distance measure above its mean value. We then use the corresponding regression coefficient which, due to the double-log function form of the regression model, can be interpreted as an elasticity to extrapolate an estimated proportional change in the dependent variable series. Further, we calculate the effect given the estimated value for each coefficient and for the 95 percent confidence interval that corresponds to each coefficient. Results are presented in Table 10.2.

For the international migration series, as the zero-inflated negative binomial regression technique was employed to generate the coefficient estimates, we exponentiate the negative binomial (NB) coefficients and the logit coefficients to obtain the corresponding predicted changes in the dependent variable series.

The top panel in Table 10.2 presents the coefficient estimates and associated lower bound and upper bound values for each of the four composite measures of cultural distance and each of the facets of economic globalization that we have considered. These values are reproduced from the tables presented in Chapters 6 through 8. The middle panel in Table 10.2 presents the mean value and standard deviation for each measure. These values, initially presented in Chapter 5, vary across the facets of economic globalization since the data samples varied. That is, there was a different number of observations for which complete data were available when, say, the 4-factor Hofstede measure of cultural distance was employed in the regression model to when the GLOBE measure was employed.

Panel C of Table 10.2 presents the corresponding proportional effects of one standard deviation increases above the mean values for each measure on the identified facet of economic globalization. Further, the 95 percent confidence interval for each coefficient estimate is used to produce a range of predicted proportional changes. For example, all else constant, a one standard deviation change in the GLOBE measure of cultural distance between a given pair of countries is estimated to reduce bilateral trade flows between the countries by 3.73 percent to 6.23 percent. Similarly, a one standard deviation increase in the Inglehart measure of cultural distance between a given pair of countries, all else constant, is estimated to reduce the level of FDI flows between the countries by 21.54 percent to 32.61 percent. It is notable that the estimated proportional effects for the levels of FDI flows and stocks are much higher, for all measures of cultural distance, than the effects estimated for bilateral trade and for migration.

Looking to the negative binomial coefficient of the Inglehart cultural distance measure reported in Panel C, we can say that if cultural distance were to increase by one percent then the expected immigrant inflow between the typical pair of source and destination countries in our sample, holding all else constant, would decrease by a factor of 0.8468. Similarly, a one percent increase in the 6-factor

Table 10.2 Estimated proportional effects of a standard deviation increase, composite cultural distance measures

Panel A: Coefficient Estimates and 95 Percent Confidence Intervals

Cultural Distance Measure . . .		*Economic Globalization Facet . . .*				
			FDI		*Migration*	
		Trade	*Inflows*	*Stocks*	*NB Coef.*	*Logit Coef.*
ln Inglehart Cultural $Distance_{ijt}$	Coefficient	−0.0926	−0.5514	−0.4423	−0.1663	0[a]
	Lower bound	−0.1140	−0.6641	−0.5542	−0.2051	0[a]
	Upper bound	0.0713	−0.4387	−0.3304	−0.1275	0[a]
ln Hofstede 4-factor Cultural $Distance_{ij}$	Coefficient	−0.0245	−0.4591	−0.4653	−0.0788	0.0621
	Lower bound	−0.0353	−0.5194	−0.5257	−0.0959	−0.003
	Upper bound	−0.0138	−0.3988	−0.4049	−0.0617	0.1273
ln Hofstede 6-factor Cultural $Distance_{ij}$	Coefficient	−0.0419	−0.7679	−0.7993	−0.1677	0.0928
	Lower bound	−0.0574	−0.8439	−0.8718	−0.1900	0.0051
	Upper bound	−0.0263	−0.6919	−0.7268	−0.1454	0.1804
ln GLOBE Cultural $Distance_{ij}$	Coefficient	−0.1416	−1.1598	−1.0547	−0.1138	−0.5051
	Lower bound	−0.1771	−1.37638	−1.2415	−0.1689	−0.6995
	Upper bound	−0.1060	−0.94322	−0.8679	−0.0587	−0.3107

[a] Corresponding coefficient estimate is not statistically significant from zero.

Panel B: Descriptive Statistics

					Migration	
		Trade	*Inflows*	*Stocks*	*NB Coef.*	*Logit Coef.*
Inglehart Cultural $Distance_{ijt}$	Mean	1.7997	1.7351	1.7348	.	.
	Std. Dev.	0.9029	0.852	0.8734	.	.

(continued)

Table 10.2 (continued)

					Migration	
		Trade	*Inflows*	*Stocks*	*NB Coef.*	*Logit Coef.*
Hofstede 4-factor Cultural Distance$_{ij}$	Mean	2.1349	2.3692	2.3924	.	.
	Std. Dev.	1.5634	1.6548	1.6619	.	.
Hofstede 6-factor Cultural Distance$_{ij}$	Mean	2.0951	2.1757	2.1399	.	.
	Std. Dev.	1.2008	1.2713	1.2584	.	.
GLOBE Cultural Distance$_{ij}$	Mean	24.203	25.4188	25.3702	.	.
	Std. Dev.	8.514	8.6487	8.6327	.	.

Panel C: Estimated Change in Economic Globalization Measure

			FDI		*Migration*	
		Trade[b]	*Inflows*[b]	*Stocks*[b]	*NB Coef.*[c]	*Logit Coef.*[c]
ln Inglehart Cultural Distance$_{ijt}$	Est. effect	−4.6457	−27.0758	−22.2680	−0.8468	.
	LB effect	−5.7193	−32.6098	−27.9025	−0.8146	.
	UB effect	3.5771	−21.5418	−16.6335	−0.8803	.
ln Hofstede 4-factor Cultural Distance$_{ij}$	Est. effect	−1.7941	−32.0665	−32.3224	−0.9242	1.0641
	LB effect	−2.5850	−36.2782	−36.5160	−0.9086	0.9970
	UB effect	−1.0106	−27.8547	−28.1289	−0.9401	1.1358
ln Hofstede 6-factor Cultural Distance$_{ij}$	Est. effect	−2.4015	−44.8698	−47.0040	−0.8456	1.0972
	LB effect	−3.2899	−49.3106	−51.2687	−0.8269	1.0051
	UB effect	−1.5074	−40.4289	−42.7394	−0.8647	1.1977
ln GLOBE Cultural Distance$_{ij}$	Est. effect	−4.9811	−39.4620	−35.8882	−0.8924	0.6034
	LB effect	−6.2299	−46.8311	−42.2440	−0.8446	0.4968
	UB effect	−3.7288	−32.0929	−29.5324	−0.9430	0.7329

[b] Values provided in Panel C are the estimated percent changes in trade flows, FDI inflows, and FDI stock values. See text for details of the calculations. [c] Values provided in Panel C are the estimated factor changes given a one percent increase in the corresponding measure of cultural distance.

Hofstede measure of cultural distance is estimated to correspond with a decrease in the level of the immigrant inflow that ranges from a factor of 0.8269 to a factor of 0.8647. Thus, the higher the value for the cultural distance measure, the less migration is predicted to occur between the source and destination countries.

Continuing with the results for the 6-factor Hofstede measure, but now turning our attention to the logit coefficient, we can say that, given a one percent increase in the measure, all else constant, the odds that there would be no migration between the source and destination country would increase by a factor of 1.0972. In other words, the higher the value for the cultural distance measure the greater the likelihood that there is no migration between the countries. While the coefficient estimates from the negative binomial estimations are consistent in sign (Panel A), and largely in effects (Panel C), across the composite measures of cultural distance, the same is not true when considering the logit coefficients. Specifically, while the coefficients of the two Hofstede cultural distance measures are, as expected, positive and significantly different from zero, the logit coefficient for the Inglehart measure is not significant from zero, and the logit coefficient for the GLOBE measure is significant from zero but is negative. Thus, there appears to be little support for an extensive margin effect of cultural distance on international migration flows.

Concluding thoughts

In this work, we have provided information that extends the related academic literature by seeking a more detailed understanding of the posited relationships between cultural differences and economic globalization. In doing so, we have addressed several related research questions. The primary research question involved whether or not cross-societal cultural differences have a negative influence on economic globalization. More specifically, segmenting this broad question into three pieces, we examined a possible relationship between cultural differences and bilateral trade flows, the potential influence of cultural differences on FDI flows and stocks, and how cultural differences may affect international migration flows. We also addressed, as far as possible, the related question of whether economic globalization leads to cultural homogeneity. In a sense, the work presented here is an exploration. It has attempted to add information on topics and relationships for which somewhat limited information previously existed.

We do find compelling evidence that cultural distance, as representative of cultural differences between countries, is negatively related to all three of the facets of economic globalization that we have considered. Generally speaking, these findings are robust. Thus, we can state our conclusions with confidence. In addition to the findings that relate to our primary research question, we also have found related information, such as the negative extensive margin effect of cultural distance on bilateral trade flows or the lack of an extensive margin effect of cultural distance on international migration flows. When addressing the question of cultural homogenization as a potential consequence of economic globalization, the results were, at best, inconclusive. Even so, the analysis did yield the result of no evidence being found to support the cultural homogenization hypothesis, and the corresponding information is provided here.

Given the importance of culture and the tremendous potential benefits that accompany globalization, it would appear very important to develop as complete an understanding of each topic as is possible. Further, and perhaps more importantly, the development of an understanding of the interrelation between the two topics, which we have addressed to some degree in this work, is likely to be of considerable value. The results that are presented here are, collectively, an effort towards this end. As is noted in the Preface, we hope that the information provided here is of interest to students, researchers, academicians, and, generally, to members of the public, and that it is useful for policy makers.

References

Albrow, Martin and Elizabeth King (1990) *Globalism, Knowledge, and Society*. London: Sage.

Anderson, James E. (1979) "A Theoretical Foundation for the Gravity Equation", *American Economic Review* 69(1): 106–16.

Anderson, James E. (2011) "The Gravity Model", *Annual Review of Economics* 3(1): 133–160.

Anderson, James E. and Eric van Wincoop (2003) "Gravity with Gravitas: A Solution to the Border Puzzle", *American Economic Review* 93(1): 190–92.

Arvis, Jean-Francois, Yann Duvall, Ben Shepherd, and Chorthip Utoktham (eds.) (2013) "Trade Costs in the Developing World: 1995–2010", World Bank Policy Research Working Paper No. 6309, Washington, DC: The World Bank.

Balasubramanyam, V.N. (2001) "Foreign Direct Investment in Developing Countries: Determinants and Impact", Paper presented at the OECD Global Forum on International Investment: New Horizons and Policy Challenges for Foreign Direct Investment in the 21st Century", 26–27 November, Mexico City, Mexico.

Banks, James A. and Cherry A. McGee Banks (1989). *Multicultural Education: Issues and Perspectives*. Needham Heights, MA: Allyn & Bacon.

Barlow, Maude (2002) "Cultural Diversity: The Right of Nations to Resist Cultural Homogenization", in *Alternatives to Economic Globalization: A Better World is Possible*, A Report of the International Forum on Globalization.

Barlow, Maude (2000) "Can National Cultures Survive Globalization?" Public lecture delivered at the Globalization and Live Performing Arts Conference. Melbourne, Australia. June 23.

Beine, Michel and Sara Salomone (2013) "The Network Effect in International Migration: Does Education Matter More than Gender?", *Scandinavian Journal of Economics* 115(2): 354–380.

Beine, Michel Ar, Frederic Docquier, and Maurice Schiff (2013) "International Migration, Transfer of Norms, and Home Country Fertility", *Canadian Journal of Economics* 46 (4): 1406–1430.

Beine, Michel Ar, Frederic Docquier, and Caglar Ozden (2011) "Diasporas", *Journal of Development Economics* 95(1): 30–41.

Beine, Michel Ar, Frederic Docquier, and Caglar Ozden (2010) "Diaspora Effects in International Migration: Key Questions and Methodological Issues", *Swiss Journal of Economics and Statistics* 146(4): 639–659.

Belot, Michele and Sjef Ederveen (2012) "Cultural Barriers in Migration between OECD Countries", *Journal of Population Economics* 25(3): 1077–1105.

Bénassy-Quéré, Agnès, Maylis Coupet, and Thierry Mayer (2005) "Institutional Determinants of Foreign Direct Investment", CEPII Working Paper No. 5.

Bergstrand, Jeffrey H. (1985) "The Gravity Equation in International Trade: Some Microeconomic Foundations and Empirical Evidence", *Review of Economics and Statistics* 67(3): 474–81.

Bergstrand, Jeffrey H. and Peter Egger (2007) "A Knowledge-and-Physical-Capital Model of International Trade Flows, Foreign Direct Investment, and Multinational Enterprises", *Journal of International Economics* 73(2): 278–308.

Beugelsdijk, Sjoerd, Henri de Groot, Gert-Jan Linders, and Arjen Slangen (2004) "Cultural Distance, Institutional Distance and Trade", European Regional Science Paper No. ersa04p265.

Bevan, Alan A. and Saul Estrin (2004) "The Determinants of Foreign Direct Investment into European Transition Economies", *Journal of Comparative Economics* 32(4): 775–787.

Blonigen, Bruce A. (2005) "A Review of the Empirical Literature on FDI Determinants", *National Bureau of Economic Research*, Working Paper No. 11299. Cambridge, MA: NBER.

Blonigen, Bruce A. and Jeremy Piger (2011) "Determinants of Foreign Direct Investment", *National Bureau of Economic Research*, Working Paper No. 16704. Cambridge, MA: NBER.

Bodvarsson, Örn B. and Hendrik van den Berg (2009) "Why People Immigrate: The Evidence", in: Bodvarsson, ÖB and van den Berg, H. (eds.) *The Economics of Immigration: Theory and Policy*. Springer, Berlin, pp 59–77.

Boisso, Dale A. and Michael J. Ferrantino (1997) "Economic Distance, Cultural Distance, and Openness in International Trade: Empirical Puzzles", Journal of Economic Integration 12(4): 456–484.

Boyd, William and Muriel M. Mackenzie (1930) *Towards a New Education: A Record and Synthesis of the Discussions on the New Psychology and the Curriculum at the Fifth World Conference of the New Education Fellowship held at Elsinore, Denmark, in August 1929*. London, New York: A.A. Knopf.

Brainard, S. Lael and David A. Riker (1997) "Are U.S. Multinationals Exporting U.S. Jobs?" NBER Working Paper No. 5958. Cambridge, MA: NBER.

Brinkerhoff, David B., Suzanna T. Ortega, and Rose Weitz (2014) *Essentials of Sociology*, Belmont, CA: Wadsworth/Cengage Learning.

Business & Economics Research Advisor (BERA) (2004) "Defining Globalization", *Business & Economics Research Advisor* (1): Summer.

Cambridge American English Dictionary (Cambridge AED) (2015) "Culture", Online. Available at: http://dictionary.cambridge.org/us/dictionary/american-english/culture. Accessed April 2015.

Candau, Fabien (2013) "Trade, FDI, and Migration", *International Economic Journal* 27(3): 441–461.

Caragliu, Andrea, Chiara Del Bo, Henri L.F. de Groot, Gert-Jan Linders (2013) "Cultural Determinants of Migration", *The Annals of Regional Science* 51(1): 7–32.

Carr, David, James R. Markusen, and Keith E. Maskus (2001) "Estimating the Knowledge-Capital Model of the Multinational Enterprise", *American Economic Review* 91(3): 693–708.

Centre d'Etudes Prospectives et d'Informations Internationales (CEPII) (2013) Gravity Dataset. Online. Available at: http://www.cepii.fr/CEPII/en/bdd_modele/presentation.asp?id=8. Accessed March 2013.

Choudary, Ifte (2015) "Culture", Online. Available at: http://www.tamu.edu/faculty/choudhury/culture.html. Accessed April 2015.

Conference Board (2014) "The Conference Board Total Economy Database", Online. Available at: http://www.conference-board.org/data/economydatabase/. Accessed January 2015.

Cowen, Tyler (2002) *Creative Destruction: How Globalization is Changing the World's Cultures*. Princeton, NJ: Princeton University Press.

Crafts, Nicholas (2000) "Globalisation and Growth in the Twentieth Century", IMF Working Paper WP/00/44. Washington D.C.: International Monetary Fund.

Cuaresma, Jesus Crespo, Mathias Moser, and Anna Raggl (2013) "On the Determinants of Global Bilateral Migration Flows", Working Paper No. 5. WWWforEurope.

Cyrus, Teresa L. (2012) "Cultural Distance and Bilateral Trade", *Global Economy Journal* 12(4) Article 3.

Damen, Louise (1987). Culture Learning: The Fifth Dimension on the Language Classroom. Reading, MA: Addison-Wesley.

Deardorff, Alan V. (1995) "Determinants of Bilateral Trade: Does Gravity Work in a Classical World?", in *The Regionalization of the World Economy*, ed. by Jeffrey Frankel. Chicago: University of Chicago Press.

Desmet, Klaus, Michel Le Breton, Ignacio Ortuno Ortin, and Shlomo Weber (2011), "The Stability and Breakup of Nations: A Quantitative Analysis", *Journal of Economic Growth* 16(3): 183–213.

Disdier, Anne-Celia, Silvio Tai, Lionel Fontagne, and Thierry Mayer (2010) "Bilateral Trade of Cultural Goods", *Review of World Economics* 145(4): 575–595.

Dollar, David (2001) "Globalization, Inequality, and Poverty Since 1980", Development Research Group, The World Bank. November.

Dow, Douglas (2015) "Psychic Distance Stimuli", Melbourne Business School. Online. Available at: https://sites.google.com/site/ddowresearch/home/scales. Accessed January 2015.

Dreher, Axel (2006) "Does Globalization Affect Growth? Empirical Evidence from a new Index", *Applied Economics* 38(10): 1091–1110."

Dreher, Axel, Noel Gaston and Pim Martens (2008), *Measuring Globalisation – Gauging its Consequences*. New York: Springer.

Dunlevy, James A. (2006) "The Impact of Corruption and Language on the Pro-Trade Effect of Immigrants: Evidence from the American States", *Review of Economics and Statistics* 88(1): 182–186.

Easterly, William and Ross Levine (1997) "Africa's Growth Tragedy: Policies and Ethnic Divisions", *Quarterly Journal of Economics* 12(4): 1203–50.

Eicher, Theo S., Lindy Helfman, and Alex Lenkoski (2012) "Robust FDI Determinants: Bayesian Model Averaging in the Presence of Selection Bias", *Journal of Macroeconomics* 34(3): 637–651.

Einstein, Albert (1917) "Kosmologische Betrachtungen zur allgemeinen Relativitätstheorie" ("Cosmological Considerations in the General Theory of Relativity"), *Koniglich Preußische Akademie der Wissenschaften, Sitzungsberichte* (Berlin): 142–152.

Ernst & Young (E&Y) (2015) "Looking beyond the Obvious – Globalization and New Opportunities for Growth", Online. Available at: http://www.ey.com/GL/en/Issues/Driving-growth/Globalization—Looking-beyond-the-obvious—2012-Index. Accessed April 2015.

Fatehi, Kamal and Jose Sanchez (2012) "Convergence Forces: The Slow March toward Homogeneity, or De Facto Standardization?" *Competition Forum* 10(2). American Society for Competitiveness.

Faubert, Violaine (2011) "Learning from the First Globalization (1870–1914)", Trésor-Economics No. 93. Paris: Ministère de l'Économie, des Finances et de l'Industrie.

Feenstra, Robert C. (2004) *Advanced International Trade: Theory and Evidence*. Princeton, NJ: Princeton University Press.

Feenstra, Robert C., Robert Inklaar, and Marcel P. Timmer (2013), "The Next Generation of the Penn World Table", Online. Available at: www.ggdc.net/pwt. Accessed January 2015.

Ferenczi, Imre and Walter F. Willcox (1929) International Migration, Vol. 1, New York: National Bureau of Economic Research.

Ghemawat, Pankaj and Steven A. Altman (2014) *DHL Global Connectedness Index 2014: Analyzing Global Flows and their Power to Increase Prosperity*, Bonn, Germany: Deutsche Post DHL.

Giddens, Anthony (1990) *Sociology*. Cambridge, MA: Polity.

Graff, Michael, A.G. Kenwood, and A.L. Lougheed (2014) *Growth of the International Economy, 1820–2015*, 5th edition. New York: Routledge.

Grogger, Jeffrey and Gordon H. Hanson (2011) "Income Maximization and the Selection and Sorting of International Migrants", *Journal of Development Economics* 95(1): 42–57.

Guiso, Luigi, Paola Sapienza, and Luigi Zingales (2009) "Cultural Biases in Economic Exchange?", *The Quarterly Journal of Economics* 124(3): 1095–1131.

Guo, Rongxing (2012) *Introduction to Intercultural Economics*. Heidelberg, NY: Springer.

Guo, Rongxing (2006) *Cultural Influences on Economic Analysis – Theory and Empirical Evidence*. New York: Palgrave-Macmillan.

Guo, Rongxing (2004) "How Culture Influences Foreign Trade – Evidence from the US and China", *Journal of Socio-economics* 33(6): 785–812.

Hatton, Timothy J. and Jeffrey G. Williamson (2002) "What Fundamentals Drive World Migration?", CEPR Discussion Paper no. 3559.

Head, Keith (2003) "Gravity for Beginners", Unpublished manuscript.

Head, Keith and John Ries (2008) "FDI as an Outcome of the Market for Corporate Control: Theory and Evidence", *Journal of International Economics* 74(1): 2–20.

Head, Keith and John Ries (1998) "Immigration and Trade Creation: Econometric Evidence from Canada", *Canadian Journal of Economics* 31(1): 47–62.

Head, Keith and Thierry Mayer (2000) "Non-Europe: The Magnitude and Causes of Market Fragmentation in Europe", *Weltwirtschaftliches Archiv* 136, p: 285–314.

Hedrick, Philip W. (2011) *Genetics of Populations*. Boston, MA: Jones & Bartlett Publishers.

Held, David, Anthony G. McGrew, David Goldblatt, and Jonathan Perraton (1999) *Global Transformations: Politics, Economics, and Culture*. Stanford, CA: Stanford University Press.

Hofstede, Geert (2012). "National Cultures and Corporate Cultures", in Larry A. Samovar, Richard E. Porter, and Edwin R. McDaniel (eds.), *Communication Between Cultures*. Belmont, CA: Wadsworth.

Hofstede, Geert (2001) *Culture's Consequences: Comparing Values, Behaviors, Institutions, and Organizations Across Nations*, Thousand Oaks, CA: Sage Publications.

Hofstede, Geert (1980) *Culture's Consequences: International Difference in Work Related Values*, Beverly Hills, CA: Sage Publications.

Hofstede, Geert and Michael Harris Bond (1988) "The Confucius Connection: From Cultural Roots to Economic Growth". *Organizational Dynamics* 16(4): 5–21.

Hofstede, Geert, Gert Jan Hofstede, and Michael Minkov (2010). *Cultures and Organizations: Software of the Mind*, (Revised, 3rd ed.) New York: McGraw-Hill.

House, Robert J., Paul John Hanges, Mansour Javidan, Peter W. Dorfman, and Vipin Gupta (eds.) (2004) *Culture, Leadership, and Organizations: The GLOBE Study of 62 Societies*, Thousand Oaks, CA: Sage Publications.

Huxley, Julian Sorell (1955) "Guest Editorial: Evolution, Cultural and Biological", *Yearbook of Anthropology*, 2–25.

Inglehart, Ronald and Christian Welzel (2005) *Modernization, Cultural Change and Democracy*. New York: Cambridge University Press.

Inglehart, Ronald, Miguel Basanez, Jaime Diez-Medrano, Loek Halman, and Ruud Luijkx (eds.) (2004) *Human Beliefs and Values: A Cross-cultural Sourcebook Based on the 1999-2002 Values Surveys*, Mexico City: Siglo Veintiuno Editores S.A. de C.V.

Inglehart, Ronald and Baker, Wayne E. (2000) "Modernization, Cultural Change, and the Persistence of Traditional Values", *American Sociological Review* 65(1): 19–51.

International Organization for Migration (IOM) (2013) *World Migration Report 2013 – Migrant Well-being and Development*, Geneva: International Organization for Migration.

Jacks, David S., Christopher M. Meissner, and Dennis Novy (2006) "Trade Costs in the First Wave of Globalization", NBER Working Paper No. 12602. Cambridge, MA: National Bureau of Economic Research.

Kahouli, Bassem and Samir Maktouf (2015) "The Determinants of FDI and the Impact of the Economic Crisis on the Implementation of RTAs: A Static and Dynamic Gravity Model", *international Business Review* 24(3): 518–529.

Kleinert, Jorn and Farid Toubal (2010) "Gravity for FDI", *Review of International Economics* 18(1): 1–13.

Kluckhohn, Clyde and William H. Kelly (1945). "The Concept of Culture", in Ralph Linton (ed.). *The Science of Man in the World Crisis*. New York: Columbia University Press.

Kogut, Bruce and Harbir Singh (1988) "The Effect of National Culture on the Choice of Entry Mode", *Journal of International Business Studies* 19: 411–432.

KPMG (2011) "Corporate and Indirect Tax Survey 2011", Publication Number 110603. KPMG International Cooperative.

Kroeber, A.L., and Clyde Kluckhohn (1952) "Culture: A Critical Review of Concepts and Definitions", Harvard University Peabody Museum of American Archeology and Ethnology Papers 47.

Lankhuizen, Maureen B.M. and Henri L.F. de Groot (2014) "Cultural Distance and International Trade: A Non-linear Relationship", *Letters in Spatial and Resource Sciences* 10.1007/s12076-014-0129-8.

Lechner, Frank (2001) "Globalization Issues". Emory University. Online. Available at: http://sociology.emory.edu/faculty/globalization/issues05.html. Accessed April 2015.

Lederach, John Paul (1995). *Preparing for Peace: Conflict Transformation across Cultures*. Syracuse, NY: Syracuse University Press.

Lewer, Joshua J. and Hendrik van den Berg (2008) "A Gravity Model of Immigration", *Economics Letters* 99(1): 164–167.

Linnemann, Hans (1966) *An Econometric Study in International Trade Flows*, Amsterdam: North-Holland Publishing.

Linton, Ralph (1945) *The Cultural Background of Personality*. New York: Routledge.

Maddison, Agnus (1995) *Monitoring the World Economy 1820-1992*. Development Center Studies, Organization for Economic Co-operation and Development, Paris.

Magnussen, Peter, Rick T. Wilson, Srdan Zdravkovic, Joyce Xin Zhou, and Stanford A. Westjohn (2008) "Breaking Through the Cultural Clutter", *International Marketing Review* 25(2): 183–201.

Mauro, Paolo (1995) "Corruption and Growth", *Quarterly Journal of Economics* CX, 681–712.

Mayda, Anna Maria (2010) "International Migration: A Panel Data Analysis of the Determinants of Bilateral Flows", *Journal of Population Economics* 23(4): 1249–1274.

Mayer, Thierry and Soledad Zignano (2011) "Notes on CEPII's Distance Measures: The *GeoDist* Database", CEPII Working Paper No. 25.

McDonald, John F and Robert A. Moffitt (1980) "The Use of Tobit Analysis", *The Review of Economics and Statistics* 62(2): 318–321.

Melitz, Jacques and Farid Toubal (2012) "Native Language, Spoken Language, Translation and Trade", CEPII Working Paper No. 17.

Merriam-Webster (2015a) "culture", Online. Available at: www.merriam-webster.com/dictionary/culture. Accessed April 10, 2015.

Merriam-Webster (2015b) "globalization", Online. Available at: www.merriam-webster.com/dictionary/globalization. Accessed April 10, 2015.

Mitterand, Francois (1993) Speech given at Gdansk, Poland, September 21, cited in J. P. Singh, *Globalization, Cultural Identities, and Negotiations: The Evolution of European Preferences on Cultural Industry Negotiations.* Working paper.

Murphy, Robert (1986) *Culture and Social Anthropology: An Overture.* 2nd ed. Englewood Cliffs, NJ: Prentice Hall.

Nei, Masahiro (1972) "Genetic Distance between Populations", *The American Naturalist* 106(949): 283–292.

Newton, Isaac (1687) *Philosophiæ Naturalis Principia Mathematica*, Londini: Jussu Societatis Regiae ac Typis Josephi Streater.

Novy, Dennis (2013) "Gravity Redux: Measuring International Trade Costs with Panel Data", *Economic Inquiry,* 51, 101–121.

Organisation for Economic Co-operation and Development (OECD) (2015a) "OECD StatExtracts: FDI Flows and Stocks by Partner Country". Online. Available at: http://www.oecd-ilibrary.org/statistics. Accessed February 2015.

Organisation for Economic Co-operation and Development (OECD) (2015b) "International Migration Database". Online. Available at: http://www.oecd-ilibrary.org/statistics. Accessed February 2015.

Otten, Sebastian (2013) "Language and Cultural Barriers in International Factor Movements", Working Paper.

Oxford English Dictionary (2015) "globalization, *n.*" OED Online. Oxford University Press. Online. Available at: http://dictionary.oed.com/ Accessed January 2015.

Parson, Talcott (1949) *Essays in Sociological Theory*. Glencoe, IL: Free Press.

Pedersen, Peder J., Mariola Pytlikova, and Nina Smith (2008) "Selection and Network Effects – Migration Flows into OECD Countries, 1990–2000", *European Economic Review* 52(7): 1160–1186.

Pöyhönen, Pentti (1963a) "Toward a General Theory of International Trade", *Ekonomiska Samfundets Tidskrift*, Tredje Serien, Argang 16: 69–77.

Pöyhönen, Pentti (1963b) "A Tentative Model for the Flows of Trade between Countries", *Weltwirtschatftliches Archiv* 90(1): 93–99.

Ratha, Dilip and William Shaw (2007) "South-South Migration and Remittances", Migration Policy Institute. Online. Available at: http://www.migrationpolicy.org/article/south-south-migration-and-remittances. Accessed March 2015.

Roberts, G.W. and J.A. Byrne (1966) "Summary Statistics on Indenture and Associated Migration Affecting the West Indies, 1834-1918", *Population Studies* 20(1): 125–34.

Robertson, Roland (1992) *Globalization: Social Theory and Global Culture.* London: Sage Publishers.

Romaine, Suzanne (2000) *Language and Society – An Introduction to Sociolinguistics*, 2nd ed. Oxford, UK: Oxford University Press.

Ruyssen, Ilse (2013) *Determinants of International Migration.* (Doctoral dissertation, Ghent University).

Scholte, Jan Aart (2002) "What is Globalization? The Definitional Issue – Again", CSGR Working Paper No. 109/02. December.

Seabrook, Jeremy (1998) "The Racketeers of Illusion", *New Internationalist*. Online. Available at: http://newint.org/features/1998/12/05/illusion/. Accessed April 2015.

Shangquan, Gao (2000) "Economic Globalization: Trends, Risks and Risk Prevention", CDP Background Paper No. 1 ST/ESA/2000/CDP/1, United Nations Development Policy and Analysis Division.

Spolaore, Enrico and Romain Wacziarg (2011) "Long-Term Barriers to the International Diffusion of Innovations", National Bureau of Economic Research, Working Paper No. 17271. Cambridge, MA: NBER.

Spolaore, Enrico and Romain Wacziarg (2009) "The Diffusion of Development", *The Quarterly Journal of Economics* 124(2): 469-529.

Sprenger, Ekaterina (2013) "The Determinants of International Migration in the European Union: An Empirical Analysis", Institute for East and Southeast European Studies Working Paper No. 325.

Tadesse, Bedassa and Roger White (2015) "Trade Costs, Genetic Distance, and Immigrants", Working Paper.

Tadesse, Bedassa and Roger White (2012) "Do Immigrants Enhance International Trade in Services? The Case of US Tourism Services Exports", *International Journal of Tourism Research* 14(6): 567–585.

Tadesse, Bedassa and Roger White (2010a) "Cultural Distance as a Determinant of Bilateral Trade Flows: Do Immigrants Counter the Effect of Cultural Distance?" *Applied Economics Letters* 17(2): 147–152.

Tadesse, Bedassa and Roger White (2010b) "Does Cultural Distance Hinder Trade in Goods? A Comparative Study of Nine OECD Member Nations", *Open Economies Review* 21(2): 237–261.

Tadesse, Bedassa and Roger White (2008) "Do Immigrants Counter the Effect of Cultural Distance on Trade? Evidence from US State-level Exports", *Journal of Socio-Economics* 37(6): 2304-2318.

Tang, Linghui (2012) "The Direction of Cultural Distance on FDI: Attractiveness or Incongruity?", *Cross Cultural Management: An International Journal* 19(2): 233–256.

Tinbergen, Jan (1962) *Shaping the World Economy: Suggestions for an International Economic Policy*, New York: Twentieth Century Fund.

Trudgill, Peter (2000) *Sociolinguistics: An Introduction to Language and Society*. New York: Penguin.

United Nations (UN) (2013) "The number of international migrants worldwide reaches 232 million", *Population Facts* No. 2013/2. United Nations Department of Economic and Social Affairs – Population Division (September).

United Nations (UN) (2012) *Migration and Human Mobility*, New York: United Nations.

United Nations (UN) (2012) *United Nations Commodity Trade Statistics Database*. Online. Available at: http://comtrade.un.org/db/. Accessed May 2012.

United States Bureau of Census and Statistics (US Census) (1975) *Historical Statistics of the U.S., Colonial Times to 1970, Bicentennial Edition, Part 2*. Washington, DC.

United States Bureau of Census and Statistics (US Census) (1960) *Historical Statistics of the U.S., Colonial Times to 1957*, Washington, DC.

University of Michigan Ross School of Business, World Tax Database Search (2015) Online. Available at: http://www.bus.umich.edu/otpr/otpr/default.asp. Accessed February 2015.

Useem, John and Ruth Hill Useem (1963) "Men in the Middle of the Third Culture: The Roles of American and Non-Western People in Cross-cultural Administration", *Human Organization* 22(3): 169–179.

Van Krieken, Robert (2006) *Sociology: Themes and Perspectives*, 3rd edition. Frenchs Forest, New South Wales, Australia: Pearson Education.

Veugelers, Reinhilde (1991) "Locational Determinants and Ranking of Host Countries: An Empirical Assessment", *Kyklos* 44: 363–82.

Vollrath, Thomas and Charlie Hallahan (2011) "Reciprocal Trade Agreements: Impacts on Bilateral Trade Expansion and Contraction in the World Agricultural Marketplace", Economic Research Report No. (ERR-113). United States Department of Agriculture Economic Research Service.

Waters, Malcolm (2001) *Globalization (Key Ideas)*. London: Routledge.

White, Roger (2013) "Is Cultural Distance a Determinant of International Migration Flows? Evidence from Denmark, Germany, and the Netherlands", *Economics Bulletin* 33, 3: 2156–2168.

White, Roger (2010) *Migration and International Trade: The US Experience Since 1945*. Edward Elgar Publishing: Cheltenham, UK and Northampton, MA, USA.

White, Roger and Bedassa Tadesse (2008) "Immigrants, Cultural Distance and US State-Level Exports of Cultural Products", *North American Journal of Economics and Finance* 19(3): 331–348.

White, Roger and Nicole Yamasaki (2014) "Source-Destination Cultural Differences, Immigrants' Skill Levels, and Immigrant Stocks: Evidence from Six OECD Member Host Countries", *National Institute Economic Review* 229, 1: R53-R67.

World Bank (2015a) "Trends in average MFN applied tariff rates in developing and industrial countries, 1981–2010". Online. Available at http://go.worldbank.org/LGOXFTV550. Accessed: February 2015.

World Bank (2015b) "Tariff Rate, Applied, Weighted Mean, All Products (percent)". Online. Available at http://data.worldbank.org/indicator/TM.TAX.MRCH.WM.AR.ZS. Accessed February 2015.

World Bank (2015c) "World Bank Income Classifications",. Online. Available at http://siteresources.worldbank.org/DATASTATISTICS/Resources/OGHIST.xls. Accessed April 2015

World Bank (2014) "World Development Indicators". Washington, DC. Online. Available at http://databank.worldbank.org. Accessed April 2014.

World Bank (2002) *Globalization, Growth, and Poverty: Building an Inclusive World Economy*, Washington, DC: International Bank for Reconstruction and Development/The World Bank and New York: Oxford University Press.

World Bank (2000) *Beyond Economic Growth: Meeting the Challenges of Global Development*, Washington, DC: International Bank for Reconstruction and Development/The World Bank.

World Trade Organization (WTO) (2015) *Regional Trade Agreements Information System*. Online. Available at: http://rtais.wto.org/UI/PublicAllRTAList.aspx. Accessed February 2015.

World Values Survey Association (WVSA) (2014) *World Values Survey Waves 1–3 1981–1998*, Madrid, Spain. Online. Available at http://www.worldvaluessurvey.org. Accessed April 2014.

Zlotnik, Hania (2005) "International Migration Trends since 1980", Selected Papers of the UNFPA Expert Group Meeting, pp. 13–28. UNFPA: New York.

Index